GENDER, CONFLICT, AND PEACEKEEPING

War and Peace Library
Series Editor: Mark Selden

GENDER, CONFLICT, AND PEACEKEEPING

Edited by
Dyan Mazurana,
Angela Raven-Roberts,
and
Jane Parpart

ROWMAN & LITTLEFIELD PUBLISHERS, INC.
Lanham • Boulder • New York • Toronto • Oxford

ROWMAN & LITTLEFIELD PUBLISHERS, INC.

Published in the United States of America
by Rowman & Littlefield Publishers, Inc.
A wholly owned subsidiary of The Rowman & Littlefield Publishing Group, Inc.
4501 Forbes Boulevard, Suite 200, Lanham, MD 20706
www.rowmanlittlefield.com

P.O. Box 317, Oxford OX2 9RU, UK

British Library Cataloguing in Publication Information Available

Library of Congress Cataloging-in-Publication Data

Gender, conflict, and peacekeeping / edited by Dyan Mazurana, Angela Raven-
    Roberts, and Jane Parpart.
    p.   cm. — (War and peace library)
    Includes bibliographical references and index.
    ISBN 0-7425-3632-7 (cloth : alk. paper) — ISBN 0-7425-3633-5 (pbk. : alk.
paper)
    1. Women and war. 2. Women and peace. 3. Women—Social conditions. 4.
Women—Violence against. 5. Peacekeeping forces. 6. Sex role. I. Mazurana, Dyan E.
II. Raven-Roberts, Angela, 1949– III. Parpart, Jane L. IV. Series.

    JZ6405.W66G45   2005
    303.6'9—dc22

                                              2004017767

Printed in the United States of America

Contents

Acronyms

ACCORD	African Centre for the Constructive Resolution of Disputes
ACRI	African Crisis Response Initiative
AFWIC	African Women in Conflict [of UNIFEM]
ANC	African National Congress
ASC	Assembly of Civil Society
ASOFERWA	Association of Solidarity for Rwandese Women
AU	African Union
AVEGA	Association of Genocide Widows of Rwanda
BMATT	British Military Advisory and Training Team
CAP	Consolidated Appeal Process
CAS	Anti-kidnapping Command [of EMP]
CEDAW	Convention on the Elimination of All Forms of Discrimination against Women
CIS	Commonwealth of Independent States
CIVPOL	United Nations Civilian Police
CMA	Civil-Military Affairs
DAW	United Nations Division for the Advancement of Women
DFAIT	Canadian Department of Foreign Affairs and International Trade
DFID	British Department for International Development
DHA	United Nations Department of Humanitarian Affairs
DPA	United Nations Department of Political Affairs
DPKO	United Nations Department of Peacekeeping Operations
DRC	Democratic Republic of the Congo

ECOMOG	Economic Community of West African States Monitoring Observer Group
ECOSOC	United Nations Economic and Social Council
ECOWAS	Economic Community of West African States
EGP	Guerrilla Army of the Poor [Guatemala]
EMP	Presidential Guard
FAA	Angolan Armed Forces
FALINTIL	Armed Forces of the Revolutionary Front for an Independent East Timor
FAO	Food and Agricultural Organization
FAR	Rebel Armed Forces [Guatemala]
FARC	Revolutionary Armed Forces of Colombia
FMLN	Farabundo Martí National Liberation Front
FNLA	National Front for the Liberation of Angola
FOIA	Freedom of Information Act
FRY	Federal Republic of Yugoslavia
FSLN	Sandinista National Liberation Front
GNU	Rwandan Government of National Unity
GoA	government of Angola
IASC	Inter-Agency Standing Committee
ICC	International Criminal Court
ICITAP	International Criminal Investigative Training Assistance Program
ICJ	International Court of Justice
ICRW	International Center for Research on Women
ICTR	International Criminal Tribunal for Rwanda
ICTY	International Criminal Tribunal for the Former Yugoslavia
IDP	internally displaced person
IFOR	International Implementation Force
IMC	International Medical Corps
INGO	international nongovernmental organization
IPTF	International Police Task Force
ISS	Institute for Security Studies [South Africa]
JCO	Joint Commission Observers
KFOR	Kosovo Force
KLA	Kosovo Liberation Army
KPS	Kosovo Police Service
MEJA	Military Extraterritorial Jurisdiction Act
MIGEPROFE	Ministry for Gender Equality and Women's Empowerment [Rwanda]
MINUGUA	United Nations Verification Mission in Guatemala

MONUC	United Nations Organization Mission in the Democratic Republic of the Congo
MPLA	People's Movement for the Liberation of Angola
MRE	mission rehearsal exercise
MSF	Doctors without Borders
MTC	mission training cell
NATO	North Atlantic Treaty Organization
NFLS	Nairobi Forward Looking Strategies
NGO	nongovernmental organization
NUPI	Norwegian Institute of International Affairs
NWV	Namibian Women's Voice
OAU	Organization of African Unity
OCHA	United Nations Office for the Coordination of Humanitarian Affairs
OHR	Office of the High Representative
OMM	Organization of Mozambican Women
ONUMOZ	United Nations Operation in Mozambique
ORPA	Organización del Pueblo en Armas
OSCE	Organization for Security and Cooperation in Europe
PBPU	Peacekeeping Best Practices Unit [of DPKO]
PGT	Guatemalan Labor Party
PLAN	People's Liberation Army of Namibia
PNH	Haitian National Police
RAF	Rwandan Army Forces
RECAMP	Reinforcement of African Military Peacekeeping Capacity
RPF	Rwandan Patriotic Front
RUF	Revolutionary United Front
RWI	Rwandan Women's Initiative
SADC	Southern African Development Community
SADF	South African Defense Forces
SFOR	Stabilization Force
SGBV	sexual and gender-based violence
SOFA	status-of-forces agreement
SRSG	special representative of the secretary-general
STD	sexually transmitted disease
SWAFT	South West African Troops
SWAPO	South West African Peoples Organization
SWC	SWAPO Women's Council
TCN	troop-contributing nation
TES	Training and Evaluation Service [of DPKO]
TfP	Training for Peace Project

TRC	Truth and Reconciliation Commission
UCMJ	Uniform Code of Military Justice
UN	United Nations
UNAMIR	United Nations Assistance Mission for Rwanda
UNAMSIL	United Nations Assistance Mission in Sierra Leone
UNAVEM	United Nations Angola Verification Mission
UNCC	United Nations Compensation Commission
UNDP	United Nations Development Program
UNDRO	United Nations Disaster Relief Coordination
UNECA	United Nations Economic Commission for Africa
UNHCR	Office of the United Nations High Commissioner for Refugees
UNICEF	United Nations International Children's Fund
UNIFEM	United Nations Development Fund for Women
UNIFIL	United Nations Interim Force in Lebanon
UNITA	National Union for the Total Independence of Angola
UNMEE	United Nations Mission in Ethiopia and Eritrea
UNMIBH	United Nations Mission in Bosnia and Herzegovina
UNMIH	United Nations Mission in Haiti
UNMIK	United Nations Interim Administration Mission in Kosovo
UNMO	United Nations military observer
UNOA	United Nations Office in Angola
UNOMA	United Nations Observer Mission in Angola
UNOMIG	United Nations Observer Mission in Georgia
UNOMIL	United Nations Observer Mission in Liberia
UNOMSA	United Nations Observer Mission to South Africa
UNTAET	United Nations Transitional Authority in East Timor
UNTAG	United Nations Transitional Assistance Group
URNG	Guatemalan National Revolutionary Unity
USAID	United States Agency for International Development
WCF	Women's Communal Funds
WFP	World Food Program
WHO	World Health Organization
WIT	Women in Transition Program [of USAID]
WPS	women's police stations

Introduction

Gender, Conflict, and Peacekeeping

Dyan Mazurana, Angela Raven-Roberts,
Jane Parpart, with Sue Lautze

A T THE CORE OF THIS BOOK IS THE KNOWLEDGE that gender is a necessary analytic tool to recognize the causes and consequences of complex political emergencies, to critically analyze national and international interventions into these violent situations, and to move effectively from war to managing systems of chronic instability to reconciliation and reconstruction. Building on insights, experiences, and literature, local and international advocates for women and women's rights are placing increased pressure on the United Nations, international organizations, and governments to design and carry out peacekeeping and humanitarian operations with attention to gender: from the impact of the conflict, to the distribution of humanitarian aid and demobilization cards, to who shapes the peace agenda and sits at the peace table, to postconflict elections and reconstruction. These advocates contend, and contributors within this book demonstrate, that peacekeeping operations and international humanitarian interventions that are not crafted and carried out with attention to the gender dimensions of the conflict and postconflict periods undermine a return to real peace, human security, and reconstruction—not only for women and girls but for the society as a whole.

The contributors to this book emphasize the role of gender in the intersection of armed conflict, complex political emergencies, and peacekeeping and humanitarian operations. They examine the historical and current debates, efforts, and obstacles regarding the mainstreaming of gender in peacekeeping and humanitarian operations. They document and analyze legal developments regarding gender, peacekeeping, and international humanitarian, criminal, and human rights law to draw attention to the pitfalls, as well as potential legal avenues to enhance the protection of women's and girls' rights during peacekeeping and humanitarian operations. They offer critical analyses of the intersection of gender and power in the context of particular armed conflicts and the peacekeeping operations sent in to restore and maintain peace. In doing so, they make apparent that inattention to, and subsequent miscalculations about, women's and girls' roles and experiences during particular conflicts and in early postconflict periods systematically undermines the efforts of peacekeeping and peace-building operations, civil society, and women's organizations to establish conditions necessary for national and regional peace, justice, and security. They explore these issues through detailed gender analyses of peacekeeping operations in Angola, Bosnia, East Timor, Ethiopia, Eritrea, Guatemala, Haiti, Kosovo, Mozambique, Namibia, Rwanda, and the former Yugoslavia.

The Roles of Women and Girls during Armed Conflict

Changes within the geopolitical post–Cold War landscape have affected the ways armed conflicts manifest and develop. Gender-based and sexual violence increasingly are used as weapons of warfare and have become defining characteristics in many conflicts. Genocide, rape, forced impregnation, forced abortion, trafficking, sexual slavery, and the intentional spread of sexually transmitted diseases (STDs), including HIV/AIDS, are integral elements of these new forms of conflict. The targeting of women, girls, men, and boys based on their gender roles within particular societies and cultures is systematic and thorough.

Yet women and girls are not only the victims of armed conflict. They play crucial roles in supporting and perpetuating violence.[1] Women and girls assume greater roles in contemporary armed conflict, including as frontline combatants, spies, messengers, porters, and "wives."[2] In countries such as Canada and the United States, women serve in every branch of the armed forces. Over the last decade, women and girls have fought in armed conflicts in Afghanistan, Bosnia and Herzegovina, Colombia, the Democratic Republic of the Congo, East Timor, Ethiopia, Eritrea, Guatemala, Iraq, Lebanon, Mozambique, Namibia, Palestine, South Africa, Sierra Leone, Sudan, Uganda, and elsewhere. Between 1990 and 2003, girl soldiers were present in fighting forces and groups in at least fifty-four countries and participated in armed conflict in thirty-six of those countries.[3] Based on political and economic motivations, women and girls have actively joined fighting forces in liberation struggles, as in East Timor, El Salvador, Eritrea, Guatemala, Mozambique, Namibia, Colombia, the Democratic Republic of the Congo, Mozambique,

Palestine, Sierra Leone, and Uganda. They engage in armed conflict for a variety of reasons, including opposition to unjust and predatory governments, and support of the political and religious goals of their movements. Women and girls also become involved by means of ideological propaganda, abduction, intimidation, and forced recruitment. They have been abducted and forced to serve in fighting forces, as in Burundi, the Democratic Republic of the Congo, Liberia, Sierra Leone, northern Uganda, Colombia, Myanmar, Sri Lanka, Iraq, and Turkey in the last decade.[4]

Although armed conflict and postconflict reconstruction processes strongly affect them, women are largely absent at the peace tables and levels of decision making within foreign affairs, defense, or international relations bodies. Likewise, the gender dimensions of the conflict and postconflict periods are usually absent. For example, although it was the first major peace accord implemented after the Fourth World Conference on Women and the Beijing Platform for Action, the Dayton Peace Accords failed to take gender into account; in fact, gender aspects of the conflict or postconflict periods were never discussed. While women are marginalized from the top levels of power, at the local level, their peace-building activities are substantial. Research into women's peace-building work in conflict and postconflict situations finds that:

> Women, although less visible than men, have long been integrally involved in seeking solutions to issues intrinsic to building peace, including ecological balance, demobilization and reintegration of former child soldiers, demilitarization and disarmament, and sustainable economic, environmental, and political development. Furthermore, women are resource managers, advocates for other women in emergency and crisis situations, leaders in political processes, and community influentials. . . . Women often develop informal or formal groups and processes that contribute to peacebuilding and the construction of democratic societies.[5]

The important contributions women make at the grassroots and informal level and their near absence at the formal level has been repeatedly noted, including by the United Nations secretary-general Kofi Annan.[6]

Regardless of the important roles women play, postconflict reconstruction processes and peacekeeping operations routinely fail to see the larger gendered political and economic structures supporting the armed conflict or the value of women's peace-building work at local and regional levels. Because for the most part the politics of gender are not recognized and the gendered causes and consequences of armed conflict and postconflict periods are overlooked, the few international and national policies and programs developed to empower women or promote women in peace building too often remain superficial because they do little to challenge and dismantle the structures that caused and fueled the violent conflict. Rather, the conditions for inequality and refueling the violence remain in place.

Women's and human rights advocates at local, national, and international levels have had varying degrees of success in influencing the policies and programs of some civilian and humanitarian agencies that participate in peacekeeping operations and those of branches of state governments responsible for humanitarian assistance. Largely because of such efforts there is an increased awareness of the gendered impacts of conflict and the postconflict situation. It is also because of these efforts that the issues of gender and peacekeeping are being raised at the highest levels of intergovernmental and governmental organizations, for example, the United Nations Security Council and government foreign affairs departments.

The Impact of Armed Conflict on Women and Girls

Sexual and Gender-Based Violence

Violations of the rights of women and girls are pervasive and form a central component of today's armed conflict. A key challenge lies in international and national agencies' developing the capacity to work with local organizations on the ground to monitor the situation of women's and girls' rights and to act in a timely, coherent, and coordinated way to ensure the application of rights within the appropriate international humanitarian and human rights standards.[7]

Women and girls of all ages are victims of gender-based and sexual violence from family members, husbands, partners, acquaintances, and, to a lesser extent, strangers during times of "peace." During times of armed conflict, rates of violence rise as members of fighting forces and groups specifically target women, adolescent girls, and, to a lesser extent, girl children.[8] The forms of violence used and the ways in which perpetrators carry out violent acts—genocide, torture, rape, mass rape, sexual slavery, enforced prostitution, enforced sterilization, enforced abortion, custodial violence, forced displacement, attacks on civilian populations, mutilations, and so on—all correspond to gender: the gender and sex of the victim, the gender of the perpetrator, and gender relations in the society and culture(s).[9] These forms of humiliation and violence take on powerful political and symbolic meanings. The deliberate initiation and endorsement of these acts by military commanders and political leaders underscores the significance of these acts as more than random assaults.

Gender and the Economic, Social, and Political Impact of Armed Conflict

In paying attention to the impact of armed conflict on women and girls, most United Nations departments and agencies and NGOs have focused their attention and reports on sexual and gender-based violence. While attention in these areas is necessary, it is equally important to recognize the economic, social, and political ways armed conflict affects women and girls.

The commodification of resources within these new wars brings some benefit to local people through the emergence of specific forms of economic organization and divisions of labor. At times, those who remain often find themselves with few options aside from working for warlords and criminal militias or entering into exploitative informal economies. Clear divisions of indentured servitude and other forms of forced labor evolve and are based on gender and generational lines. For example, women and adolescent girls are used as sexual slaves for militia commanders and soldiers in the Democratic Republic of the Congo and Angola. In Sierra Leone and in Burma, women and adolescent girls are forced to grow food, cook, and clean for soldiers and day laborers. Girls are used to carry supplies, sort and pick through gems, launder clothes, carry messages between work gangs or among fighting forces, and perform other activities deemed suitable to their size, gender, and age.

Yet, even while serving the interests of the war economy, civilian populations are terrorized by rebel groups and armed insurgents seeking to forcibly depopulate resource-rich areas in order to better control exploitation or to lower the cost of labor. A range of violent measures has been used to forcibly displace people from the diamond mines in Sierra Leone and Angola, the timber-producing areas in the Indonesian islands, and the oil fields of Colombia and southern Sudan. Sexual violence against women and girls has proved an effective mechanism for destabilizing and dispersing communities.[10]

The consequences of conflict and the resulting systems have a series of repercussions for different elements of the population. For example, shifts in demographic composition result when men and boys are killed or flee, as seen in Afghanistan, Angola, Chechnya, the Democratic Republic of the Congo, Kosovo, Palestine, Peru, Sierra Leone, Somalia, and Rwanda. Functioning nurseries and schools are rare and qualified teachers are few, especially for the internally displaced and refugees.[11] Coupled with the deliberate bombing of schools and hospitals, such demographic changes shift responsibility for these public goods back into the private sphere and back onto women. Even when the loss of men and the destruction of existing sources of income prompt new economic divisions of labor and new economic roles for women and children, these tend to be in the more unstable and high-risk informal sector. On the whole, women, as providers and caregivers, find that their workloads increase as the availability of natural resources and access to public, household, and environmental goods shrink.

As part of the assault on civilian livelihoods, wells are poisoned, lands are mined, and marketplaces are destroyed, making the daily tasks of fetching water, tilling the land, and buying and selling in markets increasingly dangerous.[12] These tasks, which are dominated by women and girls in many cultures, become all the more difficult, time consuming, and risky. Female enrollment in schools, often limited under the best of circumstances, drops in times of war because girl children and adolescents alike are forced to assume greater responsibilities to ensure household food security through their own labor, for example, by working agricultural lands, carrying out domestic labor, making carpets, or working in sweatshops. As household resources thin, adolescent girls are married off at younger and younger ages. In an attempt to provide them with some level of protection against military and rebel forces, families may marry adolescent girls at a younger age to older men. Seeing few options for survival, adolescent girls may "choose" to marry older men.[13] A combination of civil war and environmental factors, most notably drought, in Afghanistan, Somalia, Sudan, and northern Uganda, for example, has resulted in the shortening of the engagement period for prepubescent daughters.[14] Girls may also be sent off to work as domestic slaves for little or no compensation, and in such cases they are at risk of sexual abuse from their masters.[15]

Armed conflict also changes social structures and networks, with profound effects on social relations, particularly for women and girls.[16] Displacement due to armed conflict increases the number of female- and child-headed households, with the greatest increase in households headed by widows and children, because adolescent and adult males have fled, gone into exile, or are participating in or have died as a result of the fighting.[17] For example, due to war in Angola, women now head one-third of all households.[18] Females who head households in agricultural societies where cultivation is needed are increasingly hard-pressed when husbands die or become disabled, which forces them to barter for the labor of other men to help prepare their fields. This may lead to an increase of work for the women and, in particular, their daughters, who must then compensate for labor provided.[19]

The resilience and productivity of livelihood systems—that is, systems that enable people to make a living—during times of armed conflict is critical. Failure of livelihood systems results in famine; preservation of livelihoods raises chances of both survival and recovery. Livelihood systems are highly gendered and reflect the different cultural and social factors that determine the division of labor among men, women, boys, and girls, their differential access to resources, and other structural differences. While conflicts are characterized by elevated mortality rates, most people survive even protracted wars.

They do so in large part due to their own efforts rather than through human-itarian assistance.[20]

During armed conflict, the rich and powerful may be able to manipulate economies to their advantage, but these processes negatively affect the major-ity of the poor and marginalized. As the dominant actors in the marginal workforce, women are often the first to become unemployed or underem-ployed. In order to raise enough money to feed, clothe, and shelter their fam-ilies, women and girls may pursue multiple jobs or engage in risky economic endeavors such as prostitution, smuggling, and begging. The changing demo-graphic structure of communities affected by war creates additional burdens on women and girls when male family members are killed, disabled, driven into militia forces, or forced to flee. Usually girls and then boys are pulled out of school, the elderly out of retirement, and women out of the houses to seek employment, to intensify agricultural production, and to assist in the gather-ing of water, fuel, and foodstuffs.

Women, Girls, and Trafficking

The International Organization for Migration estimates that as we entered into the new century, between seven hundred thousand and two million women and children were trafficked across international borders in a process that nets several billion dollars in profit to the many criminal networks in-volved.[21] Systems of prewar gender inequality, war economies, criminal syn-dicates, and the destruction and destabilization of livelihoods combine to place women and girls at high risk for trafficking. Trafficking in human beings involves deception, coercion, forced and violent sex, sexual exploitation, and enforced prostitution. Transition, instability, disintegrating social networks, and disintegration of law and order in receiving and transit countries, which already suffer economic hardship and poverty, foster trafficking. In some cases, due to inefficiency, laxity, and often involvement of the police, as well as the tacit support of military personnel, traffickers function in those countries where they do not fear arrest, prosecution, or conviction (see Bedont, chapter 4; Vandenberg, chapter 7). Trafficked women and girls face severely compro-mised physical and mental health, in particular regarding their reproductive health due to rape, sexual abuse, STDs, including HIV/AIDS, trauma, and unwanted pregnancies.[22]

Gender, Flight, and Displacement

The United States Committee for Refugees' *World Refugee Survey 2001* re-ported more than 14.5 million refugees in 2001 and an additional 1.7 million refugees who had voluntarily repatriated during the past two years and were still in need of reintegration assistance and protection monitoring. The same source also estimates that there are approximately 20 to 24 million internally displaced persons,[23] and women make up the largest group among these displaced populations, as in Burundi, Colombia, Ethiopia, Eritrea, Peru, Rwanda, and Sri Lanka. The Office of the United Nations High Commissioner for Refugees (UNHCR) estimates that women and children constitute 80 percent of the world's refugees and internally displaced persons.[24]

Each phase of displacement affects people differently, including forced eviction, initial displacement, flight, protection, assistance, resettlement, and reintegration.[25] Refugee, returnee, and internally displaced women and girls suffer discrimination and rights abuse based on their sex during refuge and throughout their journey to and from refuge. Sex discrimination, gender-related methods of persecution, or both often cause their flight, frequently in combination with discrimination and abuse on other grounds (such as ethnicity, religion, and class). During their flight, they confront sex discrimination and gender-related persecution—often in the form of harassment, sexual extortion, or physical and sexual violence. For example, women and girls may be coerced or forced into providing sexual services to men and adolescent boys in exchange for safe passage for themselves or their family, for documentation, or for access to assistance.[26] All children are at an increased risk of becoming separated from their parents, families, or guardians.[27] Girl children who become separated from their parents face higher rates of sexual abuse and face greater risk of being forced to serve in fighting forces and groups.[28]

Women, Girls, and Health

The looting and destruction of health clinics and facilities, schools, public offices, and infrastructure during armed conflict makes it increasingly difficult for most people living in areas experiencing armed conflict to address their basic needs. Many women and girls are unable to seek medical care, often because medical facilities are destroyed or poorly equipped and staffed, or because they cannot afford treatment. Importantly, medical care is not only limited to physical service delivery but also requires the provision of information. Women and girls are often left without vital information on the prevention of STDs, HIV/AIDS, and early pregnancy. In addition, mothers are not informed about the importance of exclusive breast-feeding, complementary feeding, and other aspects of child care. This information is very important in unsanitary environments where bottle-feeding, for instance, would endanger the life of a young child. As a result, women's and girls' physical, nutritional, reproductive, and mental health are negatively affected.[29]

During famine or food shortages, women and girls are often more suscep-
tible to malnutrition than men, due to inequitable distribution of resources
within households and at the community level. The effects of malnutrition
among expectant and nursing mothers not only can threaten their own lives
but also can have severe consequences for the health and survival of their children. Repeated episodes of acute malnutrition during the preschool years
often lead to irreversible stunted growth.[30] The combination of malnutrition
and gender-based discrimination may result in stunted growth and development for girls and contribute to additional health risks for pregnant or lactat-
ing mothers. In some cases, such gender discrimination results in death.[31]
Crowding and poor conditions and sanitation within villages, towns, or
camps may increase rates of and exposure to malaria, tuberculosis, and other
communicable diseases.

United Nations Initiatives on Women, Girls, and Armed Conflict

Because the majority of contributors to this volume focus on United Nations–
led international intervention into complex political emergencies, it is useful
to locate debates and actions around gender and international intervention
within the United Nations in a larger framework of the organization's encounter with and response to issues of women, girls, and armed conflict. Core
institutional frameworks within the United Nations include the United Nations Charter, the Security Council, and the Commission on the Status of
Women, while key documents include the Nairobi Forward-Looking Strategies for the Advancement of Women,[32] the Vienna Declaration and Programme of Action,[33] the 1993 Declaration on the Elimination of Violence
against Women,[34] the Beijing Declaration and the Platform for Action and
Beijing +5, and the Windhoek Declaration and the Namibia Plan of Action
on Mainstreaming a Gender Perspective on Multidimensional Peace Support
Operations.[35] Central initiatives include, but are not limited to, those developed by member states, the establishment and rulings of the ad hoc international criminal tribunals, a series of reports by the secretary-general on issues
of peace and security, and the Report of the Panel on United Nations Peace
Operation (see Raven-Roberts, chapter 2; Hudson, chapter 5).

One of the earliest efforts to specifically address women and girls in armed
conflict took place in 1969, when the Commission on the Status of Women
began to consider whether special protection should be accorded to women
and children during armed conflict and emergency situations. Building on
this, the United Nations Economic and Social Council (ECOSOC) requested
that the United Nations General Assembly adopt a declaration on this topic.

The General Assembly responded by later adopting the Declaration on the Protection of Women and Children in Emergency and Armed Conflict in 1974. While these efforts highlighted the risk to women and children, the importance of women's involvement in peace issues was also recognized, including at the United Nations Conference on Women in Mexico in 1975. Other central events include the International Decade of Women (1976–1985), in which equality, development, and peace were central themes, and the Nairobi Forward-Looking Strategies for the Advancement of Women, adopted at the 1985 Third World Conference on Women. Throughout the 1980s, while the United Nations was ever more aware of the particular risks to women and children during armed conflict, there was a tendency to collapse women and children into a single category. While it recognized women's special responsibilities for children, this view also demonstrated a preoccupation with women in their roles as mothers and caregivers. The perspective also largely did not reflect an understanding of differential impacts among boys and girls.[36]

During the 1990s, the United Nations made a series of steps in addressing the issues of wartime violence against women and girls, including sexual and gender-based violence. Important examples include the United Nations Compensation Commission created to compensate victims of Iraq's invasion of Kuwait, which expressly included physical and mental injury arising from sexual assault (see Oosterveld, chapter 3). Additionally, the 1993 United Nations World Conference on Human Rights, Vienna, marked a watershed in explicitly recognizing many violations of women's rights as human rights violations.

The conflict in the former Yugoslavia represented the first time that consistent references began to emerge within the United Nations regarding violence against women and girls during armed conflict. In part to respond to the conflict, the Security Council established a commission of experts (the Yugoslav Commission) to investigate violations of international humanitarian law that were occurring; the commission's report collected information on more than 1,100 reports of sexual violence (see Oosterveld, chapter 3).[37]

In 1994, in the genocidal conflict in Rwanda, tens of thousands of women and girls were subjected to extreme forms of violence, including mass rape, mutilation, sexual slavery and torture, and murder. Yet for a long time, the international community remained silent and neither the Security Council nor investigations by its commission of experts referred to sexual violence. It was largely through the efforts of the NGO community that these issues were placed on the international agenda.[38]

In 1993, the Security Council established the International Criminal Tribunal for the Former Yugoslavia (ICTY) and in 1994 the International Criminal Tribunal for Rwanda (ICTR). The constituent documents and jurisprudence of the two ad hoc tribunals, the ICTY[39] and the ICTR,[40] and the statutes of the International Criminal Court (ICC)[41] and the Special Court for Sierra Leone[42] are of groundbreaking significance in the context of redress for women and girl children through the international criminal law process (see Oosterveld, chapter 3; Bedont, chapter 4). In recent times, other extralegal mechanisms that provide alternative and in some cases complementary avenues for redress have been adopted.

Another central United Nations initiative that addressed the particular situation of women in armed conflict and the international legal response thereto was the 1995 Fourth World Conference on Women held in Beijing. At this conference, women and armed conflict was identified as one of the twelve critical areas of concern to be addressed by member states, the international community, and civil society.[43] Paragraph 44 of the Beijing Platform for Action calls on "governments, the international community and civil society, including non-governmental organizations and the private sector to take strategic action," inter alia, in relation to "the effects of armed or other kinds of conflict on women, including those living under foreign occupation."[44]

The Platform for Action recognizes that civilian casualties outnumber military casualties and that women and children constitute a significant number of the victims.[45] Having diagnosed the nature of the problem of women and armed conflict, the Platform for Action proposes a number of strategic objectives and the actions to be taken by relevant actors to achieve these aims. In the context of legal responses, the Platform for Action calls for the upholding and reinforcement of the norms of international humanitarian and human rights law in relation to these offenses against women, and the prosecution of all those responsible.[46]

Girls have benefited in various ways from the developments noted above (as discussed in greater detail below). The 1989 Convention on the Rights of the Child applies to all children in all circumstances[47] and includes provisions regarding children during armed conflict. However, it was not until the 1990s that the United Nations began to give more explicit attention to the impact of armed conflict on adolescent girls and girl children. In 1993, the General Assembly invited the secretary-general to undertake a study on the impact of armed conflict on children. The resulting study[48] highlighted the ways in which girls are placed at particularly high risk during armed conflict, as well as emphasizing their numerous experiences and roles. In 1997, the secretary-general appointed a special representative for children and armed conflict with a mandate to protect and promote the rights of war-affected children and ensure that those rights are comprehensively addressed by principle actors at all levels. Furthermore, the special representative is to "promote the application of international norms and traditional value systems that provide for the protection of children in times of conflict, making the protection of children a priority concern in peace processes and peace operations and in all efforts to consolidate peace, heal and rebuild in the aftermath of conflict." The efforts of the special representative for children and armed conflict have resulted in the inclusion of child protection officers in United Nations peacekeeping mandates in Sierra Leone and the Democratic Republic of the Congo. The special representative also supported and facilitated the development of local peace initiatives, including the grassroots Sudanese Women for Peace, as well as advocated for a new law in Rwanda allowing girls to inherit property.

In 1998, the Rome Statute for the International Criminal Court included within it crimes against humanity and war crimes against women and children, including recruitment of children under fifteen years of age for hostilities. In 1999, the International Labour Organization Convention 182 named child soldiering among the worst forms of child labor and set a minimum standard of eighteen years of age for forced or compulsory recruitment. That same year, the Lomé Peace Agreement for Sierra Leone marked the first time that special provisions for children were incorporated into a peace agreement. Also in 1999, the Security Council adopted a resolution on children and armed conflict (S/RES/1261) and another on the protection of civilians during armed conflict (S/RES/1265). May 2000 marked the adoption of an Optional Protocol to the Convention on the Rights of the Child that established eighteen as the minimum age for children to participate in hostilities.

Gender Perspectives within Peace and Security:
Gender Equality, Balance, and Mainstreaming

The global commitment to incorporate gender perspectives in peace and security issues was established in the Beijing Declaration and the Platform for Action in 1995, with the endorsement of gender mainstreaming as a global strategy for promotion of gender equality. Other central events include the 1995 Fourth World Conference on Women; the 1997 United Nations Economic and Social Council call for gender mainstreaming; the 1998 recommendations by the Commission on the Status of Women for increasing women's participation in conflict prevention, peacekeeping, and postconflict peace building and reconstruction; and the support shown by numerous United Nations entities, including members of the Security Council, during the March 2000 discussions entitled "Women Uniting for Peace," regarding women's involvement in peace activities (see Raven-Roberts, chapter 2).[49]

Gender, gender equality, balance, and mainstreaming are key concepts used throughout this book. These concepts are not without complexity or debate. In order to maintain some level of conceptual clarity and depth, we offer the following definitions as a minimum foundation upon which the contributors to this collection build.

Gender

Gender is a central concept used throughout the book. Gender refers to the socially constructed differences between men and women and boys and girls. Thus, gender is about the social roles of men, women, boys, and girls and relationships between and among them. The experiences and concerns of men, women, boys, and girls before, during, and after wars and armed conflicts are shaped by their gendered social roles. These roles are in turn formed by cultural, social, economic, and political conditions, expectations, and obligations within the family, community, and nation. Because gender is not natural or biological it varies over time and across cultures. Gender is shaped by and helps shape concepts and experiences of ethnicity, race, class, poverty level, and age. The categories of women, men, boys, and girls are not without complexity or controversy. The use of monolithic terms such as "women," "men," "women's experiences," or "men's experiences" does not account for the diversity and stratification among women and men and the effects of ethnicity, race, class, poverty level, age, and geographic location. Consequently, these other factors greatly influence individual women's and men's positions and responses. Within complex political emergencies, it is important to recognize gender's crosscutting role and, most significantly, examine the effects of gender on power relations—how it is manifested and used, by whom (individuals and institutions), and how this plays out before, during, and after armed conflict.

Gender Equality

Gender equality refers to the equal rights, responsibilities, and opportunities of women, men, girls, and boys. It is a goal that has been accepted, at least rhetorically, by numerous governments and international organizations and is enshrined in international agreements and commitments.[50]

Gender Balance

The two principal strategies within the United Nations to achieve gender equality are gender balance and gender mainstreaming. Gender balance refers to the degree to which women and men participate within the full range of activities associated with the United Nations. The United Nations has committed itself to a goal of full gender balance in all professional posts.[51] Focusing on gender balance involves documenting women's existing participation and involves an examination of the barriers to women's participation and efforts made by different formal actors to increase their contributions.

Many of the organizations working within conflict and postconflict situations in the United Nations are approaching, and in a few cases have achieved, gender balance at United Nations Headquarters within professional and higher-level staff, positions classified as P1 through secretary-general.

While there has been some success in achieving gender balance at United Nations Headquarters, the same is not true in the field. Although due to different ways of classifying and counting personnel in the field, no comparable figures are available, many United Nations personnel note anecdotally that most departments and agencies have not approached gender balance in field offices. One area that is illustrative is in peacekeeping operations, where women's participation remains low. In all current missions as of 2001, the proportion of women never exceeded 6 percent of military personnel. Women made up no more than 16 percent of United Nations Civilian Police (CIVPOL) for any given operation, representing 5 percent or less of CIVPOL forces in five of the six current operations using civilian police. Where women are present in large numbers on peacekeeping missions, it tends to be in the area of the nonprofessional civilian positions, such as secretaries and lower-placed administrators. Women are rarely present at the highest levels within missions.[52]

Women's increased participation within humanitarian, peace-building, and peacekeeping operations is important to achieve the goals of various United Nations standards, mandates, and declarations regarding equality, nondiscrimination, and human rights. The increased presence of women in United Nations agencies in situations of chronic conflict and instability and reconstruction is further necessary to help ensure that women's and girls' protection and assistance needs are met and their rights upheld. For example, it is widely reported that women and girls are more likely to ask for assistance on a variety of issues or report abuses, particularly sexual abuses, to women staff (see Fitzsimmons, chapter 9; Olsson, chapter 8; Baines, chapter 11; Wilson, chapter 12).[53] While women staff are necessary in all agencies, reports from United Nations humanitarian and development agencies testify that key positions to have women in include protection officers, health staff, food distribution officers, interpreters, specialist staff, and adviser posts.[54] Field reports from a variety of United Nations agencies recommend women staff to be placed in situations where women and girls within the host nation are not permitted to interact with males outside their family.[55]

Gender balance in top positions in United Nations missions demonstrates to local populations support for equality and nondiscrimination against women and girls (see Raven-Roberts, chapter 2; Mackay, chapter 13). This can be particularly important in situations in which local constitutions and other legal instruments are being rewritten, and in which decisions about equality and rights provisions within those instruments are being debated.

Gender Mainstreaming

Gender mainstreaming is the second strategy identified by the United Nations to achieve gender equality. Gender mainstreaming is defined in the ECOSOC agreed conclusions 1997/2 as

> the process of assessing the implications for women and men of any planned action, including legislation, policies or programmes in all areas and at all levels. It is a strategy for making women's as well as men's concerns and experiences an integral dimension of design, implementation, monitoring and evaluation of policies and programmes in all political, economic and societal spheres so that women and men benefit equally and inequality is not perpetuated. The ultimate goal is to achieve gender equality.[56]

Gender mainstreaming entails bringing the perceptions, experience, knowledge, and interests of women as well as men to bear on policy making, planning, and decision making.

A focus on gender mainstreaming in situations of conflict and postconflict involves recognizing that women, girls, men, and boys experience and recover from the effects of violence and community destabilization differently according to their gender, age, ethnicity, and class status in society. Consequently, peace processes and postconflict recovery affect them differently. These differences should be understood and taken into account in all responses to armed conflict. These groups may also participate in the conflict, and in subsequent peace and recovery processes, very differently. The forums in which women and girls participate must be acknowledged and, where possible, supported along with the forums in which men and boys participate.

Although gender mainstreaming and gender balance are related, they are two distinct strategies aimed at promoting gender equality. The presence of more equal numbers of women is no guarantee that gender mainstreaming will be conducted (see Raven-Roberts, chapter 2).

United Nations Security Council Resolution 1325

Following a historic open discussion in the Security Council entitled "Women, Peace, and Security" on October 24–25, 2000, in which forty member states made strong statements supporting the mainstreaming of gender perspectives into peace support operations,[57] the Security Council adopted a resolution (S/RES/1325) on women, peace, and security. Resolution 1325 builds on a series of United Nations Security Council resolutions[58] and provides a number of important operational mandates, with implications for both individual member states and the United Nations system. An Arria Formula meeting was also held on women, peace, and security on October 23, 2000, providing an opportunity for the members of the Security Council to discuss the impact of armed conflict on women and women's role in peace processes with representatives of women's NGOs. Initiated by the president of the Security Council, Arria Formula meetings provide opportunities to have informal, confidential dialogue among Security Council members, nonmembers, and NGOs to provide information and assessment on issues related to peace and security. In the closed meeting, women from Zambia, Sierra Leone, Somalia, and Guatemala presented concrete experiences of women and girls in armed conflict. They raised concerns of grassroots movements of women committed to preventing and solving conflicts and bringing peace, security, and sustainable development to their communities.

To briefly summarize, Security Council Resolution 1325 reiterates the importance of bringing gender perspectives to the center of attention in all United Nations conflict prevention and resolution, peace-building, peace-keeping, rehabilitation, and reconstruction efforts. It calls for increased representation of women, particularly at decision-making levels, increased consultation with women, and attention to the special needs of women and girls, for example, in refugee situations. It emphasizes the respect for the human rights of women and girls, the need to draw attention to violence against women and girls, and calls for an end to impunity and the prosecution of those responsible for crimes related to sexual and other violence against women and girls. The resolution furthermore requests that the United Nations incorporate gender perspectives in negotiation and implementation of peace agreements, in all peacekeeping operations, in refugee camps, and in disarmament, demobilization, and rehabilitation initiatives. It asks the Security Council itself to ensure that Security Council missions take gender considerations into account, including through consultation with women's organizations. It specifically calls upon member states to increase voluntary financial, technical, and logistic support to gender-sensitive training efforts and to incorporate gender perspectives in national training programs. The resolution requests that the secretary-general include progress in gender mainstreaming in reporting on peacekeeping missions. It also requests that he provide member states with training guidelines and materials on the protection, rights, and needs of women and girls and invite member states to make use of these materials, as well as HIV/AIDS awareness training. It asks the secretary-general to ensure that civilian personnel of peacekeeping operations receive similar training. Finally, the resolution asked the secretary-general to prepare a study and report on the impact of armed conflict on women and girls, the role of women in peace building, and the gender dimensions of peace processes and conflict resolution.

The resulting study, *Women, Peace and Security: Study of the United Nations Secretary-General as Pursuant Security Council Resolution 1325*, and subsequent report by the secretary-general to the Security Council, *Report of the Secretary-General on Women, Peace and Security*, highlight the need for gender-based analyses and existing knowledge on gender and armed conflict and postconflict to be incorporated "into the policies, planning and implementation processes in all peace operations, humanitarian activities and reconstruction efforts."[59] Furthermore, the secretary-general calls upon the Security Council and member states to:

- identify and utilize local sources of information on the impact of armed conflict, the impact of interventions of peace operations on women and girls, and the roles and contributions of women and girls in conflict situations, including through the establishment of regular contacts with women's groups and networks;
- ensure that all peace accords brokered by the United Nations systematically and explicitly address the consequences of the impact of armed conflict on women and girls, and their contributions to the peace processes and their needs and priorities in the postconflict context;
- ensure full involvement of women in negotiations of peace agreements at national and international levels;
- incorporate gender perspectives explicitly into mandates of all peacekeeping missions, including provisions to systematically address this issue in all reports to the Security Council; and
- ensure necessary financial and human resources for gender mainstreaming, including the establishment of gender advisers/units in multidimensional peacekeeping operations and capacity-building activities.[60]

As the contributions in this book make clear, these recommendations are key markers along the road to developing peace operations and international intervention that can actually succeed in building gender-just peace in both the short and long term. Yet, again as the book's contributors reveal, there remain major stumbling blocks to reaching these recommendations. A better understanding of peace operations' structures and roles is thus a necessary starting point to locate points of entry for critique and institutional change.

Peace Processes: The Structure and Role of Peacekeeping

Peacekeeping falls within the broader rubric of peace processes that consist of a complex range of formal and informal activities. Informal initiatives include marches, demonstrations, protests, interethnic dialogue, intercultural exchange, and a variety of actions for social, political, and economic justice. A wide range of actors is involved in informal peace initiatives, including grassroots, local, national, and international organizations, peace groups, religious organizations, and multilateral agencies.[61]

Formal activities include such measures as early warning, conflict prevention, preventive diplomacy, sanctions, peace negotiations, peace accords, peacemaking, peace building, global disarmament, and peacekeeping.[62] In practice these activities include, but are not limited to, conflict resolution, peace negotiations, reconstruction of infrastructure, and the provision of humanitarian aid. These activities are conducted by political leaders, militaries, formal international organizations such as the United Nations, regional organizations such as the Organization for Security and Cooperation in Europe (OSCE), the North Atlantic Treaty Organization (NATO), and the Economic Community of West African States (ECOWAS), and governmental, nongovernmental, and humanitarian organizations.

The end of the Cold War not only precipitated new forms of armed conflict, but it also resulted in a dramatic increase in the number of peace operations and a qualitative change in the manner in which peace operations are conducted. United Nations peacekeeping operations are authorized by a resolution from the Security Council. The Security Council is responsible for the overall political direction of a United Nations peace operation.[63] It is the particular Security Council resolution(s) that provides the mandate and scope of the operation. The secretary-general maintains executive direction and command over peacekeeping operations. The United Nations Department of Peacekeeping Operations (DPKO) carries out military observer, enforcement, and peacekeeping operations, while the Department of Political Affairs (DPA) has oversight of peace-building operations, including human rights observer missions, and works with the United Nations Development Program (UNDP) and/or the Office for the Coordination of Humanitarian Affairs (OCHA).

These agencies play central roles in advising the secretary-general on the political, military, and humanitarian situation of the affected country. The recommendations of officials within DPA, DPKO, and OCHA in turn influence the composition of the secretary-general's response to the Security Council resolution and his decisions on how to structure the peace operation. DPA and DPKO also play a lead role in advising the secretary-general on selection of the chief of mission. The chief of mission is the special representative to the secretary-general (SRSG), force commander or chief military observer, which in each instance will be determined by the Security Council resolution that mandates the operation. The chief of mission reports to the secretary-general, who in turn reports back to the Security Council, the General Assembly, and contributing member states about the progress of the operation.

There are essentially three types of peace operations: observer missions, peacekeeping operations, and peace enforcement operations. Observer missions, Chapter V of the United Nations Charter, are often sent to monitor and observe cease-fires, verify troop withdrawals, or patrol borders and demilitarized zones. Observer missions can also be deployed without invoking Chapter V, as in the case of the United Nations Observer Mission to South Africa.[64] These latter missions are primarily composed of civilian personnel, who can be involved as electoral observers, or in the observation of acts of violence, human rights abuses, and so on.

Peacekeeping operations, Chapter VI, entail the presence of a multinational force of military, police, and humanitarian actors under the authority, if not always the command, of the United Nations. In peacekeeping operations three principles usually apply: consent of the parties to the presence of the peacekeeping force, impartiality of that force, and no use of force except in instances of self-defense. Peacekeeping operations are deployed to protect civilian populations, enable humanitarian components of the operation to carry out their work, and help press parties to achieve resolution of the armed conflict and move toward reconciliation. They may also be deployed to assist in political, judicial, economic, and social reconstruction. At all times, peacekeeping forces should be able to defend themselves, the other components of the operation, and the operation's mandate.[65]

Peace enforcement operations, Chapter VII, empower the United Nations to take direct action against those who are responsible for "threats to the peace, breaches of the peace or acts of aggression," including in defense of peacekeeping personnel who may come under attack. Certain aspects of peace operations that are primarily humanitarian may also be given additional peace enforcement mandates that do not require the consent of the warring parties, impartiality, or refrainment from the use of force, as in the case of the protection of "safe areas" in Bosnia and Herzegovina. Chapter VII has been used to authorize peace enforcement missions in the Korean conflict in 1950 and more recently following Iraq's invasion of Kuwait, as well as in Albania, East Timor, Haiti, Rwanda, and Somalia.

It is important to note that aspects of these operations may overlap. Likewise, an operation may transform from one type into another as circumstances change. There are enormous differences in the scope of operations.

Many contemporary multidimensional peacekeeping operations are increasingly complex, and can involve the creation of political institutions; disarmament, demobilization, and reintegration of former fighters; clearing of mines; the conduct of elections; and the promotion of sustainable development practices. Some United Nations operations have served as transitional civil administrations involved in, among other activities, establishing customs services and regulations, conducting elections, setting and collecting business and personal taxes, attracting foreign investment, adjudicating property disputes and liabilities for war damage, reconstructing and operating all public utilities, re-creating judicial and legislative structures, creating a banking system, providing health care, running schools and paying teachers, and collecting garbage.[66]

Peacekeeping operations are not only carried out by the United Nations. Although varied in composition, mandate, and resources, regional organizations such as NATO and ECOWAS have used Chapter VIII of the Charter of the United Nations to lead and undertake parts of peacekeeping operations within their regions. In 1993, the United Nations Observer Mission in Liberia (UNOMIL) was the first United Nations peacekeeping mission undertaken in cooperation with a peacekeeping operation already established by another multilateral organization, ECOWAS. The Organization of African Unity (OAU) has also sought to reinforce the United Nations' role by extending support to the peacemaking process in almost every recent African conflict. NATO, under the direction of the OSCE, has initiated three peacekeeping operations, the International Implementation Force (IFOR), Stabilization Force (SFOR)—the operation that succeeded IFOR—and the Kosovo Force (KFOR). In another example, the United Nations Observer Mission in Georgia (UNOMIG) works in close cooperation with the OSCE and the Commonwealth of Independent States (CIS).

Thinking about Gender, Conflict, and International Intervention Post-9/11

Two significant events occurred during the construction of this volume that further illuminate the central issues herein, predominately, the nature of new wars and the resulting implications for international intervention. The nature of new wars is well illustrated in the bombing of the Twin Towers and the United States Pentagon on September 11, 2001, resulting in a United States–led invasion and occupation of Afghanistan and, now, Iraq. These attacks brought to the American public, in a very graphic way, the kinds of horrors that many communities in situations of armed conflict are forced to face on a daily basis. As the events of 9/11 and the contributions in this volume make clear, one of the characteristics of the new conflicts is the civilian nature of both the perpetrators and victims of the violence. Far from the use of conventional weapons and tactics of war, we have moved to conflicts where civilians, including women and children, are the combatants, perpetrators, and intended targets of violence. We have moved to conflicts where the final weapon of mass destruction and mass terror is the body, the body as bomb.

The attacks of 9/11 and the Bush administration's response resulted in heightened discussion and definitions of terrorism that have enormous impact on today's situations of protracted armed conflicts and international response and intervention. The contributions in this volume illuminate the terrorist tactics used by those who subject communities to a daily reign of terror, through targeting the lives and livelihoods of civilians and the calculated use of extreme violence, raids, looting, and slavery. Unlike the events of 9/11, the terrorism experienced by these civilians has gone on for years and in some cases decades. Yet in the past, as now, the acts of violence they suffer have not been sufficiently recognized or addressed by the international community. Ironically, it does not appear that this will be altered by the events of 9/11. Indeed, the suffering of these communities may be pushed even further to the margins, even as this volume reveals that 9/11 is only a heightened version of a spectrum of terrorism in the new wars.

In the context of 9/11, terrorism takes on new meaning and we are being asked to focus nearly exclusively on terrorism against the United States and its allies. Such facile analysis sets up false distinctions between those who are terrorized and those who are terrorists. Indeed, the official war on terrorism coming out of the United States and, to a lesser extent, the West is being conducted in a way that takes the focus away from understanding the underlying causes and current infusions that perpetuate situations of chronic political instability, violence, and human insecurity. At the same time, huge sums are being diverted from other conflict areas to be spent on the war, occupation, and reconstruction of Iraq, and to a lesser extent Afghanistan. The aid work done in other areas and built up over years is thus weakened. Consequently, while NGOs, donor governments, and private corporations initially lined up to enter Iraq to assist in the "humanitarian endeavor" under way there, the Democratic Republic of the Congo continues to suffer deaths and casualties of catastrophic proportion, thousands of children in northern Uganda are abducted and forced to fight in the rebel forces, and famine breaks out in Ethiopia. Yet in the post-9/11 context, the political agenda shifts to focus on the official war on terrorism and away from addressing these protracted crises.

Several ironies and dangers emerge out of the post-9/11 context. One is that those who have been campaigning for the protection and promotion of women's and girls' human rights and for increased gender awareness in international relations and intervention are now seeing these same agendas manipulated to validate military invasion and occupation. The liberation of women and girls in Afghanistan and Iraq was repeatedly used as a justification for military invasion and sets a dangerous precedent of new wars of humanitarian intervention.

As international foreign policy agendas are redrawn and discussions flare around the "New World Order," we need to remember that the old world of disorder is still quite real and pressing. At the same time, very little of the "New World Order" discourse addresses this key factor. Yet new terminology and frameworks will assist us little unless we develop and refine the means to analyze the past and current states of disorder and how they are shaping the future.

Notes

1. Binta Mansaray, "Women against Weapons: A Leading Role for Women in Disarmament," in *Bound to Cooperate: Conflict, Peace and People in Sierra Leone*, ed. Anatole Ayissi and Robin-Edward Poulton, 144–49 (Geneva: United Nations Institute for Disarmament Research, 2000).

2. International Committee of the Red Cross, *Women Facing War* (Geneva: ICRC, 2001); UNICEF input for the secretary-general's study *Women, Peace and Security: Study Submitted by the Secretary-General Pursuant to Security Council Resolution 1325* (New York: UN, 2002).

3. Coalition to End the Use of Child Soldiers [or Coalition], *Child Soldiers Global Report* (London: Coalition, 2001); Coalition, "Americas Report," 2000 [database online], available at www.childsoldiers.org/americas; Coalition, "Africa Report," 2000 [database online], available at www.childsoldiers.org/africa; Coalition, "Asia Report," 2000 [database online], available at www.childsoldiers.org/asia; Coalition, "Europe Report," 2000 [database online], available at www.childsoldiers.org/europe; Coalition, "Special Report: Girls with Guns," 2000, available at www.childsoldiers.org/reports/special%20reports; Dyan Mazurana, Susan McKay, Khristopher Carlson, and Janel Kasper, "Girls in Fighting Forces: Their Recruitment, Participation, Demobilization, and Reintegration," *Peace and Conflict* 8, no. 2 (2002): 97.

4. Mazurana et al., "Girls in Fighting Forces."

5. Dyan Mazurana, Susan R. McKay, and International Centre for Human Rights and Democratic Development, "Women and Peacebuilding," in *Essays on Human Rights and Democratic Development*, no. 8 (Montreal: International Centre for Human Rights and Democratic Development [ICHRDD], 1999), 2.

6. United Nations, *Women, Peace and Security*.

7. IASC Secretariat, "Mainstreaming Gender in the Humanitarian Response to Emergencies" (final draft background paper, IASC Working Group, 36th meeting, Rome, April 22–23, 1999).

8. UN Docs. CEDAW/C.2001/1/Add.1/; CRC/C/15/Add.133; CRC/C/15/Add.116; Graça Machel, *The Impact of War on Children* (London: Hurst & Company, 2001).

9. United Nations, *Integration of the Human Rights of Women and the Gender Perspective: Violence against Women*, report of the special rapporteur on violence against women, its causes and consequences, Radhika Coomaraswamy, E/CN.4/2001/73; World Health Organization input to the secretary-general's study *Women, Peace and Security*, on file with authors.

10. See United Nations, *Integration of the Human Rights of Women and the Gender Perspective: Violence against Women*, report of the special rapporteur on violence against women, its causes and consequences, Radhika Coomaraswamy, on trafficking in women, women's migration, and violence against women, submitted in accordance with Commission on Human Rights Resolution 1997/44, February 29, 2000, E/CN.4/2000/68 and E/CN.4/2001/83; Human Rights Watch, *World Report 2000* (New York: HRW, 2000).

11. Roberta Cohen and Francis M. Deng, *Masses in Flight: The Global Crisis of Internal Displacement* (Washington, DC: Brookings Institution, 1998); UN Docs. E/CN.4/2000/83/Add.1 and E/CN.4/2001/5/Add.3.

12. United Nations, *Report of the Secretary-General to the Security Council on the Protection of Civilians in Armed Conflict*, A/56/259 (August 1, 2001).

13. Women's Commission for Refugee Women and Children, *Refugee and Internally Displaced Women and Children in Serbia and Montenegro* (New York: WCRWC, 2001); United Nations, *Women, Peace and Security*.

14. See Isis-WICCE, *Women's Experiences of Armed Conflict in Uganda, Gulu District, 1986–1999* (Kampala, Uganda: Isis-WICCE, 2001); Sue Lautze, Neamat Nojumi, Karim Najimi, and Elizabeth Stites, *Coping with Crisis: A Review of Coping Strategies throughout Afghanistan, 1999–2002* (Washington, DC: USAID, 2002).

15. Lautze et al., *Coping with Crisis.*

16. IASC Secretariat, "Mainstreaming Gender in the Humanitarian Response to Emergencies."

17. IASC Secretariat, "Mainstreaming Gender in the Humanitarian Response to Emergencies."

18. United Nations, *Women, Peace and Security.*

19. United Nations, *Situation of Human Rights in Somalia*, report of the special rapporteur, Mona Rishmawi, submitted in accordance with Commission on Human Rights Resolution 19, E/CN.4/1998/96; Brigitte Sørensen, *Women and Post-conflict Reconstruction: Issues and Sources* (Geneva: United Nations Research Institute for Social Development and the Programme for Strategic and International Security Studies, 1998).

20. See Alex deWaal, "Dangerous Precedents? Famine Relief in Somalia, 1991–1993," in *War and Hunger: Rethinking International Responses to Complex Emergencies*, ed. Joanna Macrae and Anthony Zwi, with Mark Duffield and Hugo Slim, 139–59 (London: Zed Books, 1994); Joanna Macrae, *Aiding Recovery? The Crisis of Aid in Chronic Political Emergencies* (London: Zed Books, 2001).

21. "New IOM Figures on the Global Scale of Trafficking," *Trafficking in Migrants Quarterly Bulletin* 23 (April 2001).

22. See UN Doc. E/CN.4/2000/68.

23. United States Commission for Refugees, *World Refugee Survey 2001* (April 19, 2002), available at refugees.org/world/articles/50 years__rro1__5.htm#50years.

24. "Africa: Women refugees need rights," *World News*, August 27, 2001.

25. IASC Secretariat, "Mainstreaming Gender in the Humanitarian Response to Emergencies."

26. United Nations High Commissioner for Refugees and Save the Children—UK, "The Experience of Refugee Children in Guinea, Liberia, and Sierra Leone Based on Initial Findings and Recommendations from Assessment Mission 22 October–30 November 2001" (February 2002).

27. Machel, *The Impact of War on Children*.

28. Machel, *The Impact of War on Children*.

29. IASC Secretariat, "Mainstreaming Gender in the Humanitarian Response to Emergencies"; United Nations Population Fund, "The Impact of Armed Conflict on Women and Girls: A Consultative Meeting on Mainstreaming Gender in Areas of Conflict and Rehabilitation," Bratislava, Slovakia, November 13–15, 2001.

30. United Nations Population Fund, "The Impact of Armed Conflict on Women and Girls."

31. Michael Toole and Ronald J. Waldman, "Refugees and Displaced Persons: War, Hunger and Public Health," *Journal of the American Medical Association* 270 (1993): 600.

32. *Report of the World Conference to Review and Appraise the Achievements of the United Nations Decade for Women: Equality, Development and Peace*, Nairobi, July 15–26, 1985 (UN publication, sales no. E.85.IV.10), chap. 1, sect. A, chap. 3.

33. UN Doc. A/CONF.157/24.

34. UN Doc. General Assembly Resolution 48/104.

35. UN Doc. S/2000/693.

36. United Nations Division for the Advancement of Women and the Department of Economic and Social Affairs, "Sexual Violence and Armed Conflict: United Nations Response," in *Women 2000* (New York: DAW, 1998).

37. United Nations, *Report of the Secretary-General on Rape and Abuse of Women in the Territory of the Former Yugoslavia*, E/CN.4/1994/5 (June 30, 1993). See also United Nations Division for the Advancement of Women and the Department of Economic and Social Affairs, "Sexual Violence and Armed Conflict."

38. United Nations Division for the Advancement of Women and the Department of Economic and Social Affairs, "Sexual Violence and Armed Conflict"; Human Rights Watch, *Leave None to Tell the Story: Genocide in Rwanda* (New York: HRW, 1999).

39. *Report of the Secretary-General Pursuant to Paragraph 2 of Security Council Resolution 808*, S/25704 (May 3, 1993), annex, as amended May 13, 1998.

40. See UN Doc. S/RES/955 (November 8, 1994), annex.

41. *Rome Statute of the International Criminal Court*, UN Doc. A/Conf.183/9 (July 17, 1998).

42. *Report of the Secretary-General on the Establishment of a Special Court for Sierra Leone*, S/2000/915 (October 4, 2000), annex.

43. United Nations General Assembly, *Fourth World Conference on Women, Action for Equality Development and Peace, Beijing Declaration and Platform for Action*, UN Doc. A/Conf.177/20 (1995), pars. 131, 136.

44. United Nations General Assembly, *Fourth World Conference on Women*, par. 44.

45. United Nations General Assembly, *Fourth World Conference on Women*, par. 133.

46. United Nations General Assembly, *Fourth World Conference on Women*, par. 145.

47. With the exception of the two countries that have not ratified it, the United States and Somalia.

48. United Nations, *Impact of Armed Conflict on Children*, report of the expert of the secretary-general, Graça Machel, submitted pursuant to General Assembly Resolution 48/157.

49. General Assembly press release GA/SM/157, WOM/1191 (March 7, 2000).

50. United Nations Office of the Special Adviser on Gender Issues and Advancement of Women, *Gender Mainstreaming: An Overview* (New York: UN, 2001).

51. Department of Peacekeeping Operations, Lessons Learned Unit, *Mainstreaming a Gender Perspective in Multidimensional Peace Operations* (New York: UN, 2000).

52. Dyan Mazurana with Eugenia Piza-Lopez, *Gender Mainstreaming in Peace Support Operations: Moving beyond Rhetoric to Practice* (London: International Alert, 2002).

53. See United Nations High Commissioner for Refugees, *Guidelines on the Protection of Refugee Women* (Geneva: UNHCR, 1991).

54. United Nations, *Women, Peace and Security*; United Nations High Commissioner for Refugees, *Reproductive Health in Refugee Situations: An Inter-agency Field Manual* (Geneva: UNHCR, 1999).

55. United Nations International Children's Fund, "The Gender Dimensions of Internal Displacement, concept paper and annotated bibliography, Office of Emergency Programs Working Paper Series (New York: UNICEF, 1998).

56. UN Doc. A/52/3/Rev.1.

57. Statements were made by the secretary-general, Kofi Annan, the special adviser to the secretary-general on gender issues and the advancement of women, Angela King, and the executive director of UNIFEM, Noeleen Heyzer. Statements were made by representatives of the following member states, in order of presentation: Jamaica, United States, Tunisia, Argentina, China, United Kingdom, Bangladesh, Russian Federation, Netherlands, Canada, France, Malaysia, Ukraine, Mozambique, Egypt, Democratic Republic of the Congo, South Africa, Liechtenstein, Singapore, Pakistan, Japan, Cyprus, Korea, India, New Zealand, Zimbabwe, Indonesia, United Republic of Tanzania, Australia, Croatia, Belarus, Ethiopia, Malawi, Guatemala, United Arab Emirates, Norway, Rwanda, Botswana, Nepal, and Namibia.

58. These include UN Docs. S/RES/1261, S/RES/1265, S/RES/1296, S/RES/1314, and the Statement of SC President, SC/6816, outcome document of 23rd Special Session of the General Assembly, "Women 2000: Gender Equality, Development, and Peace for the Twenty-first Century," A/S-23/10/Rev.1. Consideration should also be given to the impact on women and girls of the implementation of Article 41 of the United Nations Charter, which states that "the Security Council may decide what measures not involving the use of armed forces are to be employed to give effect to its decisions, and it may call upon the Members of the United Nations to apply such measures. These may include complete or partial interruption of economic relations and of rail, sea, air, postal, telegraphic, radio, and other means of communication, and the severance of diplomatic relations."

59. UN Doc. S/2002/114, 3.

60. UN Doc. S/2002/1154.

61. Sørensen, *Women and Post-conflict Reconstruction*; Mazurana, McKay, and International Centre for Human Rights and Democratic Development, "Women and Peacebuilding."

62. Boutros Boutros-Ghali, *An Agenda for Peace* (New York: UN, 1992), A/47/277-S/24111.

63. This material is drawn from United Nations, *Report of the Secretary-General on the Work of the Organization: Supplement to an Agenda for Peace*, position paper of the secretary-general on the occasion of the fiftieth anniversary of the United Nations, A/50/60–S/1995/1 (January 3, 1995).

64. UN Doc. S/RES/772 (1992).

65. *Report of the Panel on United Nations Peace Operations* [The Brahimi Report], A/55/305-S/2000/809 (August 21, 2000).

66. *Report of the Panel on United Nations Peace Operations*, pars. 76–77.

I

GENDER, COMPLEX POLITICAL EMERGENCIES, AND INTERNATIONAL INTERVENTION

CONTRIBUTIONS IN THIS SECTION DRAW upon current theories in militarism, peace, violence, and war economies to present critical analyses of current understandings of and responses to complex political emergencies. In particular, they highlight the role of gender in the ways that armed conflict, complex political emergencies, and peacekeeping and humanitarian operations are woven together. Within this, the contributors examine the history, current debates, efforts, and obstacles relating to mainstreaming gender in peacekeeping and humanitarian operations.

1

Gender and the Causes and Consequences of Armed Conflict

Dyan Mazurana

THE CAUSES OF ARMED CONFLICTS—those factors that generate violent conflicts and those that frustrate peace efforts—are deeper, occur earlier, and are more complex, interwoven, and transnational than the majority of us acknowledge. If we are to have any level of long-term success in building peace in societies experiencing protracted or prolonged crises, then increasingly we have to become not only curious about, but also skilled in and responsible for the social, economic, and political dynamics that fuel these conflicts. This is especially true for military and civilian actors engaged in peacekeeping and humanitarian operations, since they run a real risk of becoming incorporated into the very political and economic systems that thwart a return to sustainable peace and human security. Consequently, people in the United Nations, international NGOs, and governments need to become aware of and responsible for social, economic, and political actions that, to date, they would rather not be held accountable for.

Resistance to this responsibility is one of the central reasons why there is such stubborn opposition to and willful, token acknowledgment of the politics of femininity and masculinity in the causes and consequences of armed conflict and in a majority of past and current peacekeeping operations. Significantly, this resistance to seriously examining the politics of masculinity and femininity in generating unrest, in causing conflicts to become violent, and in the consequences of that violence during armed conflict and postconflict periods prevents those in charge of peacekeeping and humanitarian operations from (1) realistically explaining what has caused and sustained the particular conflict they have been assigned to end and, therefore, (2) fashioning peacekeeping and reconstruction policies that can succeed.

This chapter is part of growing critical conversations that challenge the dominant views regarding the causes of and responses to today's complex political emergencies. Within the United Nations discourse, a complex political emergency denotes "a conflict-related humanitarian disaster involving a high degree of break-down and social dislocation and, reflecting this condition, requiring a system-wide aid response for the international community."[1] At the same time, I aim to provide a broad, critical overview of the types of international intervention into these emergencies. In doing so, I seek to make apparent the underlying tensions between the approaches of the peacekeeping and humanitarian operations described in the rest of the book and the complex, and often misunderstood, situations into which they are sent. I argue that much of the current focus by the United Nations, Bretton Woods institutions, and government international development agencies on postconflict transition and reconstruction is misplaced. Rather, I concur with Joanna Macrae that "by the late 1990s, the problem becomes less one of how to deal with situations of 'post' conflict transition, but how to manage chronic political emergencies—in other words, how to work in the most vulnerable quasi-states experiencing protracted crises of legitimacy, security and financing."[2]

Contemporary Armed Conflicts: Challenging Assumptions

Students of contemporary armed conflict are well versed with the litany of its defining features, primarily, that these conflicts are the result of military violence, largely internal, caused by extreme poverty and underdevelopment, have high civilian causalities, and result in mass displacement. Yet such listings may conceal more than they reveal.

First, within many such accounts, there is a trend by scholars and media reporters toward blanket labeling of rebel forces as little more than drug, weapon, and gem smugglers with little to no political ideologies or critiques against the ruling factions. In these accounts, rebel forces are dehumanized as "sadistic" or "monstrous" and the forms of violence they use described as "bizarre" and "barbaric." On the contrary, rebel forces often have legitimate complaints against governments (although they may use illegitimate means to address them), and their use of violence is anything but barbaric; indeed, it is exceedingly logical (as discussed below).

Second, much focus of scholars and media reporters today is on the impact of armed violence and the resulting devastation to a country's infrastructure. Military violence does play a major role in creating the health, education, food, and infrastructure crises witnessed in today's complex political emergencies. However, military violence alone is not primarily responsible for the poor functioning of these systems prior to the conflict. The essential problem is one of the breakdown, or in some cases deliberate cannibalization, by elites of functioning political institutions to govern political, economic, and social life.

Third, internal processes of underdevelopment and maldevelopment are put forward as the root cause of violence in the current dominant paradigm of the cause of complex political emergencies in the global South. International intervention and development are thus offered as the means to remove the cause of the violence, and we see this strongly in the rationale for much of the work by the United Nations Development Program (UNDP). However, the work of David Keen, Mark Duffield, Joanna Macrae, William Reno,[3] and others reveals the multifaceted links among poverty, inequality, exploitation, violence, and protracted crises. These authors bring to light the fact that it is primarily the political elite who are orchestrating and benefiting from violence, not the poor. Since the maintenance of power, especially via post–Cold War forms of patron systems, predominantly relies on control of the means and distribution of wealth, it becomes clear that international intervention and development that does not address the distribution of power and wealth will fail to protect individuals or societies from present or future violence.

Fourth, it is a myth that today's armed conflicts are only or largely internal. "The tendency to internalize the origins of, and solutions to, conflict is problematic in that it risks idealizing both the nature of war and its resolution."[4] More accurately, what we are witnessing are necessarily and simultaneously intrastate and interstate conflicts, with regional and international involvement, by licit international corporations, foreign governments, foreign armed opposition groups, various international aid organizations, mercenaries, and licit and illicit arms, drug, and mineral dealers. While causalities fall heaviest on civilians and the war slaves of the front lines—many of whom are abducted boys and girls, as in Angola, Colombia, the Democratic Republic of the Congo, Liberia, Sierra Leone, Sudan, and Uganda—these conflicts are fought at the behest and benefit of national and international elites looking to acquire lucrative returns from exploiting valuable natural and illicit assets. In the case of national elites, such returns are then fed, in part, into patron systems to maintain positions of power and political decision making. Thus, lasting resolution of these conflicts will have to directly expose and confront those who promote and benefit, both internally and internationally.

Along these lines, some scholars are encouraging international actors and institutions within peacekeeping operations to revise their notions of neutrality. This includes recommendations to examine the historical and current economic and political roots of the conflict, as well as to acknowledge and address the politicization of humanitarian policy (discussed below). There is also the need for international actors and agencies involved in peacekeeping and humanitarian intervention to identify "winners" and "losers" in the conflict and carefully assess the roles of international institutions in supporting these groups. Key components of this approach include simultaneously confronting local, national, and international political and economic structures that fuel and benefit from the conflict and supporting peaceful, popular, and alternative indigenous solutions to build peace.[5]

A more globalized approach to understanding the causes and consequences of many of today's protracted armed conflicts focuses on the role of shadow or war economies and the resulting emerging political complexes (described below).[6] Briefly, states made weak because of the legacies of colonialism, Cold War rivalries, and processes of globalization are vulnerable to challenges and replacement. Seeing the state weaken or its legitimacy questioned internally and internationally, those in power may respond by cracking down on any group that threatens their hold on power, simultaneously increasing dissatisfaction among the populace. Lacking the funding and support provided during Cold War rivalries or from former colonial powers, those seeking to oppose or replace the state in a violent manner engage in asset accumulation through parallel or shadow economies, including trafficking in minerals, gems, timber, gold, illegal drugs, and humans. This enables these forces to purchase weaponry and pay and provide for fighters to continue asset accumulation and attacks against government or civilian populations. For example, armed groups like the National Union for the Total Independence of Angola (UNITA), the Revolutionary Armed Forces of Colombia (FARC), or the Revolutionary United Front (RUF) in Sierra Leone were able to fund their campaigns largely through their links to shadow economies in illegal drugs and minerals. Such shadow economies are now prevalent in parts of Africa, Caucasia, central Asia, eastern Europe, and Latin America.[7]

The commodities that are being fought over and that are driving war economies are starkly gendered. Diamond mining and trading is gendered, as is oil extraction, timber harvesting, and the trade in gold, minerals, drugs, weapons, and so on. The displacement of populations to assert control over areas that contain natural resources and to provide cheap or slave labor is carried out with attention to gender. At the same time, human bodies have joined the list of assets within war economies—boys, girls, women, and men as war slaves, slave labor in mines and agricultural industries, or sexual or domestic slaves. While the human rights of these people are undeniably violated, the fact that their bodies have become commodities within the war economies has deeper, more causal, and explicitly transnational implications.

Recent wars in Angola, Colombia, the Democratic Republic of the Congo, Liberia, Uganda, Sierra Leone, and Sudan, for example, are marked by extreme

levels of violence against civilian populations, most notably butchery and am-
putation of limbs; the widespread use of abducted boys and girls as soldiers,
porters, and domestic and sexual slaves, and for mine detection; and mass
rape and sexual violence of extraordinary brutality against women and girls,
including rape, gang rape, sexual mutilation, and sexual slavery by the various
armed rebel and government forces. Violent acts are tailored with detailed attention to gender and ethnicity. In other words, gender is manipulated to
serve as a weapon of war and gender is what is attacked during the violence,
for example, the castration of men and boys and the cutting of the breasts and
vaginal regions of women and girls. The gendered consequences of violent
conflict continue after fighting subsides.

Winners and losers emerge as some groups and parties benefit—
economically, socially, and politically—from today's armed conflict. Dominant groups gain from the methods of nonconventional warfare and therefore
employ calculated applications of particular forms of violence. As the political and economic power of those controlling the extralegal economies grows,
new economic and political structures arise, headed by warlords, leaders of
armed forces or groups, dictators, international mafias, or ethnonationalist
regimes. The resulting economic and political power structures, termed
"emerging political complexes,"[8] are dominated almost exclusively by men
who govern through networks of elites, often consisting of relatives, mafias,
select local or regional elites, and heads of armed factions, including the military, paramilitaries, militias, police, and secret police. In most of these places
the power was held by men before, during, and after the violence.

Significantly, these emerging political complexes are not temporary phases
in a move toward stable, representative democracies. Often, these structures
do not rely on inclusive forms of governance or legitimacy based on representation of the populace. In such climates, governance typically supplants
government as power is exercised through nonstate actors, including armed
militias and other forms of administration, while control and protection is ex-
changed for payments in kind, forced labor, or unregulated access to resources. Displays of terror, violence, and coercive power can produce the desired results, even in elections—it is the presence of instability, armed conflict,
and control via violence, fear, and selective reward systems that enables certain
individuals and groups to maintain economic and political power. In other
words, the characteristics of today's conflicts—mass displacement, instability,
targeting of civilians, use of child soldiers, and ethnic, religious, and gendered
forms of violence—are not unfortunate by-products of the conflicts; they are
both the tools and the goals.

What is crucial to understanding many of today's armed conflicts is that
those attempting to gain and assume power are forced to create the social,

economic, and political conditions in which their new forms of wealth, the redistribution of that wealth to maintain their power, and an attempt at internal and international legitimacy can be realized. Rather than chaos, anarchy, and "new barbarianism," what we are seeing is the "independent emergence of new forms of protection, authority and rights to wealth."[9] We are seeing emerging political complexes—the appearance and development of new kinds of state or nonstate entities that are able to create alternative systems of profit, power, and protection, can use systems of globalized trade to obtain the necessary inputs via shadow and parallel economies, and can defend themselves and function administratively without significant bureaucracies.[10]

The Sex Trade and War Economies:
The Perfect Conditions—Foreign Troops and No Justice

Within the context of peacekeeping operations, it is essential that those planning and executing the military, police, and humanitarian components of peacekeeping missions operate with an understanding of these new emerging political complexes, their forms of state and nonstate entities, and the war or shadow economies that sustain them. It is essential that there is a clear recognition that these systems are founded upon systems of inequality and exploitation. For example, the sex trade is often central to predatory war economies. Yet heads of peacekeeping operations and peacekeepers and humanitarian aid workers themselves tend to treat the arrival or significant increase of "prostitutes" or, in some cases more accurately, sex slaves in war zones or areas of postconflict reconstruction as a natural occurrence—in the words of former United States ambassador to the United Nations Richard Holbrooke, "Human nature is human nature. Where peacekeepers go they attract prostitutes."[11]

Lack of understanding of the politics of masculinity and femininity in the development and maintenance of war economies and patron systems and in conflict and postconflict zones contributes to the mistaken belief that the presence of women and girls "willing" to have sex with male soldiers and humanitarian aid workers is a natural, indeed harmless, transnational phenomenon. Such misconceptions prevent those in peacekeeping operations from fully understanding the predatory economies that are in place. Indeed, the trafficking in women and children into slavery and sexual slavery is transcontinental and is intimately connected to armed conflict and forced displacement.[12] Consequently, by taking part in the sex trade, peacekeepers and humanitarian aid workers support economies that maintain instability in the region, perpetuate abuses of women's, girls', and boys' human rights, further entrench systems of inequity and exploitation, and, thus, thwart a return to real peace and human security.

The recent case of Kosovo demonstrates that the presence of trafficked women and girls is an indication of larger, violent war economies. As a recent analysis of reconstruction in southeastern Europe makes clear, with the arrival of peacekeepers and other internationals, "rather than a route for traffickers, Kosova has become a destination."[13] Kosovo received this dubious distinction partly because of the arrival of "foreign bureaucrats, project contractors and soldiers all helping to rebuild the province."[14] The routes used to smuggle weapons and fighters during the war in Kosovo are now used to move illegal weapons, drugs, and "human goods," including young girls taken from orphanages.[15]

Raids by international police forces recently exposed the inhuman conditions some of these women and girls endure upon being forced into sexual slavery in Kosovo:

> The owner of one bar . . . locked [the women and girls] into a squalid unheated basement without running water, toilets, or beds to sleep in. Some of the trapped women tried to commit suicide. Others were penned in an attic. All were kept under lock and key, and women who tried to escape were beaten. In addition to working as prostitutes, some of the women were forced to perform bar "entertainment."[16]

The mafias and criminal figures that run the organized sex trade in Kosovo often have links to the former Kosovo Liberation Army (KLA) and other armed groups, which have been implicated in trafficking illegal drugs and weapons since their emergence. Local and international police and United Nations officials working to stop the trafficking in humans, drugs, and weapons report that Serbians and Albanians, former enemies, are now "working together to control prostitution" in Pristina, the capital of Kosovo.[17]

Local women running shelters for women in the Balkans who have escaped the sex trade report that "some of the women have begged the humanitarian workers to help them, and they are just ignored."[18] How did the humanitarian aid workers come in contact with these women? They were among their clients, who also included a variety of ethnic Albanians, local and international police, and German, Russian, and United States peacekeeping troops.[19] In one case, a civilian member of the NATO-led Stabilization Force (SFOR) was found to be holding two women against their will in his residence; the SFOR member had earlier purchased the women from a local bar owner for his own use. Peacekeepers have also attempted to make a profit from the sexual exploitation of women, as demonstrated when peacekeepers in the United Nations operation in Bosnia (UNMIBH) were found guilty of offering protection to and, in some cases, operating brothels (see also Vandenberg, chapter 7).

Local Bosnian women are in the forefront of demanding attention to links among forces that fueled and profited from the armed conflict, the development of these political economies, and heightened levels of human insecurity in the Balkans. In recent interviews, these women expressed their desire for NATO-led SFOR peacekeeping troops to accelerate the arrests of war criminals in order to "help draw the teeth of the criminal gangs that beleaguer their towns—'It would make our lives safer.'"[20]

Senior officials within peacekeeping operations need to recognize that within these political economies wartime rape and "recreational" prostitution have links—destabilization of regions due to warfare and economic collapse may leave women and girls with few options for obtaining much-needed income, making them targets of regional and transnational human traffickers who at times sell them back to the very forces sent to resolve the violence in the region.

It is not only peacekeepers' and humanitarian aid workers' participation in a number of illegal markets that contributes toward strengthening aggressive and predatory forces. It is well documented that food aid, international humanitarian support, the establishment of refugee camps, and even NGO support of the "civil sector" have been manipulated to support those forces most responsible for the conflict. Examples include the use of food aid as a weapon by various factions in recent wars in Angola, Bosnia and Herzegovina, Ethiopia, Mozambique, Somalia, and Sudan; the fixing of exchange rates to benefit government coffers of nations host to peacekeeping forces in Mozambique, Sudan, and Iraq; the use of refugee camps and buffer zones as locations from which armed opposition groups and paramilitaries reconvene and launch attacks, as in Burundi, the Democratic Republic of the Congo, Colombia, Kosovo, and Serbia; and the internationalization of public welfare via international and national NGOs in Kosovo, Bosnia and Herzegovina, and throughout war-torn regions in Africa.

The Merging of Security and Development:
Militarization and International Intervention

It is necessary to map the ways in which peacekeeping operations are both military and humanitarian undertakings and to chart the intersection and interweaving of the two. Only then can we turn a critical eye to these endeavors and begin to examine the implications. A central pressing question then becomes, to what extent do the United Nations, multilateral organizations, and large international NGOs recognize not only the development of these emerging political complexes but also the implications of these emerging political complexes for their planning and implementation of international intervention? The answer is that they recognize these developments in varying degrees, with greater recognition by the humanitarian community than the military establishments. In both cases, the response, in part, has been an increased merging of security and development discourses and agencies. Or, in other words, the increased militarization of international intervention and development. As Cynthia Enloe reminds us:

> Militarization is the step-by-step process by which a person or a thing gradually comes to be controlled by the military or comes to depend for its well being on militaristic ideas. The more militarization transforms an individual or a society, the more that individual or society comes to imagine military needs and militaristic presumptions to be not only normal but valuable.[21]

Nonmilitary international organizations that are engaging with peacekeeping operations increasingly run the risk of having their agendas, programs, and daily operations militarized.[22] Since the early 1990s, the international relief system both inside and outside of the United Nations has become increasingly militarized (see Raven-Roberts, chapter 2). Humanitarianism is being equated with military interventions, so much so that at times military and humanitarian agendas become indistinguishable, as in Afghanistan and Iraq recently. Ever more, military peacekeeping components are involved in the transport and distribution of humanitarian aid and supplies. In a number of peacekeeping operations, we are witnessing an increased reluctance, even refusal, by humanitarian and police components to operate in areas where peacekeeping military is not active.

Peacekeeping itself is ever more used to justify increased military spending by militaries and defense departments, including by some of the leading contributors of peacekeeping troops. For example, in December 2000, Australia, the lead nation in peacekeeping operations in East Timor (UNTAET), received its biggest military spending increase in twenty years; the primary reason given was to enable it to update its forces to focus on peacekeeping. In other instances, peacekeeping may be used as a way for cash-strapped militaries to train and maintain larger armies than they could otherwise afford, as in Indonesia, Malaysia, Nepal, Pakistan, and Thailand. At the same time, recommendations from a highly influential assessment of United Nations peacekeeping, *Report of the Panel on United Nations Peace Operations* (the Brahimi Report), privilege the role of national and regional military bodies, calling for robust forces that can be rapidly deployed and emphasizing the need to project credible force.[23]

More muscular forms of peacekeeping or peace enforcement, as currently witnessed in Africa and in NATO operations in Europe, favor military over civilian components, further militarizing and masculinizing the operations (see Hudson, chapter 5). The more militarized and masculinized the operation, the greater the likelihood of weakening any chance of incorporating gender perspectives.[24] While militaries do play necessary and important roles in peacekeeping operations, the militarization and masculinization of peace, peacekeeping, peacemaking, peace building, development, and humanitarianism should not be viewed as natural or inevitable. Indeed, such developments should be closely monitored and continuously scrutinized.

Taking seriously the experiences of local and international activists and organizations that are negotiating with these institutions in war zones teaches that they are increasingly reliant upon militaries to carry out their work and increasingly uneasy about the fact. It is likely that in engaging in debates about transforming peacekeeping operations, and calling for and participating in developing policies and programs to that end, one inevitably encounters militaries and militarized alliances and organizations. However, it is not inevitable that one's own understanding, agenda, or goals become militarized. To avoid militarization requires a constant, conscious analysis and resistance to militarism and its temptations.[25] These temptations may be especially strong for international and local actors engaged in issues of gender and peacekeeping because militarizing one's agenda, even slightly, may offer promises of a voice in important matters such as "security," and access to "first-class citizenship," "equality," resources, and some of the most powerful institutions and bodies.

At the same time, there is an increased merging of security and development within humanitarian components of complex political emergencies. During the Cold War, international relations, including humanitarian and development aid, were largely structured by the standard of national sovereignty, which determined the scope for the provision of international assistance. Populations living in countries or regions experiencing armed conflict could only receive assistance in government-held areas or in a second country in which they had sought refuge. During the 1980s, the United Nations and international NGOs increasingly negotiated access into conflict zones in an attempt to provide humanitarian aid, thus using a strategy primarily developed and used by the International Committee of the Red Cross.[26]

Changes in the post–Cold War political landscape significantly altered the goals and working methods of international aid agencies, in particular within countries experiencing or affected by armed conflict. While earlier aid agencies had a conceptual and operational reliance on the apparatus of the state, there is now growing acknowledgment that the crisis of statehood—exemplified by weak or failing public institutions, limited governmental ability to raise and re-distribute revenue, inconsistent ability to exert control over all territory, in-cluding maintaining law and order, and, in numerous cases, extensive violence carried out by a number of government and nongovernmental groups—is call-ing into question the legitimacy and ability of those governments to govern.[27]

The recent move away from channeling relief through state entities, espe-cially in countries affected by armed conflict, is arguably the first systematic response by the international aid system to the predicament of violence within failing states. The shift away from working with states to working around them has included the development of more extensive ties with in-ternational NGOs and in some cases the privatization of humanitarian aid and relief, as in Sudan after 1989. Additionally, in the early 1990s, precedent was set for using military force to secure humanitarian access where, it was argued, negotiation had failed. In Somalia, Iraqi Kurdistan, Bosnia, and Rwanda, armed forces, usually under a United Nations flag, were deployed primarily to protect humanitarian relief agencies and workers, not local civilians.[28]

While in the past United Nations departments and agencies tended to work more independently of each other, today's complex political emergencies re-quire continuous and improved coordination and cooperation. This necessity was made clear in efforts of the United Nations in the aftermath of the Gulf War and was in part responsible for the 1991 creation of the United Nations Department of Humanitarian Affairs (DHA), now the Office for the Coordi-nation of Humanitarian Affairs (OCHA), which is mandated to better coor-dinate the responses of aid agencies in emergency situations. While OCHA is the body coordinating humanitarian operations, operational United Nations departments and agencies, such as the United Nations International Chil-dren's Fund (UNICEF), UNDP, the World Food Program (WFP), and the Of-fice of the United Nations High Commissioner for Refugees (UNHCR), take on implementing tasks (see Raven-Roberts, chapter 2).

The participation of regional organizations in responding to situations of armed conflict and postconflict also grew during the 1990s. In the early 1990s, as emphasis on economic and political reform and increased support for human rights, strengthening civil society, and democratization grew, the United Nations and leading regional organizations began developing new ways of linking and working with governments, militaries, and NGOs. Signif-icant growth of NGOs and their influence in the last two to three decades has amounted to billions of dollars in international aid to the South, exceeding that distributed through the United Nations. At ten to twelve billion USD, this amount accounts for approximately 13 percent of all international develop-ment aid and at least one-half of all humanitarian assistance. Considering that this amount excludes food aid, the actual proportion of aid being channeled through NGOs is most likely higher.[29]

These developments are taking place in a climate in which policies and practice involving development and security are increasingly merging. Major departments and institutions that previously were primarily associated with development assistance, such as UNDP and the World Bank, are now taking leading roles in defining and carrying out aid policy in conflict-affected countries, including work in conflict prevention and postconflict reconstruction. At the same time, the United Nations and international agencies primarily associated with humanitarian relief have increasingly sought and used development approaches to guide their actions in conducting relief operations in conflict and postconflict situations to support the potential for recovery.[30]

Conclusion

In conclusion, many officials within peacekeeping and humanitarian operations miss the centrality of masculinity and femininity in both the conflict and "postconflict" periods, believing that issues regarding women, gender, and human rights are "soft" or marginal issues, issues that can be addressed later, after the "hard" issues have been dealt with. In so doing, they make a serious miscalculation. They fail to comprehend what has caused and sustained the particular conflict they have been assigned to address and, therefore, are unable to design missions that can tackle these factors. In other words, they fail to grasp that these emerging political complexes exist upon a foundation of inequality and exploitation. Until the United Nations, governments, and international organizations recognize and develop ways to address these underlying factors, these systems will remain in place. At the same time, these miscalculations can result in interventions' contributing to the precise chronic political emergencies they were sent in to address. This can perpetuate the states' experiences of protracted crises of legitimacy, national and human security, and financing and lead to increasingly detrimental consequences for the majority of the civilian population.[31]

There is an increased concern regarding the militarization of humanitarianism, and rightly so. The new wars of humanitarian intervention in Afghanistan and Iraq are the final fusing of militarism and humanitarianism, highlighting the struggle between the United Nations' approaches to peacekeeping and peacemaking and the new foreign policy of the United States. The model the United States is presenting to the United Nations and the world is that of militarized humanitarianism, complete with military invasion, military occupation, military control over aid distribution, military responsibility for civilian aspects of reconstruction, military base construction, infusions of weapons into the country, and military spending and technological buildup. The implications are vast. Are we to move into a world where under the guise of neoliberal governance and "humanitarian intervention" new United States–led military invasions lead to militarized peacekeeping with an agenda for regime change and social engineering far beyond what had ever been dreamt up in a United Nations peacekeeping operation? If so, how will such militarized interventions build the ground for sustainable peace, human security, and human rights? Under what circumstances do they begin to identify and address the foundational exploitations and inequalities, including those that are gender based, that these systems are based on? And under what conditions can we imagine that such militarized humanitarianism will address the foundational factor of gender in any of these analyses?

Notes

1. Mark Duffield, *Global Governance and the New Wars: The Merging of Development and Security* (London: Zed Press, 2001), 12.

2. Joanna Macrae, *Aiding Recovery? The Crisis of Aid in Chronic Political Emergencies* (London: Zed Press, 2001), 153.

3. See David Keen, *The Benefits of Famine: A Political Economy of Famine and Relief in Southwestern Sudan, 1983–1989* (Princeton: Princeton University Press, 1994); Duffield, *Global Governance*; Macrae, *Aiding Recovery?*; Joanne Macrae and Anthony Zwi, eds., with Mark Duffield and Hugo Slim, *War and Hunger: Rethinking International Responses to Complex Emergencies* (London: Zed Books, 1994); William Reno, "Reinvention of an African Patrimonial State: Charles Taylor's Liberia," *Third World Quarterly* 16, no. 1 (1995): 109–20.

4. Macrae, *Aiding Recovery?* 41.

5. Duffield, *Global Governance*; Macrae, *Aiding Recovery?*; Macrae et al., *War and Hunger*; Dyan Mazurana and Susan McKay, *Women and Peacebuilding* (Montreal: International Centre for Human Rights and Democratic Development, 1999).

6. Mark Duffield, "Post Modern Conflict: Warlords, Post-Adjustment States and Private Protection," *Journal of Civil Wars*, April 1998: 90.

7. See Duffield, *Global Governance*; Michael Klare, *Resource Wars: The New Landscape of Global Conflict* (New York: Metropolitan Books, 2001).

8. Duffield, *Global Governance*.

9. Duffield, *Global Governance*, 139.

10. Duffield, *Global Governance*; Reno, "Reinvention of an African Patrimonial State."

11. Reuters, "UN Council Calls for AIDS Training for UN Troops," July 17, 2000, available at http://www.globalpolicy.org/security/peacekpg/general/aids3.htm.

12. Cynthia Enloe, *Maneuvers: The International Politics of Militarizing Women's Lives* (Berkeley: University of California Press, 2000); United Nations, *Women, Peace and Security: Study of the United Nations Secretary-General as Pursuant Security Council Resolution 1325* (New York: UN, 2002).

13. Chris Corrin, *Gender Audit of Reconstruction Programmes in South Eastern Europe* (Fairfax, CA: Urgent Action Fund and the Women's Commission for Refugee Women and Children, 2000), 14.

14. Reuters, "NATO, U.N. Swoop in Kosovo Prostitution Crackdown," *New York Times*, online edition, November 17, 2000, available at www.nytimes.com/reuters/world/international-kosovo-.

15. Dyan Mazurana with Eugenia Piza-Lopez, *Gender Mainstreaming in Peace Support Operations: Moving beyond Rhetoric to Practice* (London: International Alert, 2002).

16. Olivia Ward, "Even Aid Workers Make Use of Sex Slaves as Europe's Human Traffickers Exploit the War Zone," *Toronto Star*, May 7, 2000.

17. Reuters, "NATO, U.N. Swoop in Kosovo Prostitution Crackdown."

18. Ward, "Even Aid Workers Make Use of Sex Slaves."

19. Ward, "Even Aid Workers Make Use of Sex Slaves."

20. Cynthia Cockburn and Dubravka Zarkov, eds., *The Post-war Moment: Militaries, Masculinities and International Peacekeeping—Bosnia and the Netherlands* (London: Lawrence and Wishart, 2002), 114.

21. Enloe, *Maneuvers*, 3.

22. Enloe, *Maneuvers*; Suzanne Williams, "Conflicts of Interest: Gender in Oxfam's Emergency Response," in Cockburn and Zarkov, *The Post-war Moment*, 85–102.

23. Mazurana with Piza-Lopez, *Gender Mainstreaming*.

24. Mazurana with Piza-Lopez, *Gender Mainstreaming*; Dyan Mazurana, "International Peacekeeping Operations: To Neglect Gender Is to Risk Peacekeeping Failure," in Cockburn and Zarkov, *The Post-war Moment*, 41–50.

25. Enloe, *Maneuvers*.

26. Macrae, *War and Hunger*.

27. Macrae, *Aiding Recovery?* 8.

28. Macrae, *Aiding Recovery?*

29. Duffield, *Global Governance*.

30. Macrae, *Aiding Recovery?*

31. Macrae, *Aiding Recovery?* 153.

2

Gender Mainstreaming in United Nations Peacekeeping Operations: Talking the Talk, Tripping over the Walk

Angela Raven-Roberts

We are always writing and reading history . . . [W]e could help change the trajectory of this history. We can do this only if we are willing to unmask "gender." We will have to pull away gender's reassuring public mask of comfortable blandness and reveal it for what it should be: a conceptual tool to make us see things at work that we would rather not see.

—Cynthia Enloe

THIS CHAPTER EXPLORES HOW THE IDEOLOGY and practice of gender mainstreaming in peace support and peacekeeping operations is pursued and perceived within the United Nations. Many writers have attested to the unevenness (and in some cases near-complete lack) of progress in mainstreaming gender within the United Nations system[1] (see Mazurana et al., introduction). In this chapter, I offer a series of explanations for the conceptual, procedural, and personal constraints that prevent this philosophy from being put into practice. This analysis is based on my experience working in the United Nations as a program officer where I was charged with implementing principles of gender mainstreaming, as well as designing and implementing various training activities that covered a range of topics from humanitarian relief and coordination to gender and children's issues in peacekeeping and postconflict environments.

Three main issues underpin the lack of success of gender mainstreaming in United Nations peacekeeping operations, and they are key to the analysis and the subsequent conclusions I present. The first is a lack of conceptual coherence among the humanitarian, human rights, political, and development approaches that the United Nations is expected to balance in its responses to armed conflict. The second is the bias against gender equality within the United Nations system, a function of the myriad of identities and associated "baggage" that staff personnel bring to their jobs, as well as of flaws in the personnel and human resource management structures. The third, which is closely associated, is the lack of effective systems of management and evaluation to appropriately standardize principles of programming, monitor programs, and hold staff accountable for adhering (or not) to practices and overall United Nations goals.

The United Nations as an Ethnographic Site

Development specialists and political scientists currently note the existence of several "regimes" and discourses that compose and inform the world of international governance structures, including the World Bank and the United Nations.[2] Within these bodies, the making and shaping of policy reflects how these institutions legitimate and justify their actions and the ways in which they advocate and publicize what they stand for and what they do.

Policy is a key aspect of the process and mechanism of governance. Polices are used to guide and justify how bureaucracies are organized and to legitimate, for example, the ways in which power and resources are managed and shared among decision makers and those responsible for implementing policies.[3] As a perspective through which society is understood, gender analysis reveals differences in how society and labor are organized between and among men and women and how power is distributed.[4] Gender and war are deeply political and politicized topics. How the United Nations manages its policies pertaining to gender and war reveals as much about the organization itself as it does about the communities and issues it has been established to assist and redress.

The United Nations, Peacekeeping, and
the Struggle for Conceptual Coherence

In confronting war and crises, the United Nations has had to reconcile multiple conceptual challenges and respond to a myriad of internal and external advocacy groups working to make it adopt a range of perspectives.[5] In the past decade alone, the United Nations has mandated itself to integrate a number of human rights, humanitarian, development, and human security perspectives. Writers have labeled these perspectives, norms, and laws as "regimes."[6]

Since 1990, peacekeeping—the use of both military and civilian agencies to respond to countries affected by wars and crises—has increasingly become standard practice. Its results are varied. From the beginning of the United Nations until 1989 there were only fifteen peacekeeping operations. With the end of the Cold War and the resulting thawing of relations on the Security Council, this figure accelerated to thirty-five in the years 1989–2001. By 2001, more than 47,575 people had been deployed in peacekeeping operations.

Cambodia, Namibia, Mozambique, Guatemala, and El Salvador are cited to portray the "success" of these missions, although such designation is questionable (see Jacobson, chapter 6; Olsson, chapter 8; Luciak and Olmos, chapter 10). On the other hand, Angola, Somalia, Bosnia, and Rwanda unquestionably have shown the dangers and pitfalls of attempting peacekeeping responses without nuanced and well-designed strategies (see Jacobson, chapter 6; Vandenberg, chapter 7). The reasons for their failure and the complexities of responding to the particular kinds of crises facing contemporary societies are subjects of much interest and debate within international relations, political science, and development. Indeed, the movement to refine and institutionalize peacekeeping as a strategy of response by the international community has come as much from the theorists of these disciplines as from the actions and advocacy of human rights groups, humanitarian organizations, and others faced with seemingly ever-escalating spaces of terror, impoverishment, violence, and abuse. In view of the recent events surrounding the invasion of Iraq by the United States and the treatment of the United Nations Security Council, there is an additional level of complexity that must now be factored into these debates.

Taking on gender issues as a platform for policy action and response is a tall order in and of itself. Tackling the challenges of protracted conflict and the consequences of failed states, widespread human rights abuses, and the displacement of millions of people as a result of war and famine is equally daunting. Putting these issues together and attempting to present a "blueprint" for a common policy approach and framework for response may seem nigh impossible. Nevertheless, this is indeed what gender mainstreaming in peacekeeping aspires to accomplish, and it does so out of a recognition that peace support operations will not be successful until they fully incorporate gender analysis into every aspect of their strategies and approaches.

To illustrate, one set of conceptual constraints within the United Nations is its inability to recognize and accept the profoundly politicized nature and characteristics of current crisis situations, including how these characteristics define and shape the forms of violence to which communities are subject. Suffering is presented as a technical issue, that is, one that is most directly remedied by technical solutions. Political nuances, for example, human rights dimensions or the allusions to the legacies of colonialism, are broadly discouraged in documents, policies, or interventions pertaining to conflict environments.

There are a number of United Nations reports that have drawn attention to the specific impact of armed conflict, including gendered impacts, and all are good at identifying the particular forms and effects of conflict and its symptoms.[7] However, they are purposefully and *by design* less explicit on the causes and functions of the violence that creates these effects.

Related to this is the United Nations' rather homogeneous categorization of disasters—war, earthquakes, and famine are presented uniformly as temporary disruptions in the otherwise smooth process of development. The lack of analytic rigor or consensus of definition is typical of many of the studies and much of the policy discourse that is put out by the United Nations and is reflective of the difficulties of having to submit reports to the scrutiny of a wide range of United Nations officials and member states, some of whom have vested interests in constraining too much political analysis. It is therefore necessary to examine what, in actuality, influences the United Nations system for managing peacekeeping operations.

United Nations policy is driven by the issuance of certain reports and studies that are, in turn, adopted as Security Council resolutions. In theory, this is the structure that informs strategic changes throughout the United Nations. These reports and studies represent the culmination of advocacy and effort by a range of pressure groups, academics, external researchers, policy institutions, community-based and international nongovernmental institutions, and other concerned authorities.

Gender came to the forefront of international attention as an important policy issue through the combined efforts of academics and activists. Subsequently, a number of important resolutions were endorsed by the United Nations. The gist of these policy instruments is to emphasize the importance of integrating gender perspectives into all aspects of United Nations programming, as well as in the personnel, recruitment, and management arenas (see Mazurana et al., introduction). This "mainstreaming" process is relevant particularly to two distinct areas: United Nations peacekeeping programs and United Nations management procedures.

In terms of programming, the various gender-focused resolutions, reports, and declarations seek to:

- make explicit that conflict is a gendered activity, that is, that men and women experience and recover from the effects of violence and community destabilization differently according to their status in society, and that postconflict recovery necessitates the full participation of both women and men;
- incorporate gender issues into all levels and types of policy analysis;
- ensure that gender concerns are addressed in planning activities, for example, in setting priorities and in identifying action steps; and

- require that all program information collected and analyzed be disaggregated by sex and that sector-specific gender studies be conducted.

In terms of management and influencing the internal culture of the United Nations, the mainstreaming of gender policies seeks to ensure:

- a gender-sensitive management culture and equality of opportunity in staff recruitment, training, and formal and informal office procedures;
- that program budgets and resource allocation reflect commitment to gender-equality goals;
- that personnel procedures and career development policies are gender sensitive; and
- that, where necessary, special mechanisms are in place to deal with specific gender-sensitive issues such as sexual harassment and abuse of power by managers.

The effectiveness of the combined United Nations policy instruments remains in question. For example, after key United Nations resolutions on gender and peacekeeping had been adopted, most notably Security Council Resolution 1325, the United Nations secretary-general convened an expert group under the leadership of Lakhadar Brahimi to study the United Nations' response to peace operations, and the nature of the environments under which such operations were undertaken. The group did an extensive survey of the operational, policy, and organizational responses to armed conflict and made a number of recommendations targeting doctrinal and organizational issues. The resulting Brahimi Report has had its share of critics from a variety of perspectives, including advocates of a gender perspective. Although many of its recommendations were directed at the United Nations' doctrine, it is important to note that the report utterly lacked a nuanced analysis (such as produced through gender analysis) of the causes or impact of conflict or of the ways in which communities experience and respond to it. For example, insufficient attention to the role of gender-based violence in sustaining the conflict and contributing to continued human insecurity in the "postconflict" period results in lack of recognition of the need to recruit and train civilian, police, and military peacekeepers to address these issues. Neither is there attention to the fact that peacekeepers should work with civil society, including women's organizations, during the peace-building actions of the mission. Nor does the report identify the need for gender experts within the mission. Consequently, although there are a number of key areas where issues of gender are crucial, gender is mentioned only as a sensitivity issue of which military components of peacekeeping operations have to be aware in their interactions with local communities.[8]

While the Brahimi Report was under way, the United Nations Division for the Advancement of Women (DAW) was in the process of finalizing a comprehensive report that reviewed gender in specific United Nations peacekeeping missions. This study, *Mainstreaming: A Gender Perspective in Multidimensional Peace Support Operations*, was primarily implemented by the Lessons Learned Unit of the Department of Peacekeeping Operations (DPKO) and looked in depth at the United Nations missions in South Africa, Namibia, El Salvador, and Kosovo. The study and its recommendations contributed greatly to the formulation of Resolution 1325, particularly regarding mandating the United Nations to integrate a gender perspective into all aspects of its peacekeeping operations (see Mazurana et al., introduction).

Of note, the Brahimi Report neither acknowledged the DAW/DPKO study nor appeared to have been informed or influenced by the recommendations or conceptual implications arising from its conclusions. The Brahimi Report's failure to acknowledge or recognize the relevance of the DAW/DPKO report reflects the marginalization of gender issues within the United Nations. In addition, it serves as an instructive example of how several discourses on parallel themes can be initiated and executed within the United Nations without apparent concern for achieving a workable degree of coherence in their findings and policy implications. It is against this background of internal incoherence that additional perspectives must compete for recognition and integration into peacekeeping operations. To further complicate the issues, policies regarding United Nations interventions in crisis-affected countries originate from a range of bodies within the United Nations.

The Humanitarian Regime

The United Nations' response to countries requiring emergency assistance rests primarily within six operational agencies: the Office of the United Nations High Commissioner for Refugees (UNHCR), the United Nations International Children's Fund (UNICEF), the World Food Program (WFP), the World Health Organization (WHO), the Food and Agricultural Organization (FAO), and the United Nations Development Program (UNDP). Each of these agencies has its own mandate and administrative structures, as well as specific policies for targeting vulnerable groups, such as UNICEF's focus on women and children.

The first attempt to develop a framework for coordinating these agencies was the 1971 General Assembly resolution 2816, which created the Office of the United Nations Disaster Relief Coordinator (UNDRO). UNDRO's policies focused primarily on the technical aspects of responding to natural disasters, as these formed the majority of the large-scale crises that countries faced at the time. Throughout the 1980s and early 1990s, natural disasters increasingly merged with and were exacerbated by a series of wars and internal armed conflicts that affected many countries, particularly in Africa. This combination and interplay of factors led to the coining of the phrase "complex emergency," which increasingly became the accepted parlance for referring to countries facing crises marked by a combination of violence, instability, and natural disasters.

The United Nations' responses to crises-affected countries increasingly came under international scrutiny and critique from donors, nongovernmental organizations, and others evaluating humanitarian operations. The United Nations' emergency network was faulted for consistent failures of coordination, lack of appropriate and timely response mechanisms, duplication of efforts, and ineffective strategies for addressing increasingly belligerent national authorities.

In the 1990s, a new dimension to these crises was added with massive and deliberate violations of human rights and targeting of civilians. The complications arising from the United Nations' response to the Gulf crisis in 1991 became the focus for a renewed call for coordination and congruence of the United Nations' disaster system, which led to the adoption of Security Council Resolution 461/82. This resolution helped establish a new coordinating mechanism whereby UNDRO was incorporated into the new Department of Humanitarian Affairs (DHA). DHA's mandate was to coordinate and advocate for interagency strategies of response, to gather and disseminate information, and to prioritize funding requirements for donors.

When Kofi Annan took over from Boutros Boutros-Ghali as secretary-general in 1997, he launched a set of initiatives targeting reform within the United Nations. At the same time other initiatives were launched to examine key issues in conflict and peacekeeping operations. Under the reforms DHA was reorganized and became the Office for the Coordination of Humanitarian Affairs (OCHA).[9] OCHA's mandate was clarified and prioritized to focus specifically on three areas: (1) coordination of emergency response among the main United Nations agencies involved with relief operations as well as with DPKO and the Department of Political Affairs (DPA); (2) policy development for the protection of civilians and development of appropriate program strategies; and (3) advocacy for humanitarian space, negotiation for access to crisis-affected communities, and the implementation of humanitarian principles.[10]

A policy development unit was established in OCHA that was tasked with defining the main thematic sectors on which the organization would work. OCHA's policy development unit was assisted by an Inter-Agency Standing Committee (IASC) that consisted of the heads of the main United Nations agencies. These agency representatives met regularly both to review issues that OCHA was working on and suggest other themes as they became important.

In 1999, UNICEF suggested that OCHA should develop a policy position on gender issues. A concept note was prepared by the UNICEF Office for Emergency Programs that was subsequently endorsed by the IASC. Notably, at the time there was no official focal point in OCHA for gender issues even though a number of other United Nations agencies and departments had established such positions.

A few months later, a staff person UNICEF had seconded to OCHA was tasked with preparing the draft for a policy paper on gender. An interagency working group on gender was organized to review and finalize the document.[11] However, by 2001, there had yet to be designated a senior-level United Nations official to oversee gender issues in OCHA. Various attempts were made by the task group to implement training and to integrate a gender perspective into the Consolidated Appeal Process (CAP)—the primary program and fund-raising mechanism used in the field to identify emergency program needs in each disaster-affected country. One of the main constraints to the effective integration of gender issues was that the CAP process itself was overseen and directed by a separate sub–working group with responsibilities for identifying key issues, organizing training, and interpreting OCHA policy.

In the absence of a commitment from senior management at OCHA, providing a "gender perspective" become nothing more than someone (usually a junior program officer) combing through any OCHA or CAP document and inserting the words "women," "girls," and "gender" in as many places as possible so that the end product would read as gender sensitive. This practice was not limited to OCHA; other focal points in the main United Nations agencies were also alert to ensuring that all documents mentioned whether there were any specific programs for women or children that their organization was implementing.

The Human Rights Regime

Implementation of programs to protect and advocate for human rights within the United Nations is administered through a series of committees and institutions. The primary body is the Commission on Human Rights, a permanent subgroup of the Economic and Social Council (ECOSOC). As with many other themes, United Nations policy on human rights has been promoted through the workings of various conferences and subsequent adoption of resolutions. The 1979 Convention on the Elimination of All Forms of Discrimination against Women (CEDAW) was the first unilateral treaty that focused specifically on women's rights. In 1993, the World Conference on Human Rights endorsed the Vienna Declaration and Program of Action, which affirmed the principle that "the human rights of women and the girl child are an inalienable, integral and indivisible part of human rights." The Program of Action called for the full mainstreaming of women's rights into all aspects of the United Nations' work, specific gender-sensitive training for all agency personnel, and the collection of specific gender-disaggregated data needed to monitor the full participation of women in program implementation and benefits. In 1999, DAW, in fulfillment of its mandate to promote gender mainstreaming in all aspects of the United Nations' work and policies, embarked upon a series of training initiatives targeting the main bodies of the Secretariat, including DPKO and DPA, and other United Nations offices and units. The training was intended to cover all aspects of United Nations programming, management, and personnel issues.

Despite these instruments and efforts, experts on human rights have commented on the constraints and problems that the United Nations has faced in implementing the mainstreaming of women's rights. Reasons cited include, in part, lack of mandate, conceptual clarity, expertise, and coordination, as well as the underrepresentation of women in positions of authority.[12]

These problems are not limited to the human rights regime. In terms of the peacekeeping agenda, there is a similar lack of conceptual clarity. The political, humanitarian, human rights, and development agencies do not seem to have a clear understanding of the diverse ways that women's and girls' rights are affected in conflict situations or of the particular relevance of human rights instruments to the specific conditions that women and girls in protracted crisis situations find themselves.

In particular it has been difficult for agencies to appreciate the implications of the use of sexualized violence in the context of ethnically based political violence. Though the international community has endorsed the principle that rape is a crime against humanity, there is still a need to fully incorporate all the strategies that are needed to respond to victims of this kind of violence (see Bedont, chapter 4; Oosterveld, chapter 3). Policy-making institutions have yet to develop appropriate programs to address the mental and social needs of victims, bring the perpetrators to justice, and ensure adequate protection for women and girls.

The Security Regime

DPA and DPKO are responsible for geopolitical security issues in the United Nations. The challenges of the post–Cold War environment have brought a new sense of activism and interventionism on the part of the Security Council that has, in turn, resulted in a greater global involvement by these departments in a host of issues and countries. For example, the number of United Nations–managed peacekeeping operations grew exponentially during the 1990s. In order to manage these complex responsibilities and environments, each department turns to its own established policy units.

Both DPA and DPKO have attempted to introduce a gender perspective into their operations and policies, but each has done so outside of the normal processes for setting policies for each department. Each department has elected to establish gender focal points independent of the policy units. This organizational segregation limits the focal points' ability to ensure that gender issues are fully incorporated and integrated into departmental policies.[13] Because they are not located within the policy units, the gender focal points are routinely marginalized in the processes of decision making and policy formulation. For example, they often are not included in the various interagency forums where common issues related to matters of peacekeeping, humanitarianism, or human rights are discussed.

This organizational structure also influences the perceived expertise of gender focal points. The departments (understandably) look for gender specialists to fill these roles rather than seeking candidates who are strong policy experts in both gender *and* political affairs/peacekeeping. Thus, even though they may be expert in gender issues per se, the focal points are not expected (nor are they given the chance) to be informed by or to influence either the politics of interagency coordination or the various discourses and debates that exist within the humanitarian, human rights, and peacekeeping agendas.

The end result is predictable dissonance within and between the departments with respect to gender. This is neither surprising nor limited to issues of gender mainstreaming. While sharing similar mandates, DPA and DPKO have been criticized for a lack of clarity of mandates, which has, in turn, negatively affected coordination and policy regarding peacekeeping and working in conflict-affected environments.[14]

Patchwork Programs

The recent study and report by the secretary-general entitled *Women, Peace and Security*[15] highlights the many features and issues that affect women worldwide as a result of war and protracted crisis situations. A closer examination and scrutiny of the report reveals how ultimately patchy and ad hoc the organizational response is to these issues. It is clear that many agencies do have their own polices but are still lacking precise standard operating procedures, frameworks, guidelines, and monitoring mechanisms. In the case of peacekeeping operations, if the commitment to gender, to reviewing the impact of that particular context on women and children, or to working with local civilian organizations is not made in the mandate of the peacekeeping operation, these things will not be done or will be left to different levels of interpretation by different agencies. Where there are principles and guidelines in place, it is still a major challenge to ensure that they are followed and monitored.

Many United Nations organizations also tend to subcontract their work out to NGOs. These organizations may not have similar guidelines or operating procedures and little is done to monitor their work. For example, in 1995, a study among refugee populations in Mozambique revealed that despite the existence of UNHCR's guidelines on the protection of women and children, none of the NGOs in the field were using them, and field staff of UNHCR appeared to be unaware of their existence.

The challenge remains, therefore, to ensure that guidelines and operating principles and methodologies are developed and disseminated widely throughout the system. These strategies must be integrated into the core policy and standard operating procedures of each agency and not be left as separate stand-alone procedures. This means that all agency personnel must be exposed to and familiar with these guidelines, whether they are men or women and whether or not they are directly or indirectly involved in program implementation. In the case of those who are directly implementing programs, there must be measures built into the management and personnel evaluation criteria to ensure that policies are being implemented.

Reform and Resistance

Despite the resolution on special measures for the achievement of gender equality and achieving a fifty-fifty gender balance by 2000, there has been little change in the gender balance of several key departments within the United Nations, especially in DPKO and the rest of the Secretariat. A recent document produced by International Alert makes note of this issue and calls for serious reforms.[16]

The "affirmative actions" of the United Nations (e.g., focused recruiting efforts to attract more women, hiring gender focal points, mandating gender-sensitivity training, etc.) have aroused a great deal of bitterness in some male staff who see their years of accumulated experience and chances for promotion being washed away by a tide of new "token" women appointees. I witnessed this resulting resistance at its most extreme when one senior official, during our discussions on recruitment drives within the United Nations to bring in larger numbers of women, dismissed the work of the DAW (and all gender focal points who had been appointed as a result of the Security Council resolution) as the "Gender Gestapo." Whether said in jest or in seriousness, the comment was indicative of the prevailing ill feeling among many United Nations personnel on the issue of gender. It is important to explore this issue further.

Within the technical and logistic sections of many United Nations agencies and departments, jobs within emergency and especially militarized environments are seen as being "naturally male."[17] A disturbing feature of much United Nations recruitment is that there is increasing emphasis on bringing ex-military personnel into humanitarian and peacekeeping work, including within policy and program sectors. A military background is somehow considered more appropriate than expertise in conflict resolution, peace studies, community development, international relations, or anthropology (see Mazurana, chapter 1).[18] Attempts to infuse gender into peacekeeping scenarios are at times dismissed as trivial, especially by some of the older military or ex-military staff of United Nations agencies.

Although the Security Council has directed the United Nations to mainstream gender, this directive does not appear to have been taken seriously by a number of staff. In part, this is because of a pervasive sense among some staff of being above the national or international laws (see Vandenberg, chapter 7). For example, Carey observes that the "United Nations does not consider itself bound by international treaties—including anti-discrimination conventions" and that "international civil servants are exempt from state jurisdictions; and peace-keeping forces are coalitions of the willing under separate national commands."[19]

Instead, other (informal) expressions of power have strong influence on the beliefs and value systems of United Nations staff. Within the United Nations, internal power is also very closely related to the issue of identity, nationality, and which member state a staff member may officially or unofficially represent. Staff members represent a plethora of political, religious, social, and ethnic organizations and identify with many kinds of associations based on class, race, gender, professional, community, or kinship affiliations. This can bias interpretations of rules, regulations, and policies when staff struggle to reconcile their cultural values with the official cultural ethos of the United Nations. Policies relating to power and conflict are thus interpreted through a personal as well as a public lens. The personal is the political, and politics are very personalized as they ultimately relate to how individual staff members interpret and implement policies.

That even a single staff of a world governance agency would imagine that his or her position should allow him or her to consider himself or herself above the law has serious implications. It may be one thing to flaunt the parking regulations or import/export rules and regulations of a country one is working in under the mantle of diplomatic immunity, but is it the same to renounce the very codes and principles that have been established by the organization for which one is working? What is it in the culture of the United Nations itself that can permit this kind of attitude? To find an answer to this question, it is important to consider the ways in which staff are recruited and the system, or lack thereof, of supervisory accountability.

Getting—and Keeping—a Job at the United Nations

A job within the United Nations is one of the most prized employment opportunities. The salaries and benefits are among the best in the world in the public sector and the opportunities for making more money are plentiful, especially on short missions such as peacekeeping operations where staff are rewarded with special hardship allowances and other remunerations to make up for living away from their families in difficult situations.

Though there are formalized career structures and systems of recruitment, there are others ways in which people can obtain a job with the United Nations. While the more structured systems hold true for the routine administrative and political jobs within the Secretariat, in other instances people can be seconded from their governments, and there are political appointees. This is especially true for higher-level positions, where donor and government influence is very important as to who will secure what position.[20] Because of the ways in which United Nations programs are funded, there are many jobs that are dependant on particular projects and the longevity or interest of the donor. Thus, there is a high state of job insecurity at all times among the majority of United Nations personnel. In emergency and peacekeeping situations there is usually urgency about setting up a program and finding the right personnel. Established recruitment and evaluation procedures are overlooked. People can bypass systems of recruitment or be seconded from other agencies without too much attention being paid as to their relevant technical expertise or experience. Another feature that undermines the establishment of proper procedures or the ability to ensure the quality of staff is that unpopular or unsuitable staff can be—and often are—posted to field-based peacekeeping operations.

The urgency and expediency of setting up peacekeeping operations in the field thus work against both the establishment of good training and briefings beforehand and the institutionalization of policies thereafter. These jobs usually have a high personnel turnover, with many staff more interested in finishing their assignments, enduring what they consider to be a hardship post, claiming their entitlements, and coming home. The temporary nature of the assignments also reduces the likelihood that staff will develop deep knowledge of the country or the communities for whom they are working. Most peace-keeping operations are either temporarily replacing existing United Nations agencies that have been evacuated or dismantled or are advance teams setting up the logistics for the establishment of more-permanent country offices to follow.

There are also conceptual differences among the program staff, who deal with issues of protection and assistance strategies for crisis-affected communities, and the technical/administrative staff, who are responsible for the establishment of operational structures of offices, logistics, communications, and so on. The technical/administrative staff tend to feel that training in gender sensitivity or the nuanced understanding of communities is less relevant to their work.

Program Performance, Organizational Success, and Personal Advancement

Although the United Nations has made explicit its commitments to gender equality and gender mainstreaming it still has a long way to go to put these commitments into policy and practice, in particular within its organization's structures, culture, and values. Despite the small but growing number of policy guidelines and attempts at providing checklists, gender manuals, and so on, there is little to ensure that these are actually implemented. Nor are there systems of personnel evaluations whereby managers are held accountable for implementing policies. Some staff may think that it is important to incorporate gender analysis and may work hard to try to integrate these perspectives. Those who feel it is irrelevant or inappropriate will ignore the guidelines or may even go so far as to undermine others who are trying to implement them.[21] Staff comment that they are not social scientists and that they do not have the expertise to do this kind of analysis. Others claim that it is not their responsibility and assert that it is the job of the gender focal point to do it. If there is no focal point or if the focal point is already overburdened, then the analysis is not done. Thus, the appearance is that guidelines and policies have been mainstreamed and are being implemented. However, in reality, these become yet another set of competing priorities that program officers remain ill prepared to put into action.

There are also ignorance and misconceptions about gender. At one level, gender is still treated as if it were about women and women's issues and therefore it is the role of women to deal with these issues. At another level are claims that gender is now outdated and no longer an issue within the United

Nations. The surprising fact is that some senior women subscribe to the latter view and have often been among the most resistant to work with special gender focal points, external consultants, and others appointed to promote gender policies.

These beliefs and behaviors are backed up by claims from other quarters that gender is "divisive" and tends to foster conflict rather than cooperation in the office or field environment and therefore should be dropped. There are accusations that this is an inappropriate philosophy fostered by "Western feminists/radicals/lesbians" who are out to cause problems for the organization. By this same token, it is asserted that international organizations have to be careful not to impose their ideologies on communities they are working with.

In peacekeeping and humanitarian environments the "cultural inappropriateness" argument is also backed up by the view that in emergency contexts there is "no time" to do gender work, as what is needed is rapid action, life-saving food, and material distribution. Performing nuanced analysis and targeting change is too cumbersome, complex, and time consuming, indeed downright harmful to the "real work" of saving lives (see Jacobson, chapter 6). At the same time, it is felt that there is "not enough" information and analysis on how gender issues are affected or implicated in the emergency context to warrant specific strategies. Finally, a number of people believe that the gender perspective focuses too much on the portrayal of women as victims and is therefore inappropriate.

The conceptual problems and misunderstandings presented thus cover a wide variety of positions that range from a lack of knowledge of what a gender analysis and perspective entails all the way to resistance based on personal prejudice and fundamental disagreement with the philosophy of the gender perspective. These prevailing attitudes and beliefs present tremendous challenges to the task of changing the organizational ethos of the United Nations staff toward issues of gender.

Studies of other organizations have revealed the complexity of processes for institutionalizing and promoting change—particularly change that targets fundamental cultural and personal values held by their constituents.[22] Studies of development and business organizations have shown that often numerous issues arise that constrain the progress toward effecting true mainstreaming and acceptance of gender ideologies.[23]

The culture of resistance to change is also manifest in the ways that the United Nations sometimes reacts to external critiques and exercises that may challenge existing practices and program or management methodologies. The United Nations invests enormous amounts of money to bring in outside technical experts, researchers, and other professionals to assist in drafting policy documents, evaluating programs, and generally monitoring the impact of the organization's work. Drafting the terms of reference, organizing the research teams, and following up on the results and recommendations is a long and laborious endeavor clouded by interagency rivalries, disagreements, and efforts to control the outcome or shape the results. Many high-powered studies have never been allowed to be disseminated and more efforts go into refuting findings than into instituting changes to redress problems. For every United Nations program official who is genuinely trying to seek conceptual clarity or attempting to quietly reform the system from within, there is an army of others who will close ranks, veto documents, blacklist the hired consultants, and otherwise discredit studies.[24] Several examples are worth mentioning.

In 1996, a study was done of Operation Lifeline Sudan that contained exceptional analysis of the nature of the conflict in Sudan and the complicity of the international system in aiding and abetting the war and failing to protect the citizens. The study contained numerous program recommendations, follow-up actions, and frameworks for advancing an understanding of the nature of political vulnerability that could have been useful for future training and program initiatives.[25] The report was heavily censored, and follow-up discussions and efforts concentrated on only one small segment of the study referring to mechanisms of internal coordination. The authors of another study on the United Nations and strategic humanitarian coordination in the African Great Lakes region were heavily pressured by United Nations officials who were likewise displeased by the team's findings. In order to get approval for dissemination, the authors considerably weakened the final document.[26] In regard to peacekeeping, the 1999–2000 Lessons Learned study on gender and peace support operations commissioned by DPKO has still not been released, and there has been no explanation as to why neither its findings nor the important documentation of several country experiences is publicly available. Likewise, important end-of-mission reports by senior gender advisers from peacekeeping operations in East Timor and Kosovo have not been made available in any public format, thus hindering the discussion on lessons learned and good practices from those experiences.

Conclusion: Management, Organizational Culture, and Creating a "Learning Environment"

When Kofi Annan assumed responsibility as the United Nations secretary-general, there was great pressure from donor governments for him to implement a series of reforms to streamline and improve the efficiency, management, and efficacy of the organization. At the same time, there was great anticipation and expectation from within the United Nations that changes would take place, especially since Kofi Annan was known as a visionary, someone committed to seeing the United Nations make a difference in a changing and volatile global situation.

There was much talk about "change management" and creating "learning environments" within the organization. UNDP, UNICEF, WFP, and many of the other organizations in the system began a process of management evaluation exercises with mixed and varied results. In theory, gender mainstreaming and creating a gender-sensitive environment was part of these exercises, but it is difficult to ascertain how successful these policy changes have been, as many internal reports and surveys are hard for outside researchers and consultants to obtain.

Gender and management issues are still of concern to many staff within the United Nations. A recent issue of an internal United Nations news bulletin, *Equal Time*, gave great prominence to a survey that had been conducted among United Nations staff on improving the working environment and on a new program that the Human Resources division is about to launch to improve issues of staff relations, management, flexible hours for family heads, dealing with sexual harassment, equal opportunities for training, and other personnel issues.

The *Equal Time* survey, and the program that it is designed to herald, also coincides with a recent report from International Alert, *Mainstreaming Gender in Peace Support Operations: Moving beyond Rhetoric to Practice.*[27] The report makes several recommendations to the United Nations for improving the substance and quality of program initiatives as well as for addressing the gender imbalance, particularly at senior policy-level positions. The issue here is not that there are token "women" who are appointed but that consideration is given to recruiting qualified women and men who have both the experience of working in complex crisis and politically volatile situations as well as the appropriate academic and technical expertise in these issues.

In the fields of humanitarian relief and disaster management, human rights, and peacekeeping operations there is a discourse demanding increased professionalization, standard setting, and accountability within the world of agencies and institutions that are working in complex political emergencies and crisis-affected countries.[28] There is a call to set standards not only for different programs but also for the recruitment, training, and management of personnel in the field.[29] There is now a growing field of academic studies in nutrition, public health, development studies, anthropology, political science, human rights and humanitarian law, and other disciplines that address the special impacts on and needs of communities affected by war and crises. These studies also attest to the many disasters and problems that are created by agencies and agency personnel who are not aware of lessons learned and past experiences, or those who lack a nuanced understanding of the communities with whom they are working.

These findings point to a pressing need for human rights and humanitarian practitioners (including peacekeepers and those working in peace support operations) to have an awareness of the legal, political, and moral issues found in current emergency and crisis situations. For this they need to have grounding in the international legal and ethical standards for the provision of assistance and protection to civilians in armed conflict. They also need to be aware of the mandates of the different actors and "regimes" they will encounter in the course of their work, as well as of the laws and standards that underpin each regime they represent, for example, the refugee regime, the security regime, the human rights regime, and the humanitarian law regime. For the United Nations this means that there must be a common acceptance and definition of the range of skills and "profile" that program officers and personnel must possess—or can acquire through training. There should be mechanisms for ensuring that across the board all personnel achieve these competencies.

Donors and governments must ensure that the resolutions and standards and recommendations that they help nurture through the General Assembly and Security Council are institutionalized within the United Nations and its personnel. This requires adequate support for training United Nations personnel in the appropriate fields necessary to implement these recommendations. Donors should also hold United Nations management to account if programs do not reflect agreed-upon standards and strategies.

The United Nations was founded on a series of highly admirable beliefs that have been affirmed and reaffirmed over time through international treaties, resolutions, and commitments. When new staff join the organization, they sign a commitment to uphold both the principles and the laws of the United Nations. It is simply unacceptable for United Nations staff to be either ignorant or in flagrant defiance of the founding principles of the United Nations and the resolutions that underpin its mandates. Paramount among these beliefs is a commitment to equality of all humans. As international civil servants, United Nations staff are duty bound to uphold this most fundamental of all principles; that is, they must not only talk the talk but also walk the walk.

Notes

The source for the epigraph is Cynthia Enloe, "Closing Remarks: Women and International Peacekeeping," in "Women and International Peacekeeping," ed. Louise Olsson and Torunn L. Tryggestad, special issue, *International Peacekeeping* 8, no. 2 (2000).

1. Henry Carey, "*Women, Peace and Security:* The Politics of Implementing Gender Sensitivity Norms in Peace-Keeping," in "Women and International Peacekeeping," ed. Louise Olsson and Torunn L. Tryggestad, special issue, *International Peacekeeping* 8, no. 2 (2000); Julie Mertus, *War's Offensive against Women: The Humanitarian Challenge in Bosnia, Kosovo and Afghanistan* (Bloomfield, CT: Kumarian Press, 2000); Anne Gallagher, "Ending the Marginalization: Strategies for Incorporating Women into the United Nations Human Rights System," *Human Rights Quarterly* 19, no. 2 (1997): 283–333; Dyan Mazurana with Eugenia Piza-Lopez, *Gender Mainstreaming in Peace Support Operations: Moving beyond Rhetoric to Practice* (London: International Alert, 2002).

2. Mark Hobart, *An Anthropological Critique of Development: The Growth of Ignorance* (London: Routledge Press, 1993); Norman Long and Anne Long, eds., *Battlefields of Knowledge: The Interlocking of Theory and Practice in Social Research and Development* (London: Routledge Press, 1992); Katy Gardner and David Lewis, *Anthropology, Development and the Post Modern Challenge* (London: Pluto Press, 1996).

3. E. Thomas Moran and J. Fresericks Volkwein, "The Cultural Approach to the Formation of Organizational Culture," *Human Relations* 45, no. 1 (1992): 19–47; David Pitt, "Power in the UN Super Bureaucracy: A New Byzantium?" in *The Nature of the United Nations Bureaucracies*, ed. David Pitt and Thomas Weiss (Boulder, CO: Westview Press, 1986).

4. Marianne Merchand and Jane Parpart, eds., *Feminism, Postmodernism and Development* (New York: Routledge Press, 1995); Amrita Basu, ed., *The Challenge of Local Feminisms: The Woman's Movement in Global Perspective* (Boulder, CO: Westview Press, 1995).

5. Joanna Macrae and Nicholas Leader, *Shifting Sands: The Search for "Coherence" between Political and Humanitarian Responses to Complex Emergencies*, Humanitarian Policy Group, Report 8 (London: Overseas Development Institute, 2000).

6. Stephen D. Krasner, ed., *International Regimes* (Cambridge, MA: Cornell University Press, 1983); Jim Whitman, ed., *Peacekeeping and the United Nations Agencies* (London: Frank Cass Publishers, 1999).

7. Most notable among these United Nations documents are Graça Machel, *The Impact of War on Children* (London: Hurst and Company, 2001); United Nations, *Impact of Armed Conflict on Children*, report of the expert of the secretary-general, Graça Machel, submitted pursuant to General Assembly Resolution 48/157, A/51/306 (August 26, 1996); *Report of the Secretary-General on Children and Armed Conflict*, A/55/163-S/2000/712 (July 19, 2000); *Report of the Secretary-General on the Causes of Conflict and the Promotion of a Durable Peace and Sustainable Development in Africa*, A/52/871-S/1998/318 (April 13, 1998); *Report of the Secretary-General on the Prevention of Armed Conflict*, A/55/985-S/2001/574 (June 7, 2001); *Report of the Secretary-General on the Protection of Civilians in Armed Conflict*, A/56/259 (August 1, 2001); United Nations, *Women, Peace and Security: Study Submitted by the Secretary-General Pursuant to Security Council Resolution 1325* (New York: UN, 2002); and *Report of the Secretary-General on Women, Peace and Security*, S/2002/1154 (October 16, 2002).

8. Mazurana with Piza-Lopez, *Gender Mainstreaming*.

9. Whitman, *Peacekeeping and the United Nations Agencies.*

10. United Nations Office for the Coordination of Humanitarian Affairs, *OCHA: What It Is, What It Does* (New York: UNOCHA, 1998).

11. United Nations Office for the Coordination of Humanitarian Affairs, *OCHA: What It Is, What It Does.*

12. Elizabeth Riddell-Dixon, "Mainstreaming Women's Rights: Problems and Prospects within the Centre for Human Rights," *Global Governance: A Review of Multilateralism and International Organizations* 5, no. 2 (April–June 1999): 149–71; Gallagher, "Ending the Marginalization."

13. Louise Olsson, *Gendering U.N. Peacekeeping*, Report 53, Department of Peace and Conflict Research (Uppsala, Sweden: Uppsala University, 1999).

14. Larry Minear, "Humanitarian Action and Peacekeeping Operations" (background paper for the UNITAR/IPS/NIRA conference, Singapore, February 24–26, 1997, available at http://www.jha.ac/articles/a018.htm); Leon Gordenker, "Clash and Harmony in Promoting Peace: Overview," in Whitman, *Peacekeeping and the United Nations Agencies*; Lawrence Ziring, Robert Riggs, and Jack Plano, *The United Nations: International Organization and World Politics* (South Melbourne, Australia: Thomas Learning Publishers, 2000).

15. United Nations, *Women, Peace and Security.*

16. Mazurana with Piza-Lopez, *Gender Mainstreaming.*

17. Similar trends are noted among the larger international NGOs that respond to complex political emergencies; see Suzanne Williams, "Conflicts of Interest: Gender in Oxfam's Emergency Response," in *The Post-war Moment: Militaries, Masculinities and International Peacekeeping; Bosnia and the Netherlands*, ed. Cynthia Cockburn and Dubravka Zarkov, 85–102 (London: Lawrence and Wishart, 2002).

18. Feinstein International Famine Center and International Alert, "The Politicization of Humanitarian Action and Staff Security: The Use of Private Security Companies by Humanitarian Agencies" (background paper for workshop held at Tufts University, Boston, 2001), 2324; Cockburn and Zarkov, *The Post-war Moment.*

19. Carey, "'Women, Peace and Security,'" 61.

20. Maurice Bertrand, "The Recruitment Policy of United Nations Staff," in *International Administration Law and Management Practices in International Organizations*, ed. Chris de Cooker for the United Nations Institute for Training and Research (Dordrecht: Martins Nijhoff Publishers, 1990); Ziring, Riggs, and Plano, *The United Nations.*

21. Riddell-Dixon, *Mainstreaming Women's Rights.*

22. Bridget Byrne and Julie Koch Laier, with Sally Baden and Rachel Marcus, *National Machineries for Women in Development: Experiences, Lessons and Strategies for Institutionalizing Gender in Development Policy and Planning*, Bridge Report 36 (Brighton: Institute for Development Studies, University of Sussex, 1996); David Collinson and Jeff Hearn, eds., *Men as Managers, Managers as Men: Critical Perspectives on Men, Masculinities and Management* (London: Sage, 1996); Richard Fardon, ed., *Counterworks: Managing the Diversity of Knowledge* (London: Routledge Press, 1995); Caroline Moser, *Gender Planning and Development: Theory, Practice and Training* (London: Routledge Press, 1993).

23. Nancy Dixon, *The Organizational Learning Cycle: How We Can Learn Collectively* (London: McGraw-Hill, 1994); H. Brown, *Women in Private and Voluntary Sectors: Case Studies in Organizational Change* (London: Office for Public Management, 1994); Anne Marie Goetze, "Managing Organizational Change: 'The Gendered Organization of Space and Time,'" in *Gender and Development Organizations*, 17–27 (London and Belfast: Oxfam, 1997).

24. Adrian Wood, Raymond Apthorpe, and John Borton, *Evaluating International Humanitarian Action* (London: Zed Books, 2001); Larry Minear, *The Humanitarian Enterprise: Dilemmas and Discoveries* (Bloomfield, CT: Kumarian Press, 2002).

25. Ataul Karim, Mark Duffield, Susanne Jaspars, Aldo Benini, Joanne Macrae, Mark Bradbury, Douglas Johnson, and George Larbi, *Operation Lifeline Sudan: A Review*, ed. Barbara Hendrie (New York: UN Department of Humanitarian Affairs, 1996).

26. Sue Lautze, Bruce Jones, and Mark Duffield, *Strategic Humanitarian Coordination in the Great Lakes Region, 1996–1997* (New York: UNOCHA Policy and Advocacy Division, 1998).

27. Mazurana with Piza-Lopez, *Gender Mainstreaming*.

28. Minear, *Humanitarian Enterprise*; Development Initiatives, *Global Humanitarian Assistance*, (Geneva: Inter-Agency Standing Committee, 2000); Angela Raven-Roberts, "Meeting the Needs of Internally Displaced Children: Training and Capacity Building of Agency Personnel," *Forced Migration Review*, no. 15 (2002).

29. Sphere Project, *The Sphere Project: Humanitarian Charter and Minimum Standards in Emergency Response* (Geneva: Oxfam Publishing, 2002).

II

GENDER, PEACEKEEPING, AND INTERNATIONAL HUMANITARIAN, CRIMINAL, AND HUMAN RIGHTS LAW

CONTRIBUTIONS IN THIS SECTION EXAMINE legal developments regarding the intersection of gender, peacekeeping, and international humanitarian, criminal, and human rights law. They critically analyze a multiplicity of developments, approaches, and venues in international law, highlighting pitfalls as well as legal means to enhance the protection of women's and girls' rights during peacekeeping and humanitarian operations.

3

Prosecution of Gender-Based Crimes in International Law

Valerie Oosterveld

G ENDER-BASED CRIMES IN WAR are nothing new.[1] Neither is the prohibition of many of these crimes. What is new is the commitment on the part of the international community to prosecute those who commit gender-based genocide, crimes against humanity, and war crimes. Since the founding of the international criminal tribunals for the former Yugoslavia and Rwanda in 1993 and 1994, respectively, international humanitarian law relating to these crimes has developed rapidly. By the time of the final negotiations in June and July 1998 to create the Rome Statute of the International Criminal Court (ICC), there was little debate that international law had evolved to the point that gender-based persecution, rape, sexual slavery, enforced prostitution, enforced sterilization, and other forms of gendered violence should be included in that statute, both as crimes against humanity and as war crimes committed in international and internal armed conflict. There was also widespread agreement, based on lessons learned from the international criminal tribunals, that a gender-sensitive ICC involves much more than the criminalization of gender-based violations: it requires judges, officials, and staff with knowledge in and experience with issues of gender-based violence; court procedures that will not retraumatize victims and witnesses; and gender-sensitive victim and witness protection. The ICC's holistic approach represents a very significant step forward in how international law approaches the prosecution of the most serious gender-based crimes known to humankind.

Criminalization of Gender-Based Violations

The past decade has brought a profound change in the recognition and prosecution of gender-based crimes. The international criminal tribunals for the Former Yugoslavia and Rwanda (ICTY and ICTR, respectively) have issued judgments addressing rape as torture, rape as an instrument of terror, enslavement (both sexual and nonsexual), castration, and forced nudity. The crimes of gender-based persecution, enslavement, rape, sexual slavery, enforced prostitution, forced pregnancy, enforced sterilization, and other forms of sexual violence of comparable gravity have been recognized as crimes against humanity and war crimes in the ICC's Rome Statute.[2] In addition, enslavement and sexual slavery have been recognized as including trafficking in women and children.[3] The approaches of the ICC, ICTY, and ICTR provide a significantly fuller understanding than in the past of the range of gender-based crimes that can take place in wartime and peacetime, the constituent elements of these crimes, and the patterns they can follow.

While there was some earlier recognition of gender-based crimes, the first international prosecution of these crimes took place after World War II, at the International Military Tribunal for the Far East (also known as the "Tokyo Tribunal").[4] The Tokyo Tribunal found several defendants guilty of rape on the basis of command responsibility, particularly for the widespread rapes committed in Nanking. World War II also led to the codification of certain gender-based crimes. Allied Control Council Law No. 10 of 1945, which was enacted after the end of the war to provide for the trial of German war criminals in the British, American, Russian, and French zones of occupation, specifically listed rape as a crime against humanity. However, there were no prosecutions under this section.

The Fourth Geneva Convention of 1949 (governing the protection of civilians in times of war), and its Additional Protocols I and II of 1977 (respectively governing the protection of victims in international and noninternational armed conflict), explicitly addresses the issue of gender-based crimes. Under Article 27 of the Fourth Geneva Convention, "women shall be especially protected against any attack on their honour, in particular against rape, enforced prostitution, or any form of indecent assault." Article 76 of Additional Protocol I states, "Women shall be the object of special respect and shall be protected in particular against rape, forced prostitution and any other form of indecent assault" in international armed conflicts. Article 4(2)(e) of Additional Protocol II, which applies in internal armed conflicts, uses gender-neutral language in its prohibition of "outrages on personal dignity, in particular humiliating and degrading treatment, rape, enforced prostitution and any form of indecent assault." The Fourth Geneva Convention and Additional Protocols therefore provide important recognition of certain crimes—rape, enforced prostitution, and indecent assault. However, these documents also have limitations: the Fourth Geneva Convention and Additional Protocol I cover protection to women (and not men) in international armed conflict, while Additional Protocol II extends this protection to both men and women in internal armed conflict. In addition, commentators have noted that the link between the women, the crimes listed, "honour," and "respect" in the Fourth Geneva Convention and Additional Protocol I, and the crimes listed and "dignity" in Additional Protocol II, tends to shift the focus away from the fact that the crimes are acts of violence that violate victims' bodily security and autonomy.[5]

The 1974 Declaration on the Protection of Women and Children in Emergency and Armed Conflict does not mention gender-based crimes in its text. However, it does call on states to take the necessary steps to "spare women and children from the ravages of war" and to prohibit "persecution, torture, punitive measures, degrading treatment and violence" against women and children civilians. In addition, paragraph 5 states that "all forms of repression and cruel and inhuman treatment of women and children, including imprisonment, torture . . . [and] collective punishment . . . committed by belligerents in the course of military operations or in occupied territories shall be considered criminal." Despite the steps forward demonstrated by the judgment of the Tokyo Tribunal, Control Council Law No. 10, the Fourth Geneva Convention, the Additional Protocols, and the 1974 Declaration, international law on gender-based genocide, crimes against humanity, and war crimes remained relatively undeveloped until the 1990s.

An important recent development in international law has been the recognition that certain gender-based crimes occur with alarming regularity in armed conflict and that these crimes sometimes take on a pattern. Identifying these patterns has helped in gaining a better understanding of the most likely scenarios to result in gender-based genocide, crimes against humanity, and war crimes.

Predictably, the invasion of Kuwait by Iraq in 1990 led to wartime sexual violence. A United Nations report by Special Rapporteur Walter Kalin outlined several categories of rape cases:

1. Rape of foreign women, mostly young and of Asian origin, by Iraqi soldiers during the first two weeks of occupation;
2. Rape of women during house searches by Iraqi army personnel, sometimes in front of close male relatives;
3. Rape of women who were abducted from checkpoints on the street for this purpose;

4. Rape used as a method of torture: some male detainees reported that during torture sessions they were forced to watch women being raped by Iraqi military personnel.[6]

Where it had been addressed at all, wartime rape had historically been dealt with in a monolithic manner. The Kalin Report represented the beginning of a more sophisticated understanding of the means, methods, and patterns of rape in warfare.[7]

This brilliantly illustrates a central issue that the book thus far seems to ignore: the question of impunity. All of the examples are of the barbarisms of the enemy. There is no mention whatever of crimes committed by the United States and its allies. This is a perfect illustration of a central problem that is not less applicable to crimes of gender than to any others and is central to the failures of the international legal order. And the United Nations system.

In 1992, the Security Council requested that the secretary-general establish a commission of experts to examine and analyze information on violations of international humanitarian law committed during the armed conflict in the former Yugoslavia. This commission submitted two interim reports in January and October 1993 and submitted its final report in May 1994. All three reports contained discussion of widespread sexual assault, and the final report contained extensive analysis of sexual violence crimes. The *Final Report of the Commission of Experts* made several important findings that expand international legal understanding of how sexual violence can be prosecuted. First, the Commission of Experts identified five patterns of sexual assault, which apply regardless of the ethnicity of the perpetrators or the victims:

1. Sexual violence during looting and intimidation, which takes place before widespread or generalized fighting breaks out in the region;
2. Sexual assault by individuals or small groups in conjunction with fighting in an area, including the rape of women in public;
3. Sexual assault of people in detention by soldiers, camp guards, paramilitaries, and civilians who are allowed to enter the camp and choose women, take them away, rape them, and either kill them or return them to the site; gang rape within the detention site (sometimes by or in front of camp commanders) is also common, as is sexual assault of men within the detention site;
4. Sexual assault by individuals or groups committed against women for the purposes of terrorizing or humiliating them, often for the purpose of "ethnic cleansing"; women were detained in camps and raped multiple times in order to impregnate them and then held until it was too late to obtain an abortion;

5. Sexual assault of women detained in hotels or similar facilities for the sole purpose of sexually entertaining soldiers, rather than causing a reaction in the women themselves.[8]

Second, this report made it clear that men also suffer from sexual violence during armed conflict, although often in different ways and in smaller numbers. For example, men "are forced to rape women and to perform sex acts on guards or each other. They have also been subjected to castration, circumcision or other sexual mutilation."[9] The report concluded that male victims of sexual violence are also protected by international humanitarian law. Third, the report noted that many of the rapes were clearly the result of command direction or an overall policy.[10]

In May 1994, Mr. Rene Degni-Segui was appointed by the Commission on Human Rights to serve as the special rapporteur for Rwanda. His report, filed later that year, concluded that rape and sexual abuse of Rwandan women during the genocide was "the rule and its absence the exception," though sexual violence was also perpetrated against men.[11] He identified the nature of the rapes:

> The perpetration of the genocide and other crimes took on special connotations when women were the victims. The massacres took place according to the following scenario: the husbands and male children were killed first, for the most part in front of their spouses and mothers; then it was the turn of the latter, often after having been tortured and raped.[12]

The special rapporteur identified several patterns of sexual violence, including gang rape, incest (militiamen forced fathers and sons to have sexual relations with their own daughters or mothers or vice versa), forced nudity, and sexual mutilation.[13] He also noted that militia with HIV/AIDS intentionally sexually assaulted in order to cause delayed death of rape victims.[14]

The expansion of understanding of patterns of one kind of gender-based crime—rape—described above was also accompanied by recognition that, while rape is a serious and horrendous crime, it is not the only gender-based crime that is committed against women in armed conflict. In 1993, the United Nations World Conference on Human Rights adopted the Vienna Declaration and Programme of Action. The Declaration and Programme of Action strongly condemned the "systematic rape of women in war situations" and called for the perpetrators of such crimes to be punished. In addition, the final document noted that "violations of the human rights of women in situations of armed conflict are violations of the fundamental principles of international human rights law. All violations of this kind, including in particular murder,

systematic rape, sexual slavery, and forced pregnancy, require a particularly effective response."[15] Two years later, the United Nations World Conference on
Women reaffirmed these statements in the Beijing Declaration and Platform
for Action.[16] Both the Vienna and Beijing documents therefore recognized the
crimes of forced pregnancy and sexual slavery.

Prosecutions by the ICTY and ICTR have led to several convictions for
gender-based crimes. The first case heard before the ICTY, *Prosecutor v. Tadic*,
resulted in the first-ever conviction on sexual violence charges since World War
II (in this case, for male sexual abuse). Tadic was found to be part of a group
that forced a male prisoner to bite off the testicle of another male prisoner and
was therefore held liable for crimes against humanity and war crimes.[17]

The ICTR and ICTY have since decided several groundbreaking cases relating to the crimes of rape and sexual violence. The ICTR's first case, *Prosecutor
v. Akayesu*, led to the first-ever international conviction for rape as a constituent part of genocide. In that case, ICTR defined rape as "a physical invasion of a sexual nature, committed on a person under circumstances which
are coercive." Rape is construed to include "acts which involve the insertion of
objects and/or the use of bodily orifices not considered to be intrinsically sexual."[18] This definition reflects the actual experience of women in war—that
objects such as guns, bayonets, batons, and bottles have been used to rape and
mutilate women.[19] In Rwanda, there were many reports of sticks and machetes being shoved in women's vaginas during the genocide.[20] Sexual violence, which includes rape, is also defined broadly as "any act of a sexual nature which is committed on a person under circumstances which are coercive.
Sexual violence is not limited to physical invasion of the human body and may
include acts which do not involve penetration or even physical contact."[21] An
example of sexual violence that does not involve a physical invasion of the
body is forcing women to undress and do gymnastics in front of a crowd.[22]
The tribunal recognized that both physical and psychological "threats, intimidation, extortion and other forms of duress which prey on fear or desperation" constitute coercion for both crimes, and it was found that coercion may
be inherent in certain circumstances, such as armed conflict or a military presence or paramilitary presence.[23]

Other cases within the ICTY and ICTR have also considered the crime of
rape. In *Prosecutor v. Delalic, Mucic, Delic and Landzo* (referred to as the
Celebici case), the ICTY confirmed the *Akayesu* approach to defining rape, including the finding that rape could amount to torture.[24] It also found that a
person who did not commit rape could still be held liable for that crime,
under the doctrine of command responsibility.[25] In the case of *Prosecutor v.
Furundzija*, the ICTY took a different approach to the definition, setting out
the constituent elements of rape as:

1. The sexual penetration, however slight:
   a. of the vagina or anus of the victim by the penis of the perpetrator or any other object used by the perpetrator; or
   b. of the mouth of the victim by the penis of the perpetrator;
2. By coercion or force or threat of force against the victim or a third person.[26]

The ICC's *Elements of Crimes* document lists the components of rape as:

1. The perpetrator invaded the body of a person by conduct resulting in penetration, however slight, of any part of the body of the victim or of the perpetrator with a sexual organ, or of the anal or genital opening of the victim with any object or any other part of the body.
2. The invasion was committed by force, or by threat of force or coercion, such as that caused by fear of violence, duress, detention, psychological oppression or abuse of power, against such person or another person, or by taking advantage of a coercive environment, or the invasion was committed against a person incapable of giving genuine consent.[27]

Concluded in June 2000, these elements more closely resemble the *Furundzija* approach than the *Celebici* or *Akayesu* approaches. Like *Furundzija*, the ICC Elements do not include nonconsent as an element of rape, but rather integrate it as an affirmative defense.[28] However, the ICC's definition differs from *Furundzija* in two ways: the ICC language is consciously gender neutral and, rather than referring to "penetration," it uses the term "invasion."[29] "Invasion" is a compelling alternative to "penetration" because "it casts rape from the perspective of the victim—who is invaded—rather than the perpetrator—who penetrates."[30]

On February 22, 2001, the ICTY released its decision in *Prosecutor v. Kunarac*. This decision provided the first convictions of rape and enslavement as crimes against humanity. It also took the consideration of force and nonconsent in rape one step further than *Furundzija* and explicitly recognized the victim's right to sexual autonomy. The ICTY noted:

> The matters identified in the *Furundzija* definition—force, threat of force or coercion—are certainly the relevant considerations in many legal systems but the full range of provisions referred to in that judgement suggest that the true common denominator which unifies the various systems may be a wider and more basic principle of penalising violations of sexual *autonomy*.[31]

The tribunal held that sexual autonomy is violated "wherever the person subjected to the act has not freely agreed to it or is otherwise not a voluntary participant."[32] Thus, the judges in *Kunarac* amended the *Furundzija* definition of rape to: the sexual penetration, however slight (a) of the vagina or anus of the victim by the penis of the perpetrator or any other object used by the perpetrator; or (b) of the mouth of the victim by the penis of the perpetrator; where such sexual penetration occurs without the consent of the victim.[33] The judgment states that "consent for this purpose must be consent given voluntarily, as a result of the victim's free will, assessed in the context of the surrounding circumstances."[34]

Boon argues that the *Kunarac* decision makes explicit what the ICC Statute suggests: that sexual autonomy is intrinsically connected to human dignity and bodily integrity.[35] In doing so, the "ICTY thus has recast the basic principle—setting out a framework that makes clear that the victim's ability to consent, in addition to the effective exercise of that consent in light of the external circumstances of war—will differentiate legal from illegal sexual and reproductive acts."[36]

In addition to advancing international law on the link between the crime of rape and sexual autonomy, *Kunarac* also examined the crime of enslavement. The ICTY held that it consists "of the exercise of any or all of the powers attaching to the right of ownership over a person" and that this exercise of power must be intentional.[37] The tribunal listed several factors that should be taken into consideration in determining whether enslavement was committed: control of someone's movement, control of physical environment, psychological control, measures taken to prevent or deter escape, force, threat of force or coercion, duration, assertion of exclusivity, subjection to cruel treatment and abuse, control of sexuality, and forced labor.[38] The ICTY found that indications of enslavement include exaction of forced labor, including through sex, prostitution, and human trafficking.[39]

The ICTY and the ICTR have examined, sometimes in great detail, the constituent elements and surrounding circumstances of various gender-based crimes, especially rape. In doing so, they have expanded the understanding of these crimes under international law. The ICC will benefit from these advances, but it will also set new precedents when it prosecutes crimes under its statute that have yet to be fully examined by the tribunals, such as enforced prostitution, forced pregnancy, enforced sterilization, gender-based persecution, and the subset of enslavement (and sexual slavery)—human trafficking.

Gender-Sensitive Court Procedure

The prosecutors for the post–World War II international military tribunals in Nuremberg and Tokyo relied heavily on physical evidence, such as memorandums and written orders, in proving their cases. The nature of warfare has changed dramatically since that time, and therefore the nature of the evidence available has changed as well. International criminal prosecutions today rely to a large extent on the testimony of victims and witnesses, as war outside the Western nations is conducted less on paper and more through verbal communication and local action. The protection and treatment of victims and witnesses is therefore a key factor in determining the success of a prosecution, and especially so in the case of gender-based crimes, where there are often special societal pressures on victims and witnesses not to reveal or discuss the crimes committed against them. It is for this reason that rules of evidence, the treatment accorded to victims and witnesses, and other procedures must be responsive to the needs of those who have suffered gender-based crimes, to ensure that the process is as positive as possible and does not cause further emotional damage or physical danger or inhibit victims and witnesses from coming forward. In other words, procedures must be in place that provide victims and witnesses with a genuine choice between remaining silent and coming forward.[40]

The first concrete recognition that gender-sensitive procedures are required to ensure that victims come forward took place in the early 1990s, when the United Nations created the United Nations Compensation Commission (UNCC), funded by a 30 percent levy on Iraq's annual oil exports, to compensate victims of Iraq's unlawful invasion and occupation of Kuwait. The UNCC determined that it would compensate "serious personal injury," including physical or mental injury arising from sexual assault.[41] The UNCC Panel of Commissioners accepted the existence of documentary evidence that many women had been raped by Iraqi forces and instituted gender-sensitive standards of proof:

> The Panel had before it some claims where rape by members of the Iraqi military forces was asserted as the cause for the injury. These claimants did not provide any medical documentation. The Commission's medical expert was of the view that many rape victims often do not wish to seek the help of a physician, as they may wish to suppress the memory of the rape, or they are embarrassed to admit that they have been sexually assaulted. Furthermore, a physician would not have been able to offer a written assessment of the physical injuries suffered by the claimant, unless the claimant presented herself for treatment immediately after the attack, which would have been difficult during the invasion and occupation of Kuwait. Taking the above-noted factors into account, the Panel recommends compensation for claims for rape where circumstantial evidence is available.[42]

The UNCC not only recognized that sexual violence crimes arising from an international armed conflict are crimes with serious physical consequences but also provided procedures that recognized the realities of the aftermath of these crimes.

Following in the footsteps of the UNCC, the ICTY and ICTR have adopted procedural rules aimed at protecting victims and witnesses of gender-based crimes. Both tribunals routinely grant a range of protective measures for witnesses in sexual violence cases, including the use of pseudonyms, protective screens, image-altering devices, closed sessions, and video-link testimony.[43] It is especially crucial in cases involving gender-based crimes to ensure that the focus of the trial remains on the accused and blame is not redirected on the victim, as unfortunately often happens at the domestic level.[44] The ICTY and ICTR adopted Rule 96 in their Rules of Procedure and Evidence to address this issue. Rule 96 provides that, in cases of sexual assault, no corroboration of the victim's testimony shall be required, prior sexual conduct of the victim shall not be admitted into evidence, and, before evidence of the victim's consent is admitted, the accused shall satisfy the trial chamber in camera that the evidence is relevant and credible. In addition, consent shall not be allowed as a defense if the victim has been subjected to, has been threatened with, or had reason to fear violence, duress, detention, or psychological oppression or reasonably believed that, if the victim did not submit, another might be so subjected, threatened, or put in fear.

The tribunals have also addressed the fact that the role of culture must also be respected in order to ensure gender-sensitive procedures. In the *Akayesu* and *Musema* cases, victims and witnesses gave evidence in the Kinyarwandan language, in which direct words are not used for sexual organs and metaphors are used instead. The judges recognized the cultural sensitivities involved in public discussion of intimate matters and accepted the evidence given in this manner.[45]

The Rome Statute of the ICC incorporates the lessons learned from the international criminal tribunals by including procedures that are meant to ensure that victims and witnesses are, as far as possible, not retraumatized by their interaction with the ICC. Article 68 of the Rome Statute covers the treatment of victims and witnesses by the ICC during all stages of a case: initiation, investigation, prosecution, sentencing, and appeal. Article 68(1) states:

> The Court shall take appropriate measures to protect the safety, physical and psychological well-being, dignity and privacy of victims and witnesses. In so doing, the Court shall have regard to all relevant factors, including . . . gender . . . and the nature of the crimes, in particular, but not limited to, where the crime involves sexual or gender violence or violence against children.

Paragraph 2 of that article provides an exception to public hearings where closed (or in camera) hearings are required in order to protect victims and witnesses, in particular "in the case of a victim of sexual violence" and having regard to the views of the victim. Article 68(4) permits the Victims and Witnesses Unit to advise the prosecutor or the court on appropriate protective measures, security arrangements, counseling, and assistance.

Article 54(1) of the Rome Statute reiterates the obligation under Article 68 as it relates to the prosecutor, stating that the prosecutor shall take appropriate measures to ensure the effective investigation and prosecution of crimes and, in doing so, take into account the nature of the crimes—in particular where they involve sexual violence, gender violence, or violence against children—and the age, gender, health, and other circumstances of the victims and witnesses. Article 57 permits the pretrial chamber to provide for the protection and privacy of victims and witnesses. Under Article 64(2) and (6)(e), the trial chamber must ensure that the trial is fair and conducted with due regard for the protection of victims and witnesses, and the trial chamber is also empowered to provide for the protection of victims and witnesses.

The Rome Statute takes an important step forward in international law by permitting the participation of victims at various stages of the proceedings. This participation includes that provided for in the ICTY and ICTR—participation as a witness—and goes further. Article 68(3) states that, where the personal interests of the victims are affected, the court must permit their views and concerns to be presented and considered at appropriate stages of the proceedings. These views can be presented by a legal representative of the victims. The ICC Statute sets out some of those avenues for participation: at the pretrial chamber examination of whether the prosecutor can proceed with an investigation (Article 15[3]), when the court determines questions of admissibility or jurisdiction (Article 19[3]), and at the sentencing stage, prior to the court's decision on reparations (Article 75[3]) and on appeal regarding reparation orders (Article 82[4]).

Rule 70 of the ICC's Rules of Procedure and Evidence provides principles governing evidence in cases of sexual violence. Rule 70 is similar, but not identical, to Rule 96 of the ICTY and ICTR. Rule 70 states that "consent cannot be inferred by reason of any words or conduct of a victim where force, threat of force, coercion or taking an advantage of a coercive environment undermined the victim's ability to give voluntary and genuine consent." In addition, consent "cannot be inferred by reason of any words or conduct of a victim where the victim is incapable of giving genuine consent," and consent "cannot be inferred by reason of silence of, or lack of resistance by, a victim of the alleged sexual violence." Finally, credibility, character, or predisposition to sexual availability of a victim or witness cannot be inferred "by reason of the sexual nature of the prior or subsequent conduct of a victim or witness." Rule 71 echoes Rule 96 of the ICTY and ICTR, stating that (subject to Article 69[4] on admissibility of evidence) the ICC shall not admit evidence of the prior or subsequent sexual conduct of a victim or witness.

Gender-Sensitive Court Staffing

The need for gender-sensitive court staffing is crucially important in ensuring fair court procedure. The 1995 Beijing Declaration and Platform for Action called on governments and international and regional organizations to aim for gender balance when nominating candidates for judicial and other positions in, inter alia, the ICTY and ICTR.[46] In addition, states committed to ensuring that these bodies are able to address gender issues properly by providing appropriate training to prosecutors, judges, and other officials so that they can integrate a gender perspective into their work.[47]

The ICC Statute contains several provisions addressing the need for gender-sensitive court staffing. Article 36(8) asserts that states parties must take into account the need for a fair representation of female and male judges when selecting judges for the ICC.[48] In addition, the same article indicates that "States Parties shall also take into account the need to include judges with legal expertise on specific issues, including, but not limited to, violence against women or children."[49] These criteria were also deemed to apply to the staffing of the Office of the Prosecutor and the Registry.[50]

The offices of the prosecutor in the ICTY and ICTR employ a legal adviser who has focused on gender-based crimes, a position that has been very important in the indictment and prosecution of these crimes by the tribunals. This expertise was also widely seen as crucial to the ICC's Office of the Prosecutor, and Article 42(9) was therefore included: "The Prosecutor shall appoint advisers with legal expertise on specific issues, including, but not limited to, sexual and gender violence and violence against children." Similarly, the fact that the Registry is responsible for the administration of the Victims and Witnesses Unit, which deals with protective measures, security arrangements, counseling, and other appropriate assistance to victims and witnesses appearing before the court, led to the addition of Article 43(6), which states in part, "The Unit shall include staff with expertise in trauma, including trauma related to crimes of sexual violence."

The practice of the international criminal tribunals and the provisions of the Rome Statute of the ICC represent important advances in ensuring that knowledgeable and experienced judges, officials, and staff are elected to or employed by the court, and the recognition that having such people is key to ensuring gender-sensitive prosecutions.

Conclusion

The last ten years have brought important changes to the international legal understanding of gender-based genocide, crimes against humanity, and war crimes. It is now widely recognized that everyone—women, girls, boys, and men—can be a victim of gender-based crimes, and that these crimes are prohibited. The ICTY and ICTR have adopted nuanced and flexible definitions of rape and other forms of gender-based violence that reflect the evolution of thinking in the fields of international human rights and international humanitarian law. The list of crimes that may be thought of as crimes of sexual violence has expanded at the same time as the understanding of the patterns of sexual violence in armed conflict has grown. This list now includes crimes such as forced nudity, sexual mutilation, forced pregnancy, and enforced sterilization but is not limited to crimes that can be described at this time: the imagination of future perpetrators is therefore not underestimated. As well, the various decisions of the two international criminal tribunals make it clear that rape and other forms of sexual assault have physical, psychological, and other far-reaching effects.

The last decade has also brought about a number of "firsts": the first international prosecution and conviction of sexual violence crimes committed in an internal armed conflict (*Akayesu*), the first prosecution and conviction of rape as a tool of genocide (*Akayesu*), the first prosecution and conviction of sexual violence crimes committed on men (*Tadic*), the first convictions of enslavement as a crime against humanity (*Kunarac*), and the first conviction for sexual violence crimes of a commander (*Celebici*) since World War II. The *Kunarac* indictment by the ICTY was the first international indictment to deal exclusively with various sexual violence crimes, including enslavement, and was later followed by *Furundzija*, which was the first indictment focused solely on the rape and sexual assault of one woman. These prosecutions have demonstrated that gender-based violence can be prosecuted under a number of different categories of crimes, including torture and genocide. They have also made findings that do much to develop the international understanding about rape crimes, for example, the finding that armed conflict can create a situation of inherent coercion that negates the defense of consent.

The Rome Statute of the ICC represents another "first," as it takes a broad-based approach to ensuring a gender-sensitive court. While the statute would not have been as far ranging as it is without the lessons learned from the international criminal tribunals, it builds on those experiences to criminalize a wide range of gender-based crimes, provides court procedures that have the goal of avoiding retraumatization of victims and witnesses, and ensures that the court is staffed with people who have knowledge of and experience in gender-based

violence. These advances have the potential of being revolutionary. Truly gender-sensitive international justice has been a long time coming. Since the ICC's
"complementary" jurisdiction, which provides countries with the first chance
to investigate or prosecute, ensures that many of the cases of gender-based
genocide, crimes against humanity, or war crimes will likely be investigated and
prosecuted at the national level instead of within the ICC, it is crucial that the
gender-sensitive advances found in the Rome Statute are incorporated into national systems. It is only in this way that gender justice can be made global.

Notes

1. The term "gender-based crimes" refers to crimes committed against persons because of their socially constructed roles as women, men, girls, or boys. Gender-based
crimes include crimes of sexual violence, such as rape and sexual slavery, but are not
restricted to these crimes. Gender-based crimes also include nonsexual crimes, such as
the killing of boys because they are perceived as potential soldiers, or the capture of
women and girls to wash and cook for fighting forces. It is an unfortunate fact that
women and girls tend to be targeted for gender-based crimes, especially for sexual violence crimes.

2. *Rome Statute of the International Criminal Court*, UN Doc. PCNICC/INF/3 (August 17, 1999), arts. 7(1)(c), (g), and (h) and 8(2)(b)(xxii) and (e)(vi).

3. *Rome Statute of the International Criminal Court*, art. 7(2)(c); *Finalized Draft
Text of the Elements of Crimes*, UN Doc. PCNICC/2000/1/Add.2 (November 2, 2000),
arts. 7(1)(c) and (g)-2, 8(2)(b)(xxii)-2 and (e)(vi)-2.

4. Kelly Dawn Askin explains that sexual assault has been seen as a crime at various
times in various parts of the world, albeit rarely, dating back to before the Middle
Ages. The Lieber Code of 1863 is viewed as the first modern step in codifying international laws of warfare. The Lieber Code mandated that "all rape . . . [is] prohibited
under the penalty of death." The 1907 Hague Convention (IV) respecting the Laws
and Customs of War on Land states, in Article XLVI, "Family honour and rights, the
lives of persons . . . must be respected." This was widely understood to prohibit rape.
Kelly Dawn Askin, *War Crimes against Women: Prosecution in International War
Crimes* (Hague: Kluwer Law International, 1997).

5. Kristen Boon, "Rape and Forced Pregnancy under the ICC Statute: Human Dignity, Autonomy, and Consent," Columbia Human Rights Law Review 32, no. 3
(2001): 627; Judith Gardam and Michelle J. Jarvis, *Women, Armed Conflict and International Law* (Hague: Kluwer Law International, 2001), 102. However, see International Committee of the Red Cross, *Women Facing War* (Geneva: ICRC, 2001), pages
55–56, describing situations where reference to "honor" may be appropriate, and
page 57, arguing that emphasis on the reference to honor does not take into account
the fact that rape is encompassed in "willfully causing great suffering or serious injury to body or health," a grave breach under Article 147 of the Fourth Geneva Convention.

6. *Report on the Situation of Human Rights in Kuwait under Iraqi Occupation* [Kalin Report], prepared by Walter Kalin, special rapporteur of the Commission on Human Rights, in accordance with Commission Resolution 1991/67, UN Doc. E/CN.4/1992/26 (January 16, 1992), reprinted in Walter Kalin, *Human Rights in Times of Occupation: The Case of Kuwait* (London: Sweet & Maxwell, 1994), par. 182.

7. In addition to recognizing that wartime rape occurs in many different contexts, Kalin also found that the rapes committed by members of the Iraqi occupying forces during the exercise of their official functions, especially in the context of house searches or interrogations in detention, can be considered to constitute torture and cruel, inhuman, or degrading treatment (Kalin Report, par. 184). With respect to rapes committed by "off-duty" members of the Iraqi armed forces, he also concluded that "Iraq may have violated its obligation, under Article 27 of the Fourth Geneva Convention, to protect women 'against any attack on their honour, in particular against rape, enforced prostitution, or any form of indecent assault'" (Kalin Report, par. 184). In other words, it does not matter whether a soldier is on- or off-duty: if that person commits a rape, it can be considered a war crime. In the past, this question had been answered in the negative, as "off-duty" rapes were considered "private." By not giving much weight to this division between "on-duty" and "off-duty" liability, Kalin set the stage for later developments finding that the circumstances of armed conflict, and therefore the circumstances of rape, are inherently coercive and that the off-duty/on-duty dichotomy is not relevant in present-day armed conflicts.

8. *Final Report of the Commission of Experts Established Pursuant to Security Council Resolution 780 (1992)*, UN Doc. S/1994/674 (May 27, 1994), (IV)(F)(3).

9. *Final Report of the Commission of Experts*, (IV)(F).

10. *Final Report of the Commission of Experts*, (IV)(F)(3).

11. *Report on the Situation of Human Rights in Rwanda*, submitted by Rene Degni-Segui, special rapporteur of the Commission of Human Rights, under paragraph 20 of Resolution S/-31 of May 25, 1994, UN Doc. E/CN.4/1996/68 (January 29, 1996), par. 16.

12. *Report on the Situation of Human Rights in Rwanda*, par. 13.

13. *Report on the Situation of Human Rights in Rwanda*, par. 18.

14. *Report on the Situation of Human Rights in Rwanda*, par. 20.

15. *Vienna Declaration and Programme of Action*, UN Doc. A/CONF.157/23 (July 12, 1993), pars. 28, 38.

16. *Beijing Declaration and Platform for Action*, UN Doc. A/CONF.177/20 (September 15, 1995), par. 131–33.

17. *Prosecutor v. Tadic*, IT-94-1 (Trial Chamber, May 7, 1997; Appeals Chamber, February 27, 2001), pars. 726, 730.

18. *Prosecutor v. Akayesu*, ICTR-96-4-I (Trial Chamber, September 2, 1998; Appeals Chamber, June 1, 2001), pars. 686, 688.

19. Iris Chang, *The Rape of Nanking: The Forgotten Holocaust of World War II* (New York: Penguin, 1997), 91–95.

20. Human Rights Watch, *Shattered Lives: Sexual Violence during the Genocide and Its Aftermath* (New York: HRW, 1996), 62–65; *Prosecutor v. Akayesu*, par. 686.

21. *Prosecutor v. Akayesu*, par. 688.

22. *Prosecutor v. Akayesu.*

23. *Prosecutor v. Akayesu.*

24. *Prosecutor v. Delalic et al.*, IT-96-21-T (Trial Chamber, November 16, 1998; Appeals Chamber, February 20, 2001), pars. 486, 489.

25. *Prosecutor v. Delalic et al.*, pars. 769, 774–75.

26. *Prosecutor v. Furundzija*, IT-95-1-T (Trial Chamber, December 10, 1998; Appeals Chamber, July 21, 2000), par. 185.

27. *Finalized Draft Text of the Elements of Crimes*, arts. 7(1)(g)-1, 8(2)(b)(xxii)-1 and (e)(vi)-1.

28. Boon, "Rape and Forced Pregnancy under the ICC Statute," 648.

29. Boon, "Rape and Forced Pregnancy under the ICC Statute."

30. Boon, "Rape and Forced Pregnancy under the ICC Statute."

31. *Prosecutor v. Kunarac*, IT-96-23 and IT-96-23/1 (Trial Chamber, February 22, 2001), par. 440.

32. *Prosecutor v. Kunarac*, par. 457.

33. *Prosecutor v. Kunarac*, par. 460.

34. *Prosecutor v. Kunarac.*

35. Boon, "Rape and Forced Pregnancy under the ICC Statute," 675.

36. Boon, "Rape and Forced Pregnancy under the ICC Statute."

37. *Prosecutor v. Kunarac*, pars. 539–40.

38. *Prosecutor v. Kunarac*, par. 543.

39. *Prosecutor v. Kunarac*, par. 542.

40. Gardam and Jarvis, *Women, Armed Conflict and International Law.*

41. United Nations Compensation Commission, *Recommendations Made by the Panel of Commissioners concerning Individual Claims for Serious Injury or Death (Category "B" Claims)*, UN Doc. S/AC.26/1994/1 (May 26, 1994), UNCC Decision 3.

42. United Nations Compensation Commission, *Recommendations Made by the Panel of Commissioners*, 263.

43. Gardam and Jarvis, *Women, Armed Conflict and International Law.*

44. Barbara Bedont, "Engendering Justice: An Assessment of the Statute of the International Criminal Court from a Gender Perspective," in *Human Rights and Development Yearbook*, ed. Hugo Stroke and Arne Tostensen (Utrecht: Netherlands Institute of Human Rights, 2000).

45. *Prosecutor v. Akayesu*, par. 687; *Prosecutor v. Musema*, ICTR-96-13 (Trial Chamber, January 27, 2000; Appeals Chamber, November 16, 2001), par. 103.

46. *Beijing Declaration and Platform for Action*, par. 142(b).

47. *Beijing Declaration and Platform for Action*, par. 142(c).

48. *Rome Statute of the International Criminal Court*, art. 36(8)(a)(iii).

49. *Rome Statute of the International Criminal Court*, art. 36(8)(b).

50. *Rome Statute of the International Criminal Court*, art. 44(2).

4

The Renewed Popularity of the Rule of Law: Implications for Women, Impunity, and Peacekeeping

Barbara Bedont

IN THE PERIOD FOLLOWING THE END of the Cold War, many states, organizations, and individuals were busy setting up mechanisms to try to prosecute those who commit genocide, war crimes, and crimes against humanity (see Oosterveld, chapter 3). Not since the end of World War II had there been so much attention given to international justice. The advocates of these initiatives championed the principle that perpetrators of egregious crimes must not be beyond the reach of the law. The implication was that where national authorities fail to act, the international community must step in. While these ideas achieved a certain popularity among international lawyers, their reach never extended to peacekeeping.

The analysis of peacekeeping throughout this book reveals that crimes, including gender crimes, are at times committed by those charged with the responsibility of keeping the peace, thus compromising the success of peacekeeping missions and entrenching inequality between men and women in transitional societies (see Mazurana, chapter 1; Vandenberg, chapter 7).[1] Peacekeepers are often stationed in postconflict situations where the state has collapsed, the justice system is nonexistent or not operating fully, crime is rampant, and women and children are impoverished and vulnerable to abuse. These societies develop into prime routes for trafficking in drugs, weapons, natural resources, and persons. The survivors of armed conflict who suffer economic dislocation, violence, and other consequences of war are vulnerable to being recruited into prostitution.[2] Meanwhile, foreign troops stationed as part of a peacekeeping mission may feed a demand for prostitution.[3] All these factors converge to create a climate favorable for trafficking in women and children, sexual enslavement, child prostitution, and other forms of sexual violence.

In this environment, the legal regime for dealing with crimes against civilians during peacekeeping operations is particularly important from a gender perspective. The current regime generally relegates responsibility for prosecuting offending peacekeepers to the authorities of the peacekeeper's home country. This regime emanates from a set of trilateral agreements between the United Nations, the state contributing peacekeeping troops (the contributing state), and the state on whose territory the mission is located (the host state). Yet, history has shown that contributing states are remiss in prosecuting their soldiers. Discriminatory laws and practices of contributing states, when combined with the provisions in the current trilateral agreements, result in little or no legal recourse for the victims of many acts that violate international human rights standards. The result is much impunity for crimes against women and children at a key time for the future of societies in transition.

The emerging international criminal law system described in chapter 3 (see Oosterveld, chapter 3) constitutes a challenge to this dysfunctional system. If the International Criminal Court (ICC) represents an acknowledgment that individuals must be held accountable for egregious crimes no matter what their official capacity, then the impunity enjoyed by peacekeepers exposes a certain hypocrisy. This exposure has the potential to serve as an impetus to states to prosecute their peacekeepers who commit crimes. In addition, the gender provisions in the Rome Statute of the ICC[4] and the progress made under international law for prosecuting those who commit crimes against women mean that for many countries there is more possibility of impunity for gender crimes at the national level than at the international level. The strengthening of international mechanisms could therefore be beneficial to women's interests. This theoretical potential, however, is not being borne out. First, the Rome Statute contains a number of provisions that limit the power of the ICC, which, in conjunction with the trilateral agreements for peacekeeping missions, limit the ICC's potential. More importantly, in the first two years of the ICC's existence, the United States succeeded in obtaining a Security Council resolution that "requested" that the ICC not investigate or prosecute any peacekeepers from states that are not a party to the Rome Statute.[5] In 2004, the United States withdrew its attempt to renew the resolution and extend the period of immunity. This move was primarily due to intense international pressure and outrage over prisoner abuse in occupied Iraq and the internal leaking of a Justice Department torture memo in which the department's legal advisers laid out arguments to support the position that some forms of torture might be legal.[6] However, while the United States administration has for the moment retreated on this issue at the

United Nations, the precedent of granting special immunity to peacekeepers has been established.

These developments do not bode well for the problem of impunity for abuses committed by peacekeepers. The limited potential of the international criminal law system that results constitutes another example of how the international legal system, based on the principle of state sovereignty, creates artificial barriers to addressing issues important to women's lives.

Definition of Terms

According to the traditional concept of peacekeeping, peacekeepers were military personnel deployed by the United Nations, upon the consent of parties to a conflict, to keep enemy forces apart and monitor the end of an armed conflict. This concept of peacekeeping has changed drastically in the last decade as peacekeeping operations have become more multidimensional, taking on tasks normally associated with administering territory. Given the many changes occurring in the current peacekeeping environment, a clarification of terms is necessary.

The label of peacekeepers is increasingly applied to a large variety of actors, associated with either the United Nations or regional organizations, who are involved in operations in conflict or postconflict situations. However, this use of the term deviates from the traditional concept of peacekeeping as articulated by Boutros Boutros-Ghali in *An Agenda for Peace*, where peacekeeping is the "deployment of a United Nations presence in the field, hitherto with the consent of all the parties concerned, normally involving United Nations military and/or police personnel and frequently civilians as well."[7]

These peacekeeping missions are undertaken under Chapter VI of the United Nations Charter. The legal regime that is discussed in the present chapter relates to the traditional form of peacekeeping missions under Chapter VI, that is, missions with the consent of the host state. For this reason, this chapter will use the term "peacekeepers" to refer to military and civilian personnel that are present in a territory with the consent of the national authorities. Military forces that intervene in another state for whatever reason and do not have such national consent are not included in the term "peacekeepers." Moreover, while civilian personnel also commit violations of human rights against local populations, the causes and solutions to the problem of human rights abuses by civilian personnel, as well as the legal regime that governs the matter, differ from those relating to military peacekeepers. The present chapter will therefore focus on the issues and legal regime relating to military personnel of peacekeeping missions.

The Lack of Accountability for Peacekeepers' Crimes

In the majority of peacekeeping operations set up under the auspices of the United Nations, the authority for prosecuting soldiers who have committed crimes rests exclusively with the soldiers' home country. The rationale for this system is the view by contributing states that their soldiers stationed in another country as part of a peacekeeping operation should not be prosecuted by the authorities of the host state. They are therefore granted a special immunity while on peacekeeping missions. While it is understandable for states to want to spare their citizens from being subject to the criminal system of another state, the United Nations system has proved dysfunctional and incapable of providing accountability where national authorities have failed to act. Many of the abuses committed by peacekeepers go unpunished or are dealt with by sending the offending soldiers home. Examples are numerous: Pakistani peacekeepers accused of killing civilians in Somalia were never tried. Italian peacekeepers in Mozambique who sexually abused children through the use of child "prostitutes" were sent home under other pretenses but never faced criminal charges.[8] Similar crimes by Bulgarian peacekeepers in Cambodia were likewise unpunished.[9] In three separate cases in which boys were killed by American peacekeepers in Somalia, no action was taken in two cases, and in the third the soldier was demoted and fined one month's pay.[10]

In some cases, national authorities have taken action against their soldiers who have committed crimes, particularly where there has been a great deal of media attention. In a highly publicized case, Canada tried and convicted soldiers of the Canadian Airborne Regiment for torturing a Somali teenager and disbanded the regiment following an official inquiry in January 1995.[11] After photos were published showing Belgian soldiers torturing a Somali boy, Belgium tried and convicted some soldiers, while others were acquitted.[12] An American peacekeeper was tried and convicted for raping and killing a young girl in Kosovo in a case that made headlines in the United States.[13] These experiences provide some examples of accountability for crimes committed by peacekeepers. Because of the lack of documented information regarding crimes committed by peacekeepers—itself a failure of the current system—it is not possible to say whether the cases in which peacekeepers are held accountable for their crimes are the exception or the rule.

Even in those cases where action has been taken, a common reaction of national authorities has been that the abuses were "isolated incidents" and do not indicate a problem with the overall system. Such was the conclusion of the commission in Italy that examined the crimes committed by Italian peacekeepers in Somalia. Italian peacekeepers in Somalia were involved in several incidents in which civilians were sexually tortured or raped.[14] The commission, having never visited Somalia to gather information, and without looking at other missions such as Mozambique where child abuse by Italian peacekeepers was widespread, concluded that the episodes of violence were "sporadic and localized, not widespread and general."[15] It further found that senior professional officers were not involved in the violations. The Ministry of Defense meted out five disciplinary sanctions related to the incidents, ranging from formal reprimands to temporary suspensions. Italy has claimed that five public prosecutions were commenced, although information regarding the cases is unavailable.[16]

Consequences of Impunity

The impunity enjoyed by soldiers who commit crimes during peacekeeping missions is an affront to the very principles that the international community seeks to instill in the societies where missions are established. The raison d'être of peacekeeping missions is to help establish security and the rule of law in transitional societies. Peacekeeping operations are not successful if gender inequality is entrenched, if democracy remains unavailable for half of the population, and if major social problems such as prostitution and HIV/AIDS are exacerbated. Moreover, crimes committed by peacekeepers reduce the trust of the local community in the mission and set a bad example for the establishment of the rule of law in the host state. Even if soldiers are prosecuted by their national authorities back home, the local population is unlikely to be aware of any action taken. Justice not only needs to be done, but it needs to be seen to have been done. Sending soldiers home or trying them back home is simply not enough.

In addition, inadequate responses by national authorities fail to deter further crimes. Many soldiers on peacekeeping missions are under the impression that if they misbehave, they will be protected by their national governments. In gender training sessions by the United Nations, trainers have reported that peacekeepers are acutely aware of their immunity, which they understand as exempting them from being prosecuted for acts they commit while abroad.[17] Peacekeepers may have this perception as a consequence of the de facto impunity enjoyed by peacekeeping troops.

The Current Legal Regime for Peacekeeping Missions

The United Nations System

The state of affairs described above arises, in part, from a legal regime that is premised on the need to preserve state prerogatives, rather than on the cause of justice. The system can be traced back to the United Nations Charter and the 1946 Convention on the Privileges and Immunities of the United Nations.[18] Article 105 of the charter states: "The Organisation shall enjoy in the territory of each of its Members such privileges and immunities as are necessary for the fulfillment of its purposes."

Section 22, Article VI, of the United Nations' privileges and immunities convention grants immunity from legal process to United Nations personnel and to "experts" performing missions for the United Nations for acts committed in the course of the performance of their mission. "Experts" are undefined in the convention. However, the provisions regarding experts are extended to peacekeepers by way of two types of agreements concluded by the United Nations for each peacekeeping mission.

First, the United Nations enters into a status-of-forces agreement (SOFA) with the host country, currently based on a 1990 model.[19] In the case that a military member of the peacekeeping operation commits a crime, the SOFA accords "exclusive jurisdiction" to the contributing state—that is, the contributing state has the sole authority to investigate and take judicial action in the case.[20] This provision does not apply to civilian members of United Nations peacekeeping operations.[21] The second salient agreement is a contribution agreement concluded between the United Nations and the contributing state.[22] The United Nations' model contribution agreement specifies (in pars. 5 and 8) that peacekeeping personnel shall enjoy the privileges and immunities provided for in the SOFA and reaffirms that responsibility for disciplinary action of military personnel rests with the contributing state.

These model agreements are used by the United Nations and the countries concerned to prepare agreements on a case-by-case basis for each peacekeeping mission. Such agreements are usually, although not always, concluded. In the absence of any status-of-forces agreement or contribution agreement, the above privileges and immunities are not guaranteed. Ordinarily, states exercise jurisdiction with regard to crimes committed on their territory or by their citizens. The policy of the United Nations is that the privileges and immunities under the United Nations Charter and the privileges and immunities convention are applicable to its operations and personnel in the absence of any agreement, thereby exempting peacekeepers from the normal territorial jurisdiction of host states.[23] Some scholars, however, maintain that members of a peacekeeping force would be subject to the laws of the host state.[24]

Customary international law on this question is at best uncertain,[25] creating the theoretical possibility that peacekeepers could be subject to the laws of the host state. Indeed, the elaborate trilateral agreements concluded in most operations suggest that states do not consider it sufficient to rely on the United Nations' privileges and immunities convention and on customary international law. So, for example, if peacekeepers sexually abused children through prostitution (as occurred in Mozambique and Bosnia)[26] and there were no agreements in place regarding which country exercised criminal jurisdiction, the host state might be able to prosecute them.[27]

The NATO System

While the current system of criminal jurisdiction for United Nations operations has been systemized, peacekeeping operations of regional organizations such as NATO involve more ad hoc arrangements. Most often, the rights of contributing states over their soldiers are both demanded and protected. For example, in Bosnia and Herzegovina, the Dayton agreements provided that NATO military personnel would be under the exclusive jurisdiction of their national authorities.[28] Thus, in both United Nations and NATO peacekeeping missions, provisions regarding the protection of peacekeeping personnel are common.

The SOFAs regulating troops of the NATO Alliance who are stationed in other NATO member states establish a system in which jurisdiction is assigned to either the contributing state or the host state according to whether the offenses are punishable by one state or the other. For example, if the offenses are punishable by the law of the contributing state but not by the law of the host state, the contributing state exercises sole authority over the case, and vice versa.[29] The contributing state and host state assume concurrent authority in cases where the conduct is punishable by the laws of both states. In those cases, the contributing state has the "primary right" to try soldiers who commit crimes.[30] The SOFA goes on to provide:

> If the State having the primary right decides not to exercise jurisdiction, it shall notify the authorities of the other State as soon as practicable. The authorities of the State having the primary right shall give sympathetic consideration to a request from the authorities of the other State for a waiver of its right in cases where that other State considers such waiver to be of particular importance.[31]

It is important to note that the SOFAs concluded between the United States and a number of countries also contain some form of primary and secondary jurisdiction for crimes committed by United States armed forces stationed abroad.[32] As discussed below, this system—which mirrors the "complementarity principle" of the Rome Statute, discussed below—provides a viable alternative model for United Nations operations. In fact, this model was used in an agreement regarding United Nations forces based in Japan in 1953. The agreement, concluded between Australia, Canada, New Zealand, the United Kingdom, the United States, and Japan, lays out a system for criminal jurisdiction that is identical to the system laid out in the NATO SOFA.[33] These agreements reflect greater equality between the states receiving and sending troops, in contrast to the system for United Nations peacekeeping operations, which exhibits a less equal relationship in which more unfavorable terms are dictated on the state receiving peacekeeping troops.

Disadvantages of the Current System of Criminal Jurisdiction for Peacekeeping Operations from a Gender Perspective

The problems that arise from the current system of criminal jurisdiction for peacekeeping operations stem from a number of factors. First, the responsibility for prosecuting peacekeepers for sexual violence crimes often rests with the military courts of the national authorities, depending on the national laws. Military justice often lacks the basic structures and safeguards to ensure independence and fairness. For example, military courts are often less transparent than civil courts. As a male-dominated institution, the military is particularly unsuitable for prosecuting individuals in cases of violence against women. Many of the problems that arise in peacekeeping missions are the product of militarized masculinity, namely, the glorification of masculine aggression. Several feminist scholars have shown how aggressiveness—considered necessary in combat—is rewarded in militaries and privileged over so-called feminine qualities.[34] Relegating responsibility for prosecuting persons who commit violence against women to those within such a culture therefore creates problems.

For example, the Italian military proved incapable of taking proper action in response to the crimes committed by Italian peacekeepers in Somalia in 1997. A specific legal regime to prosecute the Italian peacekeepers who raped and tortured Somali civilians did not exist in Italy. In a study of the Somalia matter, Natalia Lupi points out that crimes of "violation [rape],[35] torture and maltreatment against civilians" are not provided for by the Military Penal Code that regulated the behavior of Italian peacekeepers.[36] The soldiers were therefore disciplined but not prosecuted.

Another problem is the historical and continual underprosecution of crimes against women at the national level, which inevitably carries over to peacekeeping missions. Ignorance of gender issues results in inadequate attention to crimes against women by national authorities. For example, in a case involving the alleged rape of an American peacekeeper by two Czech peacekeepers, the Czech authorities dismissed the complaint on the grounds that because the American woman had had consensual sex with one of the alleged perpetrators before, she must have consented to the incident in question.[37] This reasoning reflects a mistaken and sexist assumption that a woman who consents to sex once with someone is likely to always consent to sex.

Excluding the jurisdiction of host states could be particularly problematic in cases of sexual violence because some countries that send troops to peace-keeping operations do not criminalize all forms of sexual or gender violence. For example, in some countries, the penal codes provide that men who kill female relatives who "dishonor" the family shall not be punished. In other countries, rape and other sexual assault is not punishable where the offender marries the victim.[38] Other countries have onerous evidentiary rules that make it almost impossible to secure a conviction for sexual violence, effectively resulting in impunity for these crimes.[39]

As another important example, some countries do not take sufficient action against sexual exploitation of children. The 1989 Convention on the Rights of the Child defines children as all persons under the age of eighteen years. It obliges states to prevent all forms of sexual exploitation and sexual abuse of children, including the exploitative use of children in prostitution or other unlawful sexual practices, and the traffic in children.[40] The treaty has been ratified by 191 states, leaving only two more states for universal ratification and making it the most widely ratified human rights treaty. Despite this, many countries that provide peacekeeping personnel set the age of consent below eighteen years and have inadequate laws to protect children from prostitution and trafficking.[41] Soldiers from those countries could therefore engage in these abuses of children and there would be no legal means of redress for the victims in the likely case that the authorities failed to act.

In sum, under the current system, laws and practices of national jurisdictions of contributing states that result in impunity for certain crimes mean that soldiers from such countries could commit such acts in the territory of a host state and enjoy total impunity. It is not hard to imagine a host state objecting to or even being outraged about this state of affairs. The discriminatory laws and practices of many national justice systems regarding crimes against women make the provisions in the current model SOFA and contribution agreement particularly problematic.

An Alternative Model

The solution to this untenable situation is not evident. Allowing host states to exercise jurisdiction regarding offenses punishable under their laws but not under the laws of the contributing state may not always be desirable. A host state may have laws punishing certain acts that would constitute a violation of a person's rights or freedoms under international standards. For example, laws in some countries punish women who frequent certain public places, or who otherwise violate oppressive local customs. Subjecting peacekeepers to laws of host states could work to exclude female soldiers from peacekeeping missions and could subject peacekeepers to discriminatory laws. Perhaps more importantly, since peacekeepers often operate in situations where there has been a breakdown of the state, there is a greater likelihood that the criminal laws of such a state were flawed and discriminatory. These types of scenarios underline the original rationale for the current system.

A solution may be to adopt from the NATO model. The SOFA and contribution agreement could grant primary jurisdiction to the contributing state to prosecute its nationals and grant to the host state, in cases where the acts are prohibited under the laws of both the host and contributing states, the option of exercising jurisdiction where the contributing state waives its primary jurisdiction. Such a secondary jurisdiction could also be granted to an international tribunal like the ICC with different terms. The NATO system also includes provisions requiring the authorities of the state sending troops and the host state to cooperate with each other and to keep each other informed of the progress of cases.[42] Moreover, military authorities of the sending state can exercise criminal and disciplinary jurisdiction over persons subject to its military law within the receiving state.[43] In other words, they can conduct investigations and trials in the state where the crime occurred. This would reduce the perceptual problem that occurs when victims and the local population are unaware of the fate of peacekeepers who commit crimes.

This model would preserve some control by states over their soldiers while providing an avenue to compel the contributing state not only to take action with regard to criminal offenses committed by its personnel but also to report its progress to the host state and to the United Nations. While it may be rare that contributing states waive their jurisdiction, there have been instances where states have not insisted on their strict legal rights when faced with great public pressure. For example, in Okinawa, Japan, local groups were outraged at the alleged rape of a Japanese girl by an American soldier. The protests that followed demanded a withdrawal of the United States military base from Japan. The United States sought to appease these groups by waiving its rights and allowing Japanese authorities to arrest the soldier before he was formally indicted.[44] However, this applied to the 1995 outrage and is not a general principle. Thus, an alternative model exists that could be acceptable to states and alleviate the problem of impunity for peacekeepers who commit crimes.

International Justice Mechanisms and Peacekeeping

As with many necessary reforms at the United Nations, there is considerable opposition by member states to changing the current system, as well as inertia on the part of United Nations staff. Change will only come if there is an external impetus for change. Hence the need to examine the implications of the recent developments in international justice.

The Impact of the ICC on Peacekeeping

Does the ICC provide a solution to the problem of impunity for peace-keepers who commit crimes? Will the ICC change the current system of criminal jurisdiction over peacekeepers? Some scholars have suggested that the ICC provides an answer to the problem of impunity for peacekeepers who commit crimes because individual states are unwilling to investigate or prosecute such crimes.[45] To other scholars, however, the ICC will have no practical effect on the present system of criminal jurisdiction over peacekeepers.[46]

This debate was relevant to the issue of the United States' opposition to the ICC. The United States has sought and continues to seek concessions from states to ensure that no American can be brought before the court in any circumstances without the consent of the American government. To achieve this goal, the United States has pursued an aggressive policy of weakening the power of the ICC vis-à-vis all states.[47] As part of this policy, the United States has sought and obtained a Security Council resolution that exempts peace-keepers who come from states that are not parties to the Rome Statute from being investigated or prosecuted by the ICC. Resolution 1422 states that the Security Council:

> *Requests*, consistent with the provisions of Article 16 of the Rome Statute, that the ICC, if a case arises involving current or former officials or personnel from a contributing State not a Party to the Rome Statute over acts or omissions relating to a United Nations established or authorized operation, shall for a twelve-month period starting 1 July 2002 not commence or proceed with investigation or prosecution of any such case, unless the Security Council decides otherwise;
> *Expresses* the intention to renew the request in paragraph 1 under the same conditions each 1 July for further 12-month periods for as long as may be necessary;
> *Decides* that Member States shall take no action inconsistent with paragraph 1 and with their international obligations.[48]

This resolution was the result of negotiations surrounding the renewal of the peacekeeping mission in Bosnia and Herzegovina in July 2002. The treaty establishing the ICC came into force on July 1, 2002, around the same time that the mandate of the mission in Bosnia and Herzegovina expired. The United States threatened that it would not agree to a renewal of it or any other peacekeeping mission unless it received assurances that its personnel would never be subject to the ICC's jurisdiction. It also threatened to cut off all its funding to peacekeeping missions currently in operation. The other members of the Security Council capitulated to the demands of the United States. Resolution 1422, in force for a twelve-month period, was renewed in 2003 for another twelve-month period.[49] By 2004, however, both the international climate and the climate within the United Nations were such that the United States dropped its attempt to renew Security Council Resolution 1422. Yet the exemption granted raises a series of critical issues.

The exemption for peacekeepers from the reach of the ICC is contrary to the spirit of the ICC. The Rome Statute embodies the principle that no one is above the law by virtue of his or her position. Article 27 states that the Rome Statute "shall apply to all persons without any distinction based on official capacity." This means that peacekeepers who committed crimes under the jurisdiction of the ICC would not be immune by virtue of their position.

Article 17 of the ICC is based on the "complementarity" principle that maintains that the ICC will only act where the state that normally has authority over the case is unwilling or unable genuinely to carry out the investigation or prosecution. This creates pressure for countries to take action for fear of abdicating their control over a case. States that ratify the Rome Statute must amend their domestic laws to enable them to fulfill their responsibilities to cooperate with the ICC. Because of the complementarity principle, many states are including as part of the process of national legal reform other changes to enable them to investigate and prosecute persons who commit the crimes listed in the Rome Statute. In this way, the ICC has already been a stimulus to change.

The ICC also represents an advance in international law regarding gender crimes. The Rome Statute contains many provisions empowering and facilitating the ICC to prosecute individuals who commit sexual and gender violence. First, the ICC has jurisdiction over rape, sexual slavery, enforced sterilization, forced prostitution, forced pregnancy, other forms of sexual violence, gender persecution, and trafficking in women and children.[50] Second, the Rome Statute requires that the judges and staff of the ICC include women and persons with expertise in gender violence and violence against children.[51] Third, all organs of the court must take special measures to protect the interests of victims of sexual and gender violence.[52] Finally, the judges must apply the law in a way that does not discriminate on gender grounds.[53] The Rome Statute also contains many child-specific provisions that provide sufficient authority for the ICC to take action regarding crimes against children,[54] to adopt child-friendly measures,[55] and to include staff with expertise on violence against children.[56] The process of implementing the Rome Statute by states parties may lead to changes in national laws and practices regarding crimes against women and children. It could also have the added effect of making national authorities more diligent about prosecuting soldiers who commit such crimes.

Given the progressive treatment of gender crimes under the Rome Statute, a strong ICC that could fill the void where national authorities fail to act is in the interests of women. The strong mandate of the ICC to investigate and prosecute persons who commit gender and sexual violence means that it can help to ensure that rape and other violence against women and children during a conflict is redressed. Also, women may be able to exert more influence on the ICC than on national systems because of the provisions requiring that the judges and staff of the ICC include women and persons with expertise in gender issues.[57] For these reasons, impunity for those who commit violence against women is more likely at the national level in many states than at the international level.

However, the ICC also has limitations. The ICC will only deal with genocide, war crimes, and crimes against humanity.[58] These crimes have high "thresholds": they must meet certain criteria that take them out of the category of standard domestic crimes. Most of the crimes committed by peacekeepers are more akin to standard domestic crimes and thus are unlikely to activate the potential jurisdiction of the ICC.[59]

The first question is therefore whether peacekeepers would commit war crimes, crimes against humanity, and genocide. There are two types of crimes committed by peacekeepers that may fall within these categories—attacks on civilians that lack proportionality and involvement in trafficking or prostitution rings.

Attacks on Civilians

Under the Rome Statute, Article 8(2)(a), the term "war crimes" refers to a list of acts such as murder or torture, in particular when committed as part of a plan or policy or as part of a large-scale commission of such crimes. The prohibited acts become war crimes when committed during war. One of the acts considered a war crime is intentionally attacking civilians or launching an attack that would cause harm to civilians excessive in relation to the military advantage gained.[60] For the acts of peacekeepers to be considered war crimes, the acts would have to be committed in a war. It is important to note, however, that even one commission of such an act could constitute a war crime.

Some human rights groups have drawn attention to several situations in which peacekeepers may have committed war crimes. In Somalia, where UN forces engaged in hostilities with local factions, the United States bombed the house of the aide to General Aidid while a political meeting was being held there. The United States claimed that there was a war-council meeting taking place in the house. By other accounts, the meeting was a political meeting attended by elders from a number of local clans, representatives of women's organizations, religious leaders, and other civilians. Significantly, there was no warning before the attack.[61]

Another alleged war crime may have been committed by peacekeeping troops in Somalia following the killing of twenty-five Pakistani peacekeepers in June 1993. Pakistani troops committed acts of retaliation against civilians, killing thirty Somalis in one incident.[62] The United Nations claimed that the civilian demonstrators fired on the peacekeepers first and that Pakistani forces opened fire in self-defense, while several journalists reported that the peacekeepers fired first. According to Patricia Goldman, even if the demonstrators had small arms, the actions of the Pakistani troops were not a proportionate response. The Pakistani troops, protected behind trenches and sandbagged emplacements on roofs, fired directly into the crowd with a belt-fed machine gun. Neither the United Nations nor the Pakistani government conducted a full investigation.[63]

Trafficking in Persons and Sexual Slavery

Peacekeepers have also been known to be involved in trafficking and prostitution rings, which constitute crimes against humanity. "Crimes against humanity" is defined in the Rome Statute as acts such as murder, torture, imprisonment, enslavement, persecution, and sexual violence, when committed as part of a widespread or systematic attack directed against a civilian population. An "attack directed against a civilian population" means the multiple commission of criminal acts pursuant to or in furtherance of a state or organizational policy to commit such an attack, but it need not be a military attack.[64] Acts of sexual violence such as rape, sexual slavery, enforced prostitution, forced pregnancy, and enforced sterilization are recognized as crimes against humanity as well as war crimes.[65]

Trafficking in persons is included in the definition of enslavement under the Rome Statute. Trafficking usually involves the multiple commission of acts of enslavement, enforced prostitution, or sexual slavery, directed against the civilian population, mostly women and children. A peacekeeper who commits criminal acts as part of a trafficking ring may be committing a crime against humanity. These potential acts of peacekeepers could include committing or assisting acts of enslavement by abducting or deceiving women and children into slavery. These types of acts have been committed by peacekeepers in the past. For example, international police in Bosnia were part of the trafficking network there.[66] According to a Redd Barna report regarding the United Nations mission in Mozambique (ONUMOZ), ONUMOZ personnel were directly involved in establishing and running child prostitution and trafficking rings. Namely, the organization reports that United Nations peacekeepers collected schoolgirls at school premises and recruited them for prostitution; engaged children in sexual activities, prostitution, pornographic activities (such as videos and photographs), and live sex shows; trafficked children by recruiting them for prostitution from different provinces; and intimidated children into making false statements exonerating Italian ONUMOZ personnel. The Italian peacekeepers were withdrawn from the mission under other pretenses but were not prosecuted for their actions.[67] This failure to prosecute would mean that, subject to other conditions, the ICC could potentially step in and assume jurisdiction over such a case.

Another crime known to be committed by peacekeepers is sexual relations with enslaved persons. Peacekeepers have knowingly had sexual relations with persons who are forced into prostitution in such trafficking rings.[68] The use of prostitutes itself constitutes the crime of rape if the peacekeeper is aware that the person with whom he is having sex is not consenting. In the *Foca* case at the ICTY, the Trial Chamber found one of the accused, Dragoljub Kunarac, guilty of rape even though the victim had been active in removing his clothes and kissing him. The victim went through these motions because she had been threatened with death by another soldier if she did not "please" Kunarac. At trial, Kunarac admitted having intercourse with the victim but claimed that he thought she was acting of her own free will. The ICTY Trial Chamber found this defense unbelievable given the general context of the war and specifically the delicate situation of Muslim girls detained in Foca during that time. It was deemed irrelevant whether Kunarac had heard the other soldier threaten the victim.[69]

This case shows that courts may infer that an accused had knowledge that a victim was not consenting to sex even without direct evidence of this based on the circumstances. In effect, an objective standard is applied; if the circumstances are such that a reasonable person would know that someone was not acting of his or her own free will, then the courts will be more inclined to infer that the accused knew that the victim was not consenting to sex. Typically, persons forced into "prostitution" (more accurately described as sexual slavery) are held in circumstances that are evidently against their will such as dingy back rooms in bars or houses surrounded by guards. In such circumstances, the requisite knowledge of coercion can easily be inferred. In the case of child "prostitutes," courts need only infer that the peacekeeper was aware that the victim was underage. Sexual relations with children constitute sexual assault whether or not the children are forced outright to provide sex, given the incapacity of children to consent to sexual relations with adults.

Peacekeepers who have sex with persons enslaved in a prostitution or trafficking ring could potentially be convicted of rape by the ICC. The prosecutor would have to prove, however, that the acts of the peacekeeper were "pursuant to or in furtherance of" an organizational policy to commit sexual slavery.[70] One scholar finds it "difficult to imagine that a peacekeeping force would have as a policy to commit an attack on the civilian population."[71] This argument incorrectly interprets the criteria for crimes against humanity, however. Under the definition of crimes against humanity in Article 7 of the Rome Statute, the perpetrator of the criminal acts does not have to be the originator of the policy to commit an attack on the civilian population. It is sufficient that the perpetrator commit the acts "pursuant to or in furtherance of a State or organizational policy." Thus, the policy could be devised by an organization other than the peacekeeping force. In the case of peacekeepers, if a criminal organization pursues a policy to commit trafficking, enforced prostitution, or sexual slavery, and the peacekeeper commits an act of rape that is part of the sexual slavery or trafficking plan, then the peacekeeper's crime could constitute a crime against humanity.

Would the SOFAs and Contribution Agreements Apply in Cases of International Crimes?

The next question is whether, in the case that a peacekeeper committed a war crime or crime against humanity, the system as laid out in the SOFAs and contribution agreements would preclude prosecutions by other states or international tribunals. In 1999, Secretary-General Kofi Annan issued guidelines on the principles and rules applicable to United Nations forces when they are actively engaged in situations of armed conflict as combatants. With respect to criminal jurisdiction, the guidelines state that the exclusive jurisdiction of contributing states for crimes committed by their military personnel continues to apply in cases of violations of international humanitarian law.[72] Thus, the United Nations' position is that the SOFAs and contribution agreements continue to apply even in cases of war crimes.

Again, the United Nations' policy of seeking immunity for its troops is questionable. Like all international treaties, the trilateral agreements concluded for peacekeeping missions are only binding on the parties to the agreements, that is, on the United Nations, the host state, and the contributing states. A state that was not a party to the SOFA or the contribution agreement would not be bound by it. Thus, when the SOFA assigns "exclusive jurisdiction" to the contributing state for crimes committed by peacekeepers, the jurisdiction is "exclusive" only of the other parties to the agreement, namely, the host state and the United Nations. As mentioned earlier, states exercise jurisdiction with regard to crimes committed on their territory or by their citizens. Thus, if there were no agreements, a peacekeeper who committed a crime could potentially be tried by the host state or the contributing state. The SOFA serves to assign jurisdiction between the contributing state and the host state in favor of the contributing state. The agreement does not and could not eliminate the criminal jurisdiction of other states not parties to the agreement that may have jurisdiction over a case on other grounds. For example, some states have laws allowing them to exercise jurisdiction over cases if the victim is a citizen of their state. Thus, a third state could have the right to try a peacekeeper if the victim were a citizen of that state.[73]

In addition, criminal jurisdiction by states other than the host state or the contributing state may arise for a case involving a peacekeeper under the principle of universal jurisdiction. According to this principle, some crimes are considered so egregious that any state may assume jurisdiction to prosecute the perpetrators regardless of where they are committed and against whom. Crimes for which states may assume universal jurisdiction include the grave breaches of the Geneva Conventions and their Additional Protocols, genocide, and torture, or other inhuman treatment.[74] If a peacekeeper committed a crime for which there is universal jurisdiction, theoretically any state could prosecute that peacekeeper, and the trilateral agreements would have no legal effect.[75]

Since the "exclusive jurisdiction" of the contributing state for peacekeepers' crimes under the SOFA is not "exclusive" of all states, similarly, an international tribunal is not obliged to consider the SOFA as excluding its own jurisdiction. Thus, the trilateral system of criminal jurisdiction for peacekeeping crimes does not exclude the possibility of a third state or an international tribunal like the ICC taking action in a case involving an international crime by a peacekeeper.

Limitations of the ICC

While the ICC has progressive gender provisions, the general provisions limiting the impact of the ICC on state sovereignty are one of its greatest limitations for addressing crimes against women by peacekeepers or otherwise. The Rome Statute contains a number of provisions that limit the power of the ICC.[76] These provisions are a product of compromises made to accommodate the perceived national interests of states.[77] For example, via Article 124, states that ratify the Rome Statute may make a declaration that withholds granting the ICC automatic jurisdiction over war crimes for a period of seven years. Also, via Article 16, the Security Council may pass a resolution to delay an investigation or prosecution in a case for twelve months. These provisions lessen the impact of the ICC on peacekeeping but do not eliminate it.

The greatest limitations on the ICC's power arise at the crucial stage of "surrendering" an accused person to the court.[78] If international tribunals such as the ICC are allowed to exercise a secondary jurisdiction over peace-keepers, they run into the practical problem of apprehending an accused person. According to the SOFA and contribution agreement (pars. 41 and 42[b]), peacekeepers arrested by the UN or host state must be transferred to the authorities of the peacekeeper's home country for appropriate disciplinary action. The police who make the arrest may make a preliminary interrogation (under par. 43) but may not delay the transfer of custody. Thus, contributing states would have possession of the alleged offender. A state that is unwilling to prosecute a peacekeeper in its own courts would in all likelihood be unwilling to surrender that person to the jurisdiction of an international tribunal such as the ICC. In fact, this point was raised by the secretary-general regarding the Agreement for the Special Court for Sierra Leone. The secretary-general argued to the Security Council that the terms of the agreement allowed uncooperative states to evade the court.[79] The council dismissed his concerns.[80]

This problem with surrender to an international tribunal is not unique to peacekeeping missions. It is foreseeable that in many cases under the future ICC, a person wanted by the court will be protected by his or her national government. Indeed, if this were not the case, the person would be prosecuted by his or her national government, giving rise to the principle of complementarity and the exclusion of the ICC's jurisdiction. In most such cases, the person is not likely to be surrendered to the court.

However, in the case of peacekeeping missions, the problem of surrender to the ICC is complicated by several factors. The first is the interplay between the trilateral agreements and Article 98 of the Rome Statute. Article 98 states:

1. The Court may not proceed with a request for surrender or assistance which would require the requested State to act inconsistently with its obligations under international law with respect to the State or diplomatic immunity of a person or property of a third state, unless the Court can first obtain the cooperation of that third state for the waiver of the immunity.
2. The Court may not proceed with a request for surrender which would require the requested State to act inconsistently with its obligations under international agreements pursuant to which the consent of a contributing state is required to surrender a person of that State to the Court, unless the Court can first obtain the cooperation of the contributing state for the giving of consent for the surrender.

Article 98 was included in a failed attempt to allay American fears regarding the ICC. The provision was designed to enable the United States to conclude

SOFAs with various countries that would prevent American soldiers from being surrendered to the ICC—a prospect that the United States finds unacceptable.[81]

The answers to several questions regarding the relationship between the trilateral agreements and Article 98 are uncertain and must await the interpretive decisions by the ICC. As of July 2004, the United States has reported signing over eighty Article 98 agreements, including thirty-six with states parties to the ICC.[82] First, under subparagraph 1, it is an open question whether the privileges and immunities of peacekeepers under the SOFAs and contribution agreements would constitute "state or diplomatic immunity." State immunity refers to the immunity granted to a state and head of state from the jurisdiction of the courts of another state and includes immunity granted to a person or body acting as agent of a state.[83] The trilateral agreements that grant immunity to members of a peacekeeping force may or may not be considered agreements with respect to state immunity. The trilateral agreements would not be considered agreements with respect to diplomatic immunity under Article 98 since the latter relates to immunity for members of diplomatic missions in a foreign country.

Moreover, they may or may not be considered agreements falling within subparagraph 2, whereby the consent of a state is required to surrender a person of that state to the ICC. By one interpretation of this subparagraph, the terms of the agreement must explicitly require this consent. The current SOFA and contribution agreement do not contain such explicit language. However, another interpretation would find it sufficient if such consent ensued as a consequence of the provisions of the agreement. The consent of the contributing state to surrender a peacekeeper to the ICC could be read into the provisions granting the contributing state exclusive criminal jurisdiction over its peacekeepers and requiring that peacekeepers who have been arrested be handed over immediately to the contributing state's authorities. If the trilateral agreements are found to come within the scope of Article 98, a state that detained a peacekeeper would not be able to surrender him or her to the ICC without the consent of the peacekeeper's country. To ensure accountability, the current language of the SOFA and contribution agreement for peacekeeping missions would have to be amended so as to exclude the operation of Article 98 of the Rome Statute.

The issue would be further complicated by the readoption of any resolution similar to Resolutions 1422 and 1487. The resolutions stated that member states of the United Nations should take no action inconsistent with the injunction against investigating or prosecuting peacekeepers from states not party to the ICC. Thus, even if this type of resolution were deemed by the judges of the ICC to be ultra vires—a finding that is wholly feasible—the member states of the

United Nations would have to respect the terms of such a resolution, were one adopted, and would not be able to surrender a peacekeeper to the ICC if he or she came from a non–state party. The prospect of the ICC taking action in a case involving a peacekeeper would be severely circumscribed.

In sum, the current legal regime is insufficient for addressing the problem of crimes committed by peacekeepers. Changes to the terms of the trilateral agreements would be required to overcome the existing obstacles, including allowing a secondary jurisdiction to host states and international tribunals, as well as an explicit exception for surrender to the ICC. In light of the earlier capitulation to the United States in Resolutions 1422 and 1487, this prospect seems unlikely.

Conclusion

The efforts to strengthen the international rule of law have wavered unsteadily between accommodating state sovereignty and transcending it. Insofar as the initiatives seek to overcome the constraints of the state-centric system, they create a space for women's interests to emerge. The progressive gender provisions of the Rome Statute and the establishment of the ICC gave rise to hope that international prosecutions could fill part of the void left by national systems. At the same time, the remaining strongholds of state sovereignty continue to militate against a truly equal protection of the law. The provisions in the trilateral agreements and the Rome Statute and the precedent established in the earlier Security Council resolutions of exempting peacekeepers from being investigated or prosecuted by the ICC seriously call into doubt the potential of the ICC to alter the current situation, in which peacekeepers enjoy much impunity for crimes that particularly affect women and children. These obstacles are a challenge to the professed support for the rule of law. Our efforts to make criminals accountable are a reflection of our commitment to democracy, peace, and human security. The failure to extend the rule of law principle to peacekeeping reveals that states are more committed to protecting their power base than to achieving these objectives.

Notes

1. For example, the UN Newswire reported that in Bosnia, many of the international police were part of the trafficking network there. Twenty-four police officers with the Bosnia police task force were fired for offenses that ranged from bribery to sexual impropriety (UN Newswire, "Sex Worker Issues Unsurprising, Former UN Official Says," September 6, 2001). According to another news report, German peacekeepers regularly

visited underage girls working as prostitutes in brothels in Macedonia (AFP, "Under-age Girls in Brothels Used by KFOR Soldiers: TV Report," December 17, 2000, available at www.neww.org/pipermail/women-east-west/2000-December/000698.html). For other examples, see infra, and the following newspaper reports: "UN Outraged by Peacekeeping Atrocities," IPS report, June 26, 1997; "Good Intentions Turned to Shame," *Economist*, July 5, 1997; "Peacekeeping Atrocities: UN Soldiers Accused of Tor-ture, Murder and Sexual Exploitation of Children," *Village Voice*, June 24, 1991, 38; Dateline NBC, "Disturbing the Peace," January 11, 1999, available at http://www .freedomdomain.com/un/disturbpeace.html; "Photos Reveal Belgian Paratroopers' Abuse in Somalia," CNN, April 17, 1997; "Two Peacekeepers Detained regarding Sex Crime Charges," Associated Press, January 7, 1996; "Teenagers Used for Sex by UN in Bosnia," *London Daily Telegraph*, April 25, 2002; "UN Peacekeepers in Timor Face Pos-sible Sex Charges," Reuters, reported in *PPC Peacekeeping News*, vol. 18, no. 2 (August 3, 2001); "UN Mission to Investigate Misconduct Allegations," Reuters/MSNBC.com, September 5, 2001, reported in UN Wire, September 6, 2001.

2. Bridget Byrne, "Towards a Gendered Understanding of Conflict" in *Gender and Peace Support Operations*, a joint initiative of the governments of Canada and the United Kingdom (Ottawa: Canadian Department of Foreign Affairs and International Trade, 2000), 31.

3. Kirsten Ruecker, *(En)Gendering Peacebuilding: The Cases of Cambodia, Rwanda and Guatemala* (Ottawa: Department of Foreign Affairs and International Trade, 2000); Sandra Whitworth, "Gender, Race and the Politics of Peacekeeping," in *A Future for Peacekeeping?* ed. Edward Moxon-Browne, 176–91 (New York: St. Martin's Press, 1998); Ernst Schade, *Experiences with Regard to the United Nations Peace-Keeping Forces in Mozambique* (Oslo: Redd Barna, 1995).

4. United Nations, *Rome Statute of the International Criminal Court* (New York: UN, 1998), A/CONF.183/9, as corrected by the procès-verbaux of November 10, 1998, and July 12, 1999.

5. United Nations Security Council Resolution 1422, UN Doc. S/RES/1422 (July 12, 2002), and United Nations Security Council Resolution 1487, UN Doc. S/RES/1487 (June 12, 2003).

6. "Fanning the Flames: The Administration Opens Up a Little," *Economist*, June 26, 2004, p. 33.

7. Boutros Boutros-Ghali, *An Agenda for Peace*, UN Doc. A/47/277-S/24111 (New York: UN, 1992).

8. Schade, "United Nations Peace-Keeping Forces in Mozambique."

9. Barbara Crossette, "When Peacekeepers Turn into Troublemakers," *New York Times*, January 7, 1996, sec. 4, p. 6.

10. Patricia Goldman, "Abuse of Power: The Law and Violations by United Nations Peacekeeping Forces" (LLM diss., University of Essex, Faculty of Law, 1996), 7.

11. *R. v. Brocklebank*, 34 Dominion Law Review (4th) 377 (1996).

12. Crossette, "When Peacekeepers Turn into Troublemakers."

13. ABC News.com, "Tragedy in Kosovo: Testimony of Struggle, Suffocation," April 12, 2000, available at http://more.abcnews.go.com/sections/world/DailyNews/kosovo 000412.html.

14. Dateline NBC, "Disturbing the Peace."

15. Amnesty International, "Italy: A Briefing for the UN Committee against Torture," AI Index EUR 30/02/99 (May 1999), 11; Natalia Lupi, "Report by the Enquiry Commission on the Behaviour of Italian Peace-Keeping Troops in Somalia," *Yearbook of International Humanitarian Law* 1 (1998): 378.

16. Amnesty International, "Italy: A Briefing for the UN Committee against Torture," 10–15.

17. Interview by author, UN Department of Peacekeeping Operations, New York, October 26, 2001.

18. "Convention on the Privileges and Immunities of the United Nations," February 13, 1946, *United Nations Treaty Series* 1, p. 16.

19. United Nations, "Model Status-of-Forces Agreement for Peace-Keeping Operations: Report of the Secretary-General," UN Doc. A/45/594 (October 9, 1990).

20. UN, "Model Status-of-Forces Agreement," par. 47(b).

21. Under the model SOFA, if the accused person is a civilian, the special representative or commander of the mission shall conduct an inquiry and then agree with the authorities of the accused person's country whether criminal proceedings shall be instituted. A process for resolving disputes is laid out in the SOFA (par. 47[a]).

22. United Nations, "Model Agreement between the United Nations and Member States Contributing Personnel and Equipment to United Nations Peace-Keeping Operations: Report of the Secretary-General," UN Doc. A/46/185 (May 23, 1991).

23. See United Nations Security Council Resolution 868, UN Doc. S/RES/868 (September 29, 1993).

24. Glenn Bowens, *Legal Guide to Peace Operations* (Carlisle Barracks, PA: U.S. Army Peacekeeping Institute, 1998); James M. Simpson, "Law Applicable to Canadian Forces in Somalia, 1992–1993," study prepared for the Commission of Inquiry into the Deployment of Canadian Forces to Somalia.

25. In a Canadian case considering the issue, the Supreme Court determined that American forces in Canada were exempt from Canadian criminal jurisdiction for (1) offenses committed in their camps or on their warships, except against persons not subject to United States service law or the property of such persons; or (2) for offenses, wherever committed, against other members of their forces, their property, and the property of their government. According to this one case, therefore, customary international law, as interpreted in Canada, does not grant immunity to visiting forces for offenses against nationals of the host state (*In the Matter of a Reference as to Whether Members of the Military or Naval Forces of the United States of America Are Exempt from Criminal Prosecutions in Canadian Criminal Courts* [1943], S.C.R. 483, quoted in Simpson, "Law Applicable to Canadian Forces in Somalia," 6).

26. See Schade, "United Nations Peace-Keeping Forces in Mozambique"; and *London Daily Telegraph*, "Teenagers Used for Sex by UN in Bosnia."

27. For that matter, in cases not considered peacekeeping in the present chapter where action is taken under Chapter VII of the UN Charter without the consent of the host state (as in the case of Somalia), these agreements are not likely to be concluded, and the host state would have a strong claim to exercising criminal jurisdiction over forces who committed crimes on its territory.

28. Marten Zwanenburg, "The Statute for an International Criminal Court and the United States: Peacekeepers under Fire?" *European Journal of International Law* 10 (1999): 128–29.

29. North Atlantic Treaty Organization, "North Atlantic Treaty Status-of-Forces Agreement," June 19, 1951, *Canada Treaty Series* 13 (1953): 2, art. VII(2).

30. NATO, "North Atlantic Treaty Status-of-Forces Agreement," art. VII(3).

31. NATO, "North Atlantic Treaty Status-of-Forces Agreement," art. VII(3)(c).

32. The SOFAs generally provide that the host state can exercise criminal jurisdiction over American armed forces where the offense was committed outside the army base or where the offense is punishable by the law of the host state, but not by the law of the United States. The American SOFAs also contain a provision allowing the state with primary jurisdiction over a case to notify the other state and to waive its rights to prosecute, as in Article VII(3)(c) of the NATO SOFA. See Article XXII, "Agreement under Article IV of the Mutual Defense Treaty regarding Facilities and Areas and the Status of United States Armed Forces in the Republic of Korea," July 9, 1969, *United Nations Treaty Series* 674, p. 164; Article XVI, "Agreement under Article VI of the Treaty of Mutual Co-operation and Security between Japan and the United States regarding Facilities and Areas and the Status of United States Armed Forces in Japan," January 19, 1960, *United Nations Treaty Series* 373, p. 248; and Article VIII, "Agreement between the Government of the Commonwealth of Australia and the United States of America concerning the Status of United States Forces in Australia," May 9, 1963, *United Nations Treaty Series* 469, p. 56.

33. See annex to "Protocol between Australia, Canada, New Zealand, the United Kingdom of Great Britain and Northern Ireland, the United States and Japan on the Exercise of Criminal Jurisdiction over United Nations Forces in Japan," October 26, 1953, *United Nations Treaty Series*, 2809, p. 260.

34. Cynthia Enloe, *The Morning After: Sexual Politics at the End of the Cold War* (Berkeley: University of California Press, 1993); Whitworth, "Gender, Race and the Politics of Peacekeeping"; Ruecker, "(En)Gendering Peacebuilding." In Canada, an inquiry in 1985 into offenses within the Canadian Forces concluded that soldiers were more likely to commit sexual violence than civilians. The report stated that while there was a lower incidence of violent crime more generally, there was a relatively higher frequency of sexual offenses. In addition to the sexual assaults, a high number of physical assaults were against women; see Major-General Hewson, "Mobile Command Study: A Report on Disciplinary Infractions and Anti-social Behaviour within FMC with Particular Reference to Special Service Force and Canadian Airborne Regiment," in *Report of the Commission of Inquiry into the Deployment of Canadian Forces to Somalia*, Document Book 1 (Ottawa: Government of Canada, 1997), quoted in Whitworth, "Gender, Race and the Politics of Peacekeeping," 185.

35. In Italian, "to rape" is "violentare." I believe that Lupi meant to refer to rape, and that it was incorrectly translated to "violation" in the article.

36. Lupi, "Report by the Enquiry Commission," 376.

37. *Florida Today*, "US Peacekeeper Raped," March 6, 1996.

38. See the report of Equality Now on discriminatory laws around the world, available at www.equalitynow.org/beijing_plus5_violence_eng.html.

39. See the report of the special rapporteur on violence against women to the UN Commission on Human Rights, UN Doc. E/CN.4/1997/47 (February 12, 1997), par. 39.

40. "Convention on the Rights of the Child," November 20, 1989, *United Nations Treaty Series* 1577, p. 3, arts. 34 and 35.

41. See ECPAT International [database online], available at http://www.ecpat.net/eng/Ecpat_inter/projects/monitoring/online_database/index.asp.

42. NATO, "North Atlantic Treaty Status-of-Forces Agreement," art. VII(5) and (6).

43. NATO, "North Atlantic Treaty Status-of-Forces Agreement," art. VII(1).

44. CNN.com, "Arrest Warrant Issued for Okinawa Rape Suspect," July 2, 2001, available at http://www.cnn.com/2001/WORLD/asiapcf/east/07/02/okinawa.rape. Under the agreement between Japan and the United States on the status of United States forces in Japan, Japan can assume jurisdiction for crimes committed by American soldiers outside of the army base. However, the United States has the right to retain custody of the suspect until he or she is charged. "Agreement under Article VI of the Treaty of Mutual Co-operation and Security between Japan and the United States regarding Facilities and Areas and the Status of United States Armed Forces in Japan," art. XVI.

45. Goldman, "Abuse of Power."

46. Ray Murphy, "International Humanitarian Law Training for Multinational Peace Support Operations: Lessons from Experience," *International Review of the Red Cross*, no. 840 (December 31, 2000): 953–68; Zwanenburg, "The Statute for an International Criminal Court and the United States."

47. Ruth Wedgewood, "The Irresolution of Rome," *Law and Contemporary Problems* 64, no. 1 (2001): 193–214; David J. Scheffer, "A Negotiator's Perspective on the International Criminal Court," *Military Law Review* 167 (March 2001): 1–19; Bruce Broomhall, "Toward U.S. Acceptance of the International Criminal Court," *Law and Contemporary Problems* 64, no. 1 (2001): 141–52.

48. United Nations Security Council Resolution 1422, UN Doc. S/RES/1422 (July 12, 2002).

49. United Nations Security Council Resolution 1487, UN Doc. S/RES/1487 (June 12, 2003).

50. See *Rome Statute of the International Criminal Court*, UN Doc. PCNICC/INF/3 (August 17, 1999), arts. 7(1)(c), 7(1)(g), 7(1)(h), 7(2)(c), 8(2)(b)(xxii), and 8(2)(d)(vi).

51. *Rome Statute of the International Criminal Court*, arts. 36(8)(a)(iii), 42(9), and 43(6).

52. *Rome Statute of the International Criminal Court*, arts. 54(1)(b), 57(3)(c), 64(2), and 68.

53. *Rome Statute of the International Criminal Court*, art. 21.

54. *Rome Statute of the International Criminal Court*, arts. 6(e), 7(2)(c), 7(1)(g), 8(2)(b)(xxvi), and 8(2)(e)(vii); United Nations, "Finalized Draft Elements of Crimes," in *Report of the Preparatory Commission for an International Criminal Court*, UN Doc. PCNICC/2000/INF/3/Add.2 (July 6, 2000), art. 7(1)(g)-1, 3, 5, and 6.

55. See *Rome Statute of the International Criminal Court*, arts. 54(1)(b), 68(1) and (2); and "Finalized Draft Text of the Rules of Procedure and Evidence," UN Doc. PCNICC/INF/3/Add.1 (July 12, 2000), arts. 17(3), 19(f), 75(1), 86, 88, 89(3), and 112(4).

56. See *Rome Statute of the International Criminal Court*, arts. 36(8)(b), 42(9), and 43(6).

57. Katherine Martinez and Barbara Bedont, "Ending Impunity for Gender Crimes under the International Criminal Court," *Brown Journal of World Affairs* 6, no. 41 (1999): 74–77.

58. The definitions of genocide, war crimes, and crimes against humanity in the Rome Statute, discussed infra, were based on their definitions under international law. The definition of genocide in the Rome Statute was taken verbatim from the 1948 Genocide Convention. In the convention and the Rome Statute, "genocide" is defined as specific acts, such as killing, which are committed with the intent to destroy, in whole or in part, a national, ethnical, racial, or religious group. ("Convention on the Prevention and Punishment of the Crime of Genocide," December 9, 1948, *United Nations Treaty Series* 78, p. 277, art. 2; *Rome Statute of the International Criminal Court*, art. 6). "War crimes" are violations of the laws and customs of war set up to regulate the conduct of armed conflict, for example, as laid out in the 1949 Geneva Conventions and the 1907 Hague Conventions. "Crimes against humanity" was first used as a basis for prosecution by the military tribunals set up after World War II by the Allies to try German and Japanese leaders. ("Charter for the International Military Tribunal for the Far East," January 19, 1946, *Treaties and Other International Acts Series*, p. 1589, art. 5, established by the Proclamation by the Supreme Commander for the Allied Powers, Tokyo [January 19, 1946], reprinted in *Crimes against Humanity under International Law* [Dordrecht: Martinus Nijhoff, 1992], 604; and "Charter of the International Military Tribunal, Annexed to the Agreement for the Prosecution and Punishment of Major War Criminals of the European Axis," August 8, 1945, *United Nations Treaty Series* 82, p. 279, art. 6). It refers to certain acts committed on a widespread or systematic basis that are considered so egregious as to constitute a crime committed against humanity as a whole.

59. Zwanenburg, "The Statute for an International Criminal Court and the United States," 135.

60. *Rome Statute of the International Criminal Court*, art. 8(2)(b)(iv).

61. African Rights, *Somalia Human Rights Abuses by the United Nations Forces* (New York: African Rights, July 1993), 7.

62. Amnesty International, "Peacekeeping and Human Rights," AI Index IOR 40/01/94 (January 1994).

63. Goldman, "Abuse of Power."

64. *Rome Statute of the International Criminal Court*, art. 7; United Nations, "Finalized Draft Elements of Crimes," art. 7, par. 9.

65. *Rome Statute of the International Criminal Court*, arts. 7(1)(g), 8(2)(b)(xxii), and (e)(vi).

66. UN Newswire, "Sex Worker Issues Unsurprising."

67. Schade, "United Nations Peace-Keeping Forces in Mozambique."

68. Schade, "United Nations Peace-Keeping Forces in Mozambique"; AFP, "Underage Girls in Brothels Used by KFOR Soldiers."

69. *Prosecutor v. Kunarac et al.*, IT-96-23 and IT-96-23/1 (ICTY, February 22, 2001), pars. 644–47.

70. *Rome Statute of the International Criminal Court*, art. 7(2)(a).

71. Zwanenburg, "The Statute for an International Criminal Court and the United States," 134.

72. UN Doc. ST/SGB/1999/13 (August 6, 1999), sec. 4.

73. States that have this "passive personality" ground for criminal jurisdiction include France, Spain, and Italy.

74. See the 1949 Geneva Conventions ("Geneva Convention for the Amelioration of the Condition of the Wounded and Sick in Armed Forces in the Field," August 12, 1949, *United Nations Treaty Series* 75, p. 31; "Geneva Convention for the Amelioration of the Condition of the Wounded, Sick and Shipwrecked Members of the Armed Forces at Sea," August 12, 1949, *United Nations Treaty Series* 75, p. 85; "Geneva Convention Relative to the Protection of Civilian Persons in Time of War," August 12, 1949, *United Nations Treaty Series* 75, p. 287; "Geneva Convention Relative to the Treatment of Prisoners of War," August 12, 1949, *United Nations Treaty Series* 75, p. 135) and "Convention against Torture and Other Cruel, Inhuman or Degrading Treatment or Punishment," December 10, 1984, *United Nations Treaty Series* 1465, p. 85, GA Res. 39/46 [annex, 39 UN GAOR Supp. (no. 51) at 197, UN Doc. A/39/51 (1984)].

75. Peter Rowe, "Maintaining Discipline in United Nations Peace Support Operations: The Legal Quagmire for Military Contingents," *Journal of Conflict and Security Law* 5, no. 1 (2000): 45–62.

76. Zwanenburg, "The Statute for an International Criminal Court and the United States."

77. Zwanenburg, "The Statute for an International Criminal Court and the United States."

78. *Rome Statute of the International Criminal Court*, art. 89.

79. Secretary general to the president of the Security Council, January 12, 2001, UN Doc. S/2001/40, pars. 4–5.

80. President of the Security Council to the secretary-general, January 31, 2001, UN Doc. S/2001/95.

81. Scheffer, "A Negotiator's Perspective on the International Criminal Court."

82. Coalition for an International Criminal Court, "Status of US Bilateral Immunity Agreements," available at www.iccnow.org/documents/USandICC/BIAs.html. See also www.state.gov/t/pm/art98/.

83. Robert Jennings and Arthur Watts, eds., *Oppenheim's International Law*, 9th ed., vol. 1 (London: Longman, 1996), 341–55; Hugh Kindred et al., *International Law Chiefly as Interpreted and Applied in Canada*, 5th ed. (Toronto: Edmond Montgomery Publications, 1993), 280–84.

III

INSIDE PEACEKEEPING OPERATIONS

THIS SECTION PRESENTS CRITICAL ANALYSES of the intersection of gender and power in the context of particular armed conflicts and the peacekeeping operations sent in to restore and maintain peace. The contributors reveal how miscalculations regarding women's and girls' roles and experiences both during the conflict and in the early postconflict period undermine the efforts of larger operations in establishing the necessary conditions for peace and security nationally and regionally. Contributors provide detailed gender analyses of peacekeeping operations from Mozambique, Angola, Kosovo, and Namibia.

5

Peacekeeping Trends and Their Gender Implications for Regional Peacekeeping Forces in Africa: Progress and Challenges

Heidi Hudson

O NE INDICATION OF THE SIGNIFICANCE of African regional organizations in terms of ensuring peace and security on the continent is their increasing willingness to assume peacekeeping roles. The Organization of African Unity (OAU)[1] deployed missions in Rwanda (1990–1993), Burundi (1993–1996), the Comoros (1997–1999), the Democratic Republic of the Congo (DRC; 1999–2000),[2] and Eritrea and Ethiopia (2000 to date). The Economic Community of West African States (ECOWAS), through its Monitoring Observer Group (ECOMOG), has been active in peacekeeping in Liberia (1990–1999), and in Sierra Leone, Niger, Côte d'Ivoire, and Guinea-Bissau since 1998. On September 22, 1998, South Africa and Botswana sent troops as part of a Southern African Development Community (SADC) Combined Task Force to quell a possible coup in Lesotho. In August 1998, the SADC member states Angola, Zimbabwe, and Namibia intervened in conflict in the DRC. Although the intervention received retroactive endorsement from the SADC, it was essentially an ad hoc undertaking.[3] These efforts represent a few examples of peacekeeping where Africans have had to "do it themselves." Such "homegrown" peacekeeping initiatives have not escaped criticism, and much has been written and said about the legitimacy and credibility of these responses. Various local authors, such as Malan, Neethling, and De Coning, have also analyzed the implications of African peacekeeping efforts with respect to their meaning for broader trends in contemporary peacekeeping policy and practice.[4] However, until recently, the importance of culture in conflict and conflict resolution was underestimated. Indeed, very little explicit attention has been paid to the cultural aspect of having Africans in charge of their own peace and security.

Since culture is a very broad and often treacherous terrain of investigation, any analysis of the African peacekeeping context and trends must take cognizance of the existence of microcultures, such as age, gender, and class. The notion of military versus civilian culture can also be located within the larger spectrum of culture.[5] It is at the level of gender culture that this contribution is quite clearly located. In this respect Sowa remarks that "it is puzzling that while there is a substantial body of work on peacekeeping issues, a substantial body of work on gender . . . there is so little . . . cross fertilisation."[6]

Nowadays, it is generally accepted that to include both men and women in a peacekeeping team is beneficial with respect to achieving mission objectives. More women may lead to increased legitimacy of a mission, which may further promote conflict resolution efforts.[7] The underlying argument in this chapter is based on the assumption that women's contribution to peacekeeping is both positive and real. However, this issue necessitates some qualification. Any analysis of this kind must guard against fostering stark dichotomies of men as aggressive and women as being innately peaceful. Such stereotypes reinforce the fallacy that women are too weak to participate in any form of peacekeeping operation. A concomitant of this is the fact that gender conflict or tension between male and female peacekeepers can be a real obstacle within the close confines of an operation. Indeed, lack of social support among the women themselves is also a reality of the day-to-day dynamics in peacekeeping operations.

A common feature of international, regional, and subregional peacekeeping operations is their lack of a gender-analytic approach. Women and children, those often worst hit by conflict, are excluded from peacekeeping decision-making structures (see Mazurana et al., introduction; Raven-Roberts, chapter 2). Women's views and concerns are also absent from the processes and institutions concerned with peacekeeping in Africa. Serious research and practical efforts in the area of mainstreaming gender in African peacekeeping are a relatively new phenomenon. Both qualitative information on women's experiences within African peacekeeping missions and statistics on women's representation within specific missions are not readily available, in addition to not being systematically researched. In view of this, it is my intention in this chapter to offer a regional and comparative perspective of peacekeeping trends and their gender implications. Do these trends facilitate or impede the contribution women can make to peacekeeping operations on the continent and in the various subregions? The shift from traditional to multidimensional peacekeeping has been slow in the making. Does the mainstreaming of gender in peacekeeping face a similar fate?

On the one hand, the chapter takes a skeptical look at developments on the continent. Ambitious recommendations such as those of the Brahimi Report face enormous challenges regarding a large-scale commitment by African member states in view of a culture of political weakness and a serious lack of capacity and coordination. I advance two broad arguments in this regard. First, "new" peacekeeping, with its emphasis on complex mandates and the increased involvement of civilians in humanitarian actions, has created space for women to participate more actively in peacekeeping missions. However, an increase in numbers does not necessarily reflect heightened gender awareness. Very often it simply reflects a pragmatic shift since incorporating women into a mission can help to achieve mission objectives. Second, it is doubtful whether the percentage of women in peace operations in Africa is likely to increase in the near future given the trend toward peace enforcement. This trend will necessarily favor the military component at the expense of the civilian sector. So-called muscular peacekeeping by various subregional organizations is likely to perpetuate or reinforce the aversion to deploying women in combat situations. On the other hand, there are still many opportunities for the mainstreaming of gender, particularly in the areas of training, capacity building, and research. As long as capacity-building programs are responsive to the target groups they are intended for, these programs can go a long way in facilitating a shift from pragmatism to genuine integration of gender awareness in peacekeeping operations.

For the sake of brevity I attempt not to venture too far from the peacekeeping (field) operations themselves. In this context, I broadly define the concept "peacekeeping operation" as consisting of a complex mix of multidimensional military and civilian activities and a partnership between the military, civilian police, nongovernmental organizations, the media, and (sub)regional and international organizations. It is important to mention that the examples of intervention by subregional African organizations I refer to in this chapter should technically not be equated with peacekeeping operations.[8] But since both types of operations are operations in the realm of peace and security, for the purposes of the gender analysis, I place them under the same rubric. In addition, it also needs to be stated that a holistic understanding of women's insecurity underpins the success of any peacekeeping operation. To deal with these issues, a successful peacekeeping operation requires understanding of the gender implications of more than just the mission—and must take cognizance of the gender implications of peace building and postconflict reconstruction.

The chapter surveys some of the key developments in African peacekeeping and gender. From a methodological point of view, the discussion shifts back and forth between the general peacekeeping environment on the African continent and a peacekeeping context in which gender as a variable is taken into account. The discussion opens with a statistical summary of the state of affairs regarding women's representation in peacekeeping forces in Africa. From there it briefly traces the arguments for and against adopting a regional or subregional approach to peacekeeping. The analysis then moves to its main focus, namely the developments and trends in African peacekeeping with specific emphasis on their gender implications. I examine regional and subregional peacekeeping efforts, such as those of the OAU, ECOWAS, and SADC, through the lens of gender, highlighting progress and challenges.

Female Peacekeepers in Africa: Where Art Thou?

Statistical data indicates that peacekeeping is predominantly male in nature, reflecting the traditionally male composition of national armed forces. Men are assigned the majority of military and policing tasks; women play mostly civilian roles as legal and political advisers, election and human rights monitors, information specialists, and administrators. Women's involvement in military peacekeeping remains almost insignificant. In 1993, women composed only 1.7 percent of military contingents in a total of seventeen peacekeeping missions and less than 1 percent of police.[9]

A logical starting point for an examination of the extent and level of women's representation in peacekeeping operations would be to look at United Nations missions to Africa. Of the thirty peacekeeping operations launched by the United Nations since 1988, fourteen have been in Africa and most of them were established in the early 1990s.[10] The picture that emerges, however, is fractured due to a number of reasons. First, until recently, representation in terms of gender has not been a political (strategic) priority. In many cases, detailed statistics are currently being recompiled, because until recently females were not shown in statistics as a special group. Second, the United Nations has had little say in the selection and allocation of peacekeeping troops from various countries. Despite the absence of noncombat exclusion policies in African countries such as South Africa and Zambia, women are not routinely utilized in combat positions. In recent years 77 percent of the troops deployed in United Nations peacekeeping operations were contributed by developing countries, many of whom have dubious credentials in the area of gender representation and equity.[11] Third, detailed United Nations policy guidelines on the participation of women in peacekeeping did not exist until recently.[12]

Before 1993, women composed a mere 2 percent of military personnel in peacekeeping missions in Africa.[13] In 1993, in the United Nations Mission for the Referendum in Western Sahara (MINURSO), 10.2 percent of the troops were women—the highest of any mission during 1993.[14] This is partially explained by the fact that progressive states such as France, Australia, and the United States contributed a large component of the personnel. By September 1998, the number of female peacekeepers in this mission was still high. Women composed 8.9 percent of all peacekeepers in Western Sahara. The figures, when broken down, reveal that the majority of women held noncombat roles: professionals (0.8 percent), military police (1.2 percent), international general service (3.4 percent), local general service (1.9 percent), and field service (1.6 percent).[15] By April 2000, women held only 3 percent of military positions (including troops and observers) even though they composed 16 percent of the total staff.[16] In 1994, Ghana sent a gender-mixed infantry company of rifle soldiers to serve in the refugee camps with the United Nations Assistance Mission for Rwanda (UNAMIR).[17] In the United Nations Mission in Sierra Leone (UNAMSIL), by January 2000, 11 percent of all staff were women, whereas women constituted 1 percent of all military personnel.[18] With regard to civilian policing, women constituted 18 percent of the participants in a police officers training course held in southern Africa in November 1998.[19] The high level of female representation in the training course was upheld during Exercise Blue Crane, which took place in South Africa in 1999.

A few women occupied leadership positions in peace operations, for example in Angola and South Africa. In 1992, Margaret Anstee was appointed as special representative of the secretary-general to the United Nations Angola Verification Mission (UNAVEM II). Anstee served as chief of missions until civil war erupted following elections.[20] In South Africa, Angela King served as both the chief administrative officer and deputy secretary-general special representative.[21]

Women are fairly well represented in missions involving electoral supervision. Sixty percent of the professional staff recruited for the United Nations Transitional Assistance Group (UNTAG) in Namibia (1989–1990) were women.[22] The United Nations Observer Mission to South Africa (UNOMSA, 1992–1994) had 53 percent female representation during its first sixteen months.[23] In 2000, the initial team of 165 specialists sent by South Africa to the Democratic Republic of the Congo included thirteen women (8 percent)—one personnel officer, one doctor, seven medical sisters, one military law officer, and three logistical clerks. The South African group of sixty-eight, deployed in the DRC by April 2001, also included a few women, particularly as part of the members from the South African Military Health Service.[24] By June 2002, only four women formed part of the South African contingent in the Democratic Republic of the Congo. In Operation Fiber (Burundi), women constitute 3.4 percent (25 out of 720) of the South African peacekeeping force. These women operate in the areas of personnel, VIP protection, intelligence, counterintelligence, medical services, logistics, and infantry. Two South African women (11 percent of a total of eighteen) participated in Operation Triton as part of the South African contingent of the OAU observer mission deployed in the Comoros. In the United Nations mission to Ethiopia and Eritrea two out of the nine South African peacekeepers are women (22 percent), one a military observer and the other a staff officer.

Many factors, such as policy, strategy, and the nature of the mission, determine women's empirical presence in peacekeeping operations. Global and regional tendencies also play a crucial role in influencing the direction of peacekeeping on the African continent. Such developments, in turn, have far-reaching implications for the mainstreaming of gender in peacekeeping operations. In the next section I explicate the rationale behind adopting a regional or subregional approach to peacekeeping in Africa.

Proliferation of Regional or Subregional Actors: Necessary Evil or Contextualized Solution?

It is common knowledge that one of the most significant post–Cold War trends is the fact that peacekeeping is no longer the purview of the United Nations. In Africa, the number of troops deployed on United Nations operations has dwindled from 40,000 (in 1993) to a mere 1,600 in June 1999.[25] The United Nations' growing inability to deliver peacekeepers is largely due to diminishing institutional capacity and increased demand for peacekeeping combined with demoralization and apathy as a result of the sheer magnitude of internal problems in Africa. Large-scale United Nations withdrawal has given rise to recognition of the need for regional security complexes to take collective responsibility for solving their own security problems.

As a pragmatic response non–United Nations peacekeeping actors have proliferated. This trend is indicative of the blurring of the lines between the functions of international, regional, and subregional organizations. The question arises as to who should take responsibility for African peacekeeping in the absence of a dominant United Nations involvement. Should it be the OAU or African Union or subregional organizations such as ECOWAS and SADC? Any answer to this question is not straightforward. In southern Africa, in the aftermath of the Lesotho event, there appears to be general consensus that it is preferable to rely on the United Nations peacekeeping framework, however flawed. Yet, there is also widespread recognition that in practice parallel responses by regional and subregional organizations cannot always be avoided. De Coning highlights in this regard the fact that there exists an informal hierarchy between, for instance, the SADC as a subregional organization under the OAU/AU, and the OAU/AU as a regional organization under the United Nations.[26] It can be argued that the subregional organization—due to its geographic proximity to the conflict as well as the assumption that it is more au fait with the cultural and other dynamics of the local conditions—is better suited to deal with the situation. Olonisakin argues that political will would also be easier to muster among subregional actors if and when the need arose.[27] The disadvantage of close proximity, however, is that it often breeds tension and reduces impartiality (and credibility)—"to the extent that [the neighbors] sometimes become part of the problem, rather than part of the solution."[28]

A pyramidal security structure may sound fine in theory, but it has the potential to generate enormous bureaucratic problems. De Coning, however, reminds us that there is no hard and fast rule in this respect.[29] In the case of the Lesotho intervention, the SADC took sole responsibility, whereas the Angolan conflict has primarily been the focus of the United Nations.[30] Contextual and practical factors such as the history and the intensity of the conflict, as well as the capacity, political will, and proximity of the troop-contributing organizations or states, all play an important role. The relationship between the United Nations, OAU/AU, and African subregional organizations must therefore be seen as a holistic partnership in which all contribute in their own right. Very often, a conflict situation (such as in the Democratic Republic of the Congo) is too complex for any one of these organizations to go it alone. Especially in instances where large-scale humanitarian support is required, the United Nations' contribution remains invaluable.

The fact remains that despite the OAU's intention to focus on conflict prevention, peacemaking, and peace building, the organization has been incapable of providing and financing troops to intervene in African hostilities. The early warning system at the OAU's Centre for Conflict Management is largely a myth, hampered by the lack of political will and interstate rivalry, which prevents information from being shared. By 1997–1998, only 5 percent of the OAU's annual budget was allocated to peace initiatives.[31] This failure gives rise to the alternative suggestion to build peacekeeping capacity along subregional blocs. Critics, however, argue that it is a fallacy to believe that subregional organizations have a comparative advantage in conflict situations. Cilliers argues as follows: "But if the constituent components of the whole are weak in many cases, what chance is there that subregional groupings and African 'coalitions of the willing' would be able to make a significant contribution to stability?"[32]

Trends in international peacekeeping present African peacekeepers with enormous challenges. Africa cannot afford to go it alone, but in the face of the international withdrawal the continent is faced with little choice.

Challenges to Mainstreaming Gender in African Peacekeeping Operations

Capacity and Political Will: A Double-Edged Sword

For any peacekeeping operation to be successful, capacity (at institutional and troop level) and political will are needed, and both of these prerequisites are largely absent on the African continent. Many African nations, such as Senegal and Ghana, have considerable experience as peacekeepers in United Nations missions. The capacity of many African states to contribute troops and technical support to peacekeeping operations may also appear theoretically sound. However, in practice it is doubtful whether this is really the case. For instance, Zimbabwe, once considered the powerhouse of peacekeeping training in southern Africa, boasts an armed force that is neglected, demoralized, and poorly equipped.[33] Similarly, in South Africa, regarded by many as a potential peacekeeper in the region, capacity seems to be built upon shaky foundations. South Africa has been rather reluctant in committing itself to an operation where the country's national interest was not directly at stake.[34]

Mainstreaming gender in peacekeeping is not a simple exercise and any such attempt must acknowledge the numerous other obstacles, under circumstances of political, social, and economic instability, that need to be overcome at the same time. Structurally, subregional organizations such as ECOWAS and SADC are essentially economic organizations, now required to act as peacekeepers. At the time of intervention in Liberia, ECOWAS had no formal conflict prevention and management mechanism in place to effectively coordinate the actions of ECOMOG. In contrast, SADC's Organ on Politics, Defence, and Security exists on paper but has been paralyzed by the lack of proper integration into the overall structure of the organization. Political disunity and partiality caused problems for ECOMOG in Liberia. The rift in SADC also became apparent during the conflict in the Democratic Republic of the Congo when Zimbabwe, Angola, Namibia, and the Democratic Republic of the Congo signed a mutual defense pact. Human and financial resource constraints are a very real problem for smaller, "willing but unable" states. For instance, in 1990, prior to ECOMOG's deployment in Liberia, some countries did not have enough senior-ranking soldiers to contribute to the force. Strong regional states cannot always be relied on to step in. In west Africa, Nigeria has accepted the leadership role, whereas South Africa as leader of the SADC has always been reluctant to play the role of superpower in southern Africa.[35]

The argument that African countries will have a better understanding of each other's cultural and gender dilemmas and practices may be true, but the advantage gained by such an understanding is weakened by problems relating to capacity and the will to act. Politically, the most serious obstacle against the inclusion of women in peacekeeping operations has to do with the rhetorical commitment of many African leaders to the gender cause. Africa is inundated with examples of lip service being paid to international declarations. Under the guise of preserving tradition, a dual legal system, which perpetuates women's subservience to men, is unofficially condoned and maintained. It is therefore quite plausible that such leaders will not honor their commitment to quotas and targets for gender equality in peace missions. Although, since the late 1990s, women have become involved in the activities of the OAU's Mechanism for Conflict Prevention, Management, and Resolution through the African Women's Committee on Peace and Development, political commitment from individual states remains crucial. Apart from the absence of the will to enforce compliance, weak states do not have the capacity and resources to devise special gender structures and posts. Structures such as the Gender Desk of the SADC cannot be expected to function efficiently in the area of peacekeeping if the Organ on Politics, Defence, and Security is weak and struggling to become operational. Comprehensive adherence to basic democratic principles of transparency and accountability is clearly lacking.[36] As with the situation of the United Nations, any subregional peacekeeping force is dependent upon the contributions of member states.

General instability has a direct bearing on attitudes regarding the deployment of women. Opponents of women's inclusion may contend that calculating the risk of including women in the military component of a peacekeeping mission would unnecessarily complicate an already complex situation. In Somalia, for example, military units had to provide humanitarian assistance, as the situation was too dangerous for civilian agencies to distribute relief aid. Furthermore, Africa has limited experience in the deployment of women in military peacekeeping operations. Most of the missions in Africa where fairly large numbers of women were involved took place in stable situations with the emphasis on peace building. However, the fact that there is not much evidence of women in more hazardous peacekeeping situations in Africa does not justify overlooking the central role women have played in numerous liberation wars and ignoring international evidence that exists regarding women's positive contribution to peacekeeping operations.

Improved institutional capacity and a higher degree of political commitment to peacekeeping in general must include the application of gender-sensitive approaches in the development and implementation of peacekeeping policies.[37]

Peace Enforcement, but at What Cost?

The trend in regional and subregional peacekeeping that probably poses the biggest challenge to the mainstreaming of gender is the increase in "muscular" multilateral United Nations–sanctioned military interventions and bilateral "rogue" interventions under the auspices of subregional organizations.

New patterns of conflict resolution endeavors in Africa vacillate between multilateral and unilateral interventions. The case of ECOWAS and ECO-MOG conducting forceful operations in Sierra Leone and Liberia under the leadership of Nigeria was multilateral in nature. The ECOMOG interventions were legitimized by ex post facto Security Council resolutions. Events in the Democratic Republic of the Congo in 1998, as well as South Africa's seemingly unilateral intervention in Lesotho, testify to the emerging trend of peacekeeping operations taking place in an ad hoc manner outside the parameters of United Nations sanction. The South African intervention was later quoted as being a SADC operation. However, a small contingent of Botswana troops arrived only much later in the day.[38]

The notion of peace enforcement as practiced on the African continent is a thorny issue, not only for United Nations peacekeeping in general, but for women in particular. As I argued in the introduction, it is doubtful that the percentage of women in peace operations in Africa will increase in the near future given the trend toward peace enforcement. The use of force as a norm stands in sharp contrast to the notion that female peacekeepers are generally included in a mission due to their constructive and less aggressive approach to conflict resolution. This development affects female peacekeepers in two ways. First, peace enforcement represents a shift toward a more militaristic approach to peacekeeping. Indirectly, this will weaken both the civilian element of multidimensional peacekeeping operations and women's contribution, since it is in the civilian component that women traditionally have been most visible. Second and more directly, so-called muscular peacekeeping is likely to perpetuate or reinforce the aversion to deploying women in combat situations. Troop-contributing countries will now be even more reluctant to support gender awareness strategies and more equitable representation at the military levels of an operation. The achievement of both gender mainstreaming as a strategic priority and gender balance at the tactical level may therefore be in jeopardy.[39]

African peace enforcement efforts take place in a doctrinal lacuna, without clear guidelines and procedures. Malan proposes the development of an unambiguous intervention policy based on the principle of integrated doctrine or doctrinal consensus.[40] He points to the OAU's reluctance to move beyond the orthodoxy of a United Nations mandate. At the subregional level, the SADC has also made little progress and continues to support conventional United Nations peacekeeping doctrine. In west Africa, however, ECOMOG's doctrinal thinking has been shaped by field experience to include elements of traditional peacekeeping, peace enforcement, and intervention operations.

Would doctrinal consensus enhance or debilitate the case for mainstreaming gender? Under conditions of stringency, ad hoc peacekeeping arrangements "will inevitably reflect national interests and the dominance of larger countries in the region."[41] Therefore, in the short term, gender mainstreaming will be made subservient to more localized and immediate needs and demands and will become dependent upon the policies of subregional hegemons. In the long run, more policy coherence, stability, coordination, and credibility could, however, have a positive effect in other areas of doctrinal development such as gender mainstreaming.

For peace enforcement to work, it must be efficient and should rest on the monopoly of violence. The international community may deplore the use of force, but the primary aim of such operations should be to stabilize the situation in order to minimize loss of life within a malevolent security environment. With this aim in mind, peace enforcement necessarily involves a rejection of conventional notions of impartiality, consent, and the nonuse of force. The problem with regard to mainstreaming gender under these circumstances often lies in the mistaken perception that what is good for peacekeeping may not necessarily be good for the gender cause or vice versa. The dilemma involves a paradoxical and complex choice between the success of the mission on the one hand and the successful integration of a politically correct stance on gender on the other hand. The two issues are, however, not mutually exclusive—evidence of the contribution of women to peacekeeping operations on its own could support the adoption of a more complementary approach.

The Gender Implications of Privatizing Peacekeepers

The changes in global security in the post–Cold War era and the subsequent downsizing of many armed forces have left many military experts and personnel unemployed. This has led to the manifestation of two interdependent trends, both of which have taken root in Africa. First, rather than recruiting and training civilians in the culture of traditional peacekeeping, decision makers are looking at former soldiers to fill the ranks of peacekeepers. In the context of complex political emergencies this will invariably lead to a "remilitarization" of peacekeeping, with greater emphasis on peace enforcement and even less room for women to make a meaningful contribution (see Mazurana, chapter 1; Raven-Roberts, chapter 2).

Second, the tendency to use private military forces in situations where the state and its institutions are unable to guarantee the physical security of its citizens is on the increase. In the wake of the United Nations' inability to fulfill its role as international peacekeeper (such as in Sierra Leone), the debate has moved beyond whether mercenaries should be allowed to act as peacekeepers or not. The issue now is rather how such armies should best be controlled and regulated. Not only is the United Nations overextended on the African continent, but local African peacekeepers are also increasingly under pressure to deliver a credible indigenous peacekeeping capacity. They, too, are inevitably looking toward outsourcing peacekeeping activities on the basis of improved efficiency and professionalism and lower cost.[42]

This tendency could have dire gender implications. Since such an alternative rests on the principle of "getting the job done" for profit, the notions of efficiency and expendability clearly outweigh any moral argument against the practice of "violence for hire." Mercenaries' lack of accountability to anyone but the highest bidder poses serious challenges for the mainstreaming of gender in peacekeeping. Privatized peacekeeping forces will be even less bound by gender policies, quota systems, and training and other guidelines at the national, subregional, and international levels. Furthermore, the introduction of private peacekeepers would destroy the integrated (yet complex) nature of multidimensional peacekeeping operations, thereby making it more difficult to mainstream gender in peacekeeping. It is beyond the scope of mercenaries' job description to become involved in peace building or postconflict reconstruction. Theirs is a military task and not a sociopolitical one. This implies that multidimensional peacekeeping operations will invariably become artificially disjointed and near impossible to coordinate, with mercenaries halting violence and civilian peace builders seeking enduring political solutions, each at different stages of the conflict.

Policy Coherence and Action

It stands to reason that policy making is the foundation of all peacekeeping action. Both policy and action are underpinned by gender mainstreaming as a strategy to promote gender equality by including a gender analysis in all policies, projects, and programs. Internationally, the lack of systematic attention to gender issues, as well as the lack of coherent policies in the area of peacekeeping and gender, is quite striking. The Brahimi Report is a case in point in two instances where it has failed.

First, the report does not fully consider the implications of its ambitious proposals for African peacekeepers. Africans remain skeptical about the notion of burden sharing in an environment where Africa clearly does not enjoy strategic importance in the eyes of the international community. The skepticism is strengthened by the fact that the Brahimi Report does not significantly move away from a classical interpretation of peacekeeping, thereby relegating the majority of African conflicts to an area outside United Nations responsibility. Ironically, while the cost of ECOMOG's involvement in Liberia and

Sierra Leone amounts to billions of dollars for Nigeria's weak economy, it is quite plausible that Africans will have to shoulder much more of the burden in the future. Second, the Brahimi Report has been criticized for the scant attention paid to matters of gender (see Raven-Roberts, chapter 2). In spite of the Security Council's call for the full implementation of Resolution 1325 on women, peace, and security[43] and the council's commitment to ensuring that United Nations missions take into account gender considerations, the decision to comply and to focus national training guidelines and materials on the rights, needs, and protection of women ultimately remains in the hands of individual states (see Mazurana et al., introduction).[44]

In Africa, too, at the policy level the situation is fraught with difficulties. National structures and mechanisms for achieving gender equality are not sufficiently taken into account in regional and subregional institutions that are concerned with human security, such as the OAU, ECOWAS, and the SADC. Sowa suggests a number of policy actions to ensure gender-sensitive peacekeeping, such as better gender-sensitive analysis of conflict situations; more attention given to the interface between gender, development, and human rights; integration of gender matters into training; improved communication, documentation, and research; and initiatives to build institutional and leadership capacity. I discuss some of these issues in the next section.[45]

Progress in Mainstreaming Gender in African Peacekeeping Operations

Having outlined a rather bleak picture with respect to women's representation and problems of capacity and political will of African troop-contributing countries and regional/subregional organizations, I now shift the discussion to a more positive level. In this section I pay closer attention to the opportunities that exist for improving the preparedness of peacekeepers by systematizing gender issues in training, capacity-building exercises, documentation, research, and collaboration.

External and Internal Efforts at Building
Indigenous African Peacekeeping Capacity

Foreign efforts at building African peacekeeping capacity have not come about without controversy. While the United Nations has committed itself to staying involved in specialized training, various developed states have seized the opportunity to offer equipment and expertise in order to establish themselves as concerned yet distant players. In 1997, Britain, France, and the United States launched their "P3" initiative, aimed at coordinating the UK African

Peacekeeping Training Support Programme, the French Reinforcement of African Military Peacekeeping Capacity (RECAMP), and the African Crisis Response Initiative (ACRI, the U.S. component).[46] From February 11–22, 2002, France and Tanzania co-organized a peacekeeping exercise code-named Exercise Tanzanite. Thirteen SADC countries and two non-SADC countries, Kenya and Madagascar, took part.[47] Norway has also made a concerted effort to include African officers in its training programs.[48]

African countries also began to assert themselves in the area of peacekeeping. In October 1997, at a meeting in Harare, Zimbabwe, it was agreed that African countries would provide the bulk of the troops while the OAU would operationalize its early warning system within the Conflict Management Division by linking it to the early warning systems in the various subregional organizations.[49] A number of combined regional training exercises have been conducted since 1997. The biggest multinational peacekeeping exercise in Africa to date, namely the SADC's Exercise Blue Crane, was held in South Africa in April 1999.[50] However, since the involvement of Zimbabwe, Angola, and Namibia in peacekeeping in the Democratic Republic of the Congo, there has been very little time or money to conduct combined training in the southern African region. The worsening political situation in Zimbabwe, at present, has upset a number of Western donors, with dire consequences particularly for continued Scandinavian engagement with the SADC Regional Peacekeeping Training Centre in Harare. The British Military Advisory and Training Team (BMATT) has also withdrawn from Zimbabwe as a result of deteriorating British-Zimbabwean relations.

The United Nations Development Fund for Women (UNIFEM), the United Nations Department of Peacekeeping Operations (DPKO), the United Nations International Children's Fund (UNICEF), and the United Nations Office for the Coordination of Humanitarian Affairs (OCHA) have been involved in the integration of gender training into the predeployment induction courses for peacekeepers and military observers assigned to the Democratic Republic of the Congo.[51] However, most of the training done so far has taken place in a gender vacuum or rather in a seemingly gender-neutral environment (see Mackay, chapter 13). Ogunsanye and Mngqibisa quite rightly question whether or not women have been effectively included as part of these capacity-building initiatives.[52] Pressure to fill the gap left by the withdrawal of the United Nations has preoccupied regional and subregional capacity-building initiatives in Africa, to the extent that empowering designated groups with a potentially significant contribution to the peace-building process has fallen by the wayside. A further explanation relates to the fact that most capacity-building efforts are aimed at the narrow military dimension of peacekeeping operations. Military training takes place at the expense of a more holistic emphasis on conflict management in the form of preventive diplomacy, peacemaking, peace building, and postconflict reconstruction, areas where women's contribution, at least, has been firmly recognized.

An example of an African institution involved in capacity building in the area of conflict resolution and peacekeeping is the African Centre for the Constructive Resolution of Disputes (ACCORD), based in South Africa. This organization's peacekeeping program forms part of the Training for Peace (TfP) Project, which was established in 1995 with funding from the Royal Norwegian Ministry of Foreign Affairs. The TfP Project is the result of a partnership between ACCORD, the Norwegian Institute of International Affairs (NUPI), and the Institute for Security Studies of South Africa (ISS).[53] The peacekeeping program has conducted peacekeeping training workshops in eleven SADC countries, with an emphasis on civilian training. At the five peacekeeping training projects hosted by ACCORD in Zambia, Mozambique, Zimbabwe, Tanzania, and Mauritius in 1996 the ratio of male participants (85 percent) clearly outweighed that of female participants (15 percent). All the participants from the ministry of defense and the police were male, while only four representatives from the department of foreign affairs were female, the rest of the women being from nongovernmental organizations.[54] Since the inception of the TfP Project, only 13 percent of a total of 431 trainees have been women, and most of the women trained have represented civil society organizations, rather than government. Apparently, various attempts to encourage higher participation of women in the workshops were unsuccessful.[55]

ACCORD, in collaboration with the South African Department of Foreign Affairs and the South African National Defence Force, also hosted the Sixth Annual Conference of the International Association of Peacekeeping Training Centres from June 13–15, 2000. Of the seventy-eight participants only eight (10 percent) were women, which is indicative of the long road ahead toward gender mainstreaming in the peacekeeping arena.[56]

In the area of civil policing, countries with experience in mainstreaming gender issues in the military and peacekeeping, such as Norway and Sweden, have launched important initiatives. As mentioned earlier, in the police officers training course held in southern Africa in November 1998, women constituted 18 percent of the participants. The course was initiated within the framework of the Norwegian-funded TfP Project and organized by the ISS, together with the South African Police Services, but also had a regional outreach to SADC countries. The women at the training course also participated in Exercise Blue Crane.

The area of civil policing is a much-neglected area of mainstreaming and offers vast opportunities for improvement. Noteworthy is the fact that, under Norwegian guidance, a gender perspective was integrated into the civil policing project right from the start. The issue of gender balance was dealt with in advance and in conjunction with all participating countries, which may explain the relatively high representation of women on the course and in the training exercise. This case indicates that a proactive approach can have positive results. Contrary to the realist perception that the cultural diversity of Africa presents insurmountable obstacles, experience has shown that advance planning, consultation, cultural sensitivity, and gender awareness, as well as a critical attitude toward one's own prejudices and assumptions, can go a long way in achieving the desired results.

These examples, together with international experience, reveal a number of opportunities with respect to future training and capacity-building exercises in the subregional context:

- A systematic approach to training and capacity building is required. All peacekeeping personnel should have appropriate training in the protection, rights, and particular needs of women and girls. Ongoing gender-sensitivity training programs and training regarding women's role in peace building and postconflict reconstruction are required.
- In order to maximize benefits of joint civil-military training, such ventures must be properly coordinated and seen to be mutually beneficial. This could have a spillover effect and contribute toward the cross-pollination of gender-sensitive principles and practices.
- If training is based on real and not perceived needs, then the needs of female peacekeepers must be addressed in order to optimize women's contribution to the overall achievement of mission objectives. Capacity-building programs that consider women's life skills and education in the selection process are thought to be very constructive.
- The adoption of so-called best practice models must be sensitive to contextual (and cultural) constraints. The dilemma that peacekeepers often face is that while they are obliged to respect cultural diversity, they have to operate in a society that often does not observe women's rights.
- An integrated gender perspective must permeate all stages of the peacekeeping operation, especially the planning phase. With regard to joint civil-military training, advance planning is necessary to familiarize the parties with each other's cultures, methods of operation, and various approaches prior to their working together in a mission. In its adoption of Resolution 1325 (2000), the Security Council provides a good platform for the recognition and implementation of a gender perspective in the realm of peace and security, particularly by seeking to expand the role and contribution of women in United Nations field-based operations and by expressing its willingness to incorporate a gender perspective into peace-

keeping operations. Gender mainstreaming is needed in the early assessment of each and every situation by the DPKO and should also inform both the secretary-general's and Security Council's decisions in structuring the mandate. The mandate should thus emphasize the principles of gender equality, balance, and mainstreaming. Such reinforcement lends legitimacy to possibly controversial decisions and actions and also serves as a constant reminder to all peacekeepers.

- Since the secretary-general can only invite member states to incorporate a gender perspective into national training guidelines and materials, organizations such as the AU, ECOWAS, and the SADC must be encouraged to take the lead in terms of gender mainstreaming, by means of utilizing all military and civilian resources in the region, setting targets, and pressuring states to comply within a given time frame.

Research and Networking

The need for more in-depth research on mainstreaming of gender in peacekeeping is obvious. There is a definite need for more systematic comparative analysis in order to confirm or reject hypotheses. For instance, were the positive results of the Namibian and South African missions, where there was relative gender balance, coincidental? More empirical case studies at national and international levels will enhance the scientific value of research initiatives. Longitudinal studies may also prove valuable in developing new and strengthening existing hypotheses. In this way, archaic concepts, definitions, and doctrine, such as those related to first-generation peacekeeping, can be critically questioned and transformed. Organizations should also collect and compare data on their own and other training programs. Lessons should be systematically drawn from data, documented, and widely disseminated. This could lead to the development of "best practice" models.

The following examples briefly outline some of the key developments in the African context. Between 1995 and 1998–1999, very little follow-up was done to apply lessons learned in new United Nations missions. In June 1999, however, the study "Mainstreaming a Gender Perspective in Multidimensional Peacekeeping Operations" was launched at Uppsala University, Sweden. The event represented the culmination of efforts of the United Nations Division for the Advancement of Women (DAW) and the Lessons Learned Unit (now known as the Peacekeeping Best Practices Unit [PBPU]) of the DPKO. The main aims of this study were to enhance understanding of the role played by gender dimensions at all stages of the peacekeeping process; and to determine ways in which this understanding could be integrated at policy, strategic, and tactical levels. The gender dimensions of five peace operations in El Salvador,

Namibia, Cambodia, Bosnia and Herzegovina, and South Africa were studied, and the reports are currently being edited (although it is questionable as to whether they will be released; see Raven-Roberts, chapter 2).

Another encouraging development was the policy seminar organized by ABANTU for Development in collaboration with UNIFEM (through its African Women in Conflict [AFWIC] program) in Mombasa, Kenya, on March 30–31, 2000. The aims of this initiative were to examine the gender implications of peacekeeping in Africa; to establish a framework for analysis; and to identify policy actions and strategies for implementation regarding a gender-analytic approach to peacekeeping operations. In the spirit of collaboration, the ABANTU/UNIFEM report was presented at the DPKO and DAW international conference "Mainstreaming Gender in Peacekeeping Operations" in Windhoek, Namibia, during May 2000. Principles and guidelines discussed at this seminar as well as information gleaned from the five case studies led to the adoption of the Windhoek Declaration and Namibia Plan of Action.[57]

Opportunities for research on the African continent in this respect are legion. African researchers have the expertise to conduct extensive research on gender issues in peacekeeping. The institutional capacity is also there—in South Africa alone, a number of institutes, such as the ISS and ACCORD, have embarked on gender-related security studies. However, it is not always clear whether the will to scrutinize so-called marginal issues such as gender is strong enough to sustain long-term projects in this area. This notwithstanding, African researchers are in the enviable position of being able to learn from international experience, yet being allowed to develop indigenous approaches.

Conclusion

Peacekeeping trends on the African continent informed the gender-based analysis in this chapter. The continuous interface between the broader peacekeeping context and the specific gender dimension illustrates just how difficult it is to separate the two areas of analysis. Tendencies such as the withdrawal of the United Nations as primary peacekeeper; increased emphasis on forceful unilateral and multilateral subregional interventions; and the privatization of security, as well as problems regarding capacity and political will, were placed under the spotlight. Such developments and challenges foster an environment that is not conducive to the mainstreaming of gender.

Qualitative and quantitative analyses of both African and foreign women's role in African peacekeeping operations are severely underdeveloped, under-researched, and underreported. There are, however, encouraging signs that, through more systematic policy making and concrete implementation in the form of training, capacity building, and research collaboration, women's contribution to peacekeeping in Africa will become more visible. Think tanks such as ACCORD and the ISS have a fundamental role to play in this regard, not only to promote research and training, but also to encourage individual states to rethink archaic gendered policies and practices.

What the continent really needs is first to strengthen the institutional capacity of regional and subregional organizations. Second, it requires a reconceptualization of security in comprehensive people-centered terms. There exists substantial evidence that through their understanding of peace and security, women can make a positive contribution. By introducing gender as a unit of analysis and mainstreaming it in all areas of conflict resolution and security, we allow these so-called female values and techniques to become part of policy and military doctrine, thus benefiting all.

Notes

1. The launch of the African Union (AU), which will effectively replace the OAU, occurred in July 2002. The success of the AU is partly dependent on effectively operationalizing the initiatives of the New Partnership for Africa's Development (NEPAD). One such initiative, the Peace, Security, and Political Governance Initiative, involves a commitment to building long-term conditions for development and security, as well as a commitment to increasing the capacity of African states and institutions for the prevention, management, and resolution of conflict.

2. Eric G. Berman and Katie E. Sams, "Regional Peacekeeping in Africa," *Conflict Trends*, no. 3 (2001): 50–55.

3. Theo Neethling, "Conditions for Successful Entry and Exit: An Assessment of SADC Allied Operations in Lesotho," in *Boundaries of Peace Support Operations: The African Dimension*, ed. Mark Malan, ISS Monograph Series 44, 141–64 (Pretoria: Institute for Security Studies, 2000). The expert advice offered by Dr. Theo Neethling of the Centre for Military Studies (CEMIS), University of Stellenbosch, is acknowledged and highly appreciated.

4. Please refer to these notes for a *capita selecta* of some of their key works. In addition, Mark Malan also edited two works in the ISS Monograph Series, *Whither Peacekeeping in Africa?* (no. 36, April 1999) and *Boundaries of Peace Support Operations: The African Dimension* (no. 44, February 2000).

5. Tom Woodhouse and Tamara Duffey, *Peacekeeping and International Conflict Resolution* (New York: UNITAR Programme of Correspondence Instruction in Peacekeeping Operations, 2000).

6. Theo Sowa, "Background Paper" (paper presented at the policy seminar "Gender Implications of Peacekeeping and Reconstruction in Africa," Mombasa, Kenya, March 30–31, 2000), 10.

7. For detailed analyses of women's contribution see Louise Olsson, *Gendering UN Peacekeeping: Mainstreaming a Gender Perspective in Multidimensional Peacekeeping Operations*, Report 53 (Uppsala, Sweden: Uppsala University, Department of Peace and Conflict Research, 1999); Anita Helland and Anita Kristensen, "Women in Peace Operations," in *Women and Armed Conflicts: A Study for the Norwegian Ministry of Foreign Affairs*, ed. Anita Helland, Kari Karamé, Anita Kristensen, and Inger Skjelsbæk (Oslo: Norwegian Institute of International Affairs, 1999); Judith Hicks Stiehm, "United Nations Peacekeeping: Men's and Women's Work," in *Gender Politics in Global Governance*, ed. Mary K. Meyer and Elisabeth Prügl (New York: Rowman & Littlefield, 1999); Heidi Hudson, "Mainstreaming Gender in Peacekeeping Operations: Can Africa Learn from International Experience?" *African Security Review* 9, no. 4 (2000): 18–33; Sowa, "Background Paper"; Kemi Ogunsanye and Kwezi Mngqibisa, "Women of Peace," *Conflict Trends*, no. 1 (2001): 48–52; Kemi Ogunsanye and Kwezi Mngqibisa, "A Gender Perspective for Conflict Management," ACCORD Occasional Paper 4 (2000).

8. A possible explanation for the reluctance to typify intervention operations such as in Kosovo, Liberia, Sierra Leone, DRC, and Lesotho as bona fide peacekeeping is that such operations were motivated by politics rather than considerations of peace and security.

9. Woodhouse and Duffey, *Peacekeeping and International Conflict Resolution*; Olsson, *Gendering UN Peacekeeping*.

10. Christopher Clapham, "The United Nations and Peacekeeping in Africa," in *Whither Peacekeeping in Africa?* ed. Mark Malan, ISS Monograph Series 36, 25–44 (Halfway House, Johannesburg: Institute for Security Studies, 1999).

11. Editor, "A Summary of the Report of the Panel on UN Peace Operations [The Brahimi Report]," *National Network News* 7, no. 3 (2000), available at http://www.sfu.ca/~dann/nn7-3_5.html (accessed February 21, 2001).

12. For an overview of the slow process see Hudson, "Mainstreaming Gender in Peacekeeping Operations."

13. Ogunsanye and Mngqibisa, "Women of Peace."

14. Olsson, *Gendering UN Peacekeeping*; Stiehm, "United Nations Peacekeeping"; Helland and Kristensen, "Women in Peace Operations."

15. Department of Peacekeeping Operations, "Women in UN Peacekeeping," statistics prepared for workshop at Uppsala University, Sweden, 1999.

16. United Nations Department of Peacekeeping Operations (DPKO; Lessons Learned Unit), "Mainstreaming," unofficial working document.

17. Janet C. Beilstein, "The Role of Women in United Nations Peace-Keeping," *Women 2000*, no. 1 (1995), study carried out for the Division for the Advancement of Women, available at gopher://gopher.undp.org/00/secretar/dpcsd/daw/w2000/1995-1.en; Olsson, *Gendering UN Peacekeeping*.

18. DPKO, "Mainstreaming."

19. Helland and Kristensen, "Women in Peace Operations."

20. Ogunsanye and Mngqibisa, "Women of Peace"; Olsson, *Gendering UN Peacekeeping*.

21. Olsson, *Gendering UN Peacekeeping*.

22. Helland and Kristensen, "Women in Peace Operations."

23. This case is cited in several sources, such as Helland and Kristensen, "Women in Peace Operations"; Beilstein, "The Role of Women in United Nations Peace-Keeping"; and Stiehm, "United Nations Peacekeeping."

24. First Specialised Element to Deploy in the DRC; information available at http://www.mil.za/CSANDF/CJOps/Operations...ping/first_specialised_element_to_dep.htm.

25. J. Slabbert, "Privatising Peacekeeping Operations: A Viable Alternative in Africa for Overextended UN Capacity?" in "South African Defence College Course 2 Research Papers" (2000), available at http://www.mil.za/CSANDF/CJSupp/TrainingF...ollege/Researchpapers2000_02/slabbert.htm (accessed June 14, 2001).

26. Cedric De Coning, "Lesotho Intervention: Implications for SADC; Military Interventions, Peacekeeping and the African Renaissance," in *Contributions Towards an African Renaissance*, ed. Hussein Solomon and Marie Muller, Africa Dialogue Monograph Series 1, 39–76 (Durban: ACCORD, 2000).

27. Funmi Olonisakin, "Conflict Management in Africa: The Role of the OAU and Subregional Organisations," in *Building Stability in Africa: Challenges for the New Millennium*, ed. Jakkie Cilliers and Annika Hilding-Norberg, ISS Monograph Series 46, 83–96 (Pretoria: Institute for Security Studies, 2000).

28. Mark Malan, "Debunking Some Myths about Peacekeeping in Africa," in *From Peacekeeping to Complex Emergencies: Peace Support Missions in Africa*, ed. Jakkie Cilliers and Greg Mills (Johannesburg/Pretoria: South African Institute of International Affairs/ Institute for Security Studies, 1999), 15; Olonisakin, "Conflict Management in Africa," 84.

29. De Coning, "Lesotho Intervention."

30. It should again be noted that there is a conceptual distinction between the four UN operations in Angola (as typical UN peacekeeping missions) with UN sanction and the intervention-type operation in Lesotho, which took place with neither UN nor OAU sanction.

31. Berman and Sams, "Regional Peacekeeping in Africa." It is imperative for the newly established African Union to ensure that it does not repeat the mistakes of the OAU. The AU Mechanism for Conflict Prevention, Management, and Resolution replaces the existing OAU structure and is intended to be "a collective security and early-warning arrangement to facilitate timely and efficient response to conflict and crisis situations in Africa" (Jakkie Cilliers and Kathryn Sturman, "Towards the Inaugural Assembly of the African Union: Background Note," in *African Security Analysis Programme Reports* [Pretoria: Institute for Security Studies, 2002], 7). As one of the pillars of this mechanism, the Peace and Security Council will be empowered to operate in a wide range of areas, such as early warning and preventive diplomacy; peacemaking; peace support operations and intervention; peace building and postconflict reconstruction; and humanitarian assistance. In this context, the role of the United Nations in providing financial, logistic, and military support for the union's conflict resolution efforts must also be clearly defined in order to ensure the effective coordination of activities.

32. Jakkie Cilliers, "Regional African Peacekeeping Capacity: Mythical Construct or Essential Tool?" *African Security Review* 8, no. 4 (1999): 27.

33. Mark Malan, "Peacekeeping in Africa: Trends and Responses," in *ISS Papers*, no. 31 (1998).

34. Sandile G. Gwexe, "Prospects for African Conflict Resolution in the Next Millennium: South Africa's View," *African Journal on Conflict Resolution* 1, no. 1 (1999): 103–24. This is not to argue that South Africa's concern for its national interest is unique in international relations. It stands to reason, as the United States' position after the Somalia debacle illustrates, that there is a direct correlation between states' willingness to get involved in peace missions and the niche that states want to carve out for themselves in the international community.

35. Olonisakin, "Conflict Management in Africa."

36. Insufficient appreciation of the importance of following democratic procedures in deciding when and how to intervene also became apparent at the conference "The Operationalisation of the SADC Organ," Durban, October 1999.

37. Sowa, "Background Paper."

38. Mark Malan, "Leaner and Meaner? The Future of Peacekeeping in Africa," *African Security Review* 8, no. 4 (1999): 45–61.

39. While the concept of gender balance is well understood, the meaning of gender mainstreaming—the integration of a gender perspective into all activities and policies—is more subtle and hence more difficult to implement.

40. Mark Malan, "Towards an Integrated Doctrine for Peace Support Operations in Africa," in *Building Stability in Africa: Challenges for the New Millennium*, ed. Jakkie Cilliers and Annika Hilding-Norberg, ISS Monograph Series 46, 46–69 (Pretoria: Institute for Security Studies, 2000).

41. Jakkie Cilliers and Greg Mills, "From Peacekeeping to Managing Complex Emergencies: Peace Support Missions in Africa," in *From Peacekeeping to Complex Emergencies: Peace Support Missions in Africa*, ed. Jakkie Cilliers and Greg Mills (Johannesburg/Pretoria: South African Institute of International Affairs/ Institute for Security Studies, 1999), 4.

42. Slabbert, "Privatising Peacekeeping Operations."

43. United Nations Security Council, "Security Council, Responding to 'Brahimi Report,' Adopts Wide-Ranging Resolution on Peacekeeping Operations," press release SC/6948 (November 13, 2000).

44. Ogunsanye and Mngqibisa, "Women of Peace."

45. Sowa, "Background Paper."

46. Eric G. Berman and Katie E. Sams, *Constructive Disengagement: Western Efforts to Develop African Peacekeeping*, ISS Monograph Series 33 (Halfway House, Johannesburg: Institute for Security Studies, 1998); Malan, "Peacekeeping in Africa: Trends and Responses"; Cilliers and Mills, "From Peacekeeping to Managing Complex Emergencies."

47. African Centre for the Constructive Resolution of Disputes, "Trends in Peacekeeping," *Conflict Trends*, no. 1 (2001): 3–5; M. P. Mgobozi, "Exercise TANZANITE Shows the Commitment of the French Government," *SA Soldier* 9, no. 5 (2002): 8–10.

48. Helga Hernes, "Nordic Perspectives on African Capacity-Building," in *Resolute Partners: Building Peacekeeping Capacity in Southern Africa*, ed. Mark Malan, ISS Monograph Series 21, 59–66 (Halfway House, Johannesburg: Institute for Security

Studies, 1998); Peter Cross, "Regional Co-operation and Partnerships for Peacekeeping Training" (paper presented at the sixth annual conference of the International Association of Peacekeeping Training Centres, Kruger National Park, South Africa, June 13–15, 2000, available at http://www.accord.org.za/programmes/peacekeeping/events/iaptc_report.htm [accessed July 3, 2001]).

49. Cilliers and Mills, "From Peacekeeping to Managing Complex Emergencies"; Malan, "Peacekeeping in Africa: Trends and Responses."

50. Malan, "Peacekeeping in Africa: Trends and Responses"; Malan, "Leaner and Meaner? The Future of Peacekeeping in Africa"; Theo Neethling, "Exercise Blue Crane: Forward with Peacekeeping in Southern Africa?" *ISSUP Bulletin*, no. 5 (1999).

51. Noeleen Heyzer, "Keynote Address" (presented at the policy seminar "Gender Implications of Peacekeeping and Reconstruction in Africa," Mombasa, Kenya, March 30–31, 2000, available at http://www.undp.org/unifem/speaks/peacek00.html [accessed June 14, 2001]).

52. Ogunsanye and Mngqibisa, "Women of Peace."

53. Ogunsanye and Mngqibisa, "Women of Peace."

54. African Centre for the Constructive Resolution of Disputes, "ACCORD Annual Report 1996," unpublished.

55. Ogunsanye and Mngqibisa, "A Gender Perspective for Conflict Management."

56. Cross, "Regional Co-operation and Partnerships for Peacekeeping Training."

57. United Nations Doc. A/55/138-S/2000/693. Other international developments from which Africans could benefit include the following: First, the study on women, peace, and security as called for by Security Council Resolution 1325 (2000) was being coordinated by the Office of the Special Adviser on Gender Issues and Advancement of Women within the framework of the Inter-Agency Taskforce on Women, Peace, and Security. The study focuses on the impact of armed conflict on women and girls; the gender dimensions of peace processes and conflict resolution; and the role of women in peace building. Second, UNIFEM is preparing case studies from peace missions and publishing the findings in its biennial report, *Progress of the World's Women*. Third, DPKO is working on a manual of standard operating procedures for peacekeeping missions, with specific reference to operational tools and mechanisms for the mainstreaming of gender (e-mail communication with Marlene Nilsson [DPKO] and Carolyn Hannan [DAW]).

6

Gender, War, and Peace in Mozambique and Angola: Advances and Absences

Ruth Jacobson

T HIS CHAPTER DOES NOT ATTEMPT to minimize the opposition that feminists currently encounter when they try to introduce a gendered analysis into peacekeeping and peace building, a situation amply demonstrated by other chapters in this collection.[1] Nevertheless, I first argue that, in the context of war and peace in Mozambique, there have been some long-term paradigm shifts that can be described as advances. The section on Angola that follows establishes the embedded constraints on bringing about major policy changes where international humanitarian organizations can cite "the tyranny of the urgent" as a justification for the gaps in their institutional learning as regards gender (see Raven-Roberts, chapter 2). The final section looks at the dilemmas facing feminist scholarship and feminist practitioners (female and male) working at field level within these agencies.

Any feminist project concerned with war and peace is located within the realities of a late-capitalist, globalized, post–Cold War world characterized by ever-more-stark inequalities of resources and power affecting the lives of entire populations in the South. A transformational feminist perspective must be cognizant of these inequalities in its praxis, which implies, I believe, acute dilemmas that lie beyond the parameters of gender, noticeably those of the global North–South power relationships that characterize the post–Cold War era. For the purposes of this volume, the chapter is primarily concerned with unpacking the arguments contained in my title, with particular thematic attention to the necessity of including the male experiences of war and peace.

This argument is informed by three categories of evidence. First, as noted elsewhere,[2] feminist scholarship in the fields of international relations, politics, and women's studies has provided us with a set of tools for interrogating the dichotomized lexicon of war/peace, security/insecurity, and the front line/home front. This scholarship does not dismiss the importance of policy formulation but by definition is more concerned with those underlying paradigms that produce the policies. Second, I draw on the stream of gray literature[3] currently in circulation. Third, I draw on my own fieldwork in Mozambique between 1983 and the present and more recently in Angola.

Mozambique at War: Trajectories of Continuity

Writing of the region now occupied by northern Mozambique and parts of Malawi and Zambia in the late 1890s (the immediate precolonial period), the historian Marcia Wright has concluded:

> To be born a woman and to be dislodged from a conventional social setting in the late nineteenth century was to be exposed to the raw fact of negotiability. Hence the quest for protectors, the expressions of gratitude towards those who were merciful and the strong pressure for conformity and minimization of the cost to head of the household or other man responsible for a woman.[4]

It may seem perverse to refer to such a long-past epoch to support arguments about gender and peacekeeping missions that have such current urgency. Yet it is important to maintain a historical grounding in the face of claims about the characteristics of "new" wars in Africa.[5] As elsewhere, post–Cold War paradigm shifts in Mozambique have had the unfortunate effect of producing accounts of contemporary violent conflict that veer toward the mythology of a conflict-free golden past. Wright's emphasis on "the raw fact of negotiability"[6] for women is a salutary reminder. Conquest could mean a number of outcomes. For women from the communities that experienced defeat in the expansionary wars of the precolonial period, conquest did not generally imply actual death. This was because their labor—in the fields, household, and in reproduction—was an asset to be preserved. The fact of being female was thus a form of protection, albeit often under harsh conditions of enslavement or forced incorporation into the conqueror's household. Male members of the conquered groups did not necessarily benefit from this form of negotiability; if they represented a possible future military threat, they could be killed immediately.[7] Furthermore, male labor was less valuable because then, as now, the greater burden of productive labor fell on women. However, when they survived, men and boys of conquered communities might still be able to carry on economic and social activities and eventually become heads of households themselves.[8] We see, therefore, that protection and survival in Mozambique was gendered in precolonial times.

During this mid- to late-nineteenth-century period, there were, of course, no external international peacekeepers, but there were socioeconomic and ritual mechanisms for the restoration of relationships between warring communities. These mechanisms were eventually to become important factors in the construction of traditional forms of peace building (see below).

The imposition of the Portuguese colonial order on the region, giving the current boundaries of Mozambique, deprived all African women and men of agency, transforming them into providers of labor for the colonial enterprise.[9] It was not until the start of the Mozambican war of national liberation in the later 1960s that African men and women could become actors in their own right. A significant number of women became essential elements in the organization of the struggle waged militarily by the independence force of Frelimo.

Women played significant roles through transporting of arms, provisioning of Frelimo's forces, and, more rarely, actual incorporation into the military campaign (although not in frontline combat). The ideological parameters of the liberation struggle and the earlier phase of national independence constructed women as giving unqualified support for the armed struggle, overriding any debate as to whether any of the terms of the patriarchal bargain had actually changed.[10] Despite this, it is important to recognize that the experience of the liberation struggle left Mozambican women of that generation with a distinctive legacy, one which also did not place notions of women as peacemakers at its center.

When the liberation movement of Frelimo formed a one-party Marxist-Leninist state in 1975, it specifically claimed to be the one institution that would provide protection through the emancipation of women.[11] As wives and mothers within Frelimo's modernizing project of the 1970s, they were to contribute to the transformation of society—but without resorting to the bourgeois and non-African practice of feminism.[12] Thus, overt discussion of power relationships within the home or of male sexual conduct was out of bounds. Although women needed to "preserve the peace" by avoiding direct confrontation, their experiences of citizenship under the modernizing one-party state still contained important elements that reduced their negotiability and vulnerability. Effective state-led primary health campaigns reducing infant mortality and promoting birth spacing brought the aim of controlling family size closer.[13] Girls who had enrolled in schools and market women in adult literacy campaigns had at least the prospect of participation along with men in the public sphere.[14]

These prospects were brutally curtailed by the regional politics and geopolitics of the 1980s, as the South African surrogate forces of Renamo launched a war of destabilization against the Frelimo government.[15] During the late 1970s and earlier 1980s, the impact of this war remained relatively localized, and Frelimo was still in a position to dictate whether international humanitarian agencies would become involved.[16] There is debate as to the extent to which the Frelimo state actually managed to fulfill this function with respect to the great majority of the population affected by the war, particularly in rural areas, during this earlier phase, but it remains the fact that during this period, the impact of external agencies was limited.[17] In the areas of the country that had fallen under Renamo's control, no external intervention was possible.

The position of the state women's organization, the Organizacao das Mulheres Moçambicanas (henceforth OMM), continued to be heavily constrained by its status as a state body. At its national conference in 1983, the leadership and delegates unsurprisingly backed the government line that Renamo was a totally illegitimate force of South African–backed bandits and that there could no compromise until a military victory had been achieved—once again, no configuration of women as peacemakers.

At the same event, however, there were the first signs that OMM members were prepared to break the silence around gendered power relationships within the home and Mozambican society, noticeably in relation to violence against women, the widespread practice of arranging marriages for girls just past puberty (*casamento prematuro*), and the social condoning of male sexual conduct (*amantismo*). Had this debate been able to continue, it could have changed the course of women's relationship with their protecting state; however, this debate was truncated by the combined forces of the Frelimo leadership and the escalating national crisis.

As the conflict escalated in the mid-1980s, it took on the characteristics now categorized as a complex political emergency: "a multi-dimensional crisis with profound human suffering, where the roots of the upheaval are political and with intense contestation around the state."[18] The scale and intensity of suffering now covered virtually the entire country and continued to be characterized by modalities of gendered vulnerability. Many of these are now familiar from research on other complex political emergencies, ranging from widespread sexual violence against women, forcible recruitment of male and female adults and children by both sides, psychological torture of young boys and girls, and massive displacement and loss of livelihood.[19]

My research during the later 1980s suggests that although the outcomes of the complex political emergency were seen by Mozambicans as unmistakably gendered, this perception could not be elided into categorical statements about a starkly differentiated scale of suffering for men and women.[20] On the contrary, women recounted numerous instances of self-sacrifice on the part of men attempting to protect their families, even when they had considerably better chances of escape from the aggressors.[21] At the same time, Wright's "raw facts of negotiability" continued to affect women in ways that were distinct from the male experience.[22] To cite just one example, if women escaped from the conflict zones to the larger cities, they entered into a socially and economically precarious situation of dependence on extended families, whereas men could start afresh with new relationships.

As the humanitarian crisis intensified, the Frelimo government had no option other than to open the door to external agencies. This resulted in a veritable flood of international agencies[23] ranging from the leading United Nations bodies, such as the Office of the United Nations High Commissioner for Refugees (UNHCR), to large-scale international NGOs, to smaller-scale enterprises, for example, programs specializing in the rehabilitation of child soldiers. This influx effectively took over the role of protector from the state, and the interventions undoubtedly saved the lives of hundreds of thousands of adults and children. It is not surprising, therefore, that in interviews women refugees frequently referred to the agencies as "our mothers and fathers,"[24] once again reminding us of Wright's analysis of frequent "expressions of gratitude."[25]

On the whole, the agencies involved in emergency relief replicated patriarchal assumptions about the nature of family relationships. For example, distribution of food and other goods to families who had fled from the enemy to a place of safety was automatically conducted with the assumption that the normal family was male headed; special provisions could only be made for widows. Likewise, the issue of sexual violence and coercion within camps for refugee and internally displaced women was not addressed by any institutional or training guidelines and was routinely dismissed as an issue of culture.

Yet, at the international level, during this same period (the later 1980s and earlier 1990s), an important exchange between feminists within development studies and in relation to human rights activism was taking place.[26] The planning and activism around the United Nation's Vienna conference of 1992 and the documentation for the United Nation's Fourth Conference on Women in 1995 (the Beijing conference) opened up opportunities within relief and refugee agencies to analyze the gendered effects of armed conflict (see Mazurana et al., introduction; Raven-Roberts, chapter 2). The argument was taken beyond immediate humanitarian terms: "The burden placed on women to provide for the basic needs of their families increases exponentially, there is considerable spillover effects for their daughters. Consequently, girls are moved even further away from the realization of their socio-political rights."[27] Much of this analysis may seem self-evident when seen retrospectively, but it was in marked contrast to earlier paradigms in Mozambique. The shift further strengthened the position of feminists at the policy-making level.

For example, under their influence, UNHCR issued its guidelines on refugee women in 1991. This was followed by the integration of specific requirements in UNHCR documents; for example, the "Draft Field Manual" of 1995 places the obligation on field staff to take measures to prevent sexual assault against women and girls, for example, in the siting of latrine areas. It also states, "As a general rule field staff should act on the assumption that SGBV [sexual and gender-based violence] is a problem, unless they have conclusive proof that this is not the case."[28]

Unsurprisingly, these changes at the level of policy documents did not automatically lead to the transformation of actual institutional practices (see Raven-Roberts, chapter 2). For example, an internal evaluation commissioned by the World Food Program (WFP) for the Beijing conference, based in part on the experiences of Mozambican refugees, concluded that "although WFP does have explicit guidelines on gender, women and aid, research for this report found that targeting women in emergencies is not a priority, either as beneficiaries or as employees in the food distribution process."[29]

This failure to convert rhetoric into reality obviously casts doubt on my argument for advances. Nevertheless, gender relations became something that was increasingly difficult to ignore during the course of the Mozambican complex political emergency. Staff of the agencies began to see the gendered power relationships within refugee camps and emergency settlements; for example, they noted how food and water distribution systems forced women and girls to spend long hours in queues while young men were taking advantage of skills training opportunities.[30] Concurrently, changes in the registration procedures for nongovernmental organizations, linked with the availability of external funding, were leading to a fundamental change in the capacity of women's organizations to voice disagreement with Frelimo's earlier position and with the OMM.

Another feature that can be described as an advance was the breaking of silence around sexual violence as a weapon of war. Considerably before the international attention to this feature of armed conflict in Europe, the OMM had been involved in a research program that documented the large-scale (widespread) rape and sexual servitude inflicted by Renamo.[31] I argue, therefore, that even without taking the very long view (from Wright's precolonial 1890s), it is possible to maintain that the analysis of war and peace shifted during the Mozambican complex political emergency toward a perspective that at least began to integrate gendered relationships of power. It is all the more frustrating, therefore, to note how the advent of formal peacekeeping interventions affected that pattern.

Peacekeeping, Political Settlements,
and Peace Building, 1992–1994 and After

When the possibility of a political settlement with Renamo emerged in the early 1990s, the great majority of Mozambican men were as desperate as the women for it to be grasped.[32] Although the earlier initiatives were located within Mozambique itself, regional and geopolitical factors meant that the principal dynamic became the pressure from the international community on the two protagonists.[33] Eventually, a political package of demobilization and multiparty elections was reached in 1992, through the Rome Accords. Demobilization of both armies, crucial to the political settlement, required a program to be devised, financed, and supervised by the United Nations. Mozambican soldiers were to be concentrated into collection areas, where arrangements would be made for them and their families to return to their areas of origin. Families were defined by the United Nations body responsible, the United Nations Development Program (UNDP), as one male soldier plus one wife and up to five children. Demobilized soldiers were to receive benefits of cash, goods, and tools to encourage their transition to civilian life.

There is no evidence in the documentation of this process that the relevant United Nations authorities acknowledged what was common knowledge to any Mozambican: that many soldiers had in fact accumulated not one but two—or more—wives and families in the course of the war, indeed, even during the demobilization process itself. Moreover, women and girls who were with soldiers in the demobilization centers might well have been forcibly seized from their homes in completely different areas from the chosen destination of their captors/husbands. During the demobilization (principally in 1993 and 1994), eyewitnesses from the staff of the UNDP, who were handling the logistics of the decommissioning process, reported harrowing scenes while soldiers decided on which was to be their official family. Women were forced onto lorries to accompany departing ex-soldiers while screaming, "But I want to go back to *my* home!" Those women and children who were not chosen were left behind to fend for themselves; church and welfare organizations reported a significant increase in destitution and prostitution in those areas.

A second element of external intervention concerns the demands for sexual services made by United Nations peacekeeping forces. During the 1992–1994 period, Mozambican women's organizations and international NGOs (such as the British-based Save the Children Fund) operating in the central province of Nampula became concerned at the increase of prostitution in the vicinity of the United Nations barracks. Many of those involved as prostitutes were unmistakably minors, including girls observed visiting the barracks en route from their schools. Complaints to the local commander did not produce the desired results, and it was only when complaints were made public in the Mozambican press that there began to be concern at higher levels of the United Nations mission. Investigation by the Mozambican authorities confirmed the reports that the troops were breaking Mozambican law with regard to sexual minors; however, the response was only to withdraw that contingent of peacekeepers and return them to their home countries, not to carry out any of the sanctions available under military regulations (see Bedont, chapter 4).[34]

These features of external intervention in Mozambique strengthen the broader case made by this volume: A feminist critique cannot be confined to the actual peacekeeping operations; it must encompass militarism and masculinity. There are, however, some other elements in the literature on women and war that I find problematic, particularly in the context of Mozambique. As Donna Pankhurst notes, "A common request for peace activists and commentators . . . is that there should be more of a female presence at the sites of peace-making, as well as at discussions which may take place as part of peace-building."[35] In these terms, the Mozambican political settlement certainly marginalized women. During the period when the initiative still lay within the country itself, churches and civil society organizations called for negotiations to start "in the name of our Mozambican mothers." The discourse of maternalism was then to some extent intensified by the central role that the Catholic Church played in the negotiating process.[36] The notion of Mozambican women having an autonomous political agency was largely nonexistent, and there were no women involved at any stage in the actual negotiations.[37] It is important to emphasize that the overwhelming majority of Mozambican men were similarly excluded. Once again, geopolitics affected the terms of the political settlement by insisting on a particular form of democratic transition. Mozambicans as a whole spoke of having to squeeze themselves to fit into a ready-made suit of clothes imported from the West.[38] It is highly unlikely that even the presence of women could have altered this process of conditionality, which was to be repeated in the imposition of the neoliberal economic model on the postconflict government,[39] a feature that I return to in the final section.

The second problematic element concerns what Pankhurst refers to as "the new celebration of peaceful women."[40] In an understandable revulsion against what is seen as the unprecedented horrors of the so-called new wars, she notes, there has been a surge in both analysis and policy debates toward the allegedly sex-specific capacities of women for achieving sustainable peace. As yet, however, I cannot find any coherent links between these capacities in the historical configurations of Mozambican women and men in relation to violence and peace. It is certainly the case that a certain (male) element within the higher military echelons of both Frelimo and Renamo had a strong economic interest in the continuation of the conflict.[41] However, to collapse this into a dichotomous relationship based on a male preference for the continuance of violence is totally unjust to the overwhelming majority of Mozambican men. Indeed, the peace process allowed a more open attention to the historical social and ritual ceremonies that had allowed for healing of fractured communities in the past. Several of these centered on the integration of children born as a result of forced marriage with outsiders. Gender obviously played a vital role in these, but in a much more complex form than an axiomatic female capacity for forgiveness.

In this section, I have argued that despite the overall scale of suffering experienced during the Mozambican complex political emergency and the gender blindness of aspects of the peacekeeping intervention, a long-term view should not underestimate the advances that helped to create an environment that enables gender issues to be raised at different levels of postconflict society. For example, the presence of women members of the national legislature (from both Frelimo and Renamo) contributed to the debate around the reform of the land laws during the mid-1990s in ways that would have been impossible under earlier conditions. However, these advances are fragile, a fact that is underlined when one turns to feminist analysis and activism in the Angolan complex political emergency.

Angola: Emergencies and Absences

Up to early 2002, Angolans commonly referred to their country's condition as one of permanent emergency. The country experienced war from the 1960s onward, including full-scale military invasions from South Africa. Like Mozambique, it suffered during the Cold War, with the United States supporting and arming Jonas Savimbi's National Union for the Total Independence of Angola (UNITA) and the former Soviet Union doing the same for the one-party government of the People's Movement for the Liberation of Angola (MPLA).[42] The end of the Cold War and the demise of the apartheid regime did not represent a definitive turning point in Angola as it did in Mozambique. A political settlement appeared possible in the early 1990s, resulting in a United Nations–sponsored demobilization mission, but these hopes disappeared in the disastrous return to war by Savimbi's UNITA after it lost in the electoral process. "The real nail in the Angolan conflict was [that] the solution of the conflict never enjoyed high priority in the agenda of the countries that mattered," concluded Margaret Anstee, the first woman to hold the post of United Nations secretary-general's special representative.[43]

During much of the mid- to late-1990s, internal war ravaged the country, and there was massive displacement of populations from the rural areas and smaller towns to the few places of refuge. The military balance swung toward the MPLA government[44] in the later 1990s, and a military victory seemed increasingly possible, although by no means certain. It was only the completely unanticipated death in battle of Savimbi in February 2002 that definitively closed this chapter in Angola's history and opened the way for the cease-fire signed with the remaining UNITA commanders in April 2002. At the time of writing (mid-2002), there finally seems to be a firm prospect of a military and political settlement. However, in the global environment of 2002, the prospects for a high-level commitment by the international community to assist with demobilization are unsure.

Given this extended time frame, it might reasonably be assumed that international aid and humanitarian organizations have had ample time to learn about gender and armed conflict from other programs and integrate this into their policies. In particular, one might expect a willingness to build on the work of existing Angolan women's organizations. Regrettably, the available evidence[45] strongly suggests that this is not the case. Instead, there is a marked contrast between the productive interface in Mozambique linking feminist human rights activism and heightened gender awareness and the absence of international learning on the part of international agencies operating in Angola.

Despite the similarities of colonial history between Angola, Mozambique, and other countries in southern Africa, Angola has a distinctive regional orientation, culture, and society. It is therefore entirely acceptable if the humanitarian agencies reject a one-size-fits-all approach to their programs. Yet it seems perverse that in lieu of the integration of the experiences of Mozambique and of other complex political emergencies with regard to gender, there was a tendency to reinvent the wheel and to neglect the resources that were at hand in favor of importing external expertise. Agency evaluations and field staff routinely stated that the urgency of humanitarian demands left no scope for attending to gender (see Raven-Roberts, chapter 2). Even when their organizations' guidelines affirmed that the protection of displaced and refugee women from the risk of sexual assault or coercion was obligatory, high-level staff continued to state that they saw no necessity to do this.[46] Where gender did appear, it was elided with women (and women with mothers). This kind of elision puts an examination of men and masculinity out of bounds, making it difficult, if not impossible, to grasp the structures of gendered power relationships that have permeated the lives of women and men during the Angolan conflict.[47]

Another example was the sidelining of existing bodies of knowledge, such as that produced by Angolan women researchers. Several of these women have been involved for decades with regional projects such as Women and Law in

Southern Africa and have produced research that would provide highly relevant data for the design of relief and rehabilitation programs. To cite just one example, there is important research into the patterns of indigenous inheritance practices that act as a major constraint on women's economic position; yet this research appeared to be unknown by representatives of external agencies funding microcredit programs for women.

In this context, it is worth recalling that institutional learning within development (as opposed to emergency) agencies was inseparable from a realization of the central *operational* relevance of gendered relationships of power to the outcome of development interventions. Once it was established that development programs could be put in jeopardy if gender was not addressed, then the efficiency imperative came into play.[48] Yet it has been extremely difficult to transfer this learning to the field of emergency humanitarian assistance, even where there is a strong commitment on the part of the agency to link first aid with longer-term development (Raven-Roberts, chapter 2).[49]

Agencies that were concerned with gender issues (both international and national) largely conceptualized the Angolan family as corresponding broadly with the Western monogamous model, thus ignoring processes of disruption that started, at least, under colonialism.[50] The Western model of the family is actually in a very small minority in Angola. Instead, there is the phenomenon of multiple families. Men who have been separated from their first families, whether voluntarily or not, acquire new wives and families. It is not common for each family to receive adequate support from the man involved, which would have been the norm for polygamous households in earlier times. These factors, combined with the death rates among adult males, have led to a marked growth in female-headed households of both categories: de facto, where there is an official husband but one who is not in any physical or economic sense involved in supporting his wife and children, and de jure, where the woman has been widowed or officially divorced. In fact, it is likely that this combined category represents at least as many as one out of every three households.[51] In addition, Angolan men who have been displaced from rural areas are now able to have sexual relationships before and outside marriage that fall outside the earlier system of normative social constraints. Indeed, this practice of having a wife/wives plus girlfriend(s) has entered into popular speech in the capital city and Luanda province as *Luanda um, Luanda dois, Luanda tres,* and so on.

Although Angolan women forcefully express themselves in face-to-face conversations about male sexual conduct when they have the opportunity, and some women's organizations are breaking the silence, there remain strong social constraints around publicly identifying men's sexual conduct as a major factor in family insecurity. In my fieldwork, these constraints appeared to be strongest among the personnel (female and male) of emergency and relief organizations most closely associated with religious groupings. This is not confined to the organizations operating under the auspices of the Catholic Church or the (smaller) more mainstream Protestant presence in Angola; it was also noticeable in Seventh Day Adventist and African-based charismatic churches.

In line with previous attention to the male experiences of war and peace in Mozambique, it is relevant to look at what has happened to soldiers in the opposing forces of the MPLA government and UNITA. Technically, they had the right to be demobilized from government forces at the end of their military service or if injured or disabled in combat. However, there are numerous accounts of soldiers whose period of service was arbitrarily extended or who were left destitute in remote areas.[52] This, together with forced conscription by both sides in the war, constitutes a major form of violence, much of which has gendered causes and consequences.

To illustrate, the MPLA government's amnesty law was supposed to enable Savimbi's UNITA soldiers to surrender without risk of retribution, but both anecdotal and documented evidence points to large-scale human rights abuses in this process, including the arbitrary execution of UNITA soldiers and the rape of their female dependents.[53] Such reports raise central questions for any future demobilization process supervised by the international community.

A gendered analysis is therefore necessary to fully confront cycles of violence. National and local Mozambican women's organizations, supported by international donors and working with the wives and families of demobilized or disabled ex-soldiers, feel that the women are particularly at risk of physical and emotional violence from their partners. Their explanation of this situation is linked to, but not based solely on, poverty, since this is a widespread condition. Additionally, they correlate militarized masculinity and the men's depression and alcoholism in an implicit analysis of masculinity. In the event of either a negotiated or imposed settlement and demobilization, peacekeeping forces will be operating in areas that have been sites of endemic gendered violence carried out by both sides in the war.[54] It is also inconceivable that the phenomenon of multiple families will not be found in both armed forces, thus raising the same issues for the funding and implementation of a demobilization package.

What are the prospects for adequate gender-informed training and preparation? While there are mechanisms in place within the United Nations Department of Peacekeeping Operations (DPKO) to provide some gender-informed training, they are currently fragmented and underfunded. It therefore seems highly likely that any Angolan venture will be as dismissive of the gender implications of its presence and functions as was the intervention in

Mozambique. This will have particular implications for all involved, perhaps most notably for the thousands of girls and boys who have been forcibly abducted by both sides in the combat. While there is still hope for advocacy in support of Angolan women's organizations that are encountering the realities of demobilization firsthand, the overall prospects for demobilization are not encouraging.

Conclusion: Old and New Dilemmas

In this chapter, I have attempted to present the historical and nonlinear processes that have affected men's and women's experiences of war, peace, and peacekeeping in Mozambique and Angola. I have noted that, in Mozambique, there are grounds for the kind of cautious optimism that Julie Mertus has also found in a widely different context[55] and that our understanding of gendered experiences cannot exclude men and masculinity. In Angola, the situation prior to 2002 gave grounds for considerable concern, and it appears doubtful that lessons learned regarding gender in Mozambique will be used to inform the response to Angola.

Turning now to old dilemmas, it will come as no surprise that the phenomenon of disappearing women is a global one, whether it is the marginalization of female combatants or of civilian women who have maintained the social and economic fabric of society during wars.[56] I have tried to demonstrate that while there are major institutional practices in both Angola and Mozambique that contribute to this process, change is still possible.

For feminist policy makers and field staff concerned with the issues raised by this volume, there are some new dilemmas. To what extent can they challenge the standard justification of humanitarian priorities in order to reveal deeply embedded gendered practices within their own institutions? And, given the risk of backlash, what risks will they run? I hope that feminist scholarship will be able to provide some (nonlethal) ammunition for this task.

Notes

1. I would like to acknowledge the help of the anonymous reviewer and of Dyan Mazurana on earlier versions of this chapter.
2. Ruth Jacobson, "Conflict, Peace and Gender: Venturing into Dangerous Lands," *International Feminist Journal of Politics* 3, no. 1 (2001): 131–34.
3. This category is made up of internal and consultants' reports to donors, program evaluations, commissioned research, etc., that originates from within humanitarian agencies and institutions. These documents do not generally reach the public domain.

They may reach academic circles, but not systematically, so it is difficult to carry out any kind of literature review.

4. George Wright, *The Destruction of a Nation: United States' Policy towards Angola Since 1945* (London: Pluto Press, 1996), 73.

5. Mary Kaldor, *New and Old Wars: Organized Violence in a Global Era* (Cambridge: Polity Press, 1999).

6. Wright, *Destruction of a Nation*, 73.

7. Norman Etherington, P. Maylam, J. du Bruyn, A. Webster, and S. Meintjes, "The 'Mfecane' Aftermath: Towards a New Paradigm," *South African Historical Journal* 25 (1991): 154–67; Ruth Jacobson, "Conceptualising Women's Citizenship in Southern Africa" (PhD diss., University of Bradford, 1997).

8. Jacobson, "Conceptualising Women's Citizenship"; Claire C. Robertson and Martin A. Klein, "Women's Importance in African Slave Systems," in *Women and Slavery in Africa*, ed. Claire C. Robertson and Martin A. Klein (Madison: University of Wisconsin Press, 1983).

9. Jacobson, "Conceptualising Women's Citizenship."

10. Jacobson, "Conceptualising Women's Citizenship." This process was common over southern Africa; see, for South Africa, Teboho Maitse, "Revealing Silence: Voices from South Africa," in *States of Conflict: Gender, Violence and Resistance*, ed. Susie Jacobs, Ruth Jacobson, and Jen Marchbank, 199–214 (London: Zed Books, 2000).

11. Jacobson, "Conceptualising Women's Citizenship."

12. Ruth Jacobson, "Case Study on Angola and Mozambique, with Special Reference to Gender Issues," COPE Working Paper 15, (Leeds: University of Leeds, 1998).

13. Julie Cliff, N. Kanji, and Mike Muller, "Mozambican Health Holding the Line," *Review of African Political Economy*, no. 36 (1986): 7–23.

14. Jacobson, "Case Study on Angola and Mozambique."

15. Joseph Hanlon, *Beggar Your Neighbours: Apartheid Power in Southern Africa* (London: James Currey, 1986).

16. Joseph Hanlon, *Mozambique: Who Calls the Shots?* (London: James Currey, 1991).

17. See, for contrasting views, Hanlon, *Mozambique: Who Calls the Shots?* and C. Geffray, *A causa das armas: Antropologia da guerra contemporanea em Moçambique* (Porto: Edicoes Afrontamento, 1991).

18. Jacobson, "Case Study on Angola and Mozambique," 1.

19. Meredith Turshen and Clotilde Twagiramariya, eds., *What Women Do in War Time: Gender and Conflict in Africa* (London: Zed Books, 1998); Frances Stewart and Valpy Fitzgerald, eds., *War and Underdevelopment: The Economic and Social Consequences of Conflict in Less Developed Countries* (Oxford: Oxford University Press, 2000).

20. Ruth Jacobson, "Complicating 'Complexity': Integrating Gender into the Analysis of the Mozambican Conflict," *Third World Quarterly* 20, no. 1 (1999): 175–87.

21. Jacobson, "Conflict, Peace and Gender: Venturing into Dangerous Lands."

22. Wright, *Destruction of a Nation*, 73.

23. The numbers operating rose from 7 in 1980 to 70 in 1985 and 180 by 1990 (Hanlon, *Mozambique: Who Calls the Shots?* 64).

24. Refugee households, interviewed by author, Maputo and Magude, October 1989.

25. Wright, *Destruction of a Nation*, 73.

26. Jacobson, "Case Study on Angola and Mozambique," 1.

27. World Vision International, *The Effects of Armed Conflict on Girls* (Geneva: World Vision, 1996), 7.

28. Cited in Jacobson, "Case Study on Angola and Mozambique," 32.

29. Jacobson, "Complicating 'Complexity,'" 181; Women's Commission for Refugee Women and Children, *Refugee Women in Mozambique: Assessing the Implementation of the UNHCR Guidelines on the Protection of Refugee Women* (New York: WCRWC, 1994).

30. S. Makanya, "Rural Mozambican Women in Refugee Camps in Zimbabwe: A Case-Study of Issues of Assistance," prepared for the Expert Group Meeting on Refugee and Displaced Women and Children, Vienna, July 2–6, 1990. In the gray literature of this period that I have read, and in my field interviews, this kind of observation almost always came from a female informant/researcher. However, there is clearly insufficient evidence to make any categorical statement about differential positions of male and female agency staff.

31. Ivette Illas Jeichande, *Relatorio da consultoria da OMM-UNICEF sobre mulheres deslocadas* (Maputo: UNICEF, n.d.) This kind of research program on Renamo violence needs to be placed within the context of two simultaneous propaganda wars of the 1980s. Supporters of Frelimo, who saw Renamo as primarily an instrument of the South African apartheid regime, presented Renamo's brutality toward civilian populations as a deliberate strategy of destabilization (see, for example, Hanlon, *Beggar Your Neighbours: Apartheid Power in Southern Africa*) but did not address the conduct of government forces toward women and girls. Renamo's propagandists within the United States and parts of western Europe presented the organization as "freedom fighters" and denied the documented evidence (Alex Vines, *Angola Explained: The Rise and Fall of the Peace Process* [New York: Human Rights Watch, 1999]). Women's own interests were thus manipulated by both sides.

32. More details of the actual electoral process are given in Ruth Jacobson, *Gender and the 1994 Mozambican Elections*, Working Paper 7 (Leeds: Centre for Democratisation Studies, Leeds University, 1996).

33. Alex Vines, *Renamo: From Terrorism to Democracy in Mozambique* (Bloomington: Indiana University Press, 1991).

34. There are parallels with the case of United Nations peacekeepers in Cambodia: E. Arnvig, "Child Prostitution in Cambodia: Did the UN Look Away?" *International Children's Rights Monitor* 10, no. 3 (1993): 4–6.

35. Donna Pankhurst, *Women, Gender and Peacebuilding*, Working Paper 5, Centre for Conflict Resolution, Department of Peace Studies (Bradford: University of Bradford, 2000), 17.

36. Vines, *Renamo: From Terrorism to Democracy in Mozambique*.

37. Jacobson, *Gender and the 1994 Mozambican Elections*.

38. Jacobson, *Gender and the 1994 Mozambican Elections*.

39. Joseph Hanlon, *Peace without Profit: How the IMF Blocks Rebuilding in Mozambique* (Oxford: James Currey and Heinemann, 1996).

40. Donna Pankhurst, "The 'Sex War' and Other Wars: Towards a Feminist Approach to Peacebuilding," in *Development in Practice* (Oxford: Oxfam, Forthcoming).

41. Personal observation; Vines, *Renamo: From Terrorism to Democracy in Mozambique.*

42. Wright, *Destruction of a Nation*; Victoria Brittain, *Death and Dignity: Angola's Civil War* (London: Pluto Press, 1998).

43. Margaret Anstee, *Orphan of the Cold War: The Inside Story of the Collapse of the Angolan Peace Process* (New York: St. Martin's Press, 1996).

44. After 1992 this was an elected government, and the national legislature contained some previous members of Savimbi's UNITA who had renounced his position of continuing war.

45. At present, this principally takes the form of gray literature. Much of this has not yet found its way into the academic literature; see Ruth Jacobson and Anacleta Perreira, *Assessment on Violence against Women in Angola for NOVIB* (Den Haag, Netherlands: Novib, 2001), available from author.

46. This information was given on condition that it was unattributable but came from some of the lead agencies in the field.

47. Jacobson and Perreira, *Assessment on Violence against Women in Angola.*

48. Donna Pankhurst and Jenny Pearce, "Engendering the Analysis of Conflict: Perspectives from the South," in *Women and Empowerment,* ed. Afshar Haleh (New York: Routledge Press, 1997).

49. Fiona Gell, "Gender Concerns in Emergencies," in *Gender Works: Oxfam Experience in Policy and Practice,* ed. Fenella Porter, I. Smythe, and C. Sweetman (Oxford: Oxfam, 1999).

50. Jacobson and Perreira, *Assessment on Violence against Women in Angola.*

51. Kajsa Pehrsson, *Towards Gender Equality in Angola: A Profile on Gender Relations* (Stockholm: Swedish International Development Cooperation Agency [SIDA], 2000).

52. Jacobson and Perreira, *Assessment on Violence against Women in Angola.*

53. Vines, *Angola Explained: The Rise and Fall of the Peace Process.*

54. Vines, *Angola Explained: The Rise and Fall of the Peace Process.*

55. Julie Mertus, "Grounds for Cautious Optimism," *International Feminist Journal of Politics* 3, no.1 (2001): 99–103.

56. At the time of writing, this process appears to be under way in the aftermath of the war against terrorism in Afghanistan.

7

Peacekeeping, Alphabet Soup, and Violence against Women in the Balkans

Martina Vandenberg

O SCE, UNMIK, UNMIBH, IPTF, KFOR, SFOR, JCO, OHR.[1] A jumble of acronyms, an alphabetical soup, characterizes peacekeeping operations in the Balkans. For local civilians in the Balkans, however, those acronyms sounded like safety. Women survivors and witnesses to rape and other atrocities hoped that people indicted for war crimes and still at large would be arrested by the NATO-led troops. Those indictees—perpetrators accused of crimes against humanity, rape as a war crime, persecution, and, in some cases, genocide—seemed to pose the greatest danger to refugees and internally displaced civilians as they warily returned to their homes. International civilian personnel, civilian police, and military peacekeepers, the returnees believed, would protect them in the harsh postconflict environment.

On January 13, 2000, Staff Sergeant Frank J. Ronghi raped, sodomized, and killed Merita Shabiu, an eleven-year-old ethnic Albanian girl, after luring her into the basement of an apartment building near Vitina, Kosovo.[2] Allegations that other members of Ronghi's elite Eighty-second Airborne Division on peacekeeping duty in Kosovo had engaged in misconduct, including inappropriate pat downs of Kosovar Albanian women, prompted a full-scale investigation.[3] In a November 2000 memorandum, the commanding general of U.S. Army Forced Command concluded, "Junior leaders—both commissioned and non-commissioned—beginning with the A Company commander, participated in misconduct themselves and condoned the misconduct of their soldiers."[4] The final investigative report condemned the troops' lack of appropriate training and mandated that each unit scheduled to deploy on a peacekeeping mission undergo a mission rehearsal exercise (MRE), including class-room and practical training exercises.

The Ronghi case and subsequent investigation of the United States Army's Third Battalion directed a spotlight on abuses against women in the context of peacekeeping in the Balkans. But women in the region had long whispered about harassment and unwelcome sexual advances from military peacekeepers and international civilian staff. The violent death of Merita Shabiu transformed those whispers into international headlines. Those headlines exposed a betrayal of trust and hinted at deeper, more systemic problems.

This chapter draws from three years of research conducted in Bosnia and Herzegovina and Kosovo. I begin with background on the structure of peacekeeping operations in the Balkans and then analyze the two main concerns relating to peacekeeping raised by women in interviews in Bosnia and Kosovo: sexual assault and sexual harassment by international peacekeeping, contractor, and civilian police personnel and links with trafficking of women for forced prostitution. The chapter then turns to the tradition of impunity for these abuses, focusing on United States military and civilian personnel.[5] The United States government has privatized much of its peacekeeping force, which raises concerns about impunity for abuses committed by these independent contractors. Finally, I offer recommendations aimed at ending violations of women's human rights in postconflict zones.

My analysis separates three distinct sets of personnel implicated in the abuses outlined below: military peacekeepers, civilian contractors to the military, and international civilian police. These three groups, all involved in "peacekeeping operations," operate under very different rules and institutional structures. All of these personnel, however, share two important attributes: first, they possess relative immunity for crimes committed while on mission (see Bedont, chapter 4); and second, documentation of their misconduct remains a struggle for journalists and scholars alike due to a systematic lack of transparency, reporting, and record keeping by their institutional employers and international agencies. As a result of the lack of forthrightness from institutions and governments, innuendo and rumor plague the researcher attempting to examine this area. In this chapter I strive to examine credible evidence of sexual misconduct in all three camps and suggest recommendations to end impunity for these abuses.

Background

United Nations peace operations involve a complex mosaic of agencies and actors.[6] Although there is a tendency to blame all abuses on "peacekeepers," shorthand for soldiers, the reality is far more complex. In Bosnia and Herzegovina, the Stabilization Force (SFOR), the follow-on to a peacekeeping force created by the Dayton Peace Accords in 1995 (then IFOR or Implementation Force), includes approximately twenty thousand soldiers from NATO as well as fifteen non-NATO countries.[7] Other institutions such as the Organization for Security and Cooperation in Europe (OSCE), the Office of the High Representative (OHR), the United Nations Mission in Bosnia and Herzegovina (UNMIBH), and a myriad of other intergovernmental and nongovernmental agencies employ thousands of expatriate personnel in the country. In addition, the United States military employs a large number of civilian contractors to provide logistic support for troops in the field. Under the Dayton Peace Accords and Security Council Resolution 1088, the United Nations International Police Task Force (IPTF), an unarmed force of approximately 1,800 police officers from forty-three countries, oversees the local police and assists with investigations of human rights violations committed by law enforcement personnel.[8]

In Kosovo, the United Nations Interim Administration Mission in Kosovo (UNMIK), created by Security Council Resolution 1244 in June 1999, handles an extraordinarily complex and unprecedented mandate.[9] The NATO-led Kosovo Force (KFOR), consisting of fifty thousand men and women, includes personnel from thirty countries, eighteen of them non-NATO countries.[10] As in Bosnia, United States military contractors provide support and logistic services to bases throughout the province; the OSCE, UNMIK, and other intergovernmental and nongovernmental agencies employ thousands of expatriates. However, the UNMIK civilian police force (CIVPOL), created in 1999, has an executive mandate as the only law enforcement unit in Kosovo, which is not the case in Bosnia. UNMIK CIVPOL includes 4,452 armed police officers from forty-seven countries.[11]

Even within these structures, individuals have varying degrees of freedom of movement. Most United States soldiers based in Kosovo and Bosnia and Herzegovina rarely leave their bases except in groups to patrol. Some, including soldiers in support jobs, often do not leave the base for weeks at a time.[12] They must abide by nonfraternization and no-alcohol restrictions.[13] In contrast, until May 2000, the Joint Commission Observers—United States Special Forces personnel—lived in rented houses in fifteen critical cities throughout Bosnia and Herzegovina, where they schmoozed with local citizens and acted as a liaison between NATO and local officials.[14] Similarly, SFOR contractors and IPTF officers in Bosnia and KFOR contractors and CIVPOL officers in Kosovo live in civilian housing and mix freely with the local population.

Military Peacekeepers and Sexual Assault

The Ronghi sexual assault of a Kosovar Albanian girl was not an isolated incident but occurred in a broader context of abuse. Prosecutors introduced evidence during Ronghi's court-martial in August 2000 "that other soldiers in his unit had routinely groped the breasts and buttocks of women during searches in the town."[15] The evidence—gleaned from the then-classified investigative report on beatings, threats, and assaults of civilians in Vitina by members of the elite Eighty-second Airborne Division—was accepted as fact by both prosecution and defense.[16] Ultimately, eight other members of Ronghi's platoon in the 504th Parachute Infantry Regiment faced punishment (but not imprisonment) for their roles in the beatings and assaults.[17]

The commander of the unit, Lieutenant Colonel Michael D. Ellerbe, however, received a plum assignment at the Army War College, placing him in line for a possible promotion to general.[18] Many found Ellerbe's selection problematic in light of the recommendation in the investigative report that he face a reprimand for dereliction of duty for creating a climate in his battalion that led to the abuse of civilians.

Allegations of peacekeepers perpetrating sexual assault and rape emerged long before the Ronghi case. Not all of those cases involved local women. In March 1996, the *Washington Post* reported that one or more Czech soldiers allegedly raped a female American peacekeeper in Bosnia near the Czech barracks in the British-controlled zone.[19] And in June 2001, two British peacekeepers in Bosnia faced charges for rape of a Dutch male, a corporal, aged twenty-four.[20]

Even as the war in Bosnia and Herzegovina still raged, reports surfaced of peacekeeper sexual misconduct. As reports of systematic rape and "ethnic cleansing" in Bosnia dominated the headlines around the world, the Canadian media hailed Canadian peacekeepers for protecting three hundred patients in a dilapidated mental hospital in Bakovici, Bosnia. But later reports indicated that some of those soldiers had engaged in serious misconduct: in 1996, the commander of Canada's army admitted to reporters that thirty-four soldiers faced disciplinary action for alcohol abuse, sexual misconduct, black-market activities, and violence against patients at Bakovici.[21] A final report issued in January 1997 implicated forty-seven peacekeepers and condemned one for sexual misconduct with a patient in the mental hospital.[22]

Military Peacekeepers and Sexual Harassment

Some of the abuse did not rise to the level of sexual assault but nevertheless qualified as sexual harassment under United States law and international standards.[23] In 1996, Hungarian women employed in the kitchens serving United States troops stationed in nearby Taszar, Hungary, complained that some United States soldiers and military contractors (see infra) sexually harassed them. One woman reported that an American soldier offered her $130 to have sex with him. Another Hungarian kitchen worker told a reporter for the Associated Press that her American boss frequently groped her. She stated that he "feels me up on the pretext of a body search every day."[24] The United States Army Criminal Investigation Division undertook an investigation; one soldier faced pandering charges for soliciting sex for money from one of the Hungarian kitchen workers.[25]

In Bosnia and Herzegovina, local women interviewed in 1998 complained that peacekeepers, ostensibly in the country to protect them, made unwelcome sexual advances. In one case a local activist stated that a truck full of soldiers pulled up beside her and a friend along a road in Sarajevo and offered the women money to have sex with them.[26]

Similarly, in Kosovo, soon after the arrival of NATO troops, local women began to complain of catcalls and sexual harassment on the streets of the capital, Pristina. In other cases, however, the harassment came closer to home. In the euphoria of NATO's entry into the province, Kosovar Albanian families opened their homes and, more importantly, their bathrooms and showers to soldiers. According to one NGO leader in Pristina, the troops lived without bathing facilities or warm water in the early weeks after their arrival. Local families invited soldiers in, supplying warm water, towels, and hospitality. In one case, an American soldier, arriving as a shower guest, requested—perhaps jokingly—that the young Kosovar Albanian woman who greeted him at the door shower with him in order to wash his back.[27] This sexually suggestive remark both offended and shocked the young woman. More disturbingly, however, the uniformed soldier made the remark on the heels of a vicious "ethnic cleansing" campaign that included threats of rape, sexual assault, and torture by soldiers and paramilitaries.[28] In that context, what some might dismiss as "mild" sexual harassment took on a darker shadow of threat.

Military Peacekeepers and Sexual "Misconduct": Involvement in Trafficking and Forced Prostitution

In Bosnia and Herzegovina, internal police reports, court documents, and interviews with victims conducted in 1999 and 2001 pointed to limited involvement in trafficking by military peacekeeping personnel.[29] In one case, a trafficked woman interviewed by IPTF human rights officers reported that a Russian SFOR soldier transported her to Bosnia and Herzegovina, where he sold her and her friend to a bar and brothel owner.[30]

SFOR soldiers occasionally turned up with women in their cars, prompting accusations that they engaged in trafficking or transported trafficked and other women for purposes of prostitution. In May 2001, the Associated Press reported that a United States SFOR soldier fled the scene of an accident in Gornje Dubrave, leaving two badly injured female passengers, both Moldovan, in the wreckage in front of a bar.[31] The women, who did not have passports or residency or work permits, may have been trafficked.[32]

International Police and Sexual Assault

International police monitors stationed in the Balkans also committed abuses against local women and girls, often with impunity. In 1997, United Nations investigators received information that a fifty-three-year-old IPTF monitor, a former Miami police officer, had committed statutory rape. The United Nations investigated allegations that the officer had a sexual relationship with a thirteen-year-old Bosnian girl; the IPTF officer countered that the girl was actually seventeen years old.[33] Although DynCorp, the contractor employing all of the United States IPTF officers, stripped the monitor of his police gear and fired him, he never faced prosecution. Steve Smith, formerly a UN IPTF officer in Stolac, told the *Washington Post*, "For the Americans . . . there are no professional consequences unless they want to keep working for DynCorp. . . . The [IPTF officers] are making $85,000 in a place where everyone else is making $5,000 and they're chasing whores, they're shacking up with young women, and they're basically just having a good time."[34]

These comments raise serious concerns about the privatization of international policing operations and the implications for discipline and criminal prosecution. As discussed below, the United States is the only state to use private contractors as police officers for CIVPOL contingents.[35]

International Police and Trafficking for Forced Prostitution

In Bosnia, internal IPTF reports, interviews with monitors, and testimony of trafficking victims all indicated that some IPTF monitors went to brothels as clients. Others arranged for trafficked women to be delivered to their residences. A smaller number of IPTF monitors in Bosnia purchased women and their passports from traffickers and brothel owners. It is impossible to estimate the extent to which IPTF monitors engaged in trafficking-related offenses. But, by August 2001, more than twenty-four monitors—including German, Pakistani, Fijian, American, Spanish, and British nationals—had faced repatriation (either voluntary or forced) for misconduct ranging from bribery to sexual impropriety.[36]

One notorious case hit the headlines in Bosnia and Herzegovina. Raids of three nightclubs conducted in November 2000 resulted in the repatriation of at least six IPTF monitors—two Americans, two Spaniards, and two British officers—for "exceeding the mandate" of the IPTF.[37] United Nations officials criticized the monitors for carrying out the raids without the participation of the local police. United Nations officials vociferously denied allegations made by Milorad Milakovic, manager of the nightclubs raided, that an American IPTF monitor had demanded twenty thousand deutsche marks in protection money from him.[38] But the United Nations remained silent about allegations that the women "rescued" in the brothel raids recognized at least nine of the IPTF monitors as their clients. One of the women interviewed by United Nations investigators stated: "IPTF members were my clients too. I don't know their names, but they were Americans, Spanish, and Mexicans. Once an IPTF member has taken me to a hotel for two hours. I don't know his name, but he was staying in Prijedor. That IPTF member spoke Serbian a little bit. I don't know which country he was from."[39]

The Prijedor case represented only the tip of the iceberg. Throughout the Federation and Republika Srpska, trafficked women interviewed by IPTF human rights monitors recognized other IPTF officers as their clients in the brothels. In Doboj, IPTF monitors reported to the Joint Task Force, an investigation unit:

> We had raids in December against those [brothels] and afterwards several girls came to Doboj IPTF Station and reported to Human Rights [officers] that they had been held as sex slaves. Among others they named several IPTF personnel and language assistants who have visited or frequently visited those places. The reports and girls were taken to Sarajevo for further investigation, but we never heard something back.[40]

IPTF officers' involvement as clients in the brothels destroyed the trust of trafficked women who might have otherwise fled to IPTF stations to escape from their owners. Instead, the women had to find other routes of escape. Mara Radovanovic, director of the antitrafficking NGO Lara in Bijeljina, said, "The [trafficked women] knew that some people from IPTF were customers, so when the women escaped they went to the SFOR base."[41] While allegations of SFOR soldier involvement as clients also existed, the women apparently believed that they would be more likely to receive assistance at the base.[42]

More damning than participation as clients, however, was evidence that some IPTF monitors purchased women and their passports outright. Some attempted to justify this afterward, claiming that they had "rescued" the women. From the perspective of the trafficking victims, however, the sale often meant nothing more than a transfer from one owner to another. An

American IPTF monitor purchased one trafficked woman for six thousand deutsche marks.[43] A high-level United Nations official noted that another IPTF monitor approached him and confessed that he had purchased several women and repatriated them. He stated, "One IPTF monitor bought a couple of women and bought them tickets to go home. This IPTF officer uses the prostitutes and then buys them from the owners to send them home. He confided this to me."[44] The monitor did not face any disciplinary action.

In at least one case in Bosnia, an IPTF monitor faced allegations that he had engaged directly in trafficking. David Lamb, a Philadelphia police officer who spent two years as a human rights investigator in Bosnia, told the Associated Press of a trafficking case involving a Romanian IPTF officer who, together with his wife, managed a brothel in Bosnia and Herzegovina and allegedly recruited and trafficked women from Romania into Bosnia.[45] The Romanian Embassy in Washington, DC, denied the allegations, claiming that all of the Romanian officers had been cleared of wrongdoing.

In Kosovo, the United Nations admitted in the summer of 2001 that four civilian police monitors had faced investigation on allegations of involvement in trafficking. The allegations included charges that one American civilian police monitor had transported trafficked women from the border to the brothels in exchange for money and sex. Two American policemen and one Romanian faced allegations that they had helped the owner of a brothel. Another American and the Romanian were accused of tipping off the owner of a brothel that a raid was imminent. However, in the final public report on the matter, the United Nations officials stated that the four monitors faced disciplinary measures but that none would face criminal charges. Two of the officers were repatriated, and two received letters of reprimand.[46]

Civilian Military Contractors and Sexual "Misconduct": Trafficking of Women for Forced Prostitution

Most of the key allegations of trafficking in Bosnia and Herzegovina related to contractors, who were accused of buying and selling women, transporting trafficked women, and, in one case, violence against trafficked women. Local police in Bosnia reported that trucks with SFOR contractor license plates filled the parking lots of nightclubs in the area; trafficked women from Romania, Ukraine, and Moldova filled the nightclubs.[47] Police also reported that one SFOR contractor made pornographic films of himself having sex with allegedly trafficked women from nearby brothels. According to a United States Army Criminal Investigation Division report, the film included footage of rape: "During the encounter the male leaves the view of the camera and returns with what seemed to be a bottle of oil. At the time the male returns to the bed, where the female was locate[d], the female sees the bottle and tells the male 'no' numerous times. The male gives her a reply and begins to have intercourse with the female again."[48]

One of the contractors interviewed by the United States Army investigators during the course of the investigation admitted that he had purchased a woman from "Debeli," Bosnian for "little fat boy," the owner of the local brothel, Harley Davidson. In the final United States Army report, however, investigators concluded only:

> [Name withheld] committed the offenses of illicit possession of a weapon and procuring and pandering when he purchased an UZI, 9 mm, Automatic machine pistol . . . and the freedom of a Moldavian prostitute for 1,600 DM from the owner of Harley Davidson's bar. . . . [Name withheld] committed the offense of procuring and pandering when he solicited sexual intercourse from two female prostitutes who worked at the Harley Davidson's bar.[49]

Because the military contractors lived in private housing and could move around freely, they had more opportunity to purchase, hide, and house trafficked women. An IPTF human rights officer interviewed in Bosnia said:

> Previously we had a case, a woman was discovered in private accommodation. [The contractor] had bought her and used her. She gave her statement and he was repatriated in twenty-four hours. On May 11, there was a case where an American bought a woman. . . . They buy women for the night and it happens that they get caught in cars. Prostitution is not allowed, but not really forbidden here either. It is a small violation. But it compromises our image for people in uniform to be there.[50]

A United Nations report on trafficking also highlighted another case of an SFOR contractor who purchased two women.[51] In December 1999, local police found a Romanian woman and a Moldovan woman locked inside the apartment of an SFOR civilian contractor in Vlasenica. The women, one of whom was a girl of sixteen, claimed that they were held against their will and told local police that the SFOR contractor had paid a bar owner seven thousand deutsche marks to purchase them. NATO declined to waive his immunity, and the man left Bosnia and Herzegovina a few days later. According to the United Nations report, his employer relieved him of his duties for misconduct.[52]

Immunity and Impunity

Under the Dayton Accords, IPTF monitors and SFOR soldiers enjoy complete diplomatic immunity.[53] SFOR civilian contractors, in contrast, have only functional immunity.[54] Legal niceties of immunity aside, United States civilian contractors and police have enjoyed almost complete impunity for purchase of women as chattel and involvement in trafficking of women and girls. United States soldiers, who are subject to the Uniform Code of Military Justice (UCMJ), may face charges before courts-martial, but not so for contractors and civilian police officers.

On the civilian policing front, the United Nations promulgates a fiction that all IPTF and CIVPOL monitors face prosecution at home for the crimes they commit in Bosnia and Herzegovina or Kosovo. For United States civilian police monitors, however, this is a legal impossibility. United States courts do not have jurisdiction over the crimes the officers commit while serving abroad.[55] Ironically, United States police officers also face little danger of disciplinary proceedings by their own police units back in the United States. Because the United States lacks a federal police force, individual police officers are recruited for service in international missions from their local departments.[56] Many of the officers who serve in the United States contingent have already retired from their local departments, rendering disciplinary action an even more remote possibility.

Until Congress passed the Military Extraterritorial Jurisdiction Act (MEJA) in 2000, United States courts also lacked jurisdiction over crimes committed by military contractors. The passage of MEJA extended jurisdiction for felonies carrying a penalty of imprisonment for one year or more.[57] But in practice, the United States military has turned investigation records over to local Bosnian police for prosecution, conveniently ignoring the articles of the Dayton Accords forbidding local Bosnian law enforcement officials from detaining members of the international community.[58] Ironically, the United States Army report in the military contractor case outlined above indicated that the local government would take over the prosecutions of the contractors. But two factors eliminated the possibility of prosecution in Bosnia: First, the United States contractors returned to the United States almost immediately, effectively thwarting any effort by the Bosnian authorities to press charges. Second, because of the Dayton provisions, the local authorities had no intention of attempting to prosecute the contractors, believing it to be outside their jurisdiction. Discussing involvement in criminal activities by internationals, the state prosecutor for Republika Srpska said, "These allegations are not in the competence of the national prosecutor's office. They have immunity. . . . I am not entitled to bring charges."[59]

As a rule, United States IPTF monitors and SFOR civilian contractors face no consequences whatsoever—beyond the potential loss of their job—for participation in trafficking or for acts of sexual harassment. Julian Harston, deputy special representative of the secretary-general in Bosnia, stated in an interview: "[There's] some more sense now than one year ago. It's clear to most police [IPTF] they shouldn't be customers or friends of traffickers—you'll have a sporting chance of discipline. They are sent home. Discipline is difficult in the UN."[60]

But IPTF Deputy Commissioner Dennis Laducer confirmed that being sent home did not translate into a criminal prosecution for United States IPTF monitors: "I don't think that anyone has been prosecuted [in the United States] for this. . . . Immunity is from the UN and the immunity is not ours [the United States'] to waive. It is up to [the Department of] State whether they prosecute him. I don't know what happened. Did they pass this to Department of Justice? I don't know."[61]

Instead of facilitating prosecution of employees found to have committed misconduct, one United States contractor, DynCorp, fired two employees who sought to expose international involvement and complicity in trafficking. By August 2001, DynCorp, the contractor for both the United States IPTF contract and an SFOR logistics contract, faced two wrongful termination lawsuits alleging retaliation. One, brought by Kathy Bolkovac, a former IPTF human rights officer, charged that DynCorp had fired her after she sent a memorandum on trafficking and international involvement to all the members of the United Nations mission.[62] The second, brought by Ben Johnston, a helicopter mechanic from Texas, alleged that DynCorp had terminated his employment abruptly after he went to the United States Army Criminal Investigation Division at Eagle Base in Bosnia with allegations that DynCorp employees were engaged in the buying and selling of women and girls, some as young as fourteen.[63] These cases were still pending at the time of this writing.

Privatization: Implications for Accountability

Controversy over the privatization of policing rages within the community of scholars and practitioners working on international policing issues. While some view subcontracting as an economical and efficient method to muster a police force, others have argued that the United States should create a federal police force roster for officers willing to serve abroad.[64] From the perspective of advocates for women's human rights, the current system—which maintains as its maximum penalty termination and repatriation—lacks sufficient safeguards to protect women and girls. Apart from the fundamental problem of complete impunity from criminal prosecution, the privatized system also raises questions of recruiting and vetting of personnel.[65]

SFOR civilian contractors have also enjoyed de facto if not de jure impunity for these infractions. Again, the privatization of these personnel raises questions of discipline and the fairness of mere dismissal and repatriation as punishment for acts that would otherwise be prosecuted as criminal. Given the fact that extraterritorial jurisdiction over crimes committed by civilian contractors to the military does exist in the United States, the record to date also raises serious questions about the mechanisms in place to ensure that reports of criminal activities committed while abroad follow the perpetrator home.

Recommendations

- Revisit the privatization/"federalization" debate. Serious consideration must be given to the use of private contractors as international police officers and as logistic support personnel to the military. Some scholars and practitioners have suggested eliminating the contractor system and replacing it with a federalized police force designed for rapid deployment to United Nations missions abroad. Options should be considered from the perspective of protecting civilians and women's human rights.
- Develop reporting systems designed to end impunity. Without better mechanisms to ensure that investigative reports follow these United States citizens home, perpetrators of crimes relating to trafficking and violence against women will evade prosecution.
- Waive immunity. The United Nations has shown itself completely loath to waive immunity for international personnel who engage in criminal activities while at mission. This blanket unwillingness to waive immunity must be replaced with a more nuanced approach to justice and jurisdiction.
- Enhance jurisdiction. In the case of military and civilian contractors, status-of-forces agreements should drop "exclusive jurisdiction" of contributing states and substitute "primary jurisdiction."[66] This would allow states to prosecute perpetrators where the contributing state fails to exercise jurisdiction. Safeguards must be put into place to ensure that countries do not prosecute foreign nationals on trumped-up charges.
- Introduce clear disciplinary measures. Aside from the obvious solution of improved training on women's human rights, trafficking in persons, and sexual harassment for peacekeepers, civilian contractors, and civilian police sent on peacekeeping missions, the remedies to eliminate violence against women and involvement in trafficking-related offenses by peacekeepers, civilian contractors, and police monitors must be systematic. Training programs should include the participation of experts on these issues. Disciplinary standards should be clear and transparent.
- Increase transparency of disciplinary proceedings. A lack of transparency has obfuscated the involvement of internationals in crimes against women. This failure to disclose disciplinary measures sends a message

that no one faces penalties for such behavior beyond repatriation. Prosecutions for misconduct—either in the country of the mission or in the international staff member's own country—would begin to shift that perception.

- Increase the number of qualified women staff members with training in women's human rights issues at missions. In Bosnia and Kosovo, female staff members first sounded the alarm that trafficking had mushroomed. Those female staff members, who brought with them a highly sophisticated understanding of the phenomena of violence against women and trafficking, have made an enormous impact on efforts to police the local police and the United Nations. The inclusion of women experts on sexual violence and trafficking for forced prostitution and other forms of forced labor is essential to combating this scourge. With leadership from female staff members, UNMIBH and UNMIK have both implemented reasonably successful antitrafficking measures over the past year.[67]

Notes

1. The Organization for Security and Cooperation in Europe (OSCE), United Nations Interim Administration Mission in Kosovo (UNMIK), United Nations Mission in Bosnia and Herzegovina (UNMIBH), International Police Task Force (IPTF), Kosovo Force (KFOR), Stabilization Force (SFOR), Joint Commission Observers (JCO), and Office of the High Representative (OHR).

2. Ronghi, thirty-five at the time of the incident, was tried and convicted by a court-martial in Germany. For a full account of the incident, see Steve Erlanger, "The Ugliest American," *New York Times Magazine*, April 2, 2000. Ronghi received a sentence of life without possibility of parole, which he will serve at Fort Leavenworth, Kansas. He also received a reduction in rank, forfeiture of all pay and allowances, and a dishonorable discharge. George Boehmer, "Ohio GI Gets Life Sentence for Killing Ethnic Albanian Girl in Kosovo," Associated Press, August 2000, U.S. t 2.

3. R. Jeffrey Smith, "Army Probes Behavior of U.S. Soldiers in Kosovo," *Washington Post*, January 28, 2000, A17.

4. Robert Burns, "Army May Further Punish Personnel for Misdeeds in Kosovo," Fox News, available at http://www.foxnews.com/national/12-0200/army_kosovo.sml.

5. This chapter focuses almost exclusively on United States military and civilian personnel. Much of the information was gained through Freedom of Information Act (FOIA) requests to United States government agencies. In addition, European governments refused to provide information on cases involving their nationals.

6. The Brahimi Report on United Nations peace operations notes that peace operations entail three principal activities: conflict prevention and peacemaking; peacekeeping; and peace building. As this chapter will show, abuses against women can occur in all three of these stages. See United Nations General Assembly, *Comprehen-*

sive Review of the Whole Question of Peacekeeping Operations in All Their Aspects, August 21, 2000, A/55/305-S/2000/809, par. 10.

7. The Dayton Peace Accords were signed in Paris on December 14, 1995. Annex 11 of the accords authorized the creation of the International Police Task Force; Annex 1A created the Implementation Force (IFOR). Deployment of the peacekeepers was authorized by UN Security Council Resolution 1035 (December 21, 1995). As of August 2001, the non-NATO countries participating in the Stabilization Force (SFOR) were Albania, Argentina, Austria, Bulgaria, Estonia, Finland, Ireland, Latvia, Lithuania, Morocco, Romania, Russia, Slovakia, Slovenia, and Sweden. In December 2000, the U.S. government shifted the deployment of soldiers to Bosnia and Herzegovina to the National Guard. By late 2002, the army planned to switch the entire command of the operation in Bosnia to National Guard rather than active-duty soldiers. See Steven Lee Myers, "Army Will Give National Guard the Entire U.S. Role in Bosnia," *New York Times*, December 5, 2000.

8. For an in-depth account of the formation and record of the IPTF, see Michael J. Dziedzic and Andrew Bair, "Bosnia and the International Police Task Force," in *Policing the New World Disorder: Peace Operations and Public Security*, ed. Robert B. Oakley, Michael J. Dziedzic, and Eliot M. Goldberg (Washington, DC: National Defense University Press, 1998). Also, for a critique of the IPTF's mandate, see Human Rights Watch, "Beyond Restraint: Politics and the Policing Agenda of the United Nations International Police Task Force," *Human Rights Watch Report* 10, no. 5(d) (June 1998).

9. The UN Security Council adopted Resolution 1244 on June 10, 1999, mandating that UNMIK have responsibility for civil administration, political and economic reconstruction, the judicial system, police, courts, prisons, and internal security in Kosovo. S/RES/1244 (1999). For a history of the creation of UNMIK, see Robert Perito, *The American Experience with Police in Peace Operations* (Clementsport, NS: Canadian Peacekeeping Press, 2002).

10. As of August 2001, the non-NATO countries were Argentina, Austria, Azerbaijan, Bulgaria, Estonia, Finland, Georgia, Ireland, Jordan, Lithuania, Morocco, Russia, Slovakia, Slovenia, Sweden, Switzerland, Ukraine, and the United Arab Emirates.

11. One hundred and forty-three of those officers are women.

12. Roberto Suro, "In Kosovo, an Uncertain Mission: Peacekeeping Troops Find Frustration, Little Appreciation," *Washington Post*, September 20, 2000, A1. The main U.S. base in Kosovo, the 1,000-acre Camp Bondsteel, was dubbed "The Death Star" by soldiers.

13. Cynthia Enloe notes that none of the other NATO governments who contributed soldiers to the Bosnian peacekeeping operations instituted such bans. She argues that the United States decided to implement these restrictions, which "American officials believed had worked well in Saudi Arabia during the Gulf War," in order to avoid potentially embarrassing misconduct by U.S. soldiers that might erode U.S. voter support for the mission in Bosnia. Cynthia Enloe, *Maneuvers: The International Politics of Militarizing Women's Lives* (Berkeley: University of California Press, 2000), 102–3.

14. For additional information on the role of the Joint Commission Observers, see Richard J. Newman, "Living with the Locals: A Very Public Mission," *U.S. News and*

World Report, July 6, 1998. The United States withdrew the JCOs in May 2000, stating that their mission was "accomplished." See Major Richard C. Sater, "Mission Accomplished," *Talon Magazine Online*, May 19, 2001, available at http://www.tfeagle.army .mil/tfetalon/archives/2001/tal051901/articles/psd.htm.

15. Suro, "In Kosovo, an Uncertain Mission." Women had reported similar sexually invasive and threatening bodily searches during the ethnic cleansing campaign by Serbian forces in 1999. See Human Rights Watch, *Kosovo: Rape as a Weapon of "Ethnic Cleansing"* (New York: Human Rights Watch, 2000), 15.

16. Associated Press, "Army Report Says Soldiers Abused Civilians in Kosovo," September 17, 2000.

17. Five other soldiers in the battalion were punished and three junior officers reprimanded. Thomas Ricks, "Officer Facing Discipline Gets Elite Post; Army Colonel Who Led Unit That Abused Civilians in Kosovo Picked for War College," *Washington Post*, October 19, 2000.

18. Ricks, "Officer Facing Discipline Gets Elite Post."

19. Dana Priest, "US Soldier in Bosnia Alleges Rape by Troops: American Woman Reportedly Was Attacked by Czech Soldiers Near Their Barracks," *Washington Post*, March 6, 1996. The article quoted a spokesman for the Czech contingent as stating, "The outcome is that she agreed to do it." He added that the two Czech soldiers would not be prosecuted under Czech law. The American soldier, who a U.S. Army spokeswoman reported was extremely traumatized by the attack, was evacuated to a military hospital in Hungary.

20. Danny Kemp, "Serviceman Flown Home in Bosnia Rape Claim Probe," Press Association News, June 15, 2001. The Dutch soldier alleged that the two British soldiers had raped him at the British base at Mrkonjic Grad in northwest Bosnia on June 9 or 10. Only one of the servicemen was identified. After repatriating the soldier to Britain, the British forces launched an investigation into the allegations.

21. Craig Turner, "Canada's Peacekeeper Role Marred: Abuse Reports in Somalia, Bosnia Stir Military Crisis," *Dallas Morning News*, August 4, 1996, A24.

22. Allan Thompson, "Army Chief Is Recalled for Drinking in Kosovo: Lt.-Col. Steve Bryan Ordered Home with Junior Officer," *Toronto Star*, October 2, 1999, 1. According to one account carried in the Montreal newspaper *Le Devoir*, a Canadian soldier shaved the genitals, armpits, and legs of a seventeen-year-old female patient in the mental hospital. See BosNet, "Canada's Shame," July 24, 1996, available at http://www .bosnet.org/archive/bosnet.w3archive/9607/msg00148.html.

23. Sexual harassment, which includes unwelcome sexual advances, requests for sexual favors, and other verbal or physical conduct of a sexual nature is prohibited in employment under Title VII of the U.S. code (29 C.F.R. Section 1604.11[a] [1985]). The Convention on the Elimination of All Forms of Discrimination against Women (CEDAW) has also held that sexual harassment is a form of sex discrimination prohibited under the convention. See General Recommendation 19, 1992, A/47/38.

24. Associated Press, "Hungarians Accuse Americans of Sexual Harassment and Exploitation," May 4, 1996. The workers formed a union to press their grievances. The troops were based in Hungary to support peacekeepers stationed in Bosnia and

Herzegovina. According to the press account, the vast majority of the complaints concerned U.S. military contractors rather than soldiers.

25. Department of the Army, U.S. Army Criminal Investigation Command, 515th Military Police Detachment, Case 0123-96-CID007-20027-6X2, May 20, 1996. Documents on the investigation obtained through a FOIA request.

26. S. P., interviewed by author, February 1998.

27. R. W., interviewed by author, Pristina, July 1999.

28. Human Rights Watch investigators found ninety-six credible cases of rape and other forms of sexual assault in Kosovo but concluded that the number was probably much higher. See Human Rights Watch, *Kosovo: Rape as a Weapon of "Ethnic Cleansing."*

29. Trafficking is defined in Article 3(a) of the Trafficking Protocol as "the recruitment, transportation, transfer, harboring or receipt of persons, by means of threat or use of force or other forms of coercion, of abduction, of fraud, of deception, of abuse of power or of position of vulnerability or of the giving or receiving of payments or benefits to achieve the consent of a person having control over another person, for the purpose of exploitation. Exploitation shall include, at a minimum, the exploitation of the prostitution of others or other forms of sexual exploitation, forced labor or services, slavery or practices similar to slavery, servitude or the removal of organs." General Assembly of the United Nations, *Protocol to Prevent, Suppress and Punish Trafficking in Persons, Especially Women and Children, Supplementing the United Nations Convention against Transnational Organized Crime.*

30. According to an official internal IPTF report, a Russian SFOR soldier named Sasha transported the two Ukrainian women to Bosnia and Herzegovina and sold them to the owner of the nightclub, "Cat." Dawn White, U.S. IPTF monitor who investigated the case, interviewed by author, March 19, 1999. Also, IPTF Incident Report 99/DOB/045, March 10, 1999.

31. Associated Press, "US Soldier Flees, Abandoning Injured Passengers in Crashed Car," May 30, 2001.

32. Both of the women involved in the accident gave reports to the local Bosnian police in Zivinice. One told police that she lost her passport in Lukavac, Lake Modrac; the second said that she had lost her passport in Serbia. Both of the women also noted that the driver, an American, was drunk at the time of the accident. The author obtained this transcript through a FOIA request. Zivinice Police Department, Statement Report 08-11/01-2, May 31, 2001.

33. Colum Lynch, "Misconduct, Corruption by US Police Mar Bosnia Mission," *Washington Post*, May 29, 2001, A1.

34. Lynch, "Misconduct, Corruption by US Police Mar Bosnia Mission."

35. Perito, *American Experience with Police in Peace Operations.*

36. William Kole and Aida Cerkez-Robinson, "UN Police Accused of Involvement in Prostitution in Bosnia," Associated Press, July 26, 2001.

37. Dennis Laducer, deputy commissioner of the IPTF, interviewed by author, Sarajevo, April 8, 2001.

38. Milkica Milojevic, "Milakovic Case Reached Both New York and the Investigative Judge in Prijedor: Prijedor Businessman Claims That He Is Not Guilty and That

the Process against Him Is Rigged," *Nezavisne Novine* (Republika Srpska Daily, Banja Luka), December 15, 2000.

39. Statement made by S. V. to IPTF [victim interview from Prijedor case], November 23, 2000.

40. UN Interoffice Memorandum to Vincent Coeurderoy, "Subject: Prostitution in Doboj: The Vila," March 20, 2001.

41. Mara Radovanovic, director of Lara, interviewed by author, Bijeljina, March 22, 2001.

42. The larger size of the SFOR base and the more formally structured military environment may have convinced the women to appeal to the military, rather than the international police. It is also important to note that trafficked women have pointed to high levels of involvement by local police, closing that avenue for protection as well.

43. IPTF officer, interviewed by author, Sarajevo, March 19, 2001.

44. Senior UN official, interviewed by author, Sarajevo, March 26, 2001.

45. Kole and Cerkez-Robinson, "UN Police Accused of Involvement in Prostitution."

46. F. Osmani, "Two International Policemen Expelled for Connection to Prostitution in Kosova," KosovaLive Newswire, August 13, 2001.

47. Zivinice chief of police, interviewed by author, Zivinice, March 27, 2001.

48. United States Army Criminal Investigation Command, "Agents Investigation Report," ROI 0075-00-CID597-49891, 3.

49. Department of the Army, US Army Criminal Investigations Command, 48th MP Detachment (CID), Eagle Base, Bosnia and Herzegovina, "CID Report of Investigation," 1, on file with the author.

50. IPTF human rights officer, interviewed by author, Tuzla, March 24, 2001.

51. United Nations Mission in Bosnia and Herzegovina Legal and Human Rights Office and UN Office of the High Commissioner for Human Rights in Bosnia and Herzegovina, "Report on Joint Trafficking Project," May 2000, 15, on file with the author.

52. United Nations Mission in Bosnia and Herzegovina Legal and Human Rights Office and UN Office of the High Commissioner for Human Rights in Bosnia and Herzegovina, "Report on Joint Trafficking Project."

53. IPTF officers are accorded the same status as officials of the UN as outlined in Sections 18 and 19 of the 1946 Convention on the Privileges and Immunities of the United Nations. See *General Framework for Peace in Bosnia and Herzegovina*, Annex 11.

54. Article VI of the Convention on the Privileges and Immunities of the United Nations states: Experts (other than officials coming within the scope of Article V) performing missions for the United Nations shall be accorded such privileges and immunities as are necessary for the independent exercise of their functions during the period of their missions. This immunity is functional in the sense that experts are granted immunity from "legal process of every kind" only for words and acts performed in the course of their mission. Members of the U.S. military are subject to the Uniform Code of Military Justice (UCMJ) and are tried before court-martial.

55. According to an official in the Department of State responsible for the U.S. contributions to international civilian policing operations, not a single U.S. police officer

has faced criminal prosecution in the United States for criminal activities in the Balkans.

56. In all, the United States boasts nearly eighteen thousand separate local, county, and state police departments. Perito, *American Experience with Police in Peace Operations.*

57. 18 U.S.C. Sections 3261-3267 (2000).

58. Annex 1-A of the Dayton Peace Accords establishes that NATO personnel are under the exclusive jurisdiction of their respective nations. Although one reading of the annex would indicate that this provision does not apply to civilian contractors, in practice, local police do not believe that they have the authority to arrest and prosecute any members of the international community.

59. Borislav Dimitrievic, Republika Srpska chief prosecutor, interviewed by author, Banja Luka, March 29, 2001.

60. Julian Harston, deputy special representative of the secretary-general, interviewed by author, Sarajevo, April 9, 2001.

61. Laducer, interviewed by author, April 8, 2001.

62. Kathryn Bolkovac, former IPTF officer, interviewed by author, March 19, 2001.

63. Deposition of Benjamin Dean Johnston, *Johnston v. DynCorp, Inc.*, District Court, Tarrant County, TX, March 20, 2001.

64. To implement the Presidential Decision Directive "Strengthening Criminal Justice Systems in Support of Peace Operations (PDD-71)," issued by the Clinton administration in February 2000, the State Department proposed to create a "ready roster" of U.S. police officers available to participate in CIVPOL operations. But the State Department explicitly rejected the option of seeking new legislation to "federalize" U.S. civilian police contingents. For an analysis of the PDD-71 and attempts at implementation, see Perito, *American Experience with Police in Peace Operations.*

65. Two of the highest-ranking U.S. officers stationed in Bosnia and Herzegovina had faced sexual harassment lawsuits in their U.S. police departments prior to volunteering for service in the Balkans.

66. Barbara Bedont, "International Criminal Justice: Implications for Peacekeeping," report prepared for the Canadian Department of Foreign Affairs and International Trade, December 2001.

67. UNMIK created the Trafficking and Prostitution Investigation Unit. UNMIBH created S.T.O.P., or the Special Trafficking Operations Programme.

8

The Namibian Peace Operation in a Gender Context

Louise Olsson

IT IS OFTEN HEARD THAT INCLUDING GENDER in peacekeeping would seriously implicate the United Nations in the private, rather than the public, affairs of a state. Continued "gender neutrality" safeguards against any "inappropriate," or unwelcome, involvement, and it gives the impression that as long as there is no focus on gender issues, they do not exist. This chapter argues the opposite: gender issues are in fact already present in armed conflict, and a peacekeeping operation can affect these developments—whether or not the United Nations is "gender aware." Studies find that "'unisex policies'[1] and gender-neutral legislation have differential impact on men and women and might, in some cases, worsen women's situation."[2] The chapter seeks to problematize the issue of gender in the host society with regard to United Nations attempts to assist peace through peace operations and focuses on the United Nations Transitional Assistance Group (UNTAG) in Namibia in 1989–1990. Namibian women played important roles during the armed conflict but, during the resolution process, appeared to become invisible.

Gender and Peacekeeping

During the 1990s, a process was ongoing with regard to gender in conflict resolution processes, and in peacekeeping in particular. Reports from the United Nations operations in Mozambique and Cambodia had alerted the international community to the unwanted behavior of certain peacekeepers toward local women and to undesirable effects of peacekeeping, such as increased prostitution. One reaction of the international community to the negative effects on local women was the United Nations project Mainstreaming a Gender Perspective in Multidimensional Peacekeeping Operations, which resulted in the Windhoek Declaration and the Namibian Plan of Action and contributed to the United Nations Security Council Resolution 1325 (see Mazurana et al., introduction). These documents acknowledge the complexity of gender and peacekeeping and the need to adapt the operations in accordance with the policy of gender mainstreaming.[3]

I have argued that the Namibian operation could have been a model from which many lessons regarding gender mainstreaming might have been learned, foremost regarding women's situation in the operation itself.[4] However, the importance of gender and peacekeeping is not limited to this aspect of mainstreaming. The Beijing Declaration and Platform for Action states that: "In addressing armed or other conflicts, an active and visible policy of mainstreaming a gender perspective into all policies and programs should be promoted so that before decisions are taken an analysis is made of the effects on women and men, respectively."[5]

This indicates that if the United Nations is to gender mainstream its operations, it needs not only to consider important organizational aspects, such as the recruitment process and including women in decision-making positions of the United Nations,[6] but also to adjust the operation to the situation of the women and men in the host society. Presently, however, gender awareness in peacekeeping is reminiscent of Adam Roberts's critique of how international intervention has been handled in a procrustean manner by the United Nations due to the formulation of the Charter.[7] Just as Procrustes, a notorious host from Greek mythology, fit wandering travelers to his only bed by either cutting off their legs or stretching them, so has peacekeeping followed a "one-size-fits-all" model. Gender awareness in peacekeeping needs to proceed in the opposite manner, where the operation itself is adjusted to fit the circumstances. Within this, it is important to stress that a thorough examination of the gender relations in the host country is vital. Today, when the United Nations has accepted the objective of gender mainstreaming—and thereby its goal of gender equality—procrustean solutions to the host societies' gender dynamics are no longer acceptable.

This chapter focuses on the situation of Namibian women during the conflict between the South West African Peoples Organization (SWAPO) and South Africa from the 1960s to 1988 and the resolution process in 1989–1990. It discusses issues that are important to consider in order to achieve gender mainstreaming and a more gender-equal peace. I focus on certain aspects of gender equality that are important in order to achieve gender mainstreaming and, in an antiprocrustean spirit, seek to avoid "cutting off any necessary limbs." Namibia was the first country in which a multidimensional peace-keeping operation took place, and its case is a sound starting point for discussing these issues because the conflict displays several gender dimensions in the internal arena, mainly with regard to SWAPO's handling of gender issues, as well as external development parallel to the internal where gender played a different role. The chapter focuses specifically on the changing role of women prior to, during, and after the conflict and what role the United Nations peacekeeping operations played with regard to gender equality.

Gender-Specific Features of the Namibian Conflict

Even though Namibian gendered power structures during the conflict could be characterized as patriarchal, with few women acting outside the private, family sphere, the strategy to organize women in the conflict resulted in the creation of a basis for increased equality in Namibia.[8] The struggle for Namibian independence from South Africa began in the late 1960s, when what was later to become SWAPO took up weapons against the South African army. Whether or not women participated in the conflict, as well as their role, depended on which ethnic group they belonged to, their social status, which area they lived in, and whether they had been forced to seek refuge in camps along the Angolan and Zambian borders. Significantly, a number of Namibian women were involved in the public sphere of the conflict, such as in military units. Many Namibian women were also victims of the protracted conflict.

The conflict created large numbers of internally displaced persons and refugees. These Namibian refugees, the majority of whom lived on the borders of Angola and Zambia, came to play a vital part in the struggle. In the early years of the armed conflict, the vast majority of those forced into exile were male. This was due to the fact that the main internal parties in the armed struggle against South Africa were organizations for contract workers, and only men had access to such contracts. In the mid-1970s, when the escalation of the conflict resulted in the severe repression of the civilian population in the north, this pattern began to change. Of the approximately four thousand new refugees in 1974, an estimated 20 percent were women. In the late 1970s, with the continuously severe situation in the war zone, whole families fled, together with groups of students and young people, from the north and south of the country. By 1989, women composed about 40 percent of the adult refugee population.[9]

Another aspect of the conflict with specific gender implications concerns violence. Violence in war tends to be gender specific. The majority of combat casualties tend to be male. However, due to the rise in civilian casualties in armed conflict, the number of female dead has increased dramatically. Females are also often subjected to violence in the form of abuse, rape, including mass rape, forced sterilization, and forced abortion. The aim of this form of warfare is to display power, as well as physically injure the women. The results are often serious not only for the individual but also for the society.[10] The Namibian conflict was no exception. Many sources, even if independent sources are scarce, give examples of how sexual violence was used. Many of them name Koevoet, that is, the paramilitary, as the main culprits. However, the South Africa–supported South West African Troops (SWAFT)[11] seem to have been involved as well.[12] A former female SWAPO combatant, Tekla Shikola, claims that sexual violence and rape occurred more frequently in the war zones in northern Namibia. She claims that SWAFT were the main perpetrators of this war crime. According to her, this was a strategy by South Africa to "divide and rule," making sure that it was Namibian troops who raped Namibian women.[13] Sexual violence in the Namibian conflict appears to have been used also as torture of female political prisoners.[14] Why, then, were women targeted? One reason could have been to destroy the Namibian society. Another could have been to directly threaten women because from early on in the struggle women had become an integrated part.

Organizing Women in the Struggle for Independence

Women in Namibia became more and more involved in the struggle as the conflict developed. Heike Becker, a researcher focusing on Namibian women's organizations and their development, argues that since women participated predominantly at the community level, the role of women during the early years of the independence struggle has gone largely unnoticed. One of the early signs of increasing tension between South Africa and the Namibian population concerned the forced removal of the population from the traditional villages in the 1950s. Considering that this was an issue that in many ways directly affected women by bringing conflict to the private sphere, women participated to a high degree.[15] Women also began organizing themselves during this period.[16] However, Becker observes that as the conflict regarding independence evolved in the public sphere in the 1960s, women were initially excluded from direct participation in the struggle for independence.[17] In 1970, however, the total domination of men in SWAPO was reduced. In accordance with the so-called Tanga strategy,[18] SWAPO's Consultative Congress decided to recognize a SWAPO Women's Council (SWC), which would then be responsible for organizing female participation in the struggle.[19] The result was that women became involved in the liberation movement in all positions, including as supporters, medics, and combatants. The latter was the consequence of intense lobbying by the SWC.

The SWC had its strongest support in the refugee population and in the north of Namibia, but it also operated in central and southern Namibia. The women of SWC, like male independence activists, were subject to repression, and several of the female leaders of the SWC working in Namibia also had to flee the country.[20]

The war divided Namibia into two parts, and the warfare took place mainly in the north. Furthermore, in the 1980s, the forced conscription of all men over sixteen years of age in the south of Namibia helped create a rift in Namibian society between the north and the south.[21] This rift was also evident concerning women's organizations, since in the north and in the south women were organized in different forms of associations with different agendas. While women's organizations from the north were dominated by the SWC and were mostly concerned with independence, women's organizations in the south were more concerned with issues of social justice and equality. The Namibian Women's Voice (NWV) is an example. Unlike SWAPO's women's organization, NWV focused on issues not directly related to the war, for example, the low status of "black" women, as well as social and family disintegration, prostitution, and alcoholism. Nevertheless, these problems were seen as a direct consequence of the war.[22]

In SWAPO, the gender-equality question was on the agenda beginning in 1970 but was considered subordinate to the objective of independence. To focus equally on gender equality and independence was seen as increasing the risk of losing the internal unity of SWAPO. The importance of this arrangement was, for example, pointed out by the women representatives of SWAPO in the Women's Mid-Decade Conference in Copenhagen in 1980.[23] Nevertheless, during the extended struggle, SWAPO worked for gender equality, for example, by characterizing sexism as unacceptable behavior in the SWAPO constitution adopted in 1976. From the 1970s, SWAPO also considered sexist oppression as being a separate problem from that of apartheid. Inequality between the sexes was considered to place a double burden on women even if the removal of apartheid was seen as the necessary prerequisite for an effective solution to gender-specific oppression. Furthermore, even if the official policy of SWAPO did not state gender equality as a goal equal in importance to that of independence, the practical work of the organization, which educated both young men and young women in almost equal numbers and included women in the combat units, helped change the gender construction of femininity in this small group.[24]

The gender dimension was consequently integrated into the planning and operationalization of SWAPO's work. The SWC continuously endeavored to include gender-equality issues, such as the right to education and economic equality, but gender equality remained subordinate to the fight for independence.[25] Practical issues with regard to including women in the struggle, however, had to be handled. Again sources are scarce, but one example of practical gender issues is the procedure for handling pregnant combatants. Shikola has pointed out that many children were born in SWAPO camps during the liberation struggle to both combatants and supporters.[26] These children were supported by SWAPO as long as the liberation struggle continued. In order for mothers not to be separated from their children, pregnant female combatants were removed from the front and placed in the base camps to work with child care or the training of new soldiers. There are a few reports of former combatants returning to the front when the children reached school age, however.[27] According to Shikola, being a single mother, which often was the case because longer relationships at the front were impossible, became more of a problem when former SWAPO women returned to Namibia at the end of the armed conflict. They had limited means of supporting their children, and the war had prevented any contact with the father of the children or the woman's family in Namibia. On their return to Namibia they might therefore have no one to assist them.[28]

There were many gender issues being demanded by the SWC during the conflict, and some progress was made. However, the SWC was also considering possible future developments regarding gender equality. Reviews of actual results gained by women participating in liberation struggles in neighboring countries after the liberation movement had come to power indicated that the positive changes in gender relations gained in Namibia might not automatically be permanent or result in a more gender-equal postindependent state.[29] The international community was to play an important role with regard to the resolution phase.

Namibian Women and the International Community

The SWC saw the struggle for independence as a struggle against South Africa, as well as a struggle for a new society where the "emancipation of women is of paramount importance."[30] Due to the increased importance of women's issues internationally after the Third World Conference on Women held in Nairobi in 1985, this position became acknowledged by the internal as well as external parties in the years to come (see Mazurana et al., introduction). *The Nairobi Forward Looking Strategies* (NFLS), the main document of the Nairobi conference, particularly mentions the Namibian conflict. After the Nairobi conference, international organizations visiting Namibia more often specifically asked to meet women of local organizations, and funds available for Namibian women's organizations increased.[31]

The United Nations, mainly through the Commission of the Status of Women and the secretary-general, dealt directly with the issue of women under apartheid for an extensive period of time preceding the UNTAG mission. In January 1978, the secretary-general presented a report to the Social and Economic Council entitled *The Effects of Apartheid on the Status of Women in South Africa, Namibia and Southern Rhodesia.* The report discusses gender aspects of issues such as marital status, legal capacity, and property rights, as well as health care, education, and women's role in the political struggle.[32] Although it focuses mainly on the situation of women in South Africa, it provides examples of how apartheid affected women and men differently, an insight necessary for any policy of gender mainstreaming.[33]

The Foundation for Peace

Parallel to these internal and international developments regarding women and gender equality, a separate agenda was set regarding the creation of peace. The NFLS states that it is of utmost importance to increase the number of women in peace negotiations. The responsibility for achieving this is placed mainly on the governments involved in a conflict. The NFLS claims that the interest of women should be considered as equal to that of men in wanting to contribute to international peace and cooperation.[34] In view of the examples of the different roles women and men played in the Namibian conflict, it is worth considering whether this was taken into account in negotiations for a peace agreement. Indeed, it would be important to know whether there were any women participating in the negotiations or whether women's organizations were consulted.

The Negotiations: Men as Negotiators

The process of reaching a solution was slow, and the time that elapsed between the General Assembly's resolution on Namibia in 1966 and the UNTAG operation in 1989 can be divided into three different periods. All, however, were male dominated. In the first period, 1966–1976, the question was fervently discussed in the General Assembly, and occasionally in the Security Council and in the International Court of Justice (ICJ), but there was little progress regarding the negotiations. During the second period, 1977–1981, the Contact Group, consisting of the Federal Republic of Germany, Great Britain, France, Canada, and the United States of America, initiated diplomatic attempts to solve the conflict. In the last period, 1981–1988, the resolution of the conflict became linked to the Cold War and the regional power balance, that is, foremost, the withdrawal of Cuban troops from Angola.[35] No women played a dominant role in these negotiations. Moreover, because of the sensitive international situation and South Africa's strategy to link the issue of Namibian independence to Cuban troops in Angola, there was no formal peace agreement signed specifically for Namibia involving internal Namibian actors. Instead, the peace agreements from 1988, such as the Geneva Protocol, the Brazzaville Protocol, and the Bilateral Agreement, were negotiated and signed by Cuban, Angolan, and South African representatives. Consequently, the Namibian question was solved on the level above the internal actors. None of the gender issues that had developed during the conflict were addressed in these documents. If any women were involved in the discussions on the international level, they were not in any leading positions. However, when it came to the creation of peace inside Namibia, the internal parties played a more prominent role.

Internal Actors: Female Representation

Except for SWAPO, in the later periods led by Sam Nujoma, the majority of the internal Namibian organizations were mainly excluded from top negotiations. Despite the active work of the SWAPO's Women's Council, no women were among the front people of the organization internationally during the negotiations.[36] However, a few women did participate at the highest levels of SWAPO; notable among them was Libertine Amathilda. As a medical doctor, Amathilda had been one of the most important persons in the development of medical and health care for the exiled Namibian community, and she was a member of SWAPO's Central Committee. She set an important example with regard to encouraging other women to venture outside the traditional gender roles.

Another way for women to come to a position of power was through the SWC. The leader of the SWC was automatically a member of the Central Committee and had the main responsibility to ensure that Namibian women were aware of SWAPO's policies and programs. Furthermore, she was in charge of formulating programs and policies that specifically promoted women's special interests, such as equal access to education. The SWC continuously worked to elevate the importance of gender equality, for example, by organizing gender seminars for the leadership of SWAPO. The leader of the SWC was, however, elected by the Central Committee and could subsequently be removed from office by a vote in the Central Committee (which was mainly male dominated). Gender equality was also given a lower degree of importance than independence, and feminism was considered a Western idea that risked disuniting the movement.[37]

UNTAG

The conflict was consequently resolved on a level above the local population, which was frequently not even represented, by men or women, in the negotiations. When an agreement was reached in 1988, the possibility for the United Nations to implement an operation, which had been under development since the 1970s, finally appeared.

The mandate for the mission is given in Security Council Resolution 435/1978 and gives the United Nations, through the special representative of the secretary-general (SRSG), Mr. Martti Ahtisaari, and assisted by UNTAG, the main responsibility for assisting the Namibian people in the transfer of power from South Africa. The mandate was given to the SRSG to "ensure the early independence of Namibia through free elections under the supervision and control of the United Nations."[38] In addition, UNTAG was to ensure that all hostile acts ceased, troops were confined to base, discriminatory laws abandoned, political prisoners released, refugees returned, and law and order maintained impartially. In a departure from earlier peacekeeping missions, because the mission was to help create a new state, the civilian component was to carry as much weight in the attempts by the United Nations to solve the conflict in Namibia as the military component. The peacekeeping military troops were needed in order to provide a militarily neutral environment in which the civilian components could conduct peace building by creating trust between the parties and by constructing a political environment that would support the democratic election. The United Nations Civilian Police (CIVPOL), there to limit the number of small conflicts by ensuring an impartial upholding of law and order, were also important for peace building. No reference in the mandate is made to women or gender issues. Gender neutrality seems to be assumed: the formulation of the mandate makes use of the term "people" but gives no consideration to any gender differences. The extent to which women were included in "people" consequently depended on the interpretation, and operationalization, of the mandate by United Nations departments and staff.

Certain contemporary internal developments in the United Nations focused more on the situation for women than did the mandate of the Security Council. The Economic and Social Council adopted Resolution 1989/31 on the situation for women and children in Namibia. It supported Security Council Resolution 435/1978 but also pointed to the importance of taking into consideration the different needs of men, women, and children with respect to issues such as repatriation, human rights, and the right to vote. Concerning refugees, the Economic and Social Council urged governments, INGOs, and NGOs not only to assist refugees during the repatriation to Namibia but to continue supporting women and children throughout the transitional period. Finally, it requested the secretary-general to submit a thorough report on the implementation and monitoring of the NFLS concerning women and children in Namibia.[39]

Composition

With regard to the representation of women in the mission, there were too few women in the police and military components to be able to have a defining impact. The military component of UNTAG was headed by Force Commander Lieutenant General D. Perm Chand from India and consisted of several parts: three infantry battalions (from Kenya, Malaysia, and Finland); three hundred observers (from twenty-one states); logistics (two groups, one from Canada and one from Poland); and support units. The military components were to observe that South African Defense Forces (SADF) and SWAFT were confined to their respective military bases and supervise the truce that had been negotiated. This particular task became much more problematic after the clashes in the northern war zone between South African troops and the People's Liberation Army of Namibia (PLAN) on April 1, 1989, and resulted in the deaths of several hundred PLAN fighters.

Among the countries sending military personnel, only a few, such as Australia and Canada, sent female military personnel. Regarding the behavior of the international troops, there were some problems with the military troops in Namibia, even if these were not as severe as in some of the missions to follow the UNTAG operation (see Bedont, chapter 4, and Vandenberg, chapter 7). The fact that different military contingents have different records of how they have handled relations with the local population, not to mention the treatment of local women, was not an issue of considerable relevance in the selection process in the United Nations mission to Namibia or in later missions (Raven-Roberts, chapter 2).[40] If it were, then perhaps troops could be selected that were better equipped to handled the relations with the local population. However, the financial limitations, as well as the willingness of states to contribute, restrict the United Nations' possibilities.

CIVPOL was a part of the civilian component but had its own leadership. The police had participants from twenty-five countries, such as Austria, Bangladesh, Canada, India, New Zealand, and Singapore. Police Commander Steve Fanning from Ireland headed the CIVPOL component. Among his staff was a political adviser, Ugandan lawyer Rachel Mayanja. During the election period in November, CIVPOL reached maximum strength of approximately 1,500 officers. CIVPOL included a few women, most of them from New Zealand. No CIVPOL officers with special knowledge regarding gender-specific violence were sent by any national contingent.

Currently, there is an ongoing debate regarding the importance of including gender specialists in CIVPOL. One argument raised is that due to the degree of sexual violence in armed conflict and during the resolution phase, it is important to include such expertise. Deputy Inspector Shantilweh, who is coordinator of the Women and Child Protection Unit in the Namibian police in Windhoek, and who is herself a former refugee, argues that among the police officers chosen for a mission, there need to be a number of officers trained to deal with cases of sexual abuse, domestic violence, and gender-specific violence, especially since these forms of crimes are integral parts of armed conflict. She suggests that countries that have units specially trained for such jobs should be asked to send personnel with this expertise.[41]

The civilian component, responsible for elections and administration, had a much higher degree of women than the (nearly) all-male military and police components. It had a high degree of women in leadership positions: 30 percent of the regional directors and 40 percent of the civilian staff were women. This high percentage of women is almost unprecedented and was the result of a more unbiased recruitment process set up by the men responsible for the operation, namely, SRSG Ahtisaari and UNTAG Director-General Cederic Thornberry, and underlines the need for a gender-aware leadership (see Raven-Roberts, chapter 2). The leadership publicly encouraged all United Nations personnel to apply, which had not been done in earlier missions, ensuring that the process would be unbiased. The result was that many groups applied that had formerly abstained. One of these groups was an informal group within the United Nations, the Women's Group on Equal Rights. The UNTAG leadership also consciously recruited women to leadership positions based on their merit, a policy not easily accepted by all at United Nations Headquarters.[42] Moreover, this high degree of women, many of them gender aware, resulted in aspects of practical gender mainstreaming. Gender-aware female staff sought to work with Namibian women to a higher degree than did their male counterparts.

In an article focusing on gender in participatory planning, researcher June Lennie brings up issues that are relevant in the work of gender mainstreaming. According to her, two features are important: women's perspectives and the gendered power structures in society. When a peacekeeping operation interacts with the local community to achieve peace, it encounters the same problematic. For example, UNTAG's mandate was to arrange information meetings on democracy in order for the elections to be free and fair. Lennie states that if information meetings are held only in public buildings, a series of gender issues appear. First of all, what are the circumstances surrounding the meetings? Do they suit both men's and women's work roles? The second area concerns the gendered power structures and norms. What are the roles of men and women in public life? Does the meeting take place in a public arena in which women normally never participate? In Namibia, female staff, such as Isel Rivero, discovered that during the United Nations' information meetings only men participated in the discussion; the women sat quietly in the back. Additional meetings were therefore arranged in cooperation with civil associations, for example, churches, and held in public places where women were the central actors in order to also reach them with election information.[43]

Apart from logistic issues, there are consequently larger, structural issues to consider with regard to gender and peacekeeping operations. Since these change over time, as do the construction of femininity and masculinity, it is important to consider such questions as how women's situation changed, and what roles women played, during the conflict that preceded the peacekeeping operation. The inclusion of gender-aware women in UNTAG helped, to a degree, to remedy the imbalance created by the lack of gender awareness on the international level during the negotiations process.[44]

Conclusion

Two developments took place in the efforts to create an independent Namibia, one internal, which was gender aware, and one international, which was not. Women played an active role in the Namibian conflict, mainly through their involvement in SWAPO. However, in the negotiations leading up to the peace agreement few, if any, women were involved, and no gender equality issues were included. With regard to the United Nations, especially considering the Economic and Social Council resolutions, as well as the NFLS, it is regrettable that these aspects were not given more recognition in the early developments.

The United Nations had an impact on the gender relations in Namibia. Becker describes women's situation in Namibia during the transition period as dependent on three positive developments surrounding increased awareness of women's rights in Namibian society. The first was the breach of international isolation, most immediately evident with the arrival of UNTAG, which brought with it international developments regarding women's rights. Gender issues and equality had increased in importance internationally during the UN Decade for Women and these ideas now reached Namibia. UNTAG, with its high degree of women in the civilian sector, became an example of what women could do. This underlines that behavior, attitude, and gender awareness of United Nations personnel is vital with regard to gender mainstreaming (see Mazurana et al., introduction). The second development was increased political awareness of the SWAPO women in exile. This was, for example, visible in the papers produced by SWAPO, where women's issues and equality were frequently discussed. There was consequently a high degree of gender awareness and competence among the women who returned to Namibia after the war. The third development was the establishment of gender equality as an independent issue on the political agenda in Namibia. In Namibia, the only independent journal, the *Namibian*, led by Gwen Lister, reported on women's issues. Moreover, due to the Namibian women's mobilization during the conflict, the groundwork for change in the social and political environment in Namibia was laid, making it possible to continue working for women's rights after independence.[45]

In conclusion, it should be recognized that the manner in which the United Nations implements peace can affect women and men differently and that gender neutrality cannot be assumed. The United Nations risks decreasing gender equality if it does not analyze and adjust its mission to the actual gender structure and situation of the host state. Finally, researcher Mary Caprioli claims that more equal gender relations correlates with lower degrees of state militarism.[46] Therefore, it is important to consider women's rights in relation to men's rights and not give priority to one, simply as a force of habit. Gender equality most clearly needs to be seen as related to, and not separate from, peace.

Notes

The chapter is printed with permission of Frank Cass Publishers, London. The author wishes to thank Mary-Jane Fox, Isel Rivero, Peter Wallensteen, and the participants of the seminar in Cape Town, South Africa, February 2002, for their valuable help with the chapter. A special thanks to Dyan Mazurana at Tufts University and to Peter Vale at the University of Western Cape.

1. As defined in H. T. Wilson, "The Impact of Gender on Critical Theory's Critique of Advanced Industrial Societies," in *Current Perspectives in Social Theory*, vol. 12, ed. Ben Agger, 125–36 (London: JAI Press, 1992).

2. Nitza Berkovitch, *From Motherhood to Citizenship: Women's Rights and International Organizations* (Baltimore: John Hopkins University Press, 1999), 2.

3. "Gender mainstreaming" is here understood as defined in the introduction. See also Jacqui True and Michael Minstrom, "Transnational Networks and Policy Diffusion: The Case of Gender Mainstreaming," *International Studies Quarterly* 45, no. 1 (2001): 28.

4. Louise Olsson, "Gender Mainstreaming in Practice: The United Nations Transitional Assistance Group in Namibia," *Journal of International Peacekeeping* 8, no. 2 (2001): 95–110.

5. United Nations, *Beijing Declaration and Platform for Action* (New York: UN, 1996).

6. The Windhoek Declaration and the Namibian Plan of Action lists the main fields of importance regarding gender in the operational structure of peacekeeping operations and suggests implementation strategies.

7. Adam Roberts, "Humanitarian War: Military-Intervention and Human-Rights," *International Affairs* 69, no. 3 (1993): 429–49.

8. The beginning and the conclusion of war often include changes in the gender balance and gender constructions judging from other studies; see, for example, Bridget Byrne, Rachel Marcus, and Tanya Power Stevens, *Gender, Conflict and Development*, vol. 2, *Case Studies: Cambodia, Rwanda, Kosovo, Algeria, Somalia, Guatemala and Eritrea*, BRIDGE Report 35 (Brighton: University of Sussex, 1996).

9. Heike Becker, *Namibian Women's Movement, 1980–1992: From Anti-colonial Resistance to Reconstruction* (Frankfurt: IKO-Verl, 1995).

10. This is, for example, discussed in paragraph 114 and 115 in the Beijing Declaration and Platform for Action. See also Inger Skjelsbaek, "Sexual Violence in Times of War: A New Challenge for Peace Operations?" in *Women and International Peacekeeping*, ed. Louise Olsson and Torunn L. Tryggestad, 69–84 (London: Frank Cass Publishers, 2001).

11. SWAFT was the internal Namibian military to which Namibians, mainly males, were recruited by way of conscription.

12. Miranda Davis, *Third World, Second Sex* (London: Zed Books, 1983); Caroline Allison, *Women in Namibia: "It's Like Holding the Key to Your Own Jail"* (Geneva: World Council of Churches, 1986); Manfred Hinz and Nadia Gevers Leuven-Lachinski, *Koevoet versus the People of Namibia: Report of a Human Rights Mission to Namibia on Behalf of the Working Group Kairos* (Utrecht: Working Group Kairos, 1989); Tessa Cleaver and Marion Wallace, *Namibia: Women in War* (London: Zed Books, 1990).

13. Tekla Shikola, "We Left Our Shoes Behind," in *What Women Do in Wartime: Gender and Conflict in Africa*, ed. Meredith Turshen and Clotilde Twagiramariya (London: Zed Books, 1998), 144–45.

14. Hinz and Leuven-Lachinski, *Koevoet versus the People of Namibia*.

15. Becker, *Namibian Women's Movement, 1980–1992*.

16. Catherine Coquery-Vidrovitch, *African Women: A Modern History* (Boulder: Westview Press, 1997).

17. Becker, *Namibian Women's Movement, 1980–1992*.

18. Becker, *Namibian Women's Movement, 1980–1992*, 142. This strategy contained several new approaches to the struggle. Due to the UN's failure to create an independent Namibia, SWAPO decided that armed struggle was the manner in which the goal of independence was to be reached. In order to achieve this, SWAPO decided that the political and military aspects needed stronger coordination. To mobilize the people, a youth organization and an Elders Council were formed in addition to the SWC.

19. Becker, *Namibian Women's Movement, 1980–1992*.

20. Becker, *Namibian Women's Movement, 1980–1992*.

21. A forced conscription also included young women.

22. Cleaver and Wallace, *Namibia: Women in War*.

23. Becker, *Namibian Women's Movement, 1980–1992*.

24. Becker, *Namibian Women's Movement, 1980–1992*.

25. Becker, *Namibian Women's Movement, 1980–1992*.

26. Shikola, "We Left Our Shoes Behind."

27. Shikola, "We Left Our Shoes Behind," 143–44. Pregnancy could consequently be used as a means of avoiding combat duty.

28. Shikola, "We Left Our Shoes Behind."

29. Becker, *Namibian Women's Movement, 1980–1992*.

30. Pendukeni Kaulinge, then secretary for the SWC. The quote is taken from the *Namibian Today* and reprinted in Becker, *Namibian Women's Movement, 1980–1992*, 157.

31. Cleaver and Wallace, *Namibia: Women in War*.

32. United Nations, *The Effects of Apartheid on the Status of Women in South Africa, Namibia and Southern Rhodesia: Report of the Secretary-General*, United Nations Economic and Social Council, Commission on the Status of Women, 27th sess., UN Doc. E/CN.6/619 (New York: United Nations, 1978).

33. Olsson, "Gender Mainstreaming in Practice."

34. See Articles 238 and 240 in United Nations, *The Nairobi Forward Looking Strategies* (1985), available at http://www.un.org/esa/gopher-data/conf/fwcw/nfls/nfls .en (accessed January 14, 2000).

35. For a more thorough description and discussion of these events see Heribert Weiland and Matthew Braham, *The Namibian Peace Process: Implications and Lessons for the Future* (Freiburg: Arnold Bergstraesser Institute, 1994).

36. Becker, *Namibian Women's Movement, 1980–1992*.

37. Becker, *Namibian Women's Movement, 1980–1992*.

38. United Nations, UN Doc. S/RES/435 (1978).

39. United Nations, *Yearbook of the United Nations 1989* (The Hague: Martinus Nijhoff Publishers, 1997).

40. Isel Rivero, interviewed by author, Madrid, April 13, 2000.

41. Rosalia N. Shantilweh, interviewed by author, Windhoek, June 7, 2000.

42. Olsson, "Gender Mainstreaming in Practice."

43. Olsson, "Gender Mainstreaming in Practice."

44. Olsson, "Gender Mainstreaming in Practice."

45. Becker, *Namibian Women's Movement, 1980–1992*. There were also other, more direct effects of the operation, for example, its economic effects on women and men. There are major differences that depend on the structure of the gender relations. Many Namibian women in the cities, where the United Nations was concentrated, received jobs in the peacekeeping operation. Yet these jobs were mostly in administration or housekeeping. Alma Mieze, a Namibian working for the United Nations, states that because the Namibian men were more business oriented at the time of the mission, they were able to take better advantage of the situation even if the possibility to earn money existed for both men and women. Alma Mieze, interviewed by author, Windhoek, June 8, 2000.

46. Mary Caprioli, "Gendered Conflict," *Journal of Peace Research* 37, no. 1 (2000): 53–68.

IV

PEACEKEEPING OPERATIONS, INTERNATIONAL INTERVENTION, AND GENDER-JUST PEACEMAKING AND PEACE BUILDING

CONTRIBUTIONS IN THIS SECTION EXAMINE the role of peacekeeping operations and, to a lesser extent, humanitarian intervention in establishing the necessary conditions for building a gender-just peace in postconflict societies. By bringing to the fore the gendered effects of the conflict and the postconflict period, including gender dimensions of internationally brokered peace accords, these contributions provide a critical interrogation of the tensions among peacekeeping operations, international intervention, and the role of civil and women's organizations in building peace. Examples are drawn from peacekeeping operations in Angola, East Timor, Eithiopia, Eritrea, Guatemala, Haiti, Kosovo, and Rwanda.

9

The Postconflict Postscript: Gender and Policing in Peace Operations

Tracy Fitzsimmons

FROM HAITI TO BOSNIA TO EAST TIMOR, peace building has become the central challenge in regions emerging from civil war or political instability. A quick glance at the United Nations' peacekeeping efforts across the globe shows that its role in peace building in recent postconflict settings is essentially a two-pronged endeavor: at its core, peace building is first about establishing and maintaining security, and second about constituting and buttressing a democratic political system, or at least the rhetorical claims of doing so.[1] With regard to the former, security efforts cluster around demilitarization and ridding the country of ethnically and politically motivated oppression and impunity. In oversimplified terms, governments and NGOs claim postwar victory when there is a reasonable degree of certainty that the war or conflict will not recur, when free and fair elections are held, and when a person's skin color, religious persuasion, or political party affiliation is not likely to get him killed.

I say "him" because gender is noticeably absent from most discussions of postconflict peace. Postwar victories are claimed even as women experience increasing levels of some forms of physical violence, and economic and political isolation. For many women, the end of war does not mean the advent of security. War can provide pockets of peace and opportunity for women, whereas, paradoxically, peacetime may yield increasing violence, insecurity, and economic and political constraints for them (see Jacobson, chapter 6; Vandenberg, chapter 7). Women's groups in El Salvador, for example, report that after that country's civil war in 1992, levels of domestic violence increased, partly because thousands of men returned home with few job opportunities and ten years of experience in violence. In Bosnia, women claim that men, unsatisfied with the outcome of the most recent ethnic conflict, continue to fight the war in their homes.[2]

In search of postconflict security, the United Nations as well as local leaders turned to idealized visions of country, home, and family that domesticate and subordinate women.[3] While much recent attention has been given to rape and sexual torture as used as weapons of war, nonpolitical rape, domestic violence, and women's rights tend to get lost in peace-building missions. In postconflict settings, institutions charged with providing security to all offer that security unequally and unevenly to women. At the heart of this problem is the fact that conceptions of security—in theory and in practice, at the international level and at most local levels—are gendered.[4] Despite efforts to mainstream gender in peacekeeping, the special challenges, needs, and context of women's security are frequently left out of Western peace-building efforts. The most recent and notable example of this is the report of the Panel on United Nations Peace Operations, known as the Brahimi Report (see Raven-Roberts, chapter 2). While the report is nearly exhaustive in its breadth of scope, spanning peace operations from military and police to leadership and funding, it specifically mentions gender or women just once in its 280 paragraphs, encouraging the secretary-general to compile systematically a list of individuals to lead peace operations "representing a broad geographic and equitable gender distribution."[5]

In this chapter, I offer some theoretical reflections as well as policy prescriptions concerning the integration of women and women's issues into conceptions and mechanisms of domestic security in postconflict settings—in particular with regard to the United Nations Civilian Police (CIVPOL). In doing so, I draw upon field research undertaken in Haiti, Central America, and the former Yugoslavia.

Women and the Paradox of Conflict

Historically, wartime has provided pockets of economic and political opportunity to women (and to other marginalized groups). Perhaps the most well-known example of this in the United States is World War II's Rosie the Riveter. During the war, thousands of "Rosies" replaced male laborers turned soldiers. For the years that the Rosies were working on the factory floors (1942–1947), productivity rose, product cycle time dropped, and quality improved in almost every factory. Women held leadership posts in unions and made supervisory decisions about production and quality, while at the same time often running their households. Yet it was not just in the United States that women entered into new roles during war. In some parts of the world, not only has wartime meant women running households and factories from the home front, but, for some, it has presented an opportunity to participate in military operations, clandestine information gathering, and local policing efforts. During World War I, Russian women served as pilots. Women played an important role in the Resistance in France, Scandinavia, and the Balkans. Throughout the Mexican Revolution, women armed themselves to protect their families' homes and property. And more recently, the Salvadoran and Guatemalan guerrillas, the Revolutionary Armed Forces of Colombia (FARC), and Peru's Shining Path have all counted women among their combatants and leadership. Wartime has consistently afforded some women opportunities and security far beyond the societal gender confines of the era, although these opportunities are at times unwelcome.

What happens to women in postwar periods? Even for women in the years following World War II, the answer is still debated. Some argue that the war represented a watershed for women's economic, political, and social roles; they submit that opportunities and actions of women were significantly changed between the prewar and postwar periods. Others disagree, claiming that women's lives in the postwar period compared to the prewar period were more characterized by continuity than by change;[6] essentially, they portray the wartime opportunities and responsibilities of women as a "blip" on the gender-role screen. What we do know is that following World War II, women largely disappeared from the factory workforce in the United States,[7] and most women guerrillas did not become part of the postconflict security forces that arose in Guatemala or El Salvador (see Luciak and Olmos, chapter 10). In fact, the significance of conflict and war for women's opportunities is more complex. Although tangible gains tend to largely disappear, societal norms may be transformed in subtle, long-lasting ways.

As World War II came to a close, headlines in the United States read, "16,000,000 Women: What Will Happen After?"; "Getting Rid of the Women"; "Give Back the Jobs."[8] The headlines demonstrate that, perhaps not surprisingly given the time period, the postwar focus was clearly on creating opportunities for returning soldiers and not on maintaining the ground that women had gained.[9] But nearly sixty years later, the gender outlook is better: there have been four World Conferences on Women, many countries now boast cabinet-level women's ministries, many civil or penal codes include sections on violence against women, and on the whole women are healthier and better educated. Has women's recent postconflict experience reflected this upswing?

In 2000, the International Center for Research on Women (ICRW) held a conference in El Salvador on the problems that plague returning displaced women. It would come as no surprise to women in Croatia, Mozambique, or

Haiti that those attending the ICRW conference found that returning women refugees have faced a multitude of challenges in postwar periods in Central America. The debate is not whether these conflicts represent a watershed for women in the way that some studying World War II claim, but whether the postconflict phase yields significant setbacks or obstacles for women. In the realm of domestic security, it appears that women are presented with a multitude of challenges.

CIVPOL and Women after War

Most would agree that women experience war and conflict in a different way than men. Feminist theorists have long argued that reactions to war, to demilitarization, to protection of home and family are gendered. So it is not surprising that women also experience peacetime differently than men. But what some may find surprising, and disquieting, is how international actors set women up for an *unpeaceful* transition toward democracy and peacetime. Levels of domestic violence, nonpolitical rape, and sexual harassment may actually increase in postconflict periods as returning soldiers, who are overwhelmingly male, redirect their aggression to their households, demanding a return to prewar societal patterns of interaction and responsibilities. Yet the law and its enforcers offer little protection to women during this period, as they instead focus their energies on higher-profile street crimes, homicides, political corruption, gangs, and demilitarization. Women may have made great gains across many cultures, but the ways in which international actors conceive of, train, and supply new police forces in transitional societies create a gendered, if not unequal, sense of peace and security for women.

Transitions from war offer unique opportunities to reshape domestic norms, institutions, and practices, especially in the realm of internal security and policing.[10] Yet peace treaties, peacekeeping and peace-building missions, and new civilian police forces are designed primarily to ensure the national— *public*—peace, and secondarily to guarantee private peace *in the realms that are most visible to the empowered public.* In both cases, this peace is largely measured by men, of men.

How should we examine issues of gender in postconflict international activities? I herein focus on the increasingly accepted use of United Nations international police personnel in peace operations. Known as CIVPOL, these forces grew from 35 in 1988 to 3,500 in 1997 to more than 8,000 in 2001 (then deployed mainly in Bosnia, Kosovo, and East Timor).[11] These officers are recruited from United Nations member states on short-term contracts of six to eighteen months. Their activities (and whether they are armed or have arrest powers) vary from mission to mission, depending on the mandate approved by the Security Council.[12] Increasingly, the international community relies on CIVPOL not only to monitor local police forces after wars but also to train and "mentor" new or reformed local police forces. Although bilateral and regional organizations engage in police education, training, and advice, CIVPOL forces are the main vehicle for police monitoring and field training in most postconflict settings, and their salience continues to grow as of this writing.

And while peace operations are still a very male domain, there *has* been an improvement, or learning across cases, with regard to the integration of women into new civilian police forces and the parallel role of CIVPOL. By way of example below, I compare two cases in which CIVPOL was highly involved in the creation and training of the new police: Haiti (1994–1997) and Kosovo (1999–present).

Haiti

Following the ouster of Haiti's democratically elected president Jean-Bertrand Aristide in 1991, the United States led a United Nations–authorized multinational military force that restored him to power in September 1994.[13] The military force, accompanied by international police monitors under United States command, was replaced by a United Nations peacekeeping operation in February 1995. The United Nations Mission in Haiti (UNMIH) was the first ever whose mandate explicitly included creation of a new police force.[14] The Aristide government decided to disband the Haitian armed forces, replacing it with a five-thousand-member Haitian national police force (known by its French acronym, "PNH"), to be trained at a new police academy in Haiti initially run by the United States Justice Department. The law creating the Haitian National Police was adopted by the Haitian Parliament and signed by President Aristide in late 1994. President Aristide's return to the presidency signaled the end of a coup regime under which an estimated three thousand people were extrajudicially executed or tortured. For Haitian women, much of the brutality centered on rape being used as a political tool. For the many women who had been terrorized by the former military forces, the civilian PNH provided a ray of hope that security would be inclusive of women and protect them from violence.

In February of 1995, the first class of police cadets began training at the new police academy. There were no specific efforts to recruit women into the force, nor did the United Nations or the PNH set target goals for the number of women officers. By the end of the deployment of the last class, only 7 percent of the PNH were women officers, and most of the women officers were relegated to serving as desk officers and traffic police. Within the first year of deployment and reportedly under the urging of some CIVPOL personnel, some police stations endeavored to begin a system whereby women complainants could report crimes to women officers; but the practice was far from institutionalized.

CIVPOL participated in classroom training and served as the field trainers for the PNH during the two and a half years of the United Nations operation.[15] For the first classes through the academy, all the instructors were men. The four-month-long training course for all new Haitian police officers (designed and run by a United States Department of Justice agency) included less than half a day on rape and domestic sexual violence. Two women police cadets reported in interviews with me that much of that half day was spent with the male recruits making snide and sexually explicit comments. In 1996, in response to the United Nations secretary-general's concern that the four-month basic training course was "widely considered insufficient," the training program added training centers in each of Haiti's nine territorial provinces (*departements*) to focus on six priority areas: crowd control, criminal investigation, collection and analysis of information and operations, traffic, personnel management, and management of resources. Gendered issues were noticeably absent from the list, and women's security did not figure prominently in the training programs.[16]

This lack of enthusiasm for women's involvement in policing in Haiti was unfortunate, as women proved to be responsible members of the PNH. Research shows that across many cultures, women police officers use force less frequently than their male counterparts, are less authoritarian in their interactions with citizens and with officers of lower rank, possess better communication and negotiation skills, and are more likely than male officers to diffuse potentially violent situations.[17] Among the Haitian police force, these studies are borne out in practice. At the end of the first six months of deployment of the PNH, the Inspector General's Office was bogged down investigating complaints of police misconduct—but not a single one of those cases was filed against a women officer. Nor had the inspector general received any complaints of improper use of force or firearms by women officers; yet during the same period several male officers were under review for improper use of firearms. Despite this positive performance, women officers continue to receive less than a warm welcome; men officers have frequently refused to go out on patrol with women partners or to share sources or leads with them.[18]

One of the members of the Inspector General's Office in Haiti, in response to questions on women, policing, and violence in Haiti, replied, "This study is silly. Crime and politics are the most important [issues] in Haiti now. All you want to know about is women. They are not so important."[19] In Haiti, women are seen as inferior, and outside the realm of politics and crime—and therefore unimportant in discussions of security. Addressing the Security Council in December 1996, Haiti's Pierre LeLong reported that "the specific needs of the National Police had been identified, and before the end of the year, the force would be able to guarantee peace and security throughout Haiti"[20]—at a time when more than 40 percent of the population reported having experienced rape or domestic violence.[21] Following the end of CIVPOL's involvement in Haiti in 1997, fewer than 6 percent of officers were female, there were no women's police stations, and there were still remnants of a Napoleonic code that did not criminalize all violence against women.

Kosovo

After NATO's bombing campaign in response to the displacement of hundreds of thousands of Kosovar Albanians in 1999, an agreement with the Federal Republic of Yugoslavia (FRY) permitted the NATO-led Kosovo Force (KFOR) to occupy Kosovo. As part of this process, the Yugoslav armed forces, as well as almost all police forces and judicial personnel, withdrew from the territory of Kosovo, leaving a vacuum in policing, justice, and other local administration.[22] Under Security Council Resolution 1244, the United Nations acquired unprecedented powers over this territory, assuming the full range of government functions, including taxation, the administration of justice, administration of postal service, banking regulation, and payment of all public employees at the municipal level. The total absence of any recognized Kosovar organization specializing in policing or justice led the Security Council to grant unprecedented executive authority to CIVPOL. The CIVPOL mission would grow to the largest in history at roughly 4,500 officers in 2001, deployed beginning in summer 1999, and remaining there as of this writing. A central part of the mission was the creation of the new Kosovo Police Service (KPS), to consist of six thousand members trained in a police academy run by the Organization for Security and Cooperation in Europe (OSCE).[23] Again, as in Haiti, the creation of a new security force was particularly important to women, as they had been the target of politically motivated rapes during the war. While the absolute number of rape cases in Kosovo appears to have been less than in Haiti or Bosnia, the Kosovo cases happened during a much more condensed time frame. There are reported cases of the Kosovo Liberation Army (KLA) military police participating in sexual violence against teenage girls, and the FRY forces raping ethnic Albanians in Kosovo.

In the five years between the founding of Haiti's PNH and Kosovo's KPS, some advancement by the international community can be noted with regard to its commitment to gendered policing. The United Nations Interim Administration Mission in Kosovo (UNMIK) and the OSCE mandated a target of 20 percent women for the KPS. UNMIK's stated objective was that "the recruitment and selection process for the Kosovo Police Service should strive to include no less than 20% *females*. The degree of interest received during recruitment will influence the gender composition. However, specific strategies will be developed to encourage the participation of women."[24] OSCE planning documents likewise underscore the importance of including women in the KPS as a way to "enhance the capabilities of the organization and provide a balance between the agency and the population it serves."[25] UNMIK and the OSCE also encouraged increased research into violence against women and attempted to strengthen the laws criminalizing violence against women. The training of the KPS, designed by International Criminal Investigative Training Assistance Program (ICITAP) personnel in collaboration with the OSCE, included more modules on domestic violence, rape, and women's issues than had been seen in a CIVPOL mission up to that time. Of the first sixteen classes graduating into the KPS, 18 percent of the officers were women—a percentage higher than in any postconflict peace force involving the United Nations (and also higher than the average percentage in United States police forces). In September 2000, the UNMIK's joint administrator for civil society, Vjosa Dobruna, chaired a multiethnic strategic planning session on the integration of women throughout the mission;[26] at nearly the same time, CIVPOL created the Trafficking and Prostitution Investigative Unit.

However, from a women's rights perspective, the deployed KPS and the role of internationals in its founding still leave room for improvement. Initially, only 1.5 percent of UNMIK police officers were women; that percentage is now up to a still surprisingly low 3 percent. In 2001, UNMIK reduced the target number for KPS recruits to 15 percent. In the institutional structure of the KPS, there are no women's police stations and no separate sections dealing with crimes against women and children. Also, while the international community aimed appropriately high in its initial target of 20 percent women in the KPS, it neglected to institutionalize any mechanisms that would protect women officers from being sidelined into the low-status policing areas of personnel, traffic, and administration. And despite the solid numbers of women in the judiciary, OSCE reports state that the legal system in Kosovo lacks "a mechanism and means to prosecute sexual violence cases and protect the victim," which also holds true for trafficking cases. One OSCE assessment of the justice sector in Kosovo found that "there has been no practical training of judicial, police or social services personnel on issues of sexual violence, including heightening sensitivity towards alleged victims. Over the past six months, the average sentence for sexual violence cases has declined from three years to one year."[27]

Lessons for Gendering Postconflict Security

While gendered policing in peacekeeping operations clearly made some significant inroads between the Haiti mission and the Kosovo mission, it is still insufficient and subject to reversal. This study of gender and the role of CIVPOL in postconflict civilian policing yields several lessons for how to work toward institutionalizing a more gendered conception of policing.

First, peacekeeping policy makers should focus *more on violence and less on crime*. Because violence is a principal and direct concern of peace operations, and because some violence, especially domestic violence, may not be criminalized, an emphasis on violence reduction rather than fighting crime may augment security from physical harm.[28] Violence against women should be classified as a "crime" and, as such, should be dealt with in criminal court.[29] But in Kosovo, the law does not define rape within a marriage as a criminal act. In the absence of appropriate laws and social services, the KPS and international police officers "have been mediating cases involving domestic violence, either facilitating reconciliation between the parties or admonishing the husband because the wife recants her statement."[30] In less than half of the Latin American and Caribbean countries does violence against women automatically fall under the penal code; in the rest of Latin America and the Caribbean, cases of violence against women (or children) only go before a criminal court judge in cases of extreme injury, death, or threat of death.[31] In many cases, the law suggests, or requires, mediation or reconciliation measures before a criminal or civil case involving domestic violence can be brought to court. What court would suggest mediation as a first step in an assault or attempted homicide case? Almost none, unless, apparently, the case involves a woman and her husband or live-in companion.

Second, *timing and impetus are crucial*. Engendering police forces at their moment of founding or significant reform can minimize a zero-sum identity game. If gendered policing is introduced when a police force and its identity as "masculine" are not already established, the entrance of women and gender issues into the force is less likely to be perceived as a loss of identity and power for the male officers. The key is to emphasize that there are mutual interests—not an ensured loss—in gendering the new police forces. Such benefits extend not only to the women officers but also to male officers, the police institution at large, and the democratization processes more generally. Likewise, the training, composition, and leadership within CIVPOL missions should recognize and seek to address issues of gender imbalance right from the start of the mission.[32]

Third, *civil society coalitions are necessary to achieve gender security.* No civilian police force in Latin America has made progress toward gendering its force without the existence of coalitions—within and between civil society, international funding agencies, and women officers. In highly patriarchal and sexist societies, police forces see little incentive or justification to "demasculinize" their institutions without receiving pressure from outside domestic coalitions. In the Brazilian case, it was a joint effort between the women's movement, the human rights organizations, and the state-level Ministries of Justice that led to the opening of women's police stations and the doubling of the number of women cops.[33] In Guatemala, the women's movement has joined forces with the indigenous movement to demand representation in the emerging new civilian police force. But in Haiti, where few organizations and no coalitions sustained a focus on gendered security during the creation of new police forces, the percentage of women police officers and the number of police programs aimed at gendered crimes fell between 1995 and 1999. International funding and training agencies such as ICITAP and CIVPOL have yet to learn that their few efforts to gender postconflict police forces will fail if they do not also train civil society groups to work with the police and act as watchdogs of the police, as well as encourage other societal groups that are underrepresented within the criminal justice system to forge alliances with women in gendering the new police forces.[34] Furthermore, community policing models likely mean little for women's rights and gendering policing if there are no women's organizations extant or involved in the community, and if CIVPOL does not actively work with these groups to create police forces that are more representative and responsive to community (read women's) needs.

Fourth, *gendered policing cannot occur in a vacuum.* The United Nations and others who work in postconflict settings must begin to see the totality of the security issue. Too often, those responsible for constructing a domestic security system include one or two powerful, pro-women ideas—for example, changing divorce laws, allowing women to enter the police force, offering psychological counseling to rape survivors. But if the entire system is not gendered, each of these changes makes very little impact. If we are to combat violence against women, policing must be just one link in a solid chain uniting the courts, the prisons, the lawmakers, and civil society. And while this is nothing new, it bears repeating: peacekeepers and police units must see physical, political, and economic violence against women as a crime *and* as a human rights abuse. Human Rights Watch argues that, in the South African case, "violence against women has not achieved the sort of high-level political attention that the more general political violence, for example, has been given both during the transition period and under the new regime."[35] The same could be said for the way in which CIVPOL approached the training and oversight of the new civilian police forces in El Salvador, Haiti, and Bosnia.

Fifth, *training and transparency cannot be shortchanged.* In Bosnia, 60 percent of women surveyed said that they would never go to the courts, police, or Center for Social Work to report domestic violence because of their fear of the institutions, their fear of not being understood, or the perceived inability of the institutions to do anything. No woman can report a rape, sexual assault, or incident of domestic violence and expect the police to investigate it fairly. Police—predominantly male—have little or no training in investigating sexual offenses in general, or domestic violence in particular, and can themselves be an obstacle by embarrassing women or making women feel that they are partly or wholly to blame.[36] Yet the training of the Bosnian police force on gender issues, or lack thereof, was, at least initially, a CIVPOL–conceived set of courses.

Sixth, *development agencies must incorporate gender more into their antiviolence and security programs.* United States and British aid agencies have bilaterally undertaken some training in domestic violence and gender crimes, but not to the extent needed. Similarly, growing violence-reduction efforts by the World Bank have included domestic violence programming but have emphasized other categories of violence. Although the importance of women to most development agencies makes these agencies a promising mechanism for engendering security, among these major institutions only the Inter-American Development Bank has embraced a holistic notion of violence reduction that reflects the importance of reducing gender violence.[37] This bank has funded projects to combat domestic violence in several Latin American countries. As with "community policing," attention to gender in security is often placed within a police bureaucracy rather than being allowed to shape the overall concepts and operations of the organization.

Seventh, *statistics are important—and must be generated on a local and national level.* Throughout the first five years of the new Haitian National Police, crime statistics were irregularly kept and compiled. In one police station in southern Haiti, I interviewed the police chief, the head of investigations, the head of reporting (of crimes), two police officers, and one CIVPOL officer— each gave me different statistics for the number of rapes and domestic abuse cases reported, the number of arrests, and so on. And the numbers not only varied greatly within the police station but also differed from the number recorded at the office of the French Gendarmerie advisers to the Haitian police. Such statistical chaos was also present, but to a lesser extent, for non-gender-specific crimes of homicide and armed robbery. It is difficult to fight crime and to get donor support for antiviolence programs if reliable statistics are unavailable.

Eighth, *representativity is necessary, but not sufficient.* In general, *numbers matter.* Societies need not just numbers in the form of statistics, but also numbers of women, en masse, involved in policing. In October 2000, Security Council Resolution 1325 called for greater inclusion of women in peace operations in the field—noting specifically the importance of women in the military and police. The same year, the European Parliament issued a call to urge that at least 40 percent of all peacekeeping posts be filled by women. These international institutions are headed in the right direction—the mere presence of more women in policing institutions is an important first step toward signaling that the police, and the way it treats women, has entered a new era. If women suffered violence at the hands of a prior security force (such as the military or police), they are unlikely in the postconflict period to be suddenly trusting and willing to report violence committed against them to the new (supposedly) democratic police force if it is all male. In the postconflict period, the issue is about not only what violence is currently inflicted on women but also the physical and mental trauma associated with past violence that went untreated. According to South African government reports, in 1994, over 97 percent of rapes went unreported. Having a threshold number of women officers so that the new police force is not identified as "masculine," and having women officers take police report statements from women crime survivors, will contribute to women being more willing to report crimes against them.[38] Simply put, numbers (of women police) matter—and make women feel more at ease approaching the police and participating in the criminal justice system.

An Enabling Context

The underlying lesson that arises out of the Haiti and Kosovo cases is that international peacekeepers alone are unlikely to produce policing that responds to women's needs. CIVPOL missions bring together a group of mostly male police officers, hailing from diverse countries that often have their own forms of institutionalized sexism, to train a mostly male local police force how to protect citizens. It should not be surprising that the end result is less than women centered. Take, for example, one of the more progressive innovations in gendered policing over the last two decades: the creation of women's police stations or women's sections within police stations. Studies show that women's police stations encourage higher reporting levels and more citizen confidence in the police.[39] Yet, of the more than twelve countries in Latin America that have women's police stations or women's sections within police stations, only one occurred in a country in which there had been a peacekeeping mission of the United Nations or the Organization of American States. Even in the sole exception, Nicaragua, the incorporation of female ex-guerrillas shaped gender issues in policing much more than international actors did. The Nicaraguans managed to construct a system in which women officers and gender sensitivity are characteristics of the police force, not appendages of it—in large part because of the proactive and watchdog characteristics of Nicaragua's civil society and the strength of its women's movement.

However, while international peacekeepers may be unlikely to model or promote such pro-women policing, the accompanying lesson is that those same peacekeepers can provide the context that enables or encourages local actors to adopt and promote gendered policing practices.

Between the Brahimi Report and Security Council Resolution 1325, the United Nations created on paper the context and the tactics to nurture a gendered conception of policing within CIVPOL and local police forces. The most proactive of the two with regard to gender, Resolution 1325,[40] calls on the secretary-general to "incorporate a gender perspective into peacekeeping operations . . . provide training guidelines and materials on the protection, rights and the particular needs of women, . . . and to increase their [United Nations member states'] voluntary financial, technical and logistical support for gender-sensitive training efforts." The Brahimi Report outlines the general enabling goals and strategies that, if implemented, would provide a suitable environment to usher in future gendered norms. But it does not include specific policy recommendations nor tactics to achieve or even move toward such gendered policing. Subsequent reports by the secretary-general on the implementation of the Brahimi Report have focused more pointedly on issues related to gendered policing, such as, "I appeal to Member States to redouble their efforts to identify female civilian police candidates (and, in fact, female candidates in all other areas covered by the United Nations standby arrangements system)."[41]

The most important contextual contribution international peacekeepers might be able to make is to foster a proactive civil society, locally and internationally, that will function as a watchdog on behalf of gendered policing. The Brahimi Report already includes a request for peace operations leaders "to reach out to civil society and to strengthen relations with non-governmental organizations, academic institutions and the media, who can be useful partners in the promotion of peace and security for all."[42] The evidence from successful and failed efforts at engendering policing suggests that local states and local women's organizations are a central ingredient, rather than a peripheral afterthought, in building security for women in transitional societies. Despite the achievements in many postwar security reforms, much more was, and remains, possible.

Notes

Many thanks to Charles T. Call, Nadine Jubb, and Maria Cecilia dos Santos for their very helpful substantive and editorial contributions to this chapter, and to Katie Torrington for research assistance.

1. First given broad exposure in United Nations Secretary-General Boutros-Ghali's 1992 *Agenda for Peace* (New York: United Nations, 1992), the term "peace building" is still used in multiple ways.

2. Women's organizations in El Salvador (1995, 1998) and Bosnia (1999), interviewed by author.

3. This is a variation on an argument made about middle-class families in the United States in the 1950s in Elaine Tyler May, *Homeward Bound: American Families in the Cold War Era* (New York: Basic Books, 1988).

4. From a gender perspective, postconflict security can be seen as a different kind of "protection racket" (William Stanley, *The Protection Racket State: Elite Politics, Military Extortion, and Civil War in El Salvador* [Philadelphia: Temple University Press, 1996]). Stanley's conception of a protection racket state refers to imaginary or self-induced threats from which a government "protects" its citizens, using the constructed threat as an excuse or means to consolidate its control. In the case of postconflict security, the protection racket is that governments and international agencies react to very real threats of postconflict violence by constructing a citizenry that is male and essentially void of sexual or gendered violence.

5. *Report of the Panel on United Nations Peace Operations* [The Brahimi Report], A/55/305-S/2000/809 (August 21, 2000), par. 96.

6. For the watershed debate, see William Chafe, *The American Woman: Her Changing Social, Economic and Political Roles, 1920–1970* (New York: Oxford University Press, 1972). For the opposing viewpoint, see Karen Anderson, *Wartime Women: Sex Roles, Family Relations and the Status of Women during World War II* (Westport, CT: Greenwood Press, 1981) and D'Ann Campbell, *Women at War with America: Private Lives in a Patriotic Era* (Cambridge: Harvard University Press, 1984).

7. For example, women made up 12 percent of Ford's laborers during the war, which dropped to 1 percent after the war; see Sherrie A. Kossoudji and Laura J. Dresser, "Working Class Rosies: Women Industrial Workers during World War II," *Journal of Economic History* 52 (June 1992): 431–46.

8. Published in *New York Times Magazine*, 1943; *Atlantic*, 1944; *Woman's Home Companion*, 1943.

9. See Chafe, *American Woman*; Anderson, *Wartime Women*; and Campbell, *Women at War with America.*

10. Charles T. Call, "War Transitions and the New Civilian Security in Latin America," *Comparative Politics* 35, no. 1 (October 2002): 1–20.

11. Data found in Charles T. Call, "Police Aid and the New World Disorder: Institutional Learning within the U.S. International Criminal Investigative Training Assistance Program," in *Policing the New World Disorder: Peace Operations and Public Security*, ed. Robert Oakley, Michael Dziedzic, and Eliot Goldberg (Washington, DC: National Defense University, 1998), and based on information from the UN Civilian Police unit in New York, 2001.

12. For more on CIVPOL, see Nassrine Azimi, ed., *The Role and Functions of Civilian Police in United Nations Peacekeeping Operations: Debriefing and Lessons* (Cambridge, MA: Kluwer Law International and UN Institute for Training and Research, 1996); Charles T. Call and Michael Barnett, "Looking for a Few Good Cops: Peacekeeping, Peacebuilding and CIVPOL," *International Peacekeeping*, Fall 1999, 43–68; Tor Tanke Holm and Espen Barth Eide, eds., "Peacebuilding and Police Reform," *International Peacekeeping* 6, no. 4 (Winter 1999).

13. Although Haiti's conflict was not an armed uprising or war, it involved civil resistance to a brutal authoritarian regime and left in its wake a legacy of violence and post-traumatic stress. Furthermore, Haiti's international peacekeeping operation was very similar to other peacekeeping missions and was drawn upon heavily in subsequent peace operations.

14. Security Council Resolution 940, passed July 31, 1994, authorized the United Nations Mission in Haiti, with a mandate of "(a) sustaining the secure and stable environment established during the multinational phase and protecting international personnel and key installations; and (b) the professionalization of the Haitian armed forces and the creation of a separate police force" (par. 9).

15. UNMIH was replaced by smaller missions under different names through November 30, 1997. On police reform in Haiti, see Michael Bailey, Robert Maguire, and Neil Pouliot, "Haiti: Military-Police Partnership for Public Security," in *Policing the New World Disorder: Peace Operations and Public Security*, ed. Robert Oakley, Michael Dziedzic, and Eliot Goldberg, 215–52 (Washington, DC: National Defense University, 1998).

16. United Nations, *Report of the Secretary-General of the United Nations* (New York: UN, 1996), available at www.un.org/Docs/s1996416; and United Nations, *Report of the Secretary-General of the United Nations: Transition Mission in Haiti* (New York: UN, 1997).

17. Tracy Fitzsimmons, "Engendering a New Police Identity?" *Peace Review* 10, no. 2 (1998): 269–74.

18. Women police officers and male police personnel, interviewed by author, Petionville and Carrefour stations, 1996 and 1998.

19. Member of Inspector General's Office, interviewed by author, August 2000.

20. United Nations Press Release SC/6300, December 5, 1996.

21. Fitzsimmons, "Engendering a New Police Identity?"

22. For general information about Kosovo and the NATO war, see Ivo H. Daalder and Michael E. O'Hanlon, *Winning Ugly: NATO's War to Save Kosovo* (Washington, DC: Brookings Institution, 2000); Noel Malcolm, *Kosovo: A Short History* (New York: New York University Press, 2001); Tim Judah, *Kosovo: War and Revenge* (New Haven, CT: Yale University Press, 2000); Julie Mertus, *Kosovo: How Myths and Truth Started a*

War (Berkeley, CA: University of California Press, 1999).

23. The target was increased from four thousand initially to six thousand by the end of 2002. See UNMIK, *UNMIK at Two*, UNMIK Report, 2001, author files.

24. UNMIK Doc. (1999), sec. 12.4.2(b).

25. OSCE Doc. (1999), sec. 13.5.4.

26. Swanee Hunt and Cristina Posa, "Women Waging Peace," *Foreign Policy*, May–June 2001, 38–47.

27. OSCE, untitled assessment of judicial sector reform in Kosovo, author's files (2001), 60.

28. Charles T. Call, "Sustainable Development in Central America: The Challenges of Violence, Injustice and Insecurity," report prepared for Centroamerica 2020, a project of the European Commission and USAID, 2000.

29. "Violence against women" in this section refers to cases of rape (intramarital or otherwise), domestic violence, and harassment.

30. OSCE, untitled assessment, 67.

31. See research projects done by ICRW (1998) for more on this. One important point made by ICRW and the Instituto del Tercer Mundo is that there is some perversion in cases where the victim must choose between family or criminal court—thereby forcing the victim to shoulder the burden (and pressure from her community) as to whether or not her husband/lover will perhaps go to jail.

32. The first iteration of this argument was made in Fitzsimmons, "Engendering a New Police Identity?"

33. M. Cecilia MacDowell Santos, "Gender, the State, and Citizenship: Women's Police Stations in Sao Paulo, Brazil," in *Irrumpiendo en lo publico: Seis facetas de las mujeres en América Latina*, ed. Sara Poggio and Montserrat Sagot, 63–92 (San Jose: Universidad de Costa Rica, 2000).

34. United Nations Development Program [UNDP], "Security Sector Reform: Lessons Learned from Bosnia and Herzegovina and Kosovo," draft report based on a joint UNDP/Department of Peacekeeping Operations (DPKO) mission in August 2001 (New York: UNDP, 2001); and ICITAP quarterly reports of activities, 2000–2001.

35. Human Rights Watch [HRW] and HRW Women's Rights Project, *Violence against Women in South Africa* (New York: HRW, 2000), 4.

36. International Human Rights Law Group BiH Project, *Izvestaj nvo-a o zenskim ljudskim pravima u Bosni i Hercegovini* (Sarajevo: International Human Rights Law Group, 1999), 172–73.

37. See Mayra Buvenic and Andrew Morrison, "Living in a More Violent World," *Foreign Policy* 118 (2000): 58–72; and Inter-American Development Bank website, http://www.iadb.org/.

38. I say "contribute to" because, in itself, the lack of women officers does not entirely explain women's unwillingness to report such crimes. Societal pressures reflective of cultural beliefs are perhaps a stronger factor in some societies (especially in Bosnia and in Haiti); in such societies, rape, or reporting a family member for domestic violence, brings dishonor on the family.

39. For useful analyses of the rise and contributions of women's police stations, see Santos, "Gender, the State, and Citizenship"; and Nadine Jubb, "Enforcing Gendered

Meanings and Social Order: The Participation of the National Police in the Nicaraguan Women's and Children's Police Stations" (paper given at Latin American Studies Association conference, September 2001).

40. United Nations, "The International Legal Framework," in *Women, Peace and Security: Study of the United Nations Secretary-General as Pursuant to Security Council Resolution 1325* (New York: UN, 2002).

41. Report of the Panel on United Nations Peace Operations [The Brahimi Report], 21 August 2000, A/55/305-S/2000/809, para. 97.

42. The Brahimi Report, par. 269.

10

Gender Equality and the Guatemalan Peace Accords: Critical Reflections

Ilja A. Luciak and Cecilia Olmos

P EACE AND DEMOCRACY HAVE RETURNED to Central America. This is the view
held by many policy makers in the West, who focus on the end to the civil
wars that were ravaging the region during the 1980s. Is it really the case that
El Salvador, Nicaragua, and Guatemala have now joined the "third wave of democratization?"[1]

Despite the end of the Central American wars, we argue that the prevailing
optimism regarding the future of democracy in Central America might be
premature.[2] The current emphasis on democratization is justified only if we
focus on formal democracy.[3] While the institutionalization of electoral democracy in the wake of the peace accords is encouraging, it is by no means a
sufficient guarantee that the emerging political structures will reflect popular
interests. The political transitions taking place in Central America have to be
analyzed in light of the wars that ravaged the region for so many years. The
definitive resolution of these conflicts, a precondition of sustainable peace and
democracy, requires more than an end to armed struggle. Rose Spalding has
emphasized that "peace building is not an inevitable extension of regime transition, and it should not be subsumed under an electoral process."[4] Instead we
need to focus on substantive (real) democracy, which requires social and economic justice. From this perspective, a successful implementation of the Central American peace accords was a sine qua non for democratization in the region to have any meaning.

Further, it is a key argument of our chapter that democracy cannot be fully
consolidated without the full incorporation of women into the political
process. An increasing number of scholars recognize that only a gendered

analysis of democratization provides a meaningful picture of the social and political reality prevailing in a country. Thus we examine the Guatemalan peace process through a gender lens.

The guerrilla movements of El Salvador, Nicaragua, and Guatemala waged their struggle under the banner of social and economic justice for the people. Many women who sought to participate in the construction of a new society joined their fight. Now it is important to establish whether the strong participation of women during the war is being translated into effective representation in the political structures that have emerged or are still developing.

"Gender" can be understood as a socially produced category, defined in Terrell Carver's terms as "the ways that sex and sexuality become power relations in society."[5] "Equality" is used as a twofold concept. It includes "formal equality, which can be achieved by means of legislation" and "substantial equality, which aspires to being able to deal with relations between individuals in different original positions."[6] Further, Carver makes a crucial point by emphasizing that "gender is not a synonym for women." Gender analysis is not directed against men but seeks to understand relations between the two sexes. In the prevailing societal relations both women and men are negatively affected. This view also leads to the conclusion that only men and women together can transform the inherited power relations. This conviction is at the core of the current emphasis on "mainstreaming" gender. Sustainable development and democracy require the explicit integration of a gender perspective: women and men have to be in the mainstream of development. We argue that sustainable development requires substantive democracy and can be achieved only if equality between men and women becomes an integral part of societal development.

We begin with an analysis of the evolution of the Guatemalan accords. We then examine the gender content of the peace agreements and describe the principal challenges confronting the ex-combatants during the process of reintegration into society. Next, we discuss the role of the United Nations Verification Mission in Guatemala (MINUGUA). In our analysis we postulate the central argument that in the trilogy of peacemaking, peacekeeping, and peace building, the first two phases can be considered a relative success, while the future course of the last phase is still in doubt.

The Evolution of the Guatemalan Peace Agreements

The Nicaraguan Resistance disarmed between April and June 1990, in the wake of the electoral defeat of the Sandinistas in Nicaragua. The conflict between the revolutionary government and the United States–sponsored counterrevolution led to 30,865 Nicaraguans being killed.[7] These casualties were in addition to the 50,000 people who had died during the Sandinista struggle to oust dictator Anastasio Somoza from power. The Nicaraguan peace agreement was followed on January 16, 1992, by the historic peace accords, signed at Chapúltepec Castle, Mexico, between the government of El Salvador and the guerrilla forces integrated in the Frente Farabundo Martí para la Liberación Nacional (Farabundo Martí National Liberation Front, or FMLN). This agreement ended a twelve-year conflict (1979–1992) that had adversely affected a whole nation. The war ravaged the country, creating 1.5 million refugees and claiming the lives of more than 70,000 people, most of them civilians. In the wake of the accords, optimism regarding El Salvador's future was widespread. On December 29, 1996, the final Central American peace accord was completed. The guerrilla forces integrated into the Unidad Revolucionaria Nacional Guatemalteca (Guatemalan National Revolutionary Unity, or URNG) and the Guatemalan government, headed by President Alvaro Arzú, signed an agreement ending the conflict that had engulfed Guatemala for thirty-six years. The human suffering during this period was enormous. According to the report by the Commission for Historical Clarification, charged under the peace accords with establishing the truth about Guatemala's violent past, more than 200,000 Guatemalans were killed or disappeared over the course of the conflict.[8] In addition, hundreds of villages were destroyed and 1.5 million people were internally displaced or sought refuge in Mexico.[9]

In all three wars, the United States government was a major player, either backing repressive governments or sponsoring counterrevolutionary forces. In March 1999, President Bill Clinton acknowledged the destructive role played by the United States in the Guatemalan conflict. In an unprecedented gesture, President Clinton formally apologized to the Guatemalan people at a meeting, held in Antigua, Guatemala: "For the United States, it is important that I state clearly that support for military forces and intelligence units which engaged in widespread repression was wrong, and the United States must not repeat that mistake."[10]

A comparison is useful for understanding the scope of the human tragedy caused by these wars. The Vietnam War in which 58,202 North American soldiers were killed led to the "Vietnam Syndrome." The impact of the war on the North American public was so great that it took years to rebuild public support for open foreign interventions involving U.S. troops. Yet the human cost to the United States in the Vietnam War—or in the September 2001 attacks on the World Trade Center and the Pentagon—pales in comparison to the suffering wrought on the Central American societies. In terms of the U.S. population, the victims of the Nicaraguan revolutionary and counterrevolutionary wars would amount to a staggering 7.3 million. The conflict in El Salvador corresponded to

3.5 million deaths and 75 million refugees. Finally, the slaughter in Guatemala would have been the equivalent of 6 million dead North Americans. The Guatemalan peace accords were the result of negotiations that were conducted over seven years and involved three successive administrations. The first accord concerned democratization and was signed in Querétaro, Mexico, on July 25, 1991. Interestingly, it was the government of Jorge Serrano, a conservative, who took this first important step. When Serrano instigated a failed coup in May 1993, however, and was subsequently forced from office, the negotiation process stalled. President Ramiro de León Carpio resurrected the peace negotiations in 1994, with the United Nations assuming the role of moderator. Further, a group of countries officially organized as the Group of Friends of the peace process, which included Norway, Colombia, Venezuela, Spain, Mexico, and the United States, exerted pressure on the two parties to resume the talks.[11] Following two more years of arduous talks involving a third Guatemalan administration under President Alvaro Arzú, the final peace agreement was signed on December 29, 1996. The guerrilla movement agreed to demobilize its forces in three phases over a period of two months. The disarming of the combatants started on March 3, 1997, and was completed in August of the same year, in a final, originally not programmed, fourth phase.

Civil society contributed greatly to the successful initiation of the negotiations, which was not the case in Nicaragua or El Salvador. Various sectors of Guatemalan society, including the business sector, the religious community, and the labor unions, participated in talks that preceded the signing of the first accord. These conversations were essential because they "legitimized the idea of a negotiated end to the armed conflict."[12] The role of civil society was institutionalized with an accord that established the Asamblea de la Sociedad Civil (Assembly of Civil Society, or ASC). It consisted of ten diverse organizations representing the main sectors of Guatemalan society and derived its legitimacy from the January 1994 framework agreement, in which it was given "official recognition as an interlocutor by the parties to the peace talks."[13] Specifically, the ASC was charged with the mandate "to transmit to the U.N. moderator, the government and the URNG, non-binding recommendations" and "to act as guarantor for bilateral agreements to give them the character of national commitments."[14]

The Guatemalan Accords from a Gender Perspective

A few high-ranking female URNG officials, supported by a vocal women's movement, managed to put gender equality on the agenda of the peace negotiations.[15] For example, Luz Méndez, a member of the URNG's commission negotiating the peace accords, emphasized the importance of incorporating women's rights into the agreements.[16] She had learned from the Salvadoran experience, where the FMLN leadership had paid little attention to women's rights in the peace negotiations. Although Méndez and several other officials advocated the necessity to incorporate a gender perspective into the accords, this view was not representative for the URNG in general. Awareness of gender issues was not common in the guerrilla movement. This made it imperative for the advocates for women's rights to be supported from sectors within society at large.

Particularly the Assembly of Civil Society played an important role in advocating the inclusion of women's rights in the accords. A highly visible group within the ASC was the Women's Sector. URNG official Alba Estela Maldonado, then the only woman in the URNG's fifteen-member National Directorate, affirmed that "the Women's Sector, practically the only one with a permanent presence in the Assembly of Civil Society, influenced . . . the coordination and the content of some of the accords."[17] As a result, women's rights were specifically addressed in four of the seven substantive agreements that were reached between July 1991 and September 1996. The emphasis on gender issues in the Guatemalan peace accords indicated that the level of gender awareness in the region had changed since the 1992 Salvadoran agreement.

Indeed, there were a number of important passages on women's rights in the accords. In the accord establishing procedures for the resettlement of populations uprooted during the war, the parties agreed "to emphasize in particular the protection of families headed by women, as well as the widows and orphans who have been most affected."[18] Further, the Guatemalan government "committed itself to eliminating all forms of discrimination, factual or legal, against women, and to make it easier [to have] access to land, housing, [and] credit and to participate in development projects. A gender perspective will be incorporated in the policies, programs and activities of the global development strategy."[19] In the important agreement on the rights of Guatemala's indigenous peoples, considered one of the key achievements of the URNG leadership, indigenous women were given special protection. For example, sexual harassment of an indigenous woman was to be sanctioned particularly severely under Guatemalan law.[20] Women's political rights were also addressed. The accord concerning the strengthening of civil society advocated the introduction of measures of positive discrimination to increase female participation. The agreement required the signatory parties "to take the corresponding measures in order to ensure that organizations of political and social character adopt specific policies tending to encourage and favor women's participation as part of the process of strengthening civilian power."[21]

Méndez emphasized the importance of the international climate during the peace negotiations. For example, discussions on the Socioeconomic and Agrarian Accord coincided with the 1995 Fourth World Conference on Women in Beijing. The fact that gender issues were on the forefront internationally made it easier to incorporate provisions favoring women's rights into this accord.[22] A key passage of the agreement stated:

> Recognizing the insufficiently appreciated contribution of women in all spheres of economic and social activity, particularly their work in favor of improving the community, the [signatory] parties recognize the necessity to strengthen women's participation in economic and social development on terms of equality. To this end the Government commits itself to take the specific economic and social situation of women into account in the strategies, plans and development programs and to train civil servants in the analysis and planning based on this perspective. This includes: to recognize the equality of rights between woman and man in the home, the workplace, production, as well as social and political life and to assure [women] the same possibilities than men, in particular concerning access to credit, the awarding of land and other productive and technological resources.[23]

Thus, the Guatemalan accords were unique in terms of addressing the role of women in society and advocating change toward greater gender equality. The accords reflected a rethinking of women's role in society. At least on a formal level, women were acknowledged as key protagonists in Guatemala's future development.[24] Yet the challenge remained to implement the provisions in the accords in a way that would transform Guatemalan society.

Jack Spence and his colleagues have emphasized that "the Guatemalan agreement contains more wide ranging language on social and economic areas, by far, than the Salvadoran accord, but a great many of the provisions are stated in sufficiently general terms as to make them virtually unenforceable."[25] Nineth Montenegro, a member of parliament and a key figure in the fight for women's rights, concurred with this analysis:

> The peace accords in Guatemala represent a good legal, political and economic framework of the type of country we want to build but it has not taken concrete form. This has been due to a lack of political will, a lack of resources, as well as corruption in the previous and current government. The money is squandered, not on social works, not on social expenditures, but on operating expenses. And the lack of political will also is evident and thus some accords have not been honored. . . . And so the poverty continues and the population continues to be marginalized and excluded. . . . I think that what the people want is that the peace accords help them to eat, to get a job. They are not interested in theoretical pipe dreams that the people don't feel or live personally.[26]

There is strong consensus that the URNG's weakness at the bargaining table made it impossible for the guerrilla leadership to negotiate more specific, enforceable agreements, a reality that impeded the full realization of the provisions in the accords.

The correlation of forces between the government and the URNG had negative consequences for the reintegration process of URNG ex-combatants. The prospects for URNG militants were bleak in light of the fact that the "URNG was unable to get agreement in the negotiations for provisions calling for a land reform . . . because the issue is anathema to the government and the large landholders that back it."[27] Due to the resistance by the rural bourgeoisie, it was believed that only "small numbers of former combatants" would be able to obtain "land and credit for purchasing it under the accords."[28] The positive exception to the bleak reality described here was the successful distribution of land to returning refugees.[29]

The initial stage of reintegrating URNG forces into Guatemalan society—under the shared responsibility of the government, the URNG, and a group of countries supporting the accords—concluded in May 1998.[30] The reintegration program was multifaceted and included economic, educational, human rights, family reunification, documentation, health care, housing, and training components. Interviews conducted with political cadres and former URNG combatants between August 1997 and June 1998 showed that the great majority of URNG personnel had received some benefits under the reinsertion programs.[31] Overall, the international community pledged close to two billion dollars to aid Guatemala with the implementation of the peace accords.[32] Obviously, URNG members received only a fraction of these funds. In general, ex-combatants received about six hundred dollars to cover their immediate monetary needs following demobilization. They also received an equivalent amount in agricultural inputs. The most fortunate obtained credit to buy land. Those not interested in farming received training in various vocations or obtained study grants to continue their education. Inevitably, some URNG members fell through the cracks. A local URNG leader complained that "there are historic fighters that have been left out [from the reinsertion programs]."[33] As in El Salvador, there were instances of gender discrimination in the allocation of benefits. María, a young female combatant, expressed the sentiment of many female fighters when she complained that she had received no land "because they gave it to my compañero."[34]

After years in the mountains, URNG combatants had to start over under precarious circumstances. Despite these difficult circumstances, ex-combatants expressed hope that they had not fought in vain. Doña Virginia, formerly an armed combatant, explained, "Many of us had nothing or we lost everything in the war. In fact, we needed something in order to live dignified and for this we fought. Not only for us but for a lot of people that will also benefit from the productive projects."[35] Several combatants emphasized the enormous difficulty they faced in making a new life. Dozens of former fighters had to spend more than a year in hostels following their demobilization because they had nowhere to go. Almost all URNG cadres had problems obtaining the legal documents required for a successful reintegration into society. Expectations generally exceeded the limited benefits. Many former combatants, disappointed with the initial results of the demobilization process and facing the pressures of daily life, were reluctant to continue their militancy in the URNG.

As in El Salvador and Nicaragua, the URNG leadership had problems in maintaining close relations with its supporters from the war days. Several party leaders affirmed, and personal interviews with URNG cadres confirmed, that the URNG had lost part of its rank and file during the transition from a military organization to a political movement. Grassroots leaders, sympathetic to the ideas of the revolutionary Left, complained that their constituents who had fought with the URNG were not aware of the content of the URNG's political project.[36] For several months following the signing of the peace accords, the URNG lacked the organic structures necessary to maintain contact with the grassroots. The military structures from the war days had been dissolved and the structures of the emerging political party were still under construction at the local and regional levels. Rodrigo Asturias, one of the four URNG commanders during the war, acknowledged that the four groups composing the URNG "had dissolved their structures too hastily." He argued that the lack of an adequate transition period impeded the unification of the political party that emerged out of the guerrilla movement.[37] The uncertainty created by this situation was a key factor in the informal reconstitution of the four original URNG groups during 2000–2001.

Once the ex-combatants had returned to their communities, they struggled to make a new life. The great majority had no economic resources or support from their families. According to a 1999 study, 19 percent of the URNG militants interviewed felt rejected by their communities and 80 percent reported to be unemployed.[38] The daily fight for survival left them little time for activities involving the emerging party. This was particularly true for female militants.[39]

Their experiences during the war had raised the expectations of many female combatants as to their role in the construction of postwar Guatemala. Having experienced the relative freedom and equality of combat, which was characterized by the predominance of nontraditional values, many women were reluctant to return to the straitjacket of gender inequality imposed by societal norms. Yet the great majority of the female combatants had little choice but to return to their traditional roles. Julio Manuel Canales, a Salvadoran combatant, also spoke for Guatemalan women when he succinctly summarized the experience of many female combatants: "Of all those who shouldered a rifle, only to the women did they give back a broom."[40] Once women were back in the kitchen, they were given the responsibility of ensuring the daily survival of their families while their partners competed, mostly in vain, for one of the few available jobs. Relegated to the private sphere of the household, women had fewer opportunities than men to actively participate in party activities.

Thus, a number of URNG militants were disillusioned with the peace accords and showed little interest in becoming part of a new political movement. Other old cadres were simply left out, a development that caused great resentment. Those militants who were active in party building were accustomed to taking orders from the leadership and had a difficult time adjusting to the new "democratic" reality, where the neatness of following the "orientations" from the leadership was to be replaced by messy participatory decision making.

At the same time, there was an influx of new people who frequently lacked the commitment to the political project that had originally given rise to the Guatemalan guerrilla movement. One of their advantages was that they had their documentation in order, while many longtime URNG supporters lacked the legal documents required to officially join a political party. Once again, this was especially the case for female militants. It was a common practice in the Guatemalan countryside not to register female children.[41] The lack of birth certificates subsequently impeded women from fully exercising their political rights. Women were confronted with a variety of societal norms and expectations that were discriminatory in nature. Most importantly, female cadres had little choice but to resume their traditional roles in the household. Thus, few female ex-combatants became legal members of the emerging party.

In light of this reality, it is not surprising that early evaluations of the peace accords' impact sounded a pessimistic note. Leaders of the women's movement argued that "the demands of women in respect to the implementation of the accords lack tangible results. Fourteen months after they took effect, it is difficult to perceive how these commitments have been converted into actions; the reality is that six out of ten Guatemalan women live in rural areas, and the absence of public services is common."[42] The government was criticized for "failing to have an idea of how to attend to women's historical problems" and for lacking a strategy of action designed to ensure that the provisions of the accords would not remain empty words.[43] Government officials, on the other hand, faulted the women's movement for not supporting the government in its efforts to strengthen women's rights. However, some high-ranking officials recognized that the Arzú administration did not understand how to reach out to the women's movement and build the necessary alliances.[44] In the eyes of opposition legislator Olga Camey de Noack, the problems continued following the 1999 election of Alfonso Portillo to the presidency: "At the current time [May 2001] the subject of women['s rights] is a subject that has received no attention from the current government. . . . The agenda of this government has in no instant prioritized, much less sought to vindicate, the subject of women['s rights]."[45] Not surprisingly, members of the new government held opposite views. For example, Zulema de Paz, the president of the Women's Commission in the Guatemalan parliament, argued that women's rights had been greatly advanced by the accords:

> I repeat it. I have said it many times. Definitely, it is the subject of women where we have seen most progress in the accords. I have told this to the members of the [Women's] Forum and congratulated them. They have done a good job, a permanent job that has resulted in change or means that certain accords will be honored. . . . For example, at the national level, they [the women's movement] could hold a women's conference and the women could propose what policies needed to be instituted to advance the subject of gender. This had never happened. The fact that the Women's Secretariat has been created and has taken this up and included it in its policies is also important progress.[46]

It is important to understand this statement in light of Guatemala's cultural context. The historical repression of the country's twenty-one indigenous peoples that represent more than half of the total population has led some observers to compare it to South Africa during the days of apartheid. According to World Bank estimates, in the countryside, where the overwhelming majority of the indigenous population lives, about 90 percent of the population confronts abject poverty. Under these conditions, the fight for gender equality was reduced to an urban elite phenomenon. Whereas all women suffered from the prevailing culture of machismo, the fight for survival, particularly for indigenous women, took precedence over efforts to improve gender relations. Thus, the fact that gender inequities were so broadly addressed in the peace accords was indeed a remarkable achievement. Observers who compared the new reality in the wake of the peace accords with the country's past could paint an optimistic picture, whereas representatives of the women's movement who had been instrumental in getting the gender provisions into the agreements rightly demanded concrete results.

Thus, despite the rosy scenarios painted by the government and the difficult reality of Guatemala's gender relations, the predominant sentiment within the women's movement concerning the implementation of the peace accords was profound disappointment. Most of its leaders ceased to believe in the viability of the peace process. They were especially angered by the lack of response from the political parties to their efforts to put women's rights on the agenda. As a consequence, female leaders abandoned their efforts to transform the political parties and focused their energy on strengthening the movement.

Patricia Wohlers, the MINUGUA official in charge of gender and author of a 2001 study on the challenges confronting Guatemalan women in their efforts to fully participate in society, argued that despite the institutionalization of public policies with a gender perspective, the peace accords resulted in few substantive changes for women.[47] Jorge Soto, the president of the URNG, presented the view of many observers when he maintained that only those accords that did not affect the system had been implemented.[48]

The United Nations and Guatemala: Bitter Results

Great hope arose among Guatemalans when the United Nations decided to open a peace mission in the country to verify written agreements between the government and the Guatemalan National Revolutionary Unity. The United Nations began its support of the Guatemalan peace process by observing the Oslo talks in 1990. Its efforts continued during the negotiations in 1991, which resulted in the signing of the Querétaro Agreement in Mexico. Subsequently, the United Nations moderated the negotiations that began in January 1994, committed to the verification of the signed agreements, and finally installed a United Nations mission in Guatemala.

On January 10, 1994, the government of Guatemala and the URNG signed a framework agreement defining the United Nations' role as the sole moderator and verifier of all future agreements. Within this context, both parties ratified the Global Agreement on Human Rights on March 20, 1994. In addition, they established a calendar for talks and decided to sign a final agreement for firm and lasting peace before the end of the year. On September 19, the United Nations General Assembly resolved to establish the Mission for the Verification of Human Rights in Guatemala (MINUGUA) to monitor compliance with the Global Agreement on Human Rights. A novel approach was taken in the formulation of this mission: it combined the verification of human rights with institutional strengthening in a country still at war. This demonstrated the United Nations' willingness to innovate the peace mission; MINUGUA would be the first attempt to link verification with the reinforcement of state and civil society organizations.

Guatemala's political atmosphere was still precarious when the mission arrived, since the country remained under conditions of military confrontation. MINUGUA's arrival generated high expectations. Broad sectors of civil society hoped for an end to the armed conflict and the beginning of a new stage of development for the nation. The human rights verification mission began working on November 22, 1994, establishing itself in the forefront of the process to conclude an armed conflict that had pitted Guatemalans against each other for thirty-six years. The negotiations were greatly influenced by the mission's presence and actions, especially because the negotiating parties— government and guerrilla forces—reached agreements and accepted consensus under unequal conditions. The government of President León Carpio (who had assumed power after former president Serrano's self-coup in 1993) remained under the direct influence of the army, which continued with its counterinsurgency operations and maintained its power and political influence. On the other hand, the URNG forces, made up of the Ejército Guerrillero de los Pobres (EGP), Fuerzas Armadas Rebeldes (FAR), Organización del Pueblo en Armas (ORPA), and Partido Guatemalteco del Trabajo (PGT), continued to operate along guerrilla fronts, especially in the departments of Quiché, Huehuetenango, Quetzaltenango, San Marcos, Retalulheu, Sololá, Chimaltenango, Escuintla, Santa Rosa, Petén, Alta Verapaz, and Baja Verapaz. While the guerrilla forces maintained their organization, military maneuvers, and presence, striking the army severely and causing significant casualties, their leadership took part in peace negotiations abroad.

Although historically reluctant toward change, the two sectors with the most influence and real power in the country—private enterprise (particularly conservative and reactionary) and the army—had accepted the peace process due to different internal and external factors: international pressure, the regional situation, economic crisis, national insecurity, and a reduction in institutional morale. This aspect is very important since, when it came time to verify the will and commitment toward compliance with the agreements, these two sectors would be the most vehemently opposed to the stipulated changes. It must also be noted that the army accepted negotiations only under the condition that the repression and massacres it committed during the armed conflict would not be subject to subsequent legal action.

In this framework, the arrival of MINUGUA (peacemaking) expressed the United Nations' political intention to consolidate peace after years of conflict. The UN emphasized the multidisciplinary nature of the mission and a new focus that involved not only facilitating a political solution (peacekeeping) but also supporting national efforts to create social and economic conditions for firm and lasting peace (peace building).

Originally, the negotiating process involved significant participation by civil society. Over time, however, the negotiations were conducted exclusively between the government and the URNG. Any decisions reached had the characteristics of a closed negotiation. This factor would have a direct effect on the postsigning stage. It became clear that the origin of the agreements was limited to a pact between the government and guerrilla forces, an aspect that would later be identified as a key limitation to the successful implementation of the accords. The need to simply declare peace became the primary objective of both parties. The URNG leadership failed to discuss the impact and viability of the agreements with its rank and file, and the government showed no interest in explaining the accords to civil society.

By March 1996, a little over a year after its deployment, it was clear that the UN mission would be drawn into the political conflicts of Guatemalan society. The main actors sought to lure the mission to their own side, either through demands or by criticizing the verification efforts and their results. In the months before the signing of the final peace accords, there were still expectations and hopes regarding the conflict's possible resolution. In October, however, news spread of the kidnapping of Olga de Novella, a member of a wealthy family of business leaders. Responsibility for the kidnapping fell on one of the ORPA commanders, Isaías (Augusto Baldizón Núñez), who was then detained by the Presidential Guard (Estado Mayor Presidencial, or EMP). President Arzú's administration agreed to negotiate with its prisoner and released him in exchange for de Novella. Involved in this event, which had an enormous political impact, were top guerrilla leaders—especially ORPA Commander in Chief Rodrigo Asturias, who denied having known about or authorized the kidnapping—as well as Gustavo Porras, the president's private secretary, who brokered the deal without leaving recourse to justice. Added to all this was the disappearance of a member of the kidnapping team, E. Cabrera "Mincho," who accompanied Isaías and was reported by the mission to have been detained by the EMP's Antikidnapping Command (CAS). To date, Cabrera remains disappeared.

This episode endangered the negotiations. It tarnished the process, discredited Asturias, and weakened the national actors, especially the guerrilla forces, whose dedication and commitment to the peace process was compromised. The decision by both parties to achieve a final agreement prevailed, however, and the severity of the event was ignored in order to achieve peace. Among society as a whole, this attitude caused apathy, distrust, and skepticism. This was reflected in the population's muted reaction to the signing of the peace accords on December 29, 1996, and in the negative results of the Popular Consultation in May 1999, which sought to provide constitutional support to the political commitments contained in the agreements.

Conclusion

The Guatemalan and Salvadoran peace accords differed significantly. The 1992 Salvadoran accords constituted, in the words of United Nations negotiator Alvaro de Soto, "a negotiated revolution." Under its terms, the government agreed to many demands the Salvadoran guerrilla forces made. The URNG, on the other hand, lacked a comparable bargaining position. As a consequence, the peace agreements of Guatemala failed to resolve the fundamental problems that led to the wars in the first place.

MINUGUA sought to apply an iron hand to verification, yet it lacked the capacity to compel the government to comply with accepted commitments. Thus the structural causes of an unjust situation—a situation that the accords were intended to modify—remained unchanged because such change would directly affect the economic interests of the sectors that have traditionally controlled the country. Political compromise prevailed over reform.

Successive reports on the process by the secretary-general of the United Nations explain this situation and make recommendations to the government, which is ultimately responsible for the peace process's implementation. Because of the logic behind a negotiated process, one would assume that such recommendations would guide and direct the executive's actions. However, the government has paid no attention to these suggestions, and the UN has been unable to create measures ensuring the completion of the agreements. In the view of Gustavo Porras, who played a key role in the negotiation and implementation of the accords, the peace process "led to political peace but worsened the peace of the citizen."[49] Former president Ramiro de León Carpio concurred, arguing that "very little of the accords has been implemented."[50]

The lessons learned during these postwar years in Guatemala have been bitter. Seven years after the signing of the peace agreement, the need to go further than theoretical postulates is still felt. The entities created by the accords (especially the Comisión de Acompañamiento, or Accompaniment Commission) have not fulfilled their roles in guiding the peace process and its dialogues. There is a continued lack of rapprochement and pacts on the main topics, such as the public prosecutor, indigenous identity, and educational reform, which were obviated as soon as their implementation began.

The lessons learned in this process, with its broad national scope, are many and varied. Among the most significant are: the need to make all sectors participate in the gestation of acquired commitments and, in a parallel manner, the need to design measures that ensure the continuity of positions assumed during the negotiations, especially by key groups such as private enterprise, political parties, and the army. In the international arena, coherence of action must be ensured, with respect to both the United Nations system and the international community.

From a gender perspective, the URNG would benefit from paying close attention to the experiences of the revolutionary Left in El Salvador and Nicaragua. Two key lessons can be derived from these experiences for Guatemala. Efforts by female URNG militants to strengthen gender equality in the party will bear fruit if measures of positive discrimination are strictly enforced during the early stages of the fight for women's rights. For this to happen, female militants need to be well organized and prepared to seek alliances with male party leaders. Simultaneously, these partisan efforts need to be broadened and incorporated into pluralist coalitions to affect gender relations in society at large.

What are the key factors that shaped the struggle for gender equality in El Salvador, Nicaragua, and Guatemala following the peace accords? Of women in the three countries, female FMLN militants in El Salvador played the most significant role in the guerrilla movement during the war, providing them with a strong argument in favor of women's participation in the party that was built following the peace accords. Sandinista women in Nicaragua also contributed greatly during their country's insurrection, whereas female URNG militants were a distant third in terms of female participation in the guerrilla struggle. The international climate favoring increased women's participation in decision-making bodies was strongest at the time of the Guatemalan peace accords. While it translated into strong provisions in favor of women's rights in the accords themselves, it had little significance in the early development of the URNG. FMLN women, on the other hand, were able to translate international pressure for gender equality into increased political participation. In the case of Nicaragua, Sandinista women first managed to take advantage of a favorable international climate when the Sandinista National Liberation Front was out of power. Before then, the women's movement was subordinated to the revolutionary government's interests. As a consequence, many activists left the party and focused on building a strong movement. Thus, the women's movement grew, while party activists faced a difficult struggle to transform gender relations within the Sandinista party. During the 1990s, Salvadoran women were most effective in pursuing shrewd strategies to strengthen formal equality within the political parties. They did so with the support of the women's movement. In Nicaragua, women had good ideas but ultimately lacked the clout to get them adopted, while the priorities of party leaders worked against Guatemalan women's efforts to strengthen gender equality.[51]

Any evaluation of gender equality and democratization within the Guatemalan revolutionary Left has to emphasize the enormous task facing the URNG leadership and its female members and supporters. At the dawn of the new millennium, the Guatemalan peace process is still in its early stages, and the URNG has yet to complete its transition from a political-military organization into a democratic political party. In this context, gender equality has simply not been a priority in the minds of many key officials.

URNG women have confronted problems specific to the Guatemalan situation. Most importantly, party members of both sexes were initially overwhelmed by the demands that the demobilization and the creation of a political party placed on them. A central challenge facing the women who have sought to advance gender equality within the emerging party structures was that they were still in the process of getting to know each other. The problem had three roots: First, the majority of the female URNG members were reluctant to acknowledge their militancy publicly out of fear that they would be persecuted by right-wing elements. Second, the complex ethnic composition of the membership complicated internal communication since a number of female militants did not speak Spanish. According to Rachel McCleary, "the rank-and-file supporters of the URNG [speak] 16 indigenous languages."[52] Third, despite advances in the unification process and the dissolution of the historical structures of the four constituent groups, many activists were only slowly shedding their identities as members of the subgroups in order to assume full membership in the URNG. The continued infighting within the party, which led to an open split in the spring of 2002, put gender equality on the back burner.

Guatemala's civil society, which seems to be waking, will have the last word. We argue that the successful completion of the peace process requires a renegotiation of the peace accords with broad national participation rather than the current rescheduling or restatement of agreements. Whether this scenario becomes a reality will depend on the collective will of civil society to assume this historic challenge.

Notes

Research for this chapter has been conducted with the financial assistance of the European Union. The views expressed are our own and in no way reflect the official opinion of the European Union. Several passages in this chapter are taken from Ilja A. Luciak, *After the Revolution: Gender and Democracy in El Salvador, Nicaragua, and Guatemala* (Baltimore: Johns Hopkins University Press, 2001).

1. Samuel P. Huntington, *The Third Wave: Democratization in the Late Twentieth Century* (Norman: University of Nebraska Press, 1991), 3.

2. Gary Hoskin, "Democratization in Latin America," *Latin American Research Review* 32, no. 3 (1997): 209–23.

3. Ilja Luciak, *The Sandinista Legacy: Lessons from a Political Economy in Transition* (Gainesville: University Press of Florida, 1995), 17–21.

4. Rose J. Spalding, "From Low-Intensity Warfare to Low-Intensity Peace: The Nicaraguan Peace Process" (paper presented at the Woodrow Wilson International Center for Scholars conference "Comparative Peace Processes in Latin America," Washington, DC, March 13–14, 1997), 7.

5. Terrell Carver, *Gender Is Not a Synonym for Women* (Boulder: Lynne Rienner, 1996), 120.

6. Tuija Parvikko, "Conceptions of Gender Equality: Similarity and Difference," in *Equality Politics and Gender*, ed. Elizabeth Meehan and Selma Sevenhuijsen (London: Sage, 1991), 48.

7. Thomas W. Walker, ed., *Nicaragua without Illusions* (Wilmington: Scholarly Resources, 1997), 12.

8. Historical Clarification Commission, *Guatemala: Memory of Silence* (Guatemala City: Historical Clarification Commission, 1999), 72.

9. Jack Spence et al., *Promise and Reality: Implementation of the Guatemalan Peace Accords* (Cambridge, MA: Hemisphere Initiatives, 1998), 4.

10. Henrik Broder, "Clinton Apologizes for U.S. Support of Guatemalan Rightists," *New York Times*, March 10, 1999.

11. Rachel McCleary, "Guatemala's Postwar Prospects," *Journal of Democracy* 8, no. 2 (April 1997): 137.

12. Edgar Gutiérrez, "Quién quiso asaltar el cielo?" in *Guatemala: Izquierdas en transición*, ed. Edelberto Torres Rivas (Guatemala City: FLACSO, 1997): 80. Translation by Luciak.

13. Spence et al., *Promise and Reality*, 12.

14. Gutiérrez, "Quién quiso asaltar el cielo?" 81.

15. Ana Leticia Aguilar, "Un movimiento de mujeres embrionario," in *El movimiento de mujeres en Centroamérica*, ed. María Teresa Blandón and Sofía Montenegro (Managua: La Corriente, 1997), 122.

16. Luz Méndez, member of the URNG's Political Council and executive director of the National Union of Guatemalan Women (UNAMG), interviewed by authors, Guatemala City, April 4, 1997.

17. Alba Estela Maldonado, member of the URNG's Executive Council and head of the Women's Secretariat, interviewed by authors, Guatemala City, November 20, 1997.

18. United Nations, "Acuerdo para el reasentamiento de las poblaciones desarraigadas por el enfrentamiento armado" (Guatemala City: MINUGUA, 1994), 38. Translation by Luciak.

19. United Nations, "Acuerdo para el reasentamiento," 43.

20. United Nations, "Acuerdo sobre identidad y derechos de los pueblos indígenas" (Guatemala City: MINUGUA, 1995), 6.

21. United Nations, "Acuerdo sobre aspectos socioeconomicos y situación agraria" (Guatemala City: MINUGUA, 1996), 22.

22. Méndez, interviewed by authors, April 4, 1997.

23. United Nations, "Acuerdo sobre aspectos socioeconomicos," 6. Translation by Luciak.

24. Gobierno de Guatemala, *Política nacional de promoción y desarrollo de las mujeres guatemaltecas: Plan de equidad de oportunidades 1997–2001* (Guatemala City: Government of Guatemala, 1997), 2.

25. Spence et al., *Promise and Reality*, 14.

26. Nineth Montenegro, member of parliament, interviewed by authors, Guatemala City, May 7, 2001.

27. Spence et al., *Promise and Reality*, 8.

28. Spence et al., *Promise and Reality*.

29. Spence et al., *Promise and Reality*, 54.

30. Unidad Revolucionaria Nacional Guatemalteca, *Cumplimiento de los acuerdos de paz: Período mayo–agosto* (Guatemala City: URNG, 1998), 29.

31. Ilja Luciak conducted these interviews with a team of researchers in Guatemala City and in two departments. They included both female and male political cadres and ex-combatants. A total of twenty-eight people were interviewed, seventeen in 1997 and eleven in 1998.

32. David Holiday, "Guatemala's Precarious Peace," *Current History* 99, no. 634 (February 2000): 79.

33. Anonymous, interviewed by authors, n.d.

34. Anonymous, interviewed by authors, n.d.

35. Doña Virginia, interviewed by authors, n.d.

36. Regional coordinator of the peasant group CONIC, interviewed by authors, n.d.

37. Rodrigo Asturias, interviewed by authors, May 4, 2001.

38. See Luciak, *After the Revolution*.

39. Alba Estela Maldonado, interviewed by authors, Guatemala City, March 2, 1999.

40. Julio Manuel Canales, interviewed by authors, n.d.

41. Amanda Carrera, URNG official in charge of the gender group of the Fundación Guillermo Toriello, interviewed by authors, Guatemala City, March 3, 1999.

42. La Cuerda, "Demandas de la mujeres y acuerdos de paz" 1, no. 0 (Guatemala City: La Cuerda, 1998), 11.

43. La Cuerda, "Demandas de la mujeres."

44. Racquel Zelaya, government official under the Arzú administration in charge of implementing the peace accords, interviewed by authors, Guatemala City, May 2, 2001.

45. Olga Camey de Noack, member of parliament, interviewed by authors, Guatemala City, May 7, 2001.

46. Zulema de Paz, interviewed by authors, May 4, 2001.

47. Patricia Wohlers, MINUGUA official in charge of gender issues, interviewed by author, Guatemala City, May 5, 2001.

48. Jorge Soto, president of the URNG, interviewed by authors, Guatemala City, May 7, 2001.

49. Gustavo Porras, president Arzú's private secretary and key figure in the implementation of the accords, interviewed by authors, Guatemala City, May 3, 2001.

50. Ramiro de León Carpio, former president of Guatemala, interviewed by authors, Guatemala City, May 7, 2001.

51. For an in-depth analysis of these issues, see Luciak, *After the Revolution*.

52. McCleary, "Guatemala's Postwar Prospects," 138.

11

Les femmes aux mille bras: Building Peace in Rwanda

Erin K. Baines

Let yourselves be consoled, you have been sacrificed by systems it is necessary to change. Unite so as to transform problems into opportunities for action.

—Veneranda Nzambazamariya,
Rwandan winner of Millennium Peace Prize for Women

ON THE OFFICE WALL OF PRO-FEMMES Twese Hamwe, a Rwandan network of women's associations "working together for peace and equality," hangs a poster titled *Les femmes aux mille bras* (Women with a Thousand Arms). On the poster appears a profile of a Rwandan woman with multiple arms busy at work. Agriculture, domestic chores, and child care are some of the traditional activities engaged in by the many hands, but easily added are a variety of new gender roles assumed by women in postgenocide Rwanda: reconstruction of infrastructure, generation and management of income, and community leadership. To empower grassroots women and promote their participation in the future development of their country, thousands of grassroots associations and women's organizations[1] have formed, joined together by networks such as Pro-Femmes Twese Hamwe.

The poster is a clever play on the Rwandan nationalist slogan, *Rwanda: Pays des mille collines* (Land of a Thousand Hills), and it suggests that Rwandan women have an integral role in rebuilding a country devastated by mass genocide, human displacement, and economic collapse. Given deep social rifts engendered by these events, and in the absence of social welfare institutions, both traditional and new gender roles of women are sources of social and economic capital, contributing to the prospects for peace in the country. Tutsi and Hutu women have begun to work together despite the tragedy of the genocide, focusing on the commonality of their struggle as women. Together they are rebuilding their lives, their homes, their country. In doing so, they have begun a healing process, a process of building peace. Both the Rwandan Government of National Unity (GNU) and the international community appear to recognize and value the importance of women's role in peace building, and a cooperative effort has been forged between these two actors to support the efforts of Rwandan women's organizations and grassroots associations. Thus the Ministry for Gender Equality and Women's Empowerment (MIGEPROFE) works closely with the United Nations and bilateral donors to channel resources to grassroots women, build organizational capacity, and encourage political and economic participation.

This chapter analyzes the role of women in building peace in Rwanda after the genocide and conflict, and how the national (government) and global (bilateral and multilateral organizations) shape the unique contributions to peace that Rwandan women as change agents bring to the country. I investigate how ethnic, class, and gender identities intersect to form a web of power relations in postgenocide Rwanda today. I argue that the GNU tends to mask ethnic and class differences among women in national discourses on gender equality and unity. "Partnerships" between women's organizations, grassroots associations, and the GNU problematically fuse civil society to the new Rwandan state, and the government's vision of a unitary, nonethnic nation. As a result, civil society has virtually no space in which to engage in dialogue necessary for recognizing and moving beyond historical differences that have so violently excluded different ethnic groups in the past. More disconcertingly, these relationships threaten to compromise the realms of possibility for women building peace and, potentially, compromise the security of women. The international community contributes to this precarious and pernicious situation, where woman-centered approaches fail to address questions of gender, diversity, and political context required to understand the complex web of power relations in Rwanda. In short, while the initiatives of Rwandan women provide hope in a country sometimes regarded as hopeless in the wake of the genocide, it is critical to move beyond simplistic constructions of women building peace, lest Rwandan women be sacrificed once again for the good of the "nation."

Dying in Rwanda: Background to the Conflict, Genocide, and the United Nations' Futility

> Ethnicity is both the form that conflict in Rwandese society takes and yet not the cause of that conflict.
>
> —"David"[2]

Established in October 1993 to oversee the implementation of the Arusha Peace Agreement, the United Nations Assistance Mission for Rwanda (UNAMIR) was supposed to be a relatively straightforward mission. It was even seen as an opportunity to improve the reputation of the United Nations after the debacle of peacekeeping operations in Somalia and Bosnia.[3] However, the events that unfolded in the following months made a mockery of the United Nations' promises to "never again" permit genocide, and of any perception that the peacekeeping operation was able, much less willing, to protect the lives of the innocent in Rwanda.[4] But to move forward from this point, which continues to baffle conventional analysts of "peace building," we must first look to history and the constructions of gender, ethnicity, and class in the colonial and postcolonial eras.

Rwanda consists of two principal ethnic groups sharing a common history, language, and culture, the Tutsi and Hutu.[5] In the colonial era, the Tutsi minority (10 percent of the population)—thought to be members of an "alien" and superior "race" by colonialists—were privileged in political and economic realms, first by Germany and then Belgium. Thus the Hutu became the "subject" of indirect rule in the colonial period.[6] Women, regardless of ethnicity, enjoyed few spaces in the public realm; with few legal rights, they were neither subject nor citizen of the colonial state but were relegated to the private sphere. A growing number of Hutu elites resented Tutsi privilege, and, in 1959, the monarchy was overturned after the death of a famous king. Tens of thousands of Tutsi were driven into exile in Uganda, and Hutu leaders assumed state power. Independence came in 1962, and further violence erupted as political leaders vied for control, displacing more Tutsi into Uganda. In the next decade, Hutu "moderate" Juvénal Habyarimana assumed the presidency and authoritarian control of political institutions and the military, pursuing a policy of accommodation but also retribution, where Tutsi faced deliberate institutional exclusion. In 1986, Tutsi exiles helped overthrow the Ugandan government of Milton Obote, and the newly installed president, Yoweri Museveni, "encouraged" them to set up a rebel army, the Rwandan Patriotic Front (RPF). In 1990, the RPF, believing that armed conflict was the only way to return Rwanda to "Rwandans," and stop the exclusionary policies of the past, mounted an invasion to "liberate" Rwanda.

Under international pressure,[7] the RPF and Habyarimana's government entered into the Arusha Peace Agreement, which called for the immediate cessation of hostilities, repatriation of refugees, the merging of opposing armies, and a transition to a power-sharing democracy under the supervision of a neutral international peacekeeping force. Security Council Resolution 827 established UNAMIR and requested 5,500 troops. General Roméo Dallaire, force commander, first noted "international indifference" to Rwanda when troop numbers were never met and those who did arrive were poorly equipped.[8] The profundity of this indifference was felt by Dallaire in the months to come as the promised peace in Rwanda spiraled into hell. In January 1994, a high-level government official informed Dallaire of an invidious plan to subvert the implementation of the peace agreement by carrying out a mass killing of Hutu moderates and Tutsi civilians, as well as murdering Belgian peacekeepers to oust international forces who might delay this genocidal plan. "The example he gave is that in twenty minutes his personnel could kill up to 1000 Tutsis," read Dallaire's cable to the Department of Peacekeeping Operations (DPKO).[9] Reluctant to become further involved given the dismal failure of the Somali peacekeeping mission, and in light of increasing violence in the Balkans, DPKO and the Security Council regarded the information as unconfirmed speculation. Any action was thus considered outside of UN-AMIR's mandate.

Within a few short months, an unknown assailant shot down the Rwandan president's plane as it returned from peace negotiations in Arusha, Tanzania. Hutu militia groups, known as the *interahamwe*, "those who attack together," used this incident as an excuse to galvanize the Hutu population and begin a series of organized attacks on Tutsi men, women, children, and babies, moderate Hutu politicians, and United Nations peacekeepers. The international community responded by pulling out troops as quickly as possible, leaving behind only a minimal group of 270 peacekeepers under Dallaire's leadership. As the corpses of tens of thousands of Rwandans filled the streets, rivers, and churches, UNAMIR found itself in a position of pure impotence. "Dying in Rwanda without a sign or sight of relief," wrote Dallaire, "was a reality we faced on a daily basis."[10] Within one hundred days, eight hundred thousand Tutsi and moderate Hutu were killed. The RPF made a strong offensive, seized power in Kigali, and established the new GNU. The interahamwe retreated, forcing two million Hutu to flee with them into neighboring Tanzania and Zaire (now the Democratic Republic of the Congo) and destroying the infrastructure and looting the national treasury. The refugees acted as a human shield, and later their presence compelled the international community to provide assistance to refugees, despite militia control over and benefit from that assistance.

Women were both targets of the genocide and perpetrators of it. Hate literature described Tutsi women as temptresses, and Hutu men who married Tutsi women as traitors: "Tutsi uses two means against Hutu: money and Tutsi women."[11] Rape and sexual violence were widespread strategies of Hutu militias.[12] Most women were then murdered, along with their children. Sexual violence was used as a weapon to humiliate Tutsi as a group; women were sometimes raped and sexually mutilated in front of their families.[13] A church in

Kigali-Rurale is today a memorial site for more than twenty thousand persons, their bones neatly sorted and stacked in catacombs in and around the bullet-riddled building. In the center of the church, a woman and her child are entombed in the only coffin holding the remains of a genocide victim. Her butchered, lifeless body was found in a pit latrine, a large stake driven into her vagina. Tightly wrapped in her arms was her baby. So compelling was this final plight of a mother trying to protect her child, and the horror of the interahamwe's having violated her very womanhood, that she received this symbolic burial in the heart of the church.[14]

For survivors of rape and the genocide, deep psychological trauma accompanies the "shame" of rape in Rwanda. Hundreds of survivors gave birth to babies conceived of rape.[15] Stigmatization has made the lives of women grossly and unjustly difficult. For the tens of thousands of orphans—both Tutsi and Hutu—women have also taken on the additional responsibility of raising other children.[16] Yet women also participated in the genocide. The report *Not So Innocent: When Women Become Killers* documented the participation of women as murderers, informers, inciters, and supporters of the genocide.[17] Agathe Habyarimana, the president's wife, was known to be at the center of hard-line Hutu circles responsible for planning and carrying out the genocide.[18] At the same time, insurgents in the northwest also included women. The RPF had well-respected generals who were women, some of whom later became prominent political figures in the new Rwandan government.

The Arusha Peace Agreement and UNAMIR made little reference to the gender-related impacts of the conflict, or to the role of women in building peace. Yet in the aftermath of UNAMIR's failed mission to Rwanda, the gendered implications of the conflict and genocide would change the landscape of social relations with significant implications for peace building and reconstruction in the country. Today, female-headed households represent 34–64 percent of the Rwandan population depending on location, forcing Rwandan women to assume new gender roles that challenge traditional gender relations.[19] In the aftermath of the conflict and in light of the demographic changes and their implications, the United Nations, donors, and the newly formed GNU have placed a relatively significant emphasis on the potential of Rwandan women as leaders for peace.

Leaders for Peace: Rwandan Women's NGOs and Grassroots Associations

> One village can speak for many villages. One victim can speak for many victims.
>
> —Michael Ondaatje[20]

Women can lead, women can do anything! I have seen it!

—Male manager of a women's tailoring project[21]

I met a woman in Cyangugu who had fled to Bukavu, Zaire, with her husband and children during the one hundred days of horror in Rwanda. She was one of hundreds of thousands who fled that spring. In the massive refugee camp, she was caught between hostile bands of Hutu militias and the RPF and went unprotected by an international humanitarian community, led by the Office of the United Nations High Commissioner for Refugees (UNHCR), whose refugee camps were unable to stop new waves of killings. She fled yet again but had lost several of her children. She returned to Rwanda and was relocated to an *imidugudu*, a village settlement created by the new Rwandan government. The woman had to walk two hours a day to reach a small plot of land she cultivated in order to grow enough food to feed her children. Every time she went, she had to bring her small daughters along, as children left alone had been raped in her village. She had no access to health care or money to pay school fees for her children. She said she was depressed, lonely.[22] This rural woman's experience tells the story of many other survivors like her in postgenocide Rwanda. Her experience illustrates the need for women's organizations to reach out to the grassroots, but also the many challenges facing rural women in the national project of unity building, development, and women's empowerment.

In the immediate aftermath of the genocide, national women's organizations and grassroots associations emerged in great numbers and force. In Kigali, women's organizations formed prior to the genocide began to reinitiate their activities. For example, by 1995 the women's NGO Duterimbere, originally formed in the late 1980s, had resumed activities to promote the role of women in economic development; and HAGURUKA, an association of lawyers and paralegals, renewed its activities to promote women's legal rights. New organizations formed in response to the genocide, such as Avega Agahozo (AVEGA), an organization of genocide survivors and widows. Many Rwandan women's organizations that had been formed by refugees in exile relocated to Kigali after 1994. For instance, Club Mama Sportifs, founded in Burundi, now provides educational and literacy classes to Rwandan women and girls. Many of these organizations belong to the umbrella Pro-Femmes Twese Hamwe, where membership reached thirty-five organizations by 1999.[23]

Collectively, Rwandan women's organizations provide a range of assistance and services to grassroots women, particularly survivors, those widowed by the genocide, female-headed households, women and girls caring for orphans, and rural women. For example, during the emergency phase (1994–1996), Rwandan women's organizations focused on providing basic needs, such as clothing, food, and shelter, to returning women and girls, as well as survivors. Assistance continued into the development phase (1997 to date), where agricultural tools and educational materials were offered, as well as services such as legal council, microcredit, vocational training, and psychosocial counseling.

In 1996, Pro-Femmes launched the Action for Peace Campaign, designed to promote a culture of peace throughout Rwanda. The campaign fostered dialogues in local cellules and communes between women of different ethnic backgrounds and provided skills on conflict resolution. The Action for Peace Campaign also promoted women's role in national decision making and emphasized the importance of income generation to promote women's socioeconomic status. For many women, participation in activities organized by women's NGOs—such as legal trainings or income generation—opened forums for dialogue. By identifying commonalities in their struggle and working across differences, some women have been able to move forward together. For example, in a paralegal training that brought together survivors (Tutsi women) and "new returnees" (Hutu women returning from Zaire, Burundi, and Tanzania), hostility was transformed to empathy when it was pointed out that both groups suffered from a form of widowhood. Many husbands of new returnees were in jail, accused of participating in the genocide that had widowed survivors—leaving both groups of women on their own. This is not reconciliation, but it is working across differences. "Don't talk to me about reconciliation," said one survivor. "How can you expect us to welcome back the people who killed our husbands and children? We speak of coping, of finding ways of living alongside [each other]."[24] In some cases, this has led to working together to overcome common difficulties as women; and in these cases, the potential for peace is fostered.[25]

While most women's organizations tend to be located in Kigali, they strive to reach out to rural women all over the country. To this end, sister associations were formed with the assistance of the GNU and international organizations. It is estimated that in each commune, at least one hundred women's associations currently exist, or 15,400 associations throughout Rwanda.[26] Many rural women report that they feel less "lonely," and that the act of coming together has helped to build their self-esteem and provided hope.[27] "We met with each other. We understood the genocide happened everywhere, not just to us. This helped."[28] "We felt bad. One woman would say, 'I lost a husband,' another, 'I lost my children,' and another, 'I lost everyone,' and we didn't feel so alone in our pain," one member of a rural woman's association told me while I was in Taba, Gitarama.[29]

For others, however, the associations either have been a disappointment or are perceived to be outside their means. The woman I met in Cyangugu had been visited by women's organizations that had encouraged her to form her own association and to put forward proposals for a loan. She confided she could not really afford to do these things. She had neither the time to participate, nor the ability to pay back a loan. She felt these things were "a waste of time."[30] Other rural women who had been encouraged to make proposals for extremely modest agricultural projects were disappointed when the women's organization never returned to tell them the results of their efforts.[31]

Many of the associations in rural areas are resource poor and lack good communication and regular support from women's organizations in the city.[32] For example, Kigali-based Réseau des Femmes (RDF)—a well-established association of businesswomen who volunteer to work with rural women—helped establish a grassroots association called Sevota in Taba, Gitarama. While in Kigali, I was told by RDF that the association was now independent and a good example of what could be achieved in terms of capacity building and sustainability of grassroots associations. Yet a visit to Taba revealed otherwise: agricultural projects had failed due to drought, and the members—largely widows and orphan children—were unable to generate income. Members reported that they were sick, hungry, and unable to purchase basic food items.[33] I later learned that RDF had run out of funds to support Sevota and found travel to this community difficult, and so the sister association was on its own, or "independent." As the women in Taba were situated in a region sometimes considered vulnerable to attacks by bands of interahamwe, I asked about their security. They responded that security was not a concern: poverty was the problem.

To sum up, Rwandan women's organizing fills social spaces torn apart by genocide. Interviews with representatives of women's groups, United Nations staff, and government representatives gave the impression that peace is a web, where actors within the web must rebuild the self, and the social relations that make up the whole. By meeting the practical needs of women, projects help restore dignity. Dialogue is opened through collaboration. Communication reduces fear. Meeting together "consoles" by providing time to address difference and move beyond it. Peace, then, is not defined by diplomats and official agreements, nor even by the end to armed conflict. It is a process of restoring social relations, or "reweaving the torn," and women, in their traditional gender roles, are poised in positions to promote peace. And further, they move into the future as citizens of the Rwandan nation. According to leaders of AVEGA, organizing together helps move their members into the future both transformed and transforming: "At first there was a lot of tension between people, accusations. Now they think of the future, of income . . . how to improve their lives."[34] One member who had participated in AVEGA income-generation projects said, "If my husband came back, he wouldn't know me."[35]

For their efforts to move forward, Rwandan women are seen as beacons of hope. As the special representative for human rights to Rwanda noted of AVEGA:

> Sixty percent of its 2,055 members are widows of genocide victims. The rest are married to suspected killers, who are now in prison. Yet both groups till the fields together, prepare food for the wives to take to the husbands in jail, and stood together for election during the March local elections. Reconciliation of this kind is a lesson for the whole world. It belies the image of Rwanda as a country driven by ethnic hatred."[36]

In 1997, AVEGA was officially recognized by UNESCO for its work for peace and tolerance. Yet the same processes that thrust women into leadership roles for peace in their communities also propel them into the center of a public-sphere struggle to rebuild the Rwandan nation, a struggle led by the GNU but dependant upon the participation of civil society. As the next section explains, the intervention of MIGEPROFE to promote gender equality throughout Rwanda poses strains on relations among different ethnic and class groups of women by basing "unity" on a false premise of "sameness" and masking inequalities in access to social, political, and economic power.

Building National Unity: Government Initiatives on Gender Equality

> I think there is a general realization . . . that people have suffered enough. They don't want to talk about genocide, the deaths, the killing. People are looking more into the future: "how can we change our situation?" That's the preoccupation today. We don't want to see more lives being wasted and killed, the preoccupation now is to live more in the future, not in the past.
>
> —Aloysie Inyumba[37]

In the aftermath of the genocide, the Government of National Unity worked to erase the colonial past and to move toward an imagined future where Hutu and Tutsi, men and women, would be equal. As President Paul Kagame stated, "The Government of Rwanda recognizes the importance of giving equal opportunities to both women and men to work as partners in addressing national development challenges."[38] He also called for moving beyond "prolonged periods of corrupt and repressive regimes [in Rwanda that] saw the entrenchment of 'divide and rule' as the principle of governing." This belief has translated into support for specific institutions for the promotion of women's rights and the creation of equal opportunities for women, as well as the establishment of the Ministry for National Unity. As one reviews the initiatives of MIGEPROFE, it becomes evident that the project of promoting gender equality is central to that of realizing the vision of national unity.

MIGEPROFE has branches that focus on affirmative action and capacity building, legal reform and revision, political mobilization, and gender mainstreaming throughout all levels and agencies of the GNU.[39] Perhaps the most visible initiative of MIGEPROFE has been the mass organization of civil and political society at the grassroots. MIGEPROFE has been credited with strengthening weakened women's organizations and associations in the aftermath of the genocide and providing leadership and resources.[40] The government department has been centrally involved in organizing women within rural areas and supporting the work of urban-based NGOs with rural, grassroots women.

So that grassroots women would have some avenue of influence over male-dominated political structures, women's committees were established at every level of Rwandan political organization with the cooperation of international organizations and women's NGOs. Each committee consists of ten women representatives, and each representative is responsible for voicing women's perspectives on a specific issue (such as education, health, legal matters) to local government structures. In March 1999, women-only elections were held at the smallest level of political organization, the cellule, to choose ten female committee members to represent approximately 1,000–2,500 women. The committee members at the cellule level then elected representatives to form a committee at the sector level, and this process was repeated again at the commune, prefecture, and national levels. Two seats in local and prefecture government authorities are reserved for representatives of women's committees.[41]

In an interview with Suzanne Ruboneka of Pro-Femmes Twese Hamwe, Heather Hamilton learned that both the government and civil society stress the importance of women-only forums to promote women's involvement in public decision making:

> In our culture, there are still barriers for women to express themselves in public. Women still do not dare express themselves publicly, especially when there are men present. Consequently, there are no places for women to think, to look for solutions, to play a real role. Many women are illiterate, and their point of view is never considered. How can we motivate women, give them the chance to get together to express themselves, without fear?[42]

MIGEPROFE, sometimes with the cooperation of women's NGOs, selects representatives to women's committees and presents them to the electorate. A MIGEPROFE official informed me that selection of representatives is based on the candidate's level of education and employment. However, only ten women are presented for ten positions. Grassroots women then stand behind the woman they choose to support. In essence, there is little choice as to the candidate, nor privacy in making a choice. There has been no attempt to define ethnic composition of these committees. These factors together raise questions as to whether women's committees represent all women, and whose interests they serve.

The question of ethnicity and representation goes beyond being a sensitive issue in Rwanda. It is highly political and symbolic of the desire for a new social order. In preparation for my research trip, United Nations officials in Geneva warned me to never refer to ethnic groups by name. I was to use the terms "old caseload returnees" (Tutsi refugees in exile since 1959) and "new caseload returnees" (Hutu refugees who fled in 1994) or "rescapés" (Tutsi genocide survivors). In Rwanda, I found this refusal to name ethnic groups to be the case everywhere. United Nations or NGO program reports never specified the number of Tutsi versus Hutu beneficiaries, and local NGOs or associations never made reference to ethnicity. This is part of the government's promotion of a new Rwandan national identity; the assumption is that rigid social structures of the past can be transformed in the future by referring to all ethnic groups as Rwandans, rather than Hutu or Tutsi. Yet, as Catherine Newbury and Hannah Baldwin have observed, women's organizations in postgenocide Rwanda "tended to be (in practice if not official objectives) ethnically homogenous. But this is a politically sensitive issue—not something people would speak openly about."[43] As Newbury and Baldwin continue,

> In Rwandan politics today it matters what a person's (presumed) ethnic background is, where that person lived in Rwanda, and where that person came from if he or she is an exile who came home after the genocide. Understanding these distinctions can be critical to understanding the dynamics within and among women's organizations. Although Rwandan women have displayed a remarkable capacity to transcend differences and work together, distinctions based on ethnicity, class, region, place of origin, and life experiences remain salient.[44]

Moreover, ethnic differences become a basis of privilege in access to resources and political power.

Implicitly, one can glean much about these differences by reading between the lines. For example, there are a number of widow's organizations working in Rwanda today, and, at first look, the differences between them are confusing. I had the opportunity to meet with representatives of a number of organizations and ask about their central differences. All chose to distinguish themselves in reference to the date and place they were first realized: post-1994 Rwanda, pre-1994 Rwanda, or exile. The Association de Solidarité des Femmes Rwandaises (ASOFERWA) was founded in Rwanda in September 1994 to assist widows, single mothers, and orphans of the genocide. The organization has forty paid employees and extensive projects in partnership with the international community. In January 1995, Avega Agahozo (AVEGA) was also founded to assist genocide widows, and it had ten thousand members by 1999. It too enjoys substantial funding, and basic infrastructure. The widows' association ICHYUZUZO was founded in September 1990 for those who lost husbands during the conflict between the RPF and the Rwandan army forces (FAR). In an interview, representatives of ICHYUZUZO stated that their association was "open to anyone," and "the reasons for their widowhood were not important."[45] In other words, it was not exclusively an association for genocide widows, but for widows of conflict, "prison" widows,[46] or "AIDS" widows.[47] ICHYUZUZO was poorly funded, with few staff, vehicles, and equipment to carry out its work. Finally, a number of associations for widows and female heads of household were founded in exile by widows of fallen RPF soldiers. An example is BENYSHAKA, which today carries out vocational programs with orphaned girls. While not exclusively for widows, Club Mama Sportifs also offers educational services to women and girls. Burundian exiles founded the organization and transferred their activities to Rwanda in the aftermath of the genocide. This association has been very well funded. It built Rwanda's first community center by and for women and from it was making a good profit.

Women's organizations and associations are also positioned differently according to a rural/urban divide. "Clientelism" in Rwandan politics suggests that some civil organizations with strong connections to the GNU are more likely than others to receive funding or resources. As Newbury and Baldwin argue, "This is not, of course, unique to Rwanda, but it has been an enduring (and especially powerful) element of the political landscape."[48] For instance, the Unity Club, formed by the wives of cabinet members in Kigali in 1996, has enjoyed greater access to resources from MIGEPROFE, a government branch largely composed of "old caseload returnees," than do rural women's associations (composed of survivors and "new caseload returnees"). Women's organizations depend upon international funding that is very often administered by the GNU, specifically MIGEPROFE. For example, MIGEPROFE is the central implementing partner for the Rwandan Women's Initiative (RWI), a project of UNHCR. Several organizations involved in RWI complained about the opaqueness of funding decisions made by MIGEPROFE, and their desire to find new funding sources outside of the government to pursue "alternative methodologies" to that of the government.[49]

Representatives of a number of women's organizations and associations argued that the current relationship with MIGEPROFE and women's committees compromises their ability to define and realize their own mandates.[50] Women's committee members are very often members of women's associations. Since their creation, international organizations and donor states have inundated women's committees with projects, and in the meantime the GNU requires representatives to attend "trainings" and provide "trainings" to their communities on a range of development and civil issues.[51] Women's committee members are also responsible for the administration of Women's Communal Funds (WCF), a small-scale lending fund established to provide income to women in their communities. Within each commune, women are responsible for setting up, contributing to, and managing WCF. "Trainings" are provided to managers of the funds, and a MIGEPROFE representative assists in its administration. The very same women are often in demand by national women's organizations that rely upon them to administer projects in rural areas. Most often, the goals of the NGO and MIGEPROFE become one and the same through women's committees: "We never believed in reconciliation. We never believed in any justice department. Today, we give trainings. Today we believe in the need to participate [in the rebuilding of Rwanda]; it's a woman's obligation."[52]

Enveloping difference in Rwanda is a dark veil of silence and a deep fear of speaking against an omnipresent government located at every level of Rwandan social organization.[53] Thus, one must be wary of the claim that women-only spaces, such as women's committees, are "safe spaces" for all women. Moreover, spaces opened to women by grassroots associations or women's organizations are under enormous pressure to conform to a policy of unity, which silences the desire to name and work through difference. Ethnic tensions and discrimination are not transformed by policies of nonidentification; on the contrary, such a policy can make it more difficult to discern instances of discrimination. And so, while "new caseload returnees" and survivors might work alongside each other, tilling the soil together, lining up to participate in elections, they do so under a powerful panopticon where refusing to at least mimic an embrace of the new national vision invites a likely violent outcome.

This panopticon operates through elaborate political structures and civic organizations dominated by "old caseload returnees," with nominal representation of Hutu moderates.[54] Despite efforts to hold elections and decentralize power through committees, the GNU continues to demonstrate "little tolerance for people or groups who challenge the hegemonic discourse of those in power."[55] Presently, the GNU maintains a large military presence and control in a resource-rich area of the Democratic Republic of the Congo close to fifteen times the size of Rwanda, arguing that the continued presence of Hutu militia in that country poses grave security threats. Since 1994, tens of thousands of civilians have been killed both within Rwanda and the Democratic Republic of the Congo as a result of RPF military operations.[56] The GNU justifies its military presence on the grounds that the international community is

unlikely to intervene should Hutu militias try to "finish the job" of the genocide: sporadic Hutu militia incursions into the northwest of Rwanda have left
hundreds more survivors dead in the past six years.

On paper, the GNU has begun to decentralize decision making and democ-
ratize local governmental institutions. Yet reports that political or ideological
dissidents have been murdered abound.[57] The GNU promotes national reconciliation and unity through "solidarity camps," where the strange mix of returnees, released child detainees, and university students are "reeducated." Ideological training figures heavily in the camps, but attendees also learn to fire a
gun and are often required to wear military uniforms. As reported by Human
Rights Watch, one child described the camps succinctly: "They teach us things
so that it will be easy for us to join military service later."[58] Ideological training
also figures largely in women's associations and networks, and at times I was
left wondering whether women's committees were mechanisms for empowerment or consolidation of control. Throughout my travels in the country, grassroots women and girls repeated slogans regarding national development,
peace, and unity, as the following excerpt from my field notes reveals:

> Late last night, we attended the wrap-up of a two-week training for paralegals by
> the women's legal organization HAGURUKA. The attendees were women from
> all over the country, and most had brought their children with them: they were
> playing at the back of the large room as we talked. All had volunteered to come.
> They had to take time off work or away from the fields, and all of them had to
> pay their own transportation and stay there. Most of them were representatives
> on women's councils. When they returned to their communities, they would be
> responsible for "educating" others about the law and acting as legal advisers to
> their community. I asked some of them why they were here, and they answered,
> "to fight inequality!" and "to change things!" They also hoped that this new po-
> sition would help them earn respect of members of their community. At one
> point, they performed a dance and sang, "Women and girls, do not be left be-
> hind! You have a role in the development of Rwanda! Rwanda is your concern!"
> They told me they learned the song here and will teach it to members of their
> communities when they return home.[59]

The theme of this field note entry would become a familiar one as I continued my travels and repeatedly heard the same call to action in the songs and
dances of grassroots women and girls.[60] Sevota in Gitarama did enjoy the benefits of one more project, a radio station that aired programs of women's roles
and responsibilities for the development of the country.

The blurring of state and civil society in Rwanda may be justified as a
means of forging unity among Rwandan women at a critical point in the history of the country, but this "unity" is founded on the false assumption that

all Rwandan women are equal, and they are not. Thus, a contradictory view of women's organizations and associations emerges in this analysis. On the one hand, Rwandan women in grassroots associations and organizations "connect across differences" to improve their lives and that of their communities.[61] That is, they hold the potential to identify their differences and work through them together toward common goals. On the other, the GNU imposes an ideology of sameness, downplaying difference and inequalities among Rwandan women. Thus, the constructive progress made across differences by women's organizations is potentially subverted if channeled through government-sponsored networks that silence this discussion. As I argue below, this position is one often supported by international organizations, which support the role of Rwandan women in peace building from an uncritical distance.

Universal Woman: International
Organizations and Gender Equality in Rwanda

International media as well as feminist activism in and around the Fourth World Conference on Women helped to raise the attention of the international community to gender-related issues in armed conflict (see Mazurana et al., introduction).[62] At the same time, there was a growing appreciation of the initiatives of women as peace builders in their own right,[63] and of the responsibility of international organizations to support their efforts.

In all conflict situations, particular social groups hold the key to mediation of the conflict and its aftermath and hence to prevention of renewed conflict. These are often also the groups who can lead the way from emergency to development. In Rwanda, organized women appear to be such critical groups, who can serve as change agents in reconciliation as well as community development. They may therefore call for special GNU and donor assistance to facilitate a range of transitions.

In postgenocide/postconflict Rwanda, women's empowerment projects were supported by the United Nations and donors including the United Nations Development Program (UNDP) Trust Fund for Women, the United States Agency for International Development's (USAID) Women in Transition Program (WIT), and UNHCR's Rwandan Women's Initiative. Initially, these programs focused on emergency assistance to women, but eventually longer-term empowerment projects were invoked. USAID's WIT program gradually focused on funding Women's Communal Funds, where UNHCR and UNDP have continued a more holistic approach to empowerment, including legal, psychosocial, educational, and literacy projects and capacity building of MIGEPROFE and women's organizations.

A review of all three agencies' reports and/or evaluations reveals that neither political nor gender analyses were applied. Women were often presented as a universal but vulnerable social group. For example, a WIT evaluation identified the primary beneficiaries as "Rwandan women, particularly female heads of household and those caring for foster children."[64] RWI reports identified beneficiaries as "female survivors of the genocide . . . with their children born of rape . . . [and] women who work in association with them."[65] While some returnees may have gained from RWI, which returnees benefited is unclear. Further, differences and relations between survivors and returnees are not elaborated upon, despite the fragility of the relationship between these groups. Beneficiaries are not broken down according to sex, age, ethnicity, class, or geographic location, and there has been no mapping of the relationships between government bodies, women's committees, and women's organizations, for example, to determine the prevalence of clientelism.

Yet a quick breakdown of RWI projects according to implementing partner and beneficiary groups reveals that Hutu returnees were involved in a marginal way. In the first year of the RWI project cycle, when the organization had a budget of $2.6 million, GNU agencies received over $1 million for government-related projects from the fund. In contrast, women's NGOs with widows or orphans as members and beneficiaries (survivors) received just under $1 million (including $500,000 to Club Mama Sportifs, founded by Tutsi exiles in Burundi). Only $50,000 went to projects with beneficiaries described as "mixed" (returnees and widows).[66] Funding crises in later years meant RWI suffered from lack of resources, although it received an infusion of $1.6 million in 1999 and used a good portion to support women's committees, and WCF, as well as government training.

A UNHCR official in Geneva argued that RWI was "hijacked by a literate elite with first access to the funds. Resources were used for trainings and workshops [for this group] and did not reach women in the grassroots." He continued, "Rwanda is a very politicized country, there is a need to balance [assistance among] all sides."[67] Other officials disagree, contending that the resources used by MIGEPROFE were necessary to build the capacity of the government and were regarded as a long-term investment in the future of women and gender equality in the country.[68] As Minister Alyoise Inyumba put it:

> When you came out of Beijing, the whole emphasis on the UN in terms of supporting the gender issues was mainly on mechanisms, because there has always been a concentration on pieces, on projects. But the whole emphasis of the UN was mainly to support the national mechanisms that would structurally change the welfare of the family with a special emphasis on women. If you look at the legal reform this is a mechanism. If you talk about the national women's network, this is also a mechanism. Unlike other agencies, UNHCR concentrated on building

mechanisms. These are sustainable, they are not short-lived, they are not small projects. This is a new message that UNHCR has brought to the country.[69]

So the question becomes whether women's initiatives should concentrate on building state capacity and/or that of women's organizations, or on the basic needs of grassroots women. Undoubtedly there are many methodologies that work. However, key to developing such programs is a political analysis of the context in which such initiatives are funded and supported. UNHCR, USAID, and UNDP more often than not reported on process, but rarely on how such initiatives related to the wider political context that shaped such processes. Moreover, ethnicity or class relations slip off the radar screens of humanitarian or development projects: Women are the focus, but which women? And what is their relation to men, and to other women?

In this respect, all three initiatives rarely apply gender as an analytic category in their reports, though the relationships between women and men, as well as the role of men, are critical to understanding the prospects for building peace and gender equality. For instance, in every cellule, commune, and prefecture in the country, male-dominated government bodies play a central role in community development. In some communes, I found men in such positions of power to be completely lacking in knowledge of women's or gender issues, while in others, burgomasters (government heads) were strong advocates.[70] In women's projects, men were often involved in either leadership or marginal ways, with important impacts for the family, children, and community. Finally, given that Rwanda is characterized by a hierarchical and tightly knit political system that reaches every *colline* in Rwanda, how men relate to other men, and how gender-related oppression affects men and their communities, is an important avenue for investigation by international organizations, the GNU, and feminist analysts.

In short, an emphasis on the role of women in building peace should not eclipse differences among women and relations to men. By ignoring such differences, the international community subscribes to the GNU's vision of national unity, and relations of power remain unchecked, and potentially unresolved. This cannot bode well for peace in Rwanda, and potentially it compromises women's security, by asking women to become reproducers of the nation in both their private roles as mothers and wives and now their more public roles as builders of the nation.

Conclusion

In a café in Kigali, I engaged in a somewhat heated debate with international NGO workers about the "true" nature of the Rwandan state. Is it inherently benevolent but firm, or coercive and ruthless? Do the ends justify the means? On the one hand, the ideological message sent to grassroots women by MIGE-PROFE, women's communities, and NGOs is optimistic and empowering: "Women, you have a role to play in the future of your country, get to work!"[71] It challenges traditional gender roles and relations, promoting women's participation in decision making and peace building of the country. On the other hand, given the political context of the country, "collaboration" between women's organizations and associations and the GNU may be simply a means of controlling all levels of Rwandan civil associations for purposes only a child can state—"they teach us things so that it will be easy for us to join military service later." In other words, above all, the GNU has been determined to consolidate its power within the country to ward off any security threats in the future, and to ensure the nation's economic growth. The government believes this requires absolute and unquestioning support from the entire Rwandan population, including one of the most critical assets to the future development of the country, les femmes aux mille bras. Thus, the role of civil society in building peace is both enhanced in the case of Rwanda, and restricted.

There appears to be no resolution to this paradox.[72] Perhaps that does not matter if one looks for answers in the nuance. This chapter has begun to point to the shades of gray, by arguing that the policies and practices of national and global actors to support Rwandan women as leaders for peace have produced new webs of power relations that both liberate and create new technologies of violence. In these webs, gender, ethnicity, and class intersect and are transformed. For example, some Rwandan women have assumed greater ability to act in postgenocide Rwanda: "[We have become] empowered through group healing and exchanges of experiences and believe we have been left with a certain power," stated a representative of AVEGA. Moreover, by working alongside each other in "women's projects," Hutu and Tutsi women have opened spaces for all Rwandans to move into, and this has been rightly recognized and valued by Rwandan women and men, the GNU, and the international community.

At the same time, this chapter suggests that a gender analysis of peace building in Rwanda must move beyond the current focus on "women" to ask, "which women?" Differences based on ethnicity, class, and geography intersect with gender to shape relations of power, privileging some groups of women (old caseload returnees) over others (new caseload returnees and survivors), resulting in new tensions based on differing access to resources. The assumption that women's committees are spaces of security and solidarity among women belies the heightened sense of fear and insecurity among dissenters. Those who do not share the same vision as RPF, or at least the same methods, continue to live under the threat of violence. Thus, women's committees might provide space for women previously marginalized, but they also usher women into a public sphere where their bodies and actions are scrutinized, and where control of the private, of civil society, is rein-scribed by the Rwandan state. Here, not only is it a matter of diverse Rwan-dan women working alongside each other in the fields, but it is a matter of life for some, death for others.

This chapter began with a quote by Veneranda Nzambazamariya, winner of the Millennium Peace Prize for Women for her work to build peace in her country. While she was likely referring to the genocide, her words resonate too with the process of building peace today in Rwanda. They are worth repeating here once more: "Let yourselves be consoled, you have been sacrificed by sys-tems it is necessary to change. Unite so as to transform problems into oppor-tunities for action." If Rwandan women were sacrificed so in the past, is it not essential to ensure that the spaces that are opened and opportunities found do indeed transform the systems that would sacrifice them once more for "the good of the nation," and all this in the name of peace?

Notes

I would like to thank representatives of Rwandan women's organizations, the Ministry for Women and Gender Equality, UNHCR-Rwanda, and the Women's Commission for Refugee Women and Children (WCRWC) for inspiring me to write this chapter. Field notes are derived from a program review I conducted of the RWI in 2000 for the WCRWC (see Women's Commission for Refugee Women and Children and Erin Baines, *You Cannot Dance if You Cannot Stand: A Review of the Rwanda Women's Ini-tiative and the UNHCR's Commitment to Gender Equality in Post-conflict Situations* [New York: WCRWC, 2001]). A grant from the Social Sciences and Humanities Re-search Council made this written work possible.

1. The distinction between national women's organizations (or women's NGOs or simply women's organizations) and grassroots associations (or women's associations) is that the former more often are better institutionalized, are likely to be registered and recognized, and operate across different regions of Rwanda, while the latter are small, unofficial, and located only within the cellule level, though they are usually connected to other associations through a network.

2. "David" in J. Janzen and R. Janzen, *Do I Still Have a Life? Voices from the After-math of War in Rwanda and Burundi* (Lawrence: University of Kansas, 2000).

3. Carol Off, *The Lion, the Fox and the Eagle: A Story of Generals and Justice in Rwanda and Yugoslavia* (Canada: Random House Canada, 2000).

4. Human Rights Watch, *Leave No One to Tell the Story: Genocide in Rwanda* (New York: HRW, 1999); A. DesForges and African Rights, *Rwanda: Death, Despair and De-fiance*, 2nd ed. (London: African Rights, 1995).

5. For a comprehensive history of Rwanda see Gerard Prunier, *The Rwanda Crisis: History of a Genocide* (New York: Columbia University Press, 1997).

6. Mahmood Mamdani, *When Victims Become Killers: Colonialism, Nativism and the Genocide in Rwanda* (Princeton: Princeton University Press, 2001).

7. President Habyarimana was interested in maintaining the flow of international development assistance into the country given near economic collapse under the strain of structural adjustment policies, and the Organization of African Unity keenly supported peace talks.

8. Off, *The Lion, the Fox and the Eagle*; William Shawcross, *Deliver Us from Evil: Peacekeepers, Warlords and a World of Endless Conflict* (New York: Simon and Schuster, 2000).

9. Shawcross, *Deliver Us from Evil*, 129.

10. Off, *The Lion, the Fox and the Eagle*, 6.

11. Hasan Ngeze, "Hutu 'Ten Commandments,'" *Kangura*, no. 6 (December 1990); see also Heather B. Hamilton, "Rwanda's Women: The Key to Reconstruction," *Journal of Humanitarian Assistance*, 2000, 2–3.

12. Mary Balikungeri, "Rwanda Case" (paper presented to the Expert Group Meeting on Gender-Based Persecution, Toronto, Canada, November 2–12, 1997); Human Rights Watch, *Shattered Lives: Sexual Violence during the Genocide and Its Aftermath* (New York: HRW, 1996); DesForges and African Rights, *Rwanda: Death, Despair and Defiance.*

13. Catherine Newbury and Hannah Baldwin, *Aftermath: Women in Postgenocide Rwanda*, Working Paper 303 (Washington, DC: Centre for Development Information and Evaluation, U.S. Agency for International Development, 2000); Hamilton, "Rwanda's Women: The Key to Reconstruction."

14. Field notes, Kigale-Rurale, 2000.

15. Hamilton, "Rwanda's Women: The Key to Reconstruction."

16. Newbury and Baldwin, *Aftermath: Women in Postgenocide Rwanda.*

17. DesForges and African Rights, *Rwanda: Death, Despair and Defiance.*

18. Christian Jennings, *Across the Red River: Rwanda, Burundi and the Heart of Darkness* (London: Weidenfeld and Nicholson, 2000).

19. Women's Commission for Refugee Women and Children and Erin Baines, *You Cannot Dance if You Cannot Stand.*

20. Michael Ondaatje, *Anil's Ghost* (New York: Alfred A. Knopf, 2000).

21. Field notes, Kigali, 2000.

22. Field notes, Cyangugu, 2000.

23. Pro-Femmes Twese Hamwe, *Post-Beijing Activities Report* (Kigali: Pro-Femmes, 1999).

24. Women's Commission for Refugee Women and Children, *Rwanda's Women and Children: The Long Road to Reconciliation; A Field Report Assessing the Protection and Assistance Needs of Rwandan Women and Children* (New York: WCRWC, 1997), 16.

25. United Nations Economic Commission for Africa, *Postconflict Reconstruction in Africa: A Gender Perspective*, African Women's Report 1998 (Addis Ababa, Ethiopia: UNECA, 1998); Pro-Femmes, interviewed by author, Kigali, October 26, 2000.

26. Newbury and Baldwin, *Aftermath: Women's Organizations in Postconflict Rwanda*, Working Paper 304 (Washington, DC: Center for Development Information and Evaluation, U.S. Agency for International Development, 2000).

27. Field notes, Kigali, 2000.

28. Field notes, representative of rural women's association, Gitarama, 2000.

29. Field notes, Gitarama, 2000.

30. Field notes, Cyangugu, 2000.

31. Field notes, Buyumba, 2000.

32. Lack of communication and support is in part due to security-related issues in the past, when travel to regions in the northwest was dangerous. Lack of basic infrastructure such as cars or telephones and radios also contributes to poor communication.

33. Field notes, Gitarama, 2000.

34. Field notes, Kigali, 2000.

35. Field notes, Kigali, 2000.

36. United Nations, *The Special Representative's Report on the Human Rights Situation in Rwanda*, E/CN.4/2000/41 (April 2000), par. 183.

37. Aloysie Inyumba, minister for unity and reconciliation, former minister for women and family affairs, interviewed by author, 2000.

38. Paul Katame, interviewed by author, 2000.

39. Women's Commission for Refugee Women and Children and Erin Baines, *You Cannot Dance if You Cannot Stand*.

40. Pro-Femmes, interviewed by author, Kigali, October 26, 2000.

41. MIGEPROFE, interviewed by author, Kigali, October 23, 2000.

42. Heather B. Hamilton, "Refugee Women, UNHCR and the Great Lakes Crisis." Author's collection.

43. Newbury and Baldwin, *Aftermath: Women's Organizations in Postconflict Rwanda*, 5.

44. Newbury and Baldwin, *Aftermath: Women's Organizations in Postconflict Rwanda*, 10.

45. Representatives to ICHYUZUZO, interviewed by author, Kigali, 2000.

46. Women whose husbands are in jail are often likened to widows. This comparison recognizes their status of female head of household but also expresses pessimism that their husbands will ever be released. Currently, more men die in jails than are brought to trial.

47. The rate of HIV contraction and development of AIDS in Rwanda is among the highest in Africa.

48. Newbury and Baldwin, *Aftermath: Women's Organizations in Postconflict Rwanda*, 10.

49. Women's Commission for Refugee Women and Children and Erin Baines, *You Cannot Dance if You Cannot Stand*, 17.

50. Field notes, Kigali, 2000.

51. "Trainings" is a term frequently used in Rwanda to refer to a wide range of ideological and practical activities, including civil education and rights awareness but also business management, proposal writing, and reporting.

52. Interview with representatives of AVEGA, Kigali, 2000.

53. Philip Gourevitch, *We Wish to Inform You That Tomorrow We Will Be Killed With Our Families: Stories from Rwanda* (New York: Farrar, Straus and Giroux, 1998).

54. Mamdani, *When Victims Become Killers*, 271.

55. Newbury and Baldwin, *Aftermath: Women's Organizations in Postconflict Rwanda*, 10; see also Human Rights Watch, *Rwanda: Backgrounder* (New York: HRW, 2001).

56. Human Rights Watch, *Rwanda: Backgrounder*.

57. Human Rights Watch, *Rwanda: Backgrounder*.

58. Human Rights Watch, *Rwanda: Backgrounder*.

59. Field notes, Kigali, 2000.

60. Field notes, Cyangugu, Kibuye, Gitarama, Kigali, 2000.

61. For instance, Pro-Femmes built "peace villages" for widows and orphans of different ethnic groups. See Cynthia Cockburn, *The Space between Us: Negotiating Gender and National Identities in Conflict* (London: Zed Books, 1998).

62. United Nations, "Critical Area of Concern: Women and Armed Conflict," in *Beijing Declaration and Platform for Action*, UN Doc. A/CONF.177/20 (September 15, 1995). Human Rights Watch, *Shattered Lives*, is credited with spurring the UNHCR to initiate the RWI (see Women's Commission for Refugee Women and Children and Erin Baines, *You Cannot Dance if You Cannot Stand*, 1). Rwandan women provided testimonies at Beijing, and the rights of women in armed conflict settings were recognized in Critical Area E of the Platform for Action.

63. For example, in 1996, Pro-Femmes women won the UNESCO Prize for Peace and Tolerance.

64. Women in Transition (WIT), *Transition Initiatives: Rwandan Women in Transition* (Washington, DC: USAID, 1999), 7.

65. WIT, *Transition Initiatives*, 2.

66. UNHCR, *Rwandan Women's Initiative: A Challenging Practice of Mainstreaming Gender Perspectives in the Rehabilitation Efforts within a Post Genocide Society; Report* (Kigali: UNHCR, 1997).

67. UNHCR official, interviewed by author, Geneva, 2000.

68. Senior UNHCR officials, interviewed by author, Kigali and Washington, DC, 2000.

69. UNHCR official, interviewed by author, Washington, DC, April 24, 2001.

70. Field notes, Cyangugu and Byumba, 2000.

71. Field notes, Cyangugu, 2000.

72. As Peter Uvin later pointed out to me, in a case like Rwanda, both positions are probably right.

12

State Making, Peacemaking, and the Inscription of Gendered Politics into Peace: Lessons from Angola

J. Zoë Wilson

Foucault formulates his view of positive power in terms of a reversal of Clausewitz's assertion that war is politics continued by other means. According to this model, if politics is war continued by other means, then politics—and hence power—represents a peace that is imposed upon the vanquished after war. Power is "the reign of peace in civil society" where the purpose of power is not to end the conflict of war but, instead, is to reinscribe the effects of war in "social institutions, in economic inequalities, in language, in the bodies themselves of each and everyone of us."

—Mark Haugaard

THE LINKS BETWEEN VARIOUS FORMS of war and state making,[1] on the one hand, and distinctive forms of physical and systemic violence against women,[2] on the other, are well established—as are the links between states themselves and the reproduction of asymmetrical and deeply gendered relations of hierarchy and exclusion.[3] This body of knowledge provides fertile ground for understanding how colonial insurgencies and state-making efforts, anticolonial revolutions and subsequent state reforms, and, finally, international efforts to broker, enforce, and entrench peace are unlikely to enhance women's human security vis-à-vis men. My analysis concludes that peacemaking and peace-building efforts have reiterated rather than addressed distinctive vulnerabilities Angolan women experience today because such efforts are undergirded by gender-biased assumptions, the intended and unintended consequences of which have profound, if differentiated, implications for women, and society-wide implications for human security and sustainable peace.

A Short History of the Gendered Angolan State

Modern Angola is inextricably linked to its violent colonial past. From what we know of the effect of Portuguese colonial violence, state making, and economics on women, and the structures of constraint they imposed on gender relations over time, it is possible to put forth a partial model for understanding the initial layers of the gendered constraints inherent within the contemporary state nexus of political, economic, and military power. That is, contemporary Angola reflects the partial incorporation of the sexual, reproductive, and use-labor relations of colonial insurgency into political institutions, economic relations, and cultural practices. As Parpart and Staudt argue, "Gender is at the heart of state origins, access to the state and state resource allocation."[4]

In 1483, Portuguese colonialists arrived under the banner of Christianity—in a highly patriarchal Christian era when women were integrated into the predominant cosmologies and male-dominated structures of political and military power in highly constrained roles—and regarded non-Christians as "the fallen," who "lacked the cultural and juridical frames of reference to express informed consent."[5] In accordance with natural and positive law, Africans were burdens to their colonial masters; just as the wife was subordinated to the husband, so was the native to the European.[6] Behind the myth-making that justified, legitimized, and necessitated missionary work was a highly patriarchal, avaricious, and adventurous regime whose material interests in ivory and slaves, and later coffee and other agricultural exports,[7] were facilitated by the destruction and reorganization of African cultures.[8] Unconstrained by the dictates of Christian morality in their dealings with the heathen peoples of Africa, the Portuguese simulated statehood and imposed a "rule of law" over formerly autonomous indigenous social and political groups.[9] On this basis, they claimed territorial rights and sovereign prerogatives and established a formal sector that defined the parameters of power, stateness, and entitlement, which ultimately mirrored the European myths about race, class, and gender.[10]

Few if any Portuguese women came to Angola during the early stages of colonialism, and all key levers of colonial power were controlled exclusively by men, who, by and large, insisted on doing business with male African counterparts. To accomplish this, the Portuguese, like other colonial powers, often circumvented existing power structures and, when necessary, created and enriched local strongmen who would then act as "legitimate" representatives of their people, in accordance with Portuguese rule and law. Marking the incompleteness of the male-centered nascent socioeconomic and political structures, however, historical record reveals the existence of powerful women who resisted the constraints imposed upon them by the emerging system, including the legendary Queen Nzinga (about 1581–1663) and the martyred Dona Beatrice (1682–1706). The former, in particular, taking great exception to her ruling brother's weakness and complicity with the Portuguese slave trade, attempted to negotiate with the Portuguese directly, and, finally, usurping his power, she raised an army with which she would fight for the remainder of her life.[11]

Apart from a few stories of legendary proportion, however, there is little in the historical record that allows for a nuanced account of the intersubjectivities that defined gender relations during early colonialism. Africans were, by and large, illiterate, and, as Basil Davidson notes, the accounts provided by "whites, even those of missionary intention . . . were invariably the histories of themselves. Thus, the history of the Africans of Angola can be understood only with distortion and foreshortening when seen from the European records."[12] Even in these, however, women's presence is conspicuous mainly by its absence.

Agency, autonomy, resistance, and complicity within the emerging structures of power notwithstanding, then, the Portuguese, it appears, scripted indigenous women's primary roles as military booty, and objects of sexual curiosity, aggression, loathing, and domination. Indigenous women's sexual and domestic slavery was intrinsic to the emerging colonial system, as was their symbolic embodiment of indigenous and military "other," the appropriation of their bodies, labor, and wombs serving to reinforce the sense of entitlement upon which the all-male military colonial expedition was built. The historical record reveals that in early colonial society, devoid almost entirely of European women, many men took common-law African wives, who were technically slaves, and records exist of them being bought and sold like common household wares.[13] Later, these African women would be the foundation upon which the Portuguese inflicted their desire to create a new race of peoples, the *mezticos*—a race of half Portuguese/half Africans who would serve as intermediaries for indirect rule.

Regardless of the brutality involved, the Portuguese prided themselves on the way in which their young soldiers and officials raped the black women of their colonies. They hoped to create a mixed population that would entrench the culture and language of Lusitania in Africa.[14]

Still less is known about the effects an ever-present threat of sporadic violence had on gender relations within African communities during the early stages of colonialism—and much has to be deduced from later events, practices, and institutions. However, colonial military advantage gave way to the proliferation of resistance movements, small arms, and organized military revolt, and the evidence suggests that the sexual, reproductive, and use-labor relations of colonial violence go a long way toward explaining the historical memories and cultural attitudes that underpin much of Angola's resistance-era gender configuration.

From Gendered Colonial Insurgency to Gendered Resistance Movements

By 1961, Angola was a powder keg: rebellions broke out spontaneously all over Angola, and the bloodiest colonial insurgency south of the Sahara was born. Violence and terror leading to despair and divisions within Angola would leave young women uniquely disadvantaged, as Birmingham notes:

> Armies were less discriminating in their sexual demands and the female youth of Angola was the constant victim of rape, pregnancy and disease. White youths who fathered unknown meztico children were almost commended for further-ing the colonizing cause, but their illegitimate children were frequently the vic-tims of double prejudice, being rejected by both black and white communities and subject to . . . violent atrocities. . . . The legacy of war left a generation of psy-chologically warped male youths who saw women as objects to compete for and win, and of deprived female youths whose careers were dragged down by pre-mature and indiscriminate childbearing. Only a few young women learnt to use their sexuality as a weapon for influence in the struggle for influence over adult men who monopolized power.[15]

Again, however, the incompleteness of the hierarchical constitution of power relations along sexualized gendered lines is apparent. In Angola, as in many leftist struggles of the 1960s and 1970s, women and men pooled their resources, and the promise of gender equality was subsumed under the rubric of freedom from the colonial oppressor[16]—from whom all pathologies were believed to stem (see Jacobson, chapter 6). Early on, the intention of equality, especially within the People's Movement for the Liberation of Angola (MPLA),[17] seems to have been largely genuine, and many women received special training and were even selected for continuing education in the East-ern Bloc.[18]

Nevertheless, "nationalist movements have rarely taken women's experi-ences as the starting point for an understanding of how a people becomes col-onized or how it throws off the shackles of that material and psychological domination."[19] The women of Angola had once been the "sexual objects of foreign men," the "cooks and nannies of wives of foreign men," the farmers of "maize, yams and rice in small plots to support families so that their husbands could be recruited to work miles away in foreign-owned mines and planta-tions," the uniquely vulnerable nurturers and sexual consorts with illusory choices, and, paradoxically, their roles as symbols, invisible support workers, and nurturers remained intrinsic to the anticolonial undertaking.

Cynthia Enloe notes, "Nationalism has typically sprung from masculinized memory, masculinized humiliation, and masculinized hope."[20] In *Mayombe*, for example—Pepetela's award-winning novel, long considered the defining literary account of the psychology of resistance movement fighters—"the only woman to appear . . . is based in a small Congolese provincial town outside Cabinda where guerrillas are re-supplied. . . . The only truly feminine presence is that of the forest which, symbolically, provides the energy and courage."[21]

Invisible, perhaps, but women were not absent. The underbelly of Angola's resistance politics was heavily dosed with sexual oppression and exploitation within which women were distinctly and most acutely disadvantaged, a burden complicated by the ever-fraying social fabric wrought by colonial onslaught and the predatory sexual politics of militarism and embryonic nationalism.

Unfortunately, the quality of gender relations during the resistance period in Angola must still be largely inferred from the South African case, as scholars of this period have tended to overlook women's distinct experiences and contributions.[22] The South African case is instructive due to the wealth of documentation provided by the truth and reconciliation process, and the support structures that existed between independence struggles in southern Africa. Specifically, Angola was a defining member of the Front Line States and an unfaltering supporter of the African National Congress (ANC) and South West African Peoples Organization (SWAPO) freedom fighters. Just as women's experiences within colonial South Africa resembled those in Angola,[23] so did women's experiences within resistance movements.

In her analysis of women's testimonies in the truth and reconciliation process,[24] Lyn Graybill illuminates the way women wove together their distinctive experiences under apartheid with their asymmetrical and differential integration into the resistance movements—not just as women, but as mothers, wives, and political beings. The implication is that women's experiences during this period cannot be understood outside the colonial context, which, over time, disarticulated the social fabric and rearticulated women—as individual and social beings—as distinctly vulnerable in ways that affected not only their bodies but also their choices, their community status, their access to crucial resources, their support networks, the people they loved, and those who loved them. Graybill notes that "while men's lives were hard under apartheid, women suffered even greater burdens and social restrictions."[25] Although they were less often the victims of gross human rights violations, the Truth and Reconciliation Commission (TRC) concluded that women were "clearly apartheid's major economic victims."[26]

Without a doubt, many courageous women contributed politically and militarily to the struggle for democracy, but the majority were not directly involved; instead, they provided logistic and emotional support. They suffered most brutally from the socioeconomic consequences of apartheid, and their efforts need to be acknowledged.[27]

Economic vulnerabilities and severely circumscribed social roles and choices helped to reproduce sexual, reproductive, and use-labor perversities in the resistance movements:

> Abuse of female MK [Umkhonto we Sizwe (MK), an armed wing of the ANC] soldiers in MK camps in Zambia, Angola, and Tanzania (including acts of rape, euphemistically called "gender-specific offences" [by the Truth and Reconciliation Committee]) made up part of the ANC's testimony. . . . General Masondo, a former political commissar for the ANC in exile, explained that since there were 22 women to 1000 men in the camps, the "law of supply and demand" spoke for itself.

Similarly, Harding recounts the training camp experiences of Katila, an early MPLA recruit: "Still, by the time I was 15, I was aware of sex, aware that it was a problem. You see, I had no experience of this matter. At the age of sixteen I became pregnant. I gave birth to a boy, the fruit of an unhappy experience. His father was a young man, a year older than me. I can say that there were many other children born in this way."[28]

Predictably, the revolutionary promises of gender equality would be indefinitely delayed by the immediate postindependence war, but perhaps "delay" misstates the case (see Jacobson, chapter 6). In 2000, Savimbi was captured on tape rallying troops by encouraging them "to leave their women behind before marching into battle: When you take over another place, you will say, 'My God, why did I bring my wife along?'"[29]

Independence: The Gendered Political Economy of Civil/Resource War

In 1975, Portugal abandoned Angola. "The withdrawal of Portuguese authority, with the concurrent rescinding of responsibility of government, compounded by the wholesale abandonment of the country by most of colonial society and its economic agents, created a void which had serious implications for the course of the struggle between the [resistance] movements."[30] Fear and mistrust among the parties of the transitional government, fueled by the death throes of Portuguese occupation and awakening Cold War interests, led back to civil war within a few short months.[31] Simultaneously, apartheid South Africa, with the support of the United States (which ultimately backed the National Union for the Total Independence of Angola [UNITA]), advanced from the south, hoping to stem SWAPO and ANC operations in Angola and defend its interests in Namibia (then South-West Africa). The Cubans, supported by the Russians, came to the aid of the MPLA.

Ultimately, this war congealed into a military struggle between the MPLA and UNITA. War left few opportunities for state reform. Instead, both sides found quick resort to external funding and the profitable resource-extraction channels established by the Portuguese, which were designed in the first instance to maximize profit, minimize risk, finance a colonial insurgency, and prevent the majority from ever ruling. The MPLA relied on offshore oil revenues to maintain control over the state, while UNITA traded in conflict diamonds to finance its military challenge. These strategies are overwhelmingly dominated by the male military chain of command. They are intricately linked to the support and maintenance of existing hierarchies in which substantive domestic legitimacy remains tightly bound to military sectors; thus, broad-based social welfare continued to decline, while the chances for renewed political and economic complexity evaporated.

In this way, the basic structure continued to mirror the Portuguese colonial state,[32] but the situation was further complicated by the competing factions' incorporation of vast numbers of male youths into, ultimately, the largest per capita military-to-civilian ratio in Africa. What government reform was instituted tended toward centralization, along the Marxist model; most functions were geared toward the military.

There has, however, been considerable effort to change Portuguese colonial laws, especially with the introduction of a radical new family law in 1987. Similarly, the constitution guarantees equal rights regardless of race, sex, or religion.[33] However, law and order are only weakly institutionalized. During fieldwork in the northern province of Uige, for example, I discovered that the court building was still in ruins from the war of 1992 and had no lights or running water, although the justice delegate commented that some court cases were seen—mainly those involving murder. Police functions were performed by military personnel, and no police presence was provided for the villages, where the majority of people live. Incidences of domestic abuse were thought to be widespread, but it was acknowledged that no capacity existed to mediate these affairs. Therefore, in terms of the political and economic structure, formal laws and institutions provide only a shadow of what might one day materialize, while in the informal political economy, war predominantly structures people's lives.

"Indeed, in so far as these conflicts dissolve conventional distinctions between 'people', 'army' and 'government', the implications of the social transformation involved are especially radical and far reaching. The victims of this transformation, moreover, are well aware of its depth."[34] Sporadic fighting over the years led to millions of internally displaced persons, creating a situation in which ever-increasing numbers of women and children became the second and third families of itinerant soldiers.[35] Refugees and internally displaced separated from subsistence fields, and families who remained in the rural areas rely on unreliable remittances primarily from the military sector, extended kinship networks, and aid organizations. In the last years leading up to the death of Savimbi, the MPLA army (Angolan Armed Forces, or FAA) adopted a scorched-earth policy—herding people out of the countryside, purging it of UNITA supporters and subsistence farmers alike. No longer capable of providing the use-value services (even meals and shelter) and commodities that sustain the irregularly paid soldiers in the countryside, women are left with few and, in many cases, nonexistent options.[36] Children suffer too: one in five children dies before the age of five, and one in three suffers from malnutrition.[37]

Women in urban areas fare little better, and arguably worse. Subsistence opportunities are scarce in a city that was built for three hundred thousand but is now home to four to five million. The unemployment rate exceeds 84 percent. The majority of households include extended families, most of which are supported by women's and girls' income and labor.[38] Threadbare market women can be seen on corners and streets selling fish, eggs, bread, and basic staples, but these informal survival strategies provide little security. "Theirs is a difficult existence but each of them seeks their way with dignity and grace. They move about like acrobats, like true artists of balance. They make their burdens appear unreal, as if the weight became one of their limbs."[39] The underbelly of this hard life is prostitution, which is rife. One interviewee noted that many male international staff consider Angolan women ideal sexual consorts, because of Angola's supposedly low AIDS rate. For many women, this is the best deal going.

As a partial model for understanding the position of women and the gender dynamic inscripted into contemporary Angola, we find a tapestry of social order interwoven with sexual violence, use-labor exploitation, and structural exclusion of women from all key levers of political, economic, and military power. At some point, however, the effects have society-wide implications as women's lives become the site of social-fabric gaps and perversities over which everyone, at some point, must stumble and fall. This is the backdrop against which current peace initiatives must be seen.

Peacemaking/Keeping/Building in Angola

Mainstreaming a gender perspective is the process of assessing the implications for women and men of any planned action, including legislation and policies of programs, in all areas and at all levels. It is a strategy for making women's as well as men's concerns and experiences an integral dimension of the design, implementation, monitoring, and evaluation of policies and programs in all political, economic, and societal spheres so that women can benefit equally and inequality is not perpetuated. The ultimate goal is to achieve gender equality[40] (Mazurana et al., introduction; Raven-Roberts, chapter 2).

Angola is the site of no less than two international peacemaking efforts, the Bicesse Peace Agreement (1990) and the Lusaka Protocol (1994); four international peacekeeping (troop deployment) efforts, the United Nations Angola Verification Mission (UNAVEM) I, II, and III and the United Nations Observer Mission in Angola (MONUA); and one peace-building mission, the United Nations Office in Angola (UNOA), which is currently ongoing. Few component initiatives targeted women as a vulnerable group, and fewer still incorporated the Geneva-based objective of gender mainstreaming.

In the following analysis, priority will be afforded to peacemaking agreements and peace-building processes[41] because these germinate the seeds from which social transformation emanates. They identify and consolidate basic power relations and mandate priorities for immediate postwar political activities[42] and, as a result, have the greatest impact on the trajectory of social, political, and economic systems. Analyses will not be rigidly time bound, as aftereffects are felt both in the near and far futures.

Further, my analysis will not draw a sharp distinction between peace efforts and the context within which they are experienced. Peacemaking/keeping/building are complex, nested, and interrelated processes, which are ultimately difficult to delineate from each other, and from the processes of globalization at large. Issues that remain "off the table" often tell us more about what to expect from a peace effort than those explicitly addressed.

Peacemaking

It has been recognized that peace agreements sometimes contain the seeds of their own destruction.[43] The first Angolan post–Cold War peace process culminated in the Bicesse Peace Agreement, the primary achievement being the identification, consolidation, and international legitimization of key military contenders to power through the establishment of an interim administration. While elections were scheduled, Bicesse fostered few institutions of substantive or deliberative democracy, and crucial decisions about the type of system transformation that would occur predated the electoral process. The peace process never transcended an elite/military/international hierarchy of concern—the only players at the negotiating table. With respect to this style of peacemaking, William Reno noted recently,

This motive, and diplomatic approaches that prize negotiated settlements as a means of resolving grievances, provide predatory gang leaders with a measure of externally guaranteed power and stability once they become presidents or government ministers. This creates the appearance of a return of order. In fact, it often stabilises predatory rule, and marginalizes alternatives.[44]

In other words, notwithstanding its other conspicuous shortcomings, such as being forced to work with the lowest budget in the history of peacekeeping, Bicesse primarily attempted to achieve peace through the solidification and legitimization of the power of military belligerents. This logic seems to have infused itself into African conflicts where all manner of armed rebels aspire to the negotiating table, and a few light weapons and indiscriminate targeting of civilian populations can translate into a sizable and *legitimate* piece of the state pie.[45]

The thin veneer of democracy in Angola did very little to consolidate peace, and the 1992 elections led to full-scale conventional warfare. Savimbi, the leader of UNITA, lost the first round of the vote and revealed to the world that he had used the lightweight peace process as an opportunity to rearm by launching a full-scale military attack where more civilians were killed than in the previous sixteen years of conflict.[46] Paradoxically, this seems to have intensified the logic of appeasing military belligerents. In 1994 the Lusaka Protocol was initiated, and, rather than attempt a thin veneer of domestic engagement, it unashamedly pursued the appeasement of high-level belligerents to the exclusion of all else.

UNITA's leadership would receive private residences, political offices in each province, and one central headquarters. UNITA would also hold a series of posts as ministers, deputy ministers, ambassadors, provincial governors and deputy governors, municipal administrators and deputy administrators, and commune administrators. The government would retain all other positions of patronage.[47]

At the same time, the protocol continued to reinforce the unlimited power of belligerents turned political aspirants; it contained no substantive steps toward structural change and took only a nominal interest in investigating or publicizing human rights abuses. Human Rights Watch ultimately concluded, "The impunity with which rights were abused eroded confidence in the peace process and created a vicious cycle of rights abuse that steadily worsened." It also noted that "This strategy of see no evil, speak no evil appears to have backfired badly."[48]

During both peacemaking processes, a key problem for women was that "groups that grow out of genuine community efforts to defend against predators, religious movements seeking reform, or citizens' groups protesting against war face serious problems attracting the attention of diplomats."[49]

Further, women are underrepresented in military chains of command and high-level diplomatic posts,[50] which minimizes their ranks among the "qualified" and makes them unlikely candidates for peace talks—overwhelmingly conducted by credentialed white English-speaking men[51] and "government officials turned warlords" wearing fine suits and speaking English. Women, women's groups, and organizations rooted in the logic of social welfare (as opposed to military power and wealth accumulation) are more likely to speak an indigenous language, to lack crucial formal sector connections, to concentrate their organizational efforts in grassroots "peasant" organizations,[52] and, most decisively, to lack the ability or desire to disrupt agreements with violence—a key, if perverse, criterion of "getting to the table." The result is that Angolan women have been "systematically excluded from all peace process negotiations as if their citizenship does not count for anything."[53]

A second key problem is the type of "order" or political/social transformation Portuguese colonialism seeded, Bicesse rooted, and Lusaka fertilized. Bicesse and Lusaka failed to appreciate the historical legacy of Angola and the predatory nature of its state structures and ultimately failed to notice that both UNITA and the MPLA had adopted sophisticated military-dependent local/global linkages based initially on former colonial networks and Cold War patronage[54] and increasingly linked to oil and diamond commodity chains.[55] As though mirroring the colonial past, both parties derived their power almost exclusively from militarily guaranteed international linkages and neither from nonmilitary domestic linkages. The agreements exacerbated the logic of the system by leaving it intact and sending the clear message that military might would be rewarded with international legitimacy and that the new high politics of macroeconomics, direct foreign investment, and trade in oil, diamonds, and military supplies would far outshine any quiet mumblings about human rights, social welfare, or the deepening of civil society links.[56]

Despite the rooting of humanitarian catastrophe of epic proportions, throughout the peace processes "oil company executives and US state department officials [were] all but falling over themselves in jockeying to reach the Angolan feeding trough."[57] To date, Angola remains one of the richest countries in Africa thanks mainly to "dollar diplomacy" linked to private sector investment. It would not be an exaggeration to say that "American motorists, via U.S. oil companies, have effectively bankrolled the Angolan government, war and all, from the beginning."[58] Current profits exceed USD $1.4 billion per year, a figure boosted by an oil-backed debt far in excess of USD $2,819 billion.[59] Little if any of that money finds its way into social welfare or infrastructure, even in the long-held MPLA stronghold of Luanda. "Indeed, 'onshore' life in Angola is largely irrelevant to the system as it is now."[60]

Some Angolans, however, are more irrelevant than others. Sectors linked to the generation of foreign exchange have profited enormously: military, fisheries, oil, and diamonds—sectors dominated by men.[61] Thus, strictly speaking, women are numerically underrepresented in growing sectors. However, the emerging order is more gendered than liberal-minded analyses reveal. That is, patterns seeded and consolidated by the logic of the peace agreements exacerbated two interrelated and highly gendered, structurally violent trends.

First, they relied on the "strongman" or leviathan theory of state consolidation, wherein governments (rightly or inevitably) comprise iron fisted victors, paradoxically construed in paternalistic terms, and thereby expected, despite enormous evidence to the contrary, to act in the best interests of those structurally and physically at their mercy. This logic is part of the "special international relations state" that interprets national security in terms of the integrity of state borders and internal order, defined by the absence of "the state of nature," as guaranteed by military and police enforcement[62]—who, unfortunately for Angolans, are commonly experienced as social predators.[63] That is, the implicit state model adopted by the peace agreements privileged order as physical coercion over more robust, deliberative social forms rooted in the social fabric.[64] The result was an unapologetic strategy that relied on the mystical power of quasi-legitimacy[65] to transform colonial-era institutions and a rapacious and predatory military elite into a wise and caring government, meanwhile leaving all military modalities, structures of violence, and asymmetrical wealth and capital accumulation processes in place; that is, the state "order" remained lethal. Thus, for the most part nothing changed for women, who remained structurally peripheral to most levers of military/state power and symbolically entrenched as military "other."

Second, recognizing and bestowing international legitimacy under such terms dovetailed with the deepening internationalized public/private split. In Angola the formal sector comprises, almost exclusively, international commodity chains linked to military control over key territorial resources. This sector is only tangentially related to the informal/private sphere by its need for new young (male) soldiers, subsistence commodities in war zones to feed irregularly paid soldiers, and the domestic and sexual services of women. This sphere is overwhelmingly populated by women, children, and the elderly; large numbers of men have been recruited by UNITA or government forces. With the exception of a minuscule stratum of elites, the majority of Angolan women are hierarchically ordered as "prey," raw resources to be exploited within a resource-based war economy. "To be sure, as many feminist theorists have argued, women's [enforced] specialization in use-value—as opposed to exchange value—work *enables* male accumulation and thereby subsidizes capital accumulation. At some point, though, capital loses as it stifles exchange-oriented accumulation among women."[66]

The lack of voice the majority of women have in formal political and economic spheres may explain the impunity with which the MPLA, in its bid to destroy UNITA, adopted a policy of "depopulating"[67] the countryside—undertaken because "unpopulated land means no food supplies, no women, no supporters, and no recruits." The resulting displaced, or *deslocados*, walk for days through the bush to overcrowded transit camps established by UNOA, where there is simply not enough food, water, and shelter. Again, the majority are women and female-headed households. In transit camps, their invisibility is heightened as social networks are disrupted and disintegrate and dislocation prevents subsistence farmers from producing use-labor commodities; at this point the internally displaced people become relevant only as a means to mobilize international community guilt.[68]

In sum, then, instead of attempting to effect a reversal of the perversities set in motion by Portuguese colonialism, the liberation struggle, and internationalized civil war, Bicesse and Lusaka: (1) legitimized the military/economic/political elite structure, (2) de-emphasized vertical and horizontal processes of self-determination, domestic cohesion, and deliberation, (3) simultaneously fostered international business as usual, thereby deepening the role of internationalized, military-dependent commodity chains in state accumulation processes, (4) reinscribed separate and distinctive spheres characterized by male (military- and commodity chain–backed) authority on the one hand, and female reproduction, care, and use labor on the other, and (5) reiterated young women and female-headed households as uniquely vulnerable and peripheral.

There was, then, in both peace agreements a failure to take account of the gendered nature of the society with which they were meant to engage. The single-mindedness with which diplomatic strategies focused on appeasing military belligerents rendered the process blind to the values of diversity and equality. By extension, women were invisible in the process; peripheral to the *high politics* of the state/military/economy nexus. Individually and collectively, they were treated like a homogeneous whisper from the background, an undifferentiated void. However, predominant among the rural poor, the dispossessed, subsistence agricultural producers, and informal market traders, and as mothers, family providers, and primary caregivers, these women cut across social, ethnic, and rural class distinctions and thus represent and maintain webs of nonmilitary social fabric. Their trials, challenges, humiliations, and defeats will define the generation to come. By rendering them invisible, the peace processes rendered themselves blind to the people's future, a future as troubled now as it was foreseeable then.

Peace Building

UNOA, the ongoing Security Council–mandated peace-building mission, is best described as high-level constructive engagement supported by a threadbare NGO-driven[69] humanitarian presence, loosely coordinated by the United Nations. On high, its strategy is to socialize the government of Angola (GoA) in the ways of "liberal peace,"[70] mainly in terms of macroeconomic fundamentals and transparency, and third way capitalism. At the intermediate levels, its strategy is to press for citizen rights such as identity papers and the rule of law. On the ground, it coordinates and funds basic infrastructure and health services while attempting to alleviate the worst internally displaced suffering.[71]

By far the most striking feature of UNOA is the extent to which it reflects the triumph of liberal "wisdoms" and modalities, characterized by decentralized partnerships between donor governments, militaries, NGOs, and the private sector, all linked by free market, trickle-down, and soup kitchen epistemologies.[72] The second most striking feature is the extent to which this approach privileges, courts, and empowers Angola's already perverse and cannibalistic formal/military sector. In effect, the hierarchy of concern of liberal peace dictates that UNOA's main strategy of engagement is to support business as chillingly usual while appealing to the GoA's sense of "a kinder, gentler capitalism." As suasion, UNOA relies on a "system of carrots and sticks where cooperation paves the way for development assistance, and access to wider networks of global governance, while noncooperation risks varying degrees of conditionality and isolation."[73]

However, the sheer magnitude of oil and short-term oil-backed loan profits,[74] coupled with the total absence of horizontal domestic cohesion or vertical state-society linkages, means that the international community does not have any sticks it is willing to use,[75] nor does it have any less profitable sanctions it can levy. Overwhelming poverty truncates demand for imports, and Angola has no other exports.[76] Essentially powerless to effect radical changes in the structures of incentive and profit that emanate from its member states, UNOA is a sacrifice on the altar of guilt or Cold War politics and failed peacekeeping missions. It can do little more than pick up the pieces and beg reform.

Further, unregulated and cross-pollinating international commodity chains militate against the achievement of even intermediate-level goals, such as engendering civil and human rights in Angola. Under current conditions, the government of Angola is highly unlikely to support substantive empowerment of citizens who may ultimately become political rivals, especially given the international community's established habit of legitimizing belligerents. Given Angola's highly militarized demographics, transnational networks' willingness to buy natural resources from any warlord who can seize control over them, and the Western public's blind-eye consumerism, the prospect is indeed risky in the current climate.

Those who suffer the most from this maddening mix of domestic and international politics are in varying stages of being internally displaced. According to the Office of the United Nations High Commissioner for Refugees (UNHCR), in 1999 alone, one million people fled their homes, in flight from the brutality of UNITA and government forces. The total number may be as high as three to four million. Taken over a longer period, most people in Angola are in some stage of coping with dislocation. The vast majority of these are women, children, and the elderly, and, for them, things are worse than they have ever been. Recently, UNOA has incorporated a specific mandate for internally displaced persons (IDPs), providing emergency food, sometimes clean water, sometimes shelter, sometimes medicines. Issues of coordination are moot—there is never enough of anything. One elderly woman, now living in a new IDP camp in the Northern Province of Uige, had these comments: "We are a rural people and we do not get enough food; we are isolated from our families."[77]

Getting women's and civil societies' voices to the negotiating table will require significant changes in the United Nations approach. Currently, Angola has a mere forty-eight NGOs,[78] twenty-three of which deal with "community development and education," eight with "community health, environment, water, sanitation and shelter," five with "relief/emergency," two with religious matters, zero with "legal help advocacy and human rights networking," and ten with "women, family planning and child care."[79]

Field research in the province of Uige revealed that no women's organizations existed, apart from the MPLA women's wing—whose office was deserted. The sisters from the Catholic NGO Caritas advised that they had attempted to fill this vacuum with social clubs where women could find camaraderie and solace and look toward building on new friendships. The sisters reported that women mainly expressed concern over the practice of polygamy among their soldier husbands and the strain this put on scarce family resources. Both the United Nations International Children's Fund (UNICEF) and International Medical Corps (IMC) provided mother/child services, but, as of 2001, there was no family planning, and condoms were not readily available. Representatives of both organizations felt that women would be unlikely, at this point, to practice either safe sex or family planning, a factor of culture and powerlessness, but that sexually transmitted disease, childbirth, and early childhood illness and malnutrition posed significant risks of death and long-term debilitation.

Other NGOs and United Nations agencies exhibited a marked lack of capacity to deal effectively with gender issues affecting their area of expertise.

The World Food Program, for example, found that men, as household heads, insisted on receiving rations but then routinely sold foodstuffs on the black market before they reached other family members. Doctors without Borders (MSF) noted that girl children were often malnourished. While their families were given supplements, these were shared among family members, and the child remained malnourished in subsequent visits. A stream rehabilitation NGO realized that, while fetching water was the main responsibility of women, "traditional leaders are the key to motivating the people, and they often do not care how far women have to walk."[80] All acknowledged that solutions to these problems were embryonic and prey to erratic capacity and funding shifts.

At a more systemic level, part of the problem lies with internally displaced persons being stripped of any humanizing features. Mark Duffield documents a similar logic in the Sudan: "The IDP identity overcomes the problem of identity by understanding Southerners through the pre-existing categories of developmental studies—as independent households ranked in terms of varying degrees of wealth, self-sufficiency and economic vulnerability. At a stroke, all sense of history and cultural difference was lost."[81] As a category, they tell no truths about who wins and who loses.

Migrants of very diverse origins and backgrounds, speaking different languages, practicing different religions, and having different modes of livelihood, become collectively "the displaced." They are thus characterized only by their present condition, homelessness, without identity, in limbo.[82]

Ultimately, UNOA's IDP strategy is not gender mainstreamed, despite the fact that the majority of IDPs are, in fact, women. A lack of training and capacity leads staff to overwhelmingly conceptualize Angolan women as victims, devoid of agency and autonomy—a perspective that may account for unwillingness to test the boundaries claimed by men, who are overwhelmingly accepted as household heads. One NGO, for example, began with accepting men's entitlement to head water committees but later refused to rehabilitate streams in villages that did not put forth a gender-mixed committee—ultimately finding the stipulation relatively unproblematic and, in fact, a significant improvement over all-male committees. Still, overall, the tendency to rely on blanket categories, expressed, for example, in the acceptance of patriarchy and chauvinism as intractable cultural forms, is rife, while international community participation in the construction and reproduction of gendered options remains invisible to participants in the process. Self-awareness, not only as a humanitarian response, but also as a powerful participant in the process of social transformation, is, to large extent, crucially absent from intervention design. Further, in most areas there have been no gender-impact assessments or baseline studies, and no capacity is in place to recognize or document the distinctive social relations through which Angolan women continue to innovate, strategize, and employ entrepreneurial spirit, creativity, imagination, and resolve toward hope and reconstruction.

In sum, the research and analysis reveals that there are profound gaps in knowledge and that the need for an accurate and systematic mapping of crosscutting and intersecting gender inequities is acute. Nevertheless, cutting in at any point reveals that complex peacekeeping operations do reinscribe the effects of a violent past into political practice, social institutions, and economic inequalities and, ultimately, onto the bodies of the victims. On one level, structures and practices enacted in the past have, through the force of habit and custom and by collective response to a collective problematic, reproduced themselves. These problematics include malestream myths about stateness, order, power, violence, and versions of liberalism, which, through their implicit gender bias, render women's unique experiences in the world secondary or invisible. On another level, actors act as though gendered *realities* are in fact *real*—as though male entitlement and female powerlessness cannot be transcended during the painstaking process of effecting transition from emergency to peace (defined in terms of absence of open warfare). In taking this perspective, actors reproduce the *reality* they claim to merely describe.

Conclusion

What if gender were really mainstreamed into, not only the specifics of peacekeeping missions themselves, but also their overall objectives and underlying epistemologies? What if peacekeeping really represented a decisive break from the unworkable past?

Angola is at a crucial crossroads. Now that the war between UNITA and the MPLA seems to have come to an end with the recent battle death of Savimbi, demobilization and reintegration of soldiers has become a top priority. There is no evidence as of yet that this will have a gender component, or that any parallel reintegration of internally displaced, most of whom are women and female-headed households, is being considered. What will be the effect on women's own long-term strategic goals and interests? Women have played a crucial role in household survival during the decades of war, but, to be sure, their visions exceed mere survival; their actions are directed toward future goals for themselves, their families and their communities, and society as a whole.[83] If the demobilization and reintegration process follows on the heels of past peace-building initiatives, one should expect the productive spaces women have carved out for themselves to contract rapidly and considerably, as men usurp all places of power, privilege, and nonmilitary economic vitality, with the help of the United Nations.

Alternatively, an equally robust intervention with IDP communities paralleling the demobilization process, including forefront advocacy for gender equity in land and legal entitlements, visible shelters, counseling and legal redress for cases of domestic and sexual abuse, microfinance, and gender-mainstreamed community planning, would go a long way toward balancing the "playing field" and easing return, for both soldiers and their families. The complexity and dynamism of postwar environs are inherently conflictive and barbed at the political, cultural, social, and more intimate levels. Nevertheless, it is clear that society as a whole would benefit from a radical departure from the gendered political economy of war that has held it hostage for five hundred years.

Notes

I would like to thank the Canadian Social Science and Humanities Research Council, the Canadian Department of National Defence, and all the staff at the Office of the United Nations High Commissioner for Refugees in Luanda, Angola.

The source for the epigraph to this chapter is Mark Haugaard, *The Constitution of Power* (Manchester: Manchester University Press, 1997), 68.

1. John Keegan, *A History of Warfare* (Toronto: Vintage Books Canada Edition, 1994); Charles Tilly, "War Making and State Making as Organized Crime," in *Bringing the State Back In*, ed. Peter Dietrick Rueschemeyer and Theda Skocpol (New York: Cambridge University Press, 1995).

2. Cynthia Enloe, *Bananas, Beaches and Bases: Making Feminist Sense of International Politics* (Berkeley: University of California Press, 1989); Cynthia Enloe, *Does Khaki Become You? The Militarization of Women's Lives* (London: Pandora, 1988); Jacklyn Cock, *Colonels and Cadres: War and Gender in South Africa* (Cape Town: Oxford University Press, 1991); Jan Jindy Pettman, *Worlding Women* (London: Routledge, 1996).

3. Spike Peterson, introduction to *Global Gender Issues*, ed. Spike Peterson and Anne Sisson Runyan (Boulder: Westview Press, 1993); Pettman, *Worlding Women.*

4. Jane Parpart and Kathleen Staudt, "Women and the State in Africa," in *Women and the State in Africa*, ed. Jane Parpart and Kathleen Staudt (Boulder: Lynne Rienner Publishers, 1990).

5. Siba N'Zatioula Grovogui, *Sovereigns, Quasi Sovereigns and Africans* (Minneapolis: University of Minnesota Press, 1996), 53.

6. Grovogui, *Sovereigns, Quasi Sovereigns and Africans*, 31.

7. Southern African Research and Documentation Centre, *Reporting Elections in Southern Africa* (Harare: SARDC, 2000).

8. A small elite of complicit African slave traders and trading tribes amassed significant power and wealth by dealing with, and acting as intermediaries for, the Portuguese. However, by and large, relations between the Africans and Portuguese were rarely peaceful, profoundly destructive, and almost always eventually treacherous.

9. Christopher Chapham, *Africa and the International System* (Cambridge: Cambridge University Press, 1993); Assis Malaquias, "Ethnicity and Conflict in Angola: Prospects for Reconciliation," in *Angola's War Economy*, ed. Jakkie Cilliers and Christian Dietrich (Pretoria, South Africa: Institute for Security Studies, 2000).

10. Far from a cohesive or systematic imposition of a new order, the Portuguese approach to colonialism was particularly prone to pillage, plunder, and indiscriminate destructiveness until well into the twentieth century. Nevertheless, the evolution of cosmologies of legitimacy emanating from Christian thought in Europe generated broad trends in the colonized world (see Grovogui, *Sovereigns, Quasi Sovereigns and Africans*). While these were differentially applied, the *flavor* of the general trajectory of gender relations is clear. Not to exaggerate the unity or coherence of stateness, "taking the context seriously" is understanding that the "assumption of men's (more specifically, elite men's) experience as representative of human experience" lays the foundation for a particular kind of state in which women's experiences, opportunities, and visibilities are constituted as marginal. Spike Peterson, *Gendered States: Feminist (Re)Visions of International Relations Theory* (Boulder: Lynne Reinner, 1992); see also Grovogui, *Sovereigns, Quasi Sovereigns and Africans*.

11. David Sweetman, *Women Leaders in African History* (London: Heinemann Educational Books, 1987).

12. Basil Davidson, *In the Eye of the Storm: Angola's People* (Harmondsworth, UK: Penguin Books, 1975), 52.

13. David Birmingham, *Portugal and Africa* (Great Britain: Macmillan, 1999), 106.

14. Birmingham, *Portugal and Africa*, 125.

15. Birmingham, *Portugal and Africa*, 134.

16. Jeremy Harding, *Small Wars, Small Mercies* (London: Penguin Books, 1993), 29–36.

17. The anticolonial movements consisted of: the People's Movement for the Liberation of Angola (MPLA), largely representing the Mbundu; the National Union for the Total Independence of Angola (UNITA), largely representing the Ovimbundu; and the now defunct National Front for the Liberation of Angola (FNLA), largely representing the Bacongo (Malaquias, "Ethnicity and Conflict in Angola," 96).

18. Malaquias, "Ethnicity and Conflict in Angola."

19. Enloe, *Bananas, Beaches and Bases*, 44.

20. Enloe, *Bananas, Beaches and Bases*, 44.

21. Ana Mafalda Leite, "Angola," in *The Post-colonial Literature of Lusophone Africa*, ed. Patrick Chabal (Johannesburg: Witswatersrand University Press, 1996), 118.

22. Fernando Andresen Guimaraes, *The Origins of the Angolan Civil War* (Great Britain: Macmillan, 2001); Willem van der Waals, *Portugal's War in Angola 1961–1974* (Johannesburg: Ashanti Publishing, 1993).

23. Lyn Graybill, *Truth and Reconciliation in South Africa* (Boulder: Lynne Reinner Publishers, 2002), 97–112.

24. If recent calls for a truth and reconciliation process in Angola are heeded, this may go some considerable distance toward revealing the quality of historical injustices embedded in present. One hopes, however, that much of the gender bias embedded in the South African process will not be repeated (Graybill, *Truth and Reconciliation in South Africa*, 103–8).

25. Graybill, *Truth and Reconciliation in South Africa*, 100.

26. Graybill, *Truth and Reconciliation in South Africa*, 108.

27. Graybill, *Truth and Reconciliation in South Africa*, 101.

28. Harding, *Small Wars, Small Mercies*, 35.

29. "Savimbi Mocks Women and Peace on TV," *Cape Argus*, 2000, 40, 28, available at www.iol.co.za.

30. Guimaraes, *Origins of the Angolan Civil War*, 96–97.

31. For a review of the history of the Angolan conflict see Richard Cornwell, "The War for Independence" in *Angola's War Economy*, ed. Jakkie Cilliers and Christian Dietrich (Pretoria, South Africa: Institute for Security Studies, 2000); Southern African Research and Documentation Centre, *Reporting Elections in Southern Africa*.

32. Linda Heywood, *Contested Power in Angola, 1840s to the Present*, Rochester Studies in African History and the Diaspora 6 (Rochester, NY: University of Rochester Press, 2000).

33. Swedish International Development Agency, *Country Gender Analysis for Angola* (Stockholm: Swedish International Development Agency, 1992).

34. Mark Duffield, *Global Governance and the New Wars* (London: Zed Books, 2001), 136.

35. CARITAS, interviewed by author, Uige, Angola, April 2001.

36. Senior Inter-Agency Network, *Senior Inter-Agency Network on Internal Displacement: Mission to Angola 12–17 March 2001; Findings and Recommendations* (New York: UN Office for the Coordination of Humanitarian Affairs, 2001). See, for example, Peter Beaumont, "Forced on a Trail of Tears," *Mail and Guardian*, August 17–23, 2001, 13.

37. Global Witness, *All the President's Men* (London: Global Witness, 2002), 4.

38. Southern African Research and Documentation Centre, *Beyond Inequalities: Women in Angola* (Harare: SARDC, 2000).

39. Margrit Coppé, *Mulheres Lutadoras: Walking Shops*, Development Workshop photographic compendium (Brussels, Belgium: 11.11.11, n.d.).

40. IASC Secretariat, "Mainstreaming Gender in the Humanitarian Response to Emergencies" (final draft background paper, IASC Working Group, 36th meeting, Rome, April 22–23, 1999, available at http://www.reliefweb.com).

41. Due to limited space, peacekeeping will be omitted. However, it is important to note that women have composed less than 3 percent of Angola's peacekeeping missions, and the patronage of prostitutes, notably those underage, has been identified as a key problem of the UNAVEMs and MONUA. See Southern African Research and Documentation Centre, *Beyond Inequalities: Women in Angola*; Joni Seager, *The State of Women in the World Atlas* (London: Penguin Reference, 1997).

42. Brigitte Sørensen, *Women and Post-conflict Reconstruction* (Geneva: United Nations Research Institute for Social Development, 1998).

43. Fen Osler Hampson, "Peace Agreements," in *Encyclopedia of Peace and Conflict* (New York: Academic Press, 1999).

44. William Reno, "Warfare in Collapsed States, and Special Problems of Conflict Resolution," *Global Dialogue* 6, no. 2 (July 2001): 6.

45. For example, recent peace talks in the Democratic Republic of the Congo (DRC) have focused mainly on formalizing military power into political power and slicing up the metaphorical pie over which belligerents are fighting. All sides have been hostile to UN bids to involve civil society, but the process continues unhindered by this fact.

46. David Sogge, *Sustainable Peace: Angola's Recovery* (Harare: Southern African Research and Documentation Centre, 1992). For further examples of the volatility of thin, externally spawned electoral politics see Jack Snyder, *From Voting to Violence: Democratisation and Nationalist Conflict* (New York: W. W. Norton & Company, 2000).

47. Human Rights Watch, *Angola Unravels: The United Nations* (New York: HRW, 1999), 1, available at http://hrw.org/reports/1999/angola/ang1998-10.htm.

48. Human Rights Watch, *Angola Unravels: Summary* (New York: HRW, 1999), 1–4, available at http://hrw.org/reports/1999/angola/ang1998-01.htm.

49. Reno, "Warfare in Collapsed States," 7.

50. Louise Olsson, *Gendering UN Peacekeeping* (Uppsala: Department of Peace and Conflict Research, Uppsala University, 1999).

51. The Bicesse peace talks are unique in that Margaret Anstee, after being given twenty-four hours to decide whether she would take the post, led the negotiations, the disarmament, and the first elections in Angola's war-torn history. "The total budget for seventeen months of operation was only $118,000." Margaret Anstee, *The United Nations in Angola: Herding Cats* (Washington, DC: United States Institute of Peace Press, 1999), 592. In Anstee's own words, "I was the first woman to be appointed as Special Representative, of the UN Secretary-General and head a peacekeeping mission, and I am still the only woman to have had to deal with open conflict in that capacity" (610). No peacekeeping operation had been so underfunded before or since.

52. Southern African Research and Documentation Centre, *Beyond Inequalities: Women in Angola*, 37.

53. Henda Ducados, *An All Men's Show? Angolan Women's Survival in the 30-Year War*, 2, available at http://www.web.net/~iccaf/humanrights/angolainfo/angolanews feb01.htm#agenda (accessed September 15, 2004); Southern African Research and Documentation Centre, *Beyond Inequalities: Women in Angola*, 36.

54. Christopher Clapham, *Africa and the International System* (Cambridge: Cambridge University Press, 1993); Christopher Clapham, "Discerning the New Africa," *International Affairs* 74, no. 2 (1998).

55. Jakkie Cilliers and Christian Dietrich, eds., *Angola's War Economy* (Pretoria, South Africa: Institute for Security Studies, 2000); Sagaren Naidoo, "The Role of War Economies in Understanding Contemporary Conflicts," *Global Dialogue* (Institute for Global Dialogue) 5, no. 2 (September 2000).

56. Human Rights Watch, *Angola Unravels: Angolan Civil Society and Human Rights* (New York: HRW, 1999), available at http://hrw.org/reports/1999/angola/ang1998-11.htm.

57. Toronto Committee for Links between Southern Africa and Canada, *Southern Africa Report* 15, no. 4 (Toronto: TCLSAC, 2000), 1.

58. Sogge, *Sustainable Peace: Angola's Recovery*, 5.

59. Global Witness, *A Crude Awakening* (London: Global Witness, 2000), available at http://www.oneworld.org/globalwitness.

60. Sogge, *Sustainable Peace: Angola's Recovery*, 6.

61. Southern African Research and Documentation Centre, *Beyond Inequalities: Women in Angola*.

62. Pettman, *Worlding Women*.

63. Field notes, Luanda, April 2001.

64. Dyan Mazurana and Susan McKay, *Women and Peacebuilding* (Montreal: International Centre for Human Rights and Democratic Choice, 1999).

65. Jakkie Cilliers, "Resource Wars: A New Type of Insurgency," in *Angola's War Economy*, ed. Jakkie Cilliers and Christian Dietrich (Pretoria, South Africa: Institute for Security Studies, 2000), 13.

66. Parpart and Staudt, "Women and the State in Africa," 6.

67. The MPLA adopted its military strategy of total victory after repeated attempts to broker peace with UNITA—all ending in resumed UNITA military action. The human security toll of full military action in the countryside has been catastrophic. With the recent battle death of Savimbi, real peace seems finally to be looming. It remains to be seen the extent to which the MPLA will now seek to redress the humanitarian situation and redirect the peace dividend to the people. There is some hope. This recent turn of events has put the final nail in the coffin of hypotheses that posited that the MPLA fermented war as a means of securing access to the spoils of the war economy. It seems also to have confirmed what many have suspected, that Savimbi was the main belligerent and engine of the cycles of war that have plagued Angola over the years.

68. In order to compensate, the United Nations, under the UNOA peace-building operation, has ultimately undertaken all social welfare functions, only to find that the MPLA has incorporated this free UN safety net into its power and capital accumulation strategies: it indiscriminately displaces people, separating them from all possible means of subsistence, and routinely calls on the United Nations and other members of the NGO community to feed and house the newly internally displaced.

69. Nongovernmental organization.

70. Duffield, *Global Governance and the New Wars*.

71. Senior Inter-Agency Network, *Senior Inter-Agency Network on Internal Displacement*.

72. Larry Swatuk and Timothy Shaw, conclusion to *The South at the End of the 20th Century*, ed. Larry Swatuk and Timothy Shaw (London: Macmillan, 1994).

73. Duffield, *Global Governance and the New Wars*, 34.

74. Global Witness, *A Crude Awakening*.

75. Texaco, *Agenda International* 4, no. 1, February–March (London: Garden House Press, 2001): 18.

76. Economist Intelligence Unit, *Country Report: Angola*, 2001, available at http://www.eiu.com.

77. Translation from local language.
78. Approximate figures.
79. Mohamed Salih, *African Democracies and African Politics* (London: Pluto Press, 2002), 53.
80. Field interviews, Uige, Angola, April 2001.
81. Duffield, *Global Governance and the New Wars*, 212.
82. Duffield, *Global Governance and the New Wars*, 16.
83. Sørensen, *Women and Post-conflict Reconstruction.*

13

Mainstreaming Gender in United Nations Peacekeeping Training: Examples from East Timor, Ethiopia, and Eritrea

Angela Mackay

THIS CHAPTER IS BASED ON PERSONAL experience and observations and anecdotal evidence of the recent efforts by the United Nations Department of Peacekeeping Operations (DPKO) Training and Evaluation Service (TES) to provide training in gender and peacekeeping to the military and civilian police personnel on United Nations missions. I begin the paper with a brief background to situate the project, describe how the training was put together, reflect upon some of the experiences from the delivery process, and, finally, offer some thoughts on where we are, or should be, going.

Background of Gender and Peacekeeping Training Initiative

Not all meetings between foreign ministers are so auspicious. In 1998, United States Secretary of State Madeleine Albright and Canadian Foreign Minister Lloyd Axworthy, spurred, it is believed, by the unimpressive record of some peacekeepers' behavior in the field, but perhaps more significantly by the appalling experiences of local women during the most recent missions, agreed to collaborate on the development of gender-training materials for peacekeepers. Two years later, in October 2000, the finished product was delivered. The history of the development of the materials, long and tortured, resulted in the sharing of the costs and the work by the Canadian Department of Foreign Affairs and International Trade (DFAIT) and the British Department for International Development (DFID). United States Senator Jessie Helms, then chair of the Senate Foreign Relations Committee, concerned that United

States money was somehow going to be involved in a project in Canada—not a developing country—had put an end to the American participation in the project.

The timing of the delivery of this package of training materials coincided with the historic United Nations Security Council resolution 1325 (2000). This was an unprecedented event—a unanimous adoption by the Security Council of the first resolution on women, peace, and security. The role of peacekeeping militaries was a central concern in the open Security Council debate and resulted in the strong endorsement of training initiatives for peacekeepers. Such language was due, in part, to peacekeepers' dreadful record on women, which has become a familiar feature of United Nations missions of the last two decades.

The Training and Evaluation Service of DPKO had been planning to develop a training package since February 2000, when the DFAIT/DFID material was subjected to its first test run during a workshop in Ottawa, Canada. The initiative took off in October 2000. The DPKO TES material was to be specifically targeted at military and police peacekeepers, unlike the DFAIT/DFID product, which was best suited for training military, police, and civilian peacekeepers simultaneously.

It is important to note that at the time of the gender and peacekeeping training project, the TES was a very small unit, staffed with four serving military officers and a small support staff. Simply put, its mandate is to develop, deliver, and evaluate training materials for troop-contributing nations. It regularly runs United Nations Technical Assistance Training (UNTAT) courses, mainly in regional centers, aimed primarily at the training staff of the various troop-contributing nations (TCNs). These trainers then, in turn, deliver the materials to their own forces. Importantly, the training of troops is a national responsibility. The United Nations can suggest, request, cajole, or persuade TCNs to provide specific training to peacekeeping forces, but it cannot insist. Standards exist—but enforcement is another story. This creates enormous problems. There are distinctions of quality, equipment, preparedness, and education between professional and conscript armies; between the wealthy and the poorer nations; between those, no matter where from, with a tradition of training disciplined forces and those with lesser skills and dubious objectives.

The UNTAT courses are perhaps the most visible but, in fact, represent only a portion of the activity that TES is involved in. Thus, when the gender project began, it was seriously understaffed and lacked the civilian personnel to provide alternative, nonmilitary perspectives. So here it was—a blank slate, limited resources, and no one nearby with whom to confer on how to do it.

Approach

In recent memory, DPKO had undertaken a number of initiatives in its efforts to mainstream gender, but not in the form of training materials and not for such a very concrete and practical purpose as direct delivery to the troops doing the work in the field. The intent with this material was to make it available to national trainers of TCNs. This was daunting. The trainers of TCNs are officers, male to a man as far as one could tell. The range of knowledge and background in human rights had to be assumed to vary enormously from one nation to the next. The trainers' comprehension of "gender," without doing anyone a disservice, had to be assumed to be even less. These are sensitive subjects in this welter of nations, which by no means suggests they should be tiptoed around, but a central challenge was to devise material that did two things at once.

On the one hand, the trainers had to be educated about gender, human rights, and women's human rights—without being threatened—and on the other, they had to become fluent enough with the subject matter to pass it on through their own training systems.

Parallel to this was the question of methodology. Military training styles, no matter what the level, tend to the formal. Much of it is simply another subject to tick off on a checklist. This subject was different and needed to be acknowledged as such from the outset. Talking about "gender" strikes at the heart, if not the soul, of us all. Yet here we would be developing material intended for soldiers, task oriented, 90 percent male, who had most likely not given the subject too much attention in the past, and who were likely to be defensive. Yet, it was important to grab their attention, engage them, and train them, without alienation—in a maximum time frame of one day.

Would participatory training methods work? Would the soldiers be familiar with small-group work, case studies, problem solving, or reflective exercises? There was only one way to find out.

The time frame for delivery of the completed training materials was six months. It was decided to divide it into three blocks. The first two-month period was dedicated to exploring what else, if anything, existed that could be utilized—from within the United Nations or elsewhere. In addition, it was essential to talk—to talk with a variety of United Nations personnel at different levels and with different functions, from within DPKO and without, with people who had experience of peacekeeping missions, both military and civilian, with trainers, with the Division for the Advancement of Women (DAW), and with a number of other United Nations agencies. The second phase would be to research and write the content, and the third block would be dedicated to field-testing and revision. It was an ambitious time frame.

The results of so much talking and interviewing were enormously useful. No great revelations took place, but the interviews confirmed—no matter what the source—how vitally important it was to provide the training, at the same time as universally reinforcing the fact that it had to be concrete, practical, and unambiguous. It was generally agreed that there was little room for theoretical talk: this had to reach military personnel at all levels, and they needed to understand very quickly why it was relevant to them.

Some useful training ideas, more in the realm of methodology than content, were discovered among the United Nations agencies. Their styles tended to the participatory but also were designed to deal with the specific issues and questions inherent to their specialized area of work. Whether it was the World Food Program (WFP), the Office of the United Nations High Commissioner for Refugees (UNHCR), or the United Nations International Children's Fund (UNICEF), all the programs and departments have a history of participatory training methods for field staff, as well as specific mandates and responsibilities to which their training materials can be focused. That is quite different from targeting peacekeepers with such diverse backgrounds and mandates. National training for peacekeepers is varied in quality and quantity; the peacekeepers come from an array of cultural backgrounds, have not worked side by side as national contingents before, and inherit the traditional professional rigidity, task orientation, and limited vision of the military. Nonetheless, the discoveries within the agencies were helpful and welcome contributions because the field of gender training for peacekeepers increasingly looked like a desert.

Square One

It was clear that there was a need for the training and that the focus had to be practical and of immediate relevance to the "soldier on the ground"; thus, the content should be based on real-life examples as much as possible. There was some material available from other sources that could be adapted. The course was to be designed to take place over one training day; preferably, it should be modular in format so it could be delivered over time. It was to be initially made available to TCNs for their national trainers to deliver. There was the rub. This was to be a manual for trainers, so it had to include all the necessary explanations, instructions, and background in an accessible way. The theory was the main challenge. How could national troop trainers understand and learn themselves in order to deliver? At the same time, the theoretical underpinnings had to be relatively invisible if the trainers were not to be scared off.

The preliminary interviews had also identified a number of important themes: first, that gender in peacekeeping is not just about gender-based violence or women as victims. Of course not, but those are the easy sells, the subjects that, experience shows, universally grab the military attention. How was gender in peacekeeping to be covered adequately without having the trainees believe that those two issues alone define gender? A second theme had to do with discussing actions that empower women and build on their experiences of conflict and their skills and strengths—particularly important in postconflict environments, which, after all, are where current missions are mainly focused. Finally—how to get across the message that peacekeepers "serve" a population? This final message is contentious and in many ways in opposition to the science, art, and practice of the military endeavor (a point I return to later).

There are always difficult choices to be made when one is designing training materials—what to include, where to compromise, what to discard completely. The challenge was to make the most of one day. The first task was to define the terms. What are we talking about? What do we mean by gender? So the first module became "Why Gender?"

The expectation, later to be proved true, was that any military person who had heard the word and given it a moment's thought expected either that it was "women's stuff" or that it was all about sexual harassment, prejudice, and relationships within the military itself rather than with the host population. This in itself says a great deal about the military modus operandi. If nothing else was achieved but to define the terms, to clarify what gender is about and the effects of violent conflict on gender relations—then all would not be in vain.

Ideally, a definition of terms would provide the foundation for further discussion in the second module, "Gender and Human Rights," on the complex intersections among gender, human rights, and culture. This combination of themes was fraught with subjectivity and wafts of cultural imperialism and would require careful navigation.

The final module was intended to close on a positive and proactive note; it was titled "What Can I Do?" and was to be an open challenge and discussion period for participants to leave the training with the recognition that they had a personal responsibility as well as personal power to act, to be a force for not only doing no harm, but hopefully doing good.

This was a tall order but was in accord with the principles upon which the training came to be based: be honest and unequivocal but nonconfrontational; be rights based; seek to identify and exploit the positive possibilities that conflict creates; and emphasize both personal and collective responsibility. The focus of the materials, simply put, "is to inform peacekeepers about the impact of armed conflict on gender relations, to teach them basic gender analysis skills, and to sensitize them to the implications of their actions." The methodology would be a mixture of presentation, problem solving and case study analysis in small groups, individual reflection, and large group discussion.

For the use of the trainers, the training materials would include all the appropriate conventions and human rights documents and codes of conduct, as well as basic reading materials, bibliographies, references, and websites. A considerable amount of additional materials was ultimately added to help trainers select cases and exercises appropriate to the group, its expectations, rank levels, and deployment prospects and for the ambitious to build further training sessions.

The "So What?" Factor

A good friend, a retired Canadian general, sat in the back of the class when some of the early field-testing of this material took place in Bosnia. He kept asking, "So what?" And he was right. In spite of his position and experience, the subject matter was new to him. If he did not understand or see the relevance, the chances were good that others would not see it. Ever since, the "So what?" factor has been ever present. Theory can be fascinating, experiences and anecdotes telling, but throughout the training it had to be possible to answer the "So what?" question if a peacekeeper asked it. If the material could not be demonstrated to be relevant, then attention would fade, and we would have failed.

Before the entire package was completed, portions of it were tested in a number of locations—Ghana, Turin, and Bosnia. The audiences did not differ significantly in that they were predominantly military and male; women constituted 10 percent or less of the audience in all cases. The UNTAT training in Ghana was for west African TCN military and civilian police trainers; UNTAT in Turin was for an international mix of TCN and other trainers; and in Bosnia, under the auspices of the Lester Pearson Canadian International Peacekeeping Training Centre, the course "Demobilization, Disarmament and Reintegration" was for military, police, and civilian participants from the Balkan states.

The outcomes were as diverse as the audiences, but the principal message of these brief testings was that the material was on track. However, it was in the test-tube state, partial and experimental. The audiences engaged with the subject differently, as they always will. Some were attracted by the novelty, others were deeply suspicious, and, for some, it was almost possible to see the lights flashing as it helped them make sense of their own experiences and observations. The comments ranged from the depressing reaction to a case study about a raped woman identifying her attacker, "It depends how hard she resisted" (this from a police officer); to the comment of a delighted participant: "I understand now what our women talk about. I am going to teach this when I go back home."

The main practical benefits were the confidence of knowing we were heading in the right direction and the realization of the importance of getting the gender–human rights linkages clear and of reinforcing a rights-based approach.

United Nations Transitional Administration in East Timor (UNTAET)

In February 2000, the first comprehensive field test was carried out in the UN mission in East Timor. This was a somewhat artificial situation as the training was designed for predeployment, yet the UNTAET peacekeepers were already deployed in mission. This was unavoidable, given the national mandate and responsibility for providing predeployment training.

The peacekeeping headquarters in Dili organized the training sessions. A total of five training sessions were organized, all of them in Dili, three for military peacekeepers, one for UN Civilian Police (CIVPOL), and one for a group of recent graduates from the Timor Loro'sae Police School. The latter was a bonus in the sense of being a "gift" for East Timor, but also because it was a tremendous opportunity for the trainers to learn from the East Timorese and explore their attitudes and approaches to the subject. One remarkable young woman retold her own story of being attacked by a man while out jogging on the shoreline. He had stopped his car, got out, and started hitting her, yelling that women should not be out alone like that. She recognized him as a former Armed Forces of the Revolutionary Front for an Independent East Timor (FALINTIL) member and reported him. He was charged with assault, and she was to appear in court to give evidence the following day. The ensuing discussion was a heartening demonstration of a new breed of police, men and women, aware of their rights—and the rights of others—and ready to protect them. They confirmed that previously it would have been extremely rare for a woman to be out alone in this way and even rarer for her to report a man and have him charged.

Participants repeatedly pointed out the endemic problem of wife beating as a gender issue that could not be touched because it was a "part of the culture." Examples abounded of women beat, threatened, and raped. So did comments such as, "The women here are really quiet and well-behaved," "There wasn't much of a problem with rape here—only a few," and, "The Catholic Church has been a very positive influence. The priests told everyone to sleep at home and not go with the peacekeepers."

While such perceptions were common, the reality was that a colleague was confronted with a staff member's being threatened in a United Nations office by her husband, who saw her speaking with another man. The reality was a burgeoning sex trade in downtown Dili, one that included boys and girls. The reality was a population so brutalized by the abuses and cruelties of Indonesian occupation that notions of decent human treatment had become blurred, and the women were traditionally at the receiving end of anger and violence.

Yet the response to such a situation was far from adequate and indeed was highly problematic on a number of fronts. Examples include arming Australian peacekeeper civil-military affairs specialists (CMAs) with the advice not to speak to a woman alone. More dauntingly, a response among the CIVPOL personnel dealing with issues of domestic violence was to work through the elders, always men, who use traditional mediation methods. Such actions suggest many questions about the challenge of the effectiveness of traditional practices and the pervasive male authority, an authority that may perpetuate discrimination and injustice.

Such problems were not confined to dealing with local women. That a senior officer in the peacekeeping force assigned a female soldier to deal with visitors whom he believed, erroneously, to be conducting a "gender audit" while he stayed away is further evidence about how the subject was viewed in some military circles.

It was these circles we sought to train. In addition to the subject itself, a further challenge was created by having to deal with an array of ranks, English language competence, nationalities, and positions and jobs within the military. The very real problems this caused in the classroom meant that at any one time some 25 percent of participants were unable to follow what was happening. It meant also that deference to higher-ranking officers stunted discussion and argument and permitted highly questionable statements to go unchallenged. Having a colonel declare that women do not need to be represented at the "peace table," and that male politicians, bureaucrats, and local authorities are able to fully represent women's interests, stifles any inclination to disagreement by junior personnel. And there the matter lies, uncontested, on the table, tempting the trainer to lead the charge. This is not ideal. It also highlights the central concern of the capacity of trainers in TCNs to handle similar situations, especially if the trainer is of a junior rank.

The selection of participants to attend the trainings suggested that troops had been hauled off the streets at the last minute, or whoever happened to be available on that day had been sent. For the purposes of the field test, this was not the most productive approach to get constructive feedback. Airplane and truck mechanics should certainly be exposed to the generic materials predeployment, but they may not have been the best audience for these circumstances. As an Australian corporal mechanic pointed out, "There are no Sheilas under my truck."

It would be wrong to suggest that there were no inspiring moments. The training initiative was warmly welcomed by one commanding officer who had sent a soldier home after he was accused of sexual assault. The commanding officer reflected that it had been a tough decision, since it would cost that soldier his career and his family's income. The officer commented on the urgent need for such training because, he said, troops, who come from many different nations, have little idea how to behave away from the sheltered confines of home, exposed to apparently available women, and encountering other expectations concerning the conduct of social relationships.[1]

A Scandinavian officer applauded the "Personal Reflections" activity in the human rights module where everyone had the opportunity to read a short story and imagine it was told or written by a close relative or family member. Each story described a human rights violation. He claimed it to be the most moving and effective element in the training.

Another officer, in defiance of stereotypes of his region, adamantly and frequently claimed that education of girls had to be everyone's national priority, because only with educated women would communities make sustainable gains both economically and in the way women are treated.

So what did we learn from our experience in UNTAET? The principal discovery was that a distinction needed to be made between the material provided for predeployment training and in-mission training. Consequently, two streams of material were needed, retaining similar objectives, but with varied content. The in-mission course had to be context specific. No matter how useful we might think it is to make comparisons between previous missions, the peacekeepers in East Timor are not interested in what happened in Cambodia or Lebanon or Bosnia. They want real, context-specific examples to which they can immediately relate. Additionally, different people doing different jobs need a varied focus, and at different levels. People who never leave the barracks or compound have different needs from CMA personnel who are the vanguard in reaching the population and who need to build relationships of trust rapidly for the sake of everyone's security. It was also clear that the training conducted in missions must go to the battalions in the field and not be confined to what is always the more rarefied atmosphere of the headquarters location.

We learned too that a mixed group that includes at least 30 percent women participants has an entirely different dynamic and provides a richer learning experience for everyone. Sadly, this is difficult to accomplish when only 2–3 percent of military peacekeepers are female. The CIVPOL do a better job, at least in UNTAET (8 percent of CIVPOL in UNTAET were female), and with a showing of closer to 40 percent women in the classroom contributed to the liveliest group of all. Indeed, the police's knowledge of human rights issues was much better than the military's and therefore allowed for more discussion based on experience rather than reducing the training to a lesson on human rights.

Ultimately, the key lesson that two sets of material were needed—one generic for predeployment training by TCNs and the other context specific, tailored to each mission's needs—meant back to the drawing board. The next task was to design a common set of guidelines to be used in all missions to guide the collection of mission-specific data for inclusion as background, and to form the basis of new exercises. Both the guidelines and an in-mission training package consisting of a half-day course that could be delivered in "slices" would reinforce the generic predeployment training, as well as catch any troops who would otherwise fall through the cracks if no predeployment course was provided.

United Nations Mission in Ethiopia and Eritrea (UNMEE)

Testing of the in-mission package was scheduled in the United Nations Mission in Eritrea and Ethiopia. There was a significant difference from the previous field tests. In this case there was a military mission training cell (MTC) in place to assist with the organization and delivery of the training, as well as to use the guidelines to collect mission-specific background information—at least in theory that was the intent. This time civilian mission staff was included in the planning, as well as in identifying local community members to participate in the training. Their participation would serve as a reality check for the content, and, most importantly, they would provide their own perspective. The training would also be taken to the troops in visits to three different field battalions, Kenya, Netherlands/Canada, and Jordan.

Our experience demonstrated again the leap that military personnel have to make to embrace the subject matter—and that training on military subjects is perceived as a far cry from such "soft" issues as gender and human rights. The guidelines, intended to be a guide for the kind of background information that an MTC should have available before embarking on delivery, were tested. The results all around were disappointing, demonstrating both a failure to grasp the subject matter and the rejection of five-year-old NGO reports on the postliberation conflict in Eritrea as outdated. The proposed local material for exercises also proved unusable.

In spite of these drawbacks, the testing in UNMEE was a turning point. The single most successful feature was the inclusion of members of the local population in all the field training, including members of the clergy, nuns, teachers, mayors, local NGO representatives, de-mining organizations, and the national Red Cross. Noteworthy was that the personnel from the Dutch and Canadian battalion were so confined by their own national rules that they had virtually no contact with the local population during their six-month deployment—which was almost over. For many of them this training was the first time they had been able to meet and discuss anything—gender or otherwise—with someone who could provide a gateway into the culture they lived among. It was encouraging to watch, and it became clear that this kind of activity could be a catalyst for good relations between the peacekeepers and the host population.

Another advantage was the contribution of mission human rights staff who helped make the content of the training material more digestible and relevant to the military. Likewise, the delivery of the training for headquarters staff in Addis Ababa—more of a demonstration and discussion than a training because of the seniority and experience of the personnel involved—proved an invaluable contribution to the assessment of the material and to the entire concept of including the subject on the training agenda for the military. Yet having a senior United Nations military observer (UNMO) officer[2] reinforce what a Dutch soldier had already said—that military peacekeepers are far from home and isolated and that when they have time off they want to meet women for one reason only, sex, and that they are not going to think very much about gender or human rights—was unfortunately predictable.

The UNMO colonel went on to effectively advise that this was all a waste of time. What was needed, he claimed, were orders, orders that tell a soldier what he can and cannot do and what will happen if he disobeys. His claim that soldiers are basically unintelligent and unable to reason for themselves was of itself a disturbing glimpse into the world of peacekeeping. So this is what host nations are subjected to? Armies of barely coherent foot soldiers whose only hope of doing a good job is to follow orders or be punished? Surely not. Or if so, why are those who issue the orders not in the classroom? Turn his argument on its head, and we have exactly the justification needed for gender training.

Outcomes

Out of our work in UNTAET and UNMEE, what was learned? There were lessons on every front. First, the content. There was room for technical improvement, more illustration and less text, shorter, easier-to-read exercises, and better instructions, the usual methodology concerns. The gender–human rights–culture intersections needed tightening and will always be subject to local adjustments. But essentially we had two packages close to completion. The generic version for the TCNs was by far easier to complete and then make available to national trainers, who would inevitably adapt to their local circumstances and deliver in ways best suited to their own troops.

The in-mission version was another matter and would always be dependent on the competence and interest of the mission training cells. This leads to a second issue, that of training staff. These cells are staffed with military personnel who are familiar and comfortable with training military subjects. The gender and peacekeeping material is a very different subject matter with which most have little familiarity. They lacked the background and confidence to deliver this specialized training. What does that mean for the future? Will they be able to adapt? Will they enlist the support of other mission personnel who can share the teaching? Will the guidelines be used to collect—and maintain—contextual material? Will this be an identified task? In addition, this staff rotates every six or twelve months. How can continuity be ensured? Will the Australian captain in UNMEE who undertook to include this material in future induction courses for newly deployed units be replaced with someone equally enthusiastic and competent?

Third, what of training for civilian personnel? The TES has no mandate to train civilians. Furthermore, it appears that there is no mandate for this to be done in a coherent fashion by any element within the United Nations. Civilians are in need of training on this subject as much as the military, and there was considerable enthusiasm among the civilian participants in UNMEE. To have them sit side by side with the military personnel, together with the national participants, was a revelation for everyone.

Then there is the thorny subject of senior staff training. It does not seem likely in most cases, and is probably not advisable, that the colonel sits down with the corporal. But how are we to get the senior officers on board? If, as we have seen in previous missions, low-level harassment and abuse of women goes uncorrected, leading to an environment of impunity with increased incidents of assault and violation, is the senior staff not culpable? Does the fault not rest with senior personnel—military and civilian—who fail to establish and publicize codes of conduct and standards of behavior? If soldiers are trained to follow orders, where are the orders concerning the treatment of women? To reinforce this message it will be equally necessary to expose senior staff to this training. The "how" remains the challenge.

At some point the product has to leave home, to be released into the world and left to find its way. So it is with this training material. At the time of writing the in-mission package is currently being prepared for publication as a manual for trainers and as an addition to the TES website. The generic package is in the final stages of technical revision and will follow the same path.

But what of the bigger questions already outlined? The product is one issue, its usage and value is another. In order to provide support to the other existing mission training cells, the training will be delivered in both the United Nations Organization Mission in the Democratic Republic of the Congo (MONUC) and the United Nations Assistance Mission in Sierra Leone (UNAMSIL) in 2001. In late 2001 a "Train the Trainer" course will be run to ensure the availability of a pool of competent trainers. This will include MTC staff, military, police, and civilians from existing missions and member states—both men and women. The intention is for these trainers to develop confidence and comfort with the training material and to share their own insights into the subject and how to deliver it in different environments. Hopefully, this will provide support for the military trainers, will produce practical ideas on the inclusion of senior staff, and will lead to the development of a database of available, prepared trainers.

That the material is needed is increasingly evident. The word is out, and women's advocates both within and outside of the United Nations are applying pressure. In the short life of this project, additional requests for assistance in either delivering or developing similar material have come from the Australian Armed Forces, the United Nations Interim Force in Lebanon (UNIFIL), and civilian organizations in Norway, Switzerland, and South Africa.

Conclusion

The material developed will always be a work in progress, not least because the explosion of research in the world of gender, conflict, and security will continue to provide sources and insights for inclusion in the training material, but also because future missions will have different needs and different experiences.

In spite of all the challenges and drawbacks, the material was generally welcomed and in some cases received a very positive response and almost a sigh of relief—"at last, something to help us with this issue." The rather negative and depressing reactions, while troublesome, keep us all honest and eliminate complacency. But they also reinforce the need for realistic expectations. This is not a crusade. We should not count converts but rather take sustenance from the participants who, at the end of the day, have gained a glimpse of recognition, who will continue to think about the subject, who are more sensitized to the world in which they carry out their duties than they were when they came in. This was perhaps the best we could hope for at the time.

There remain two outstanding concerns. The first has to do with evaluation. How do we evaluate not the content but the results? It is complicated but possible to evaluate the delivery of the training by TCNs and MTCs and other training organizations. But how do we know if it is having the desired effect? Is the absence of abuse by peacekeepers any kind of proof? If displaced and other vulnerable populations are better protected by peacekeepers and there are fewer instances of neglect or denial of responsibility, will that tell us something? If senior personnel establish and reinforce clear codes of conduct, will this be progress for which we can claim some credit? If CMA personnel and CIVPOL engage with the women in a society, seek their input and advice as well as that of the male authority figures, will that be success? If women's voices are heard in the democratic process, if women emerge in decision-making positions, won't that be a significant step forward? If men, desolated and disturbed by their experience of warfare, can be identified and supported before their rage turns to domestic violence, will this be progress? When the employment opportunities offered by the arrival of a United Nations peacekeeping mission are constructed to offer real alternatives to prostitution by desperate women, then shall we have moved ahead?

The biggest change of all, and the greatest challenge, remains the nature of the military itself. That there is a contradiction between the warrior soldier, trained for arms and to fight and kill, and the image of the peacekeeper, trained to negotiate, protect, and defuse tension, is not news. The challenge we face is not only that the peacekeeper is asked to think outside the box of all previous training but that the populations peacekeepers are sent to work within, so frequently and readily identified as "helpless victims" in need of protection, are to be thought of as complex people to work and consult with. The international community asks the peacekeeper, on the one hand, to provide that protection, to fill the void vacated by the men at war who, in every society we can mention, are responsible for the defense of their community, while on the other hand suggesting that these are not helpless victims, but active agents, thinking, competent, strong, and able. Women. Women without their men, for whom the experience of conflict has overturned their world, yet who are survivors. We ask peacekeepers to support as well as protect, to enforce human rights they themselves may barely know exist. We tell them to be sensitive to other cultural norms, customs, and behaviors when they themselves are saturated in one of the most pervasive and powerful, masculinized professional cultures in the world, a culture to which they must truly belong if they are to fulfill their warrior function. These contradictions remain a stumbling block.

Setting out on this project was an act of faith. Its implementation has been and remains a formidable challenge, but peacekeeping never was for the faint of heart.

Notes

1. Personal conversation with author, quoted in *Peace News*, no. 2443, June–August 2001.

2. UNMOs are unarmed military observers who are sent to some of the world's worst crisis spots to collect firsthand knowledge on the levels of fighting and destruction and to report this information ultimately to the United Nations Security Council.

14

What if Patriarchy *Is* "the Big Picture"?
An Afterword

Cynthia Enloe

FEMINISTS ARE FOREVER BEING SCOLDED for missing the point. "You've got to look at the Big Picture," we are told. The presumption is that, when one is trying to make sense of societal conflict and its chances for resolution, the Big Picture holds the key to causality. If we keep our eyes on the Big Picture, we will grasp "what's really going on." We feminists, this reasoning implies, are so frequently wasting our analytic energies on the proverbial trees, when we should be paying attention to the forest.

The corollary to the scolders' admonition is that the Big Picture will provide us all with a strategic causal vantage point that puts sexism in proper perspective—that is, reveals it to be a mere blip on the landscape. Once we get smart and concentrate on the Big Picture, in other words, we feminists will come to our senses and see that sexism—its structure, its culture, and its practice—is a matter that one spends energy exploring only when the important things are sorted out. Expending serious analytic resources—time, money, staff, authority—on women's experiences in order to figure out when and where gendered dynamics are at work is a mere indulgence. And who can afford indulgence when time, money, staff, and authority are in such short supply? "This isn't a college seminar, you know. We've got a crisis here."

Of course, the important things—as prioritized by the drawers of the conventional Big Picture—are still there to be argued over. The fact that they are not so obvious, that they generate a lot of debate, is one of the things, I think, that makes it so easy to ignore the possible alternatives. The debates heard in policy and academic circles lead one to believe that genuine analytic exploration is going on: Is it oil or poverty? Rival state interests or weapons technology? Ethnic hatreds or diamonds? Security Council vetoes or capitalist investments? As fierce, and often useful, as these debates are—about which is the causal forest and which are merely the consequential trees—all of these debaters share a flawed assumption: that we gain nothing significant by investing the major resources it would take to make full sense of women's lives, to explore women's lives in a way that might upset our understandings of violence, of the state, even of the current international political economy.

The dominance of the conventional range of competing Big Pictures is one of the conditions that makes it so hard today to operationalize United Nations Security Council Resolution 1325. It was indeed a groundbreaking achievement to get this resolution passed by the male-led governmental delegations sitting on the Security Council in October 2000. Yet perhaps what was not grasped, and still is not absorbed by the members of those delegations or by the thousands of officials worldwide who found 1325 lying in their in-boxes, was the genuinely radical understanding that informed the feminist analysis undergirding 1325. That feminist understanding is this: that patriarchy—in all its varied guises, camouflaged, khaki clad, and pin-striped—is a principal cause both of the outbreak of violent societal conflicts and of the international community's frequent failures in providing long-term resolutions to those violent conflicts.

Consequently, despite the passage of 1325, the conventional Big Picture assumptions, and the routine scoldings to feminists they justify, are not to be taken lightly. Every day in boardrooms within the glass-sided buildings of United Nations Secretariat and Geneva headquarters, as well as inside the cluttered aid offices in Dili, Freetown, and Addis Ababa, these assumptions and scoldings act as effective silencers. No woman or man who wants to be taken seriously—in an international agency's budget strategizing, in tense cease-fire negotiations, in a stressful humanitarian intervention, in a research project about to come up for renewal—breaks this silence casually. When any of us is in these circumstances we usually act as though we cannot afford to be the object of dismissive scorn.

Most of us engaged in the administration, evaluation, or investigation of peacekeeping and postconflict reconstruction operations do not control well-stocked treasuries or strategic mineral deposits or a bomber wing. Our principal currency, therefore, is our intellectual acuity—as measured in the eyes of our colleagues. So we think twice before taking issue with the conventional wisdom about the alleged triviality of the gendering that goes on in the Big Picture. Instead of challenging the convention head-on, maybe we smuggle in an extra bit of funding for a study of women's nutrition in the conflict area, or we search for an unfrightening euphemism for sex trafficking, or we get the peacekeeping mandate written vaguely enough so that domestic violence prevention can be added later to the forms of violence addressed by field staffers.

But. But what if the Big Picture *is* patriarchy? That is, what if a principal engine of causality in societal conflict—and its chances for long-term resolution—*is* the contested, interlocking constructions of public and private masculinized privilege? What if the only way to throw these workings of masculinities into sharp relief *is* to take the lives of women seriously?

All of the closely observed case studies presented here strongly suggest that to understand—to pin down the exact causes of—why violent conflict erupts, why it can be perpetuated, why so many of the efforts to genuinely end this violence are frustrated, the workings of rival masculinities and rival femininities must be analyzed, in detail, over months or years. Furthermore, these careful studies reveal, the analytic eye must be attentive not just to the workings of masculinities and femininities in the disrupted local society; the analytic eye has to be turned simultaneously toward the external interveners. Just as no militia or its political-party backer is ungendered, so too no peacekeeping regiment or its authorizing bureaucracy is ungendered. Moreover, these genderings are not merely a trivial aspect of each of their workings. As we have learned from the scholar-practitioners here, all too often the unequal but mutually dependent structurings of masculinities and femininities in many conflicts serve as justifiers of priorities, as the props holding up authority, or as the fuel to motivate actions. And once we are talking about sources of prioritization, authority, and motivation, we are getting very close to causality. Now, once we have inched up on causality, we're not in the realm of investigatory indulgence; we've entered instead the sphere of the raison d'être for conducting any analytic thinking at all.

Those who try to persuade us—in a spirit of genuine urgency—to keep an eye on an ungendered Big Picture are, of course, also interested in the trees. They know that any forest is the sum of the trees plus the dynamics among all the elements that shape the relationships between those trees. These conventional Big Picture enthusiasts, however, have convinced themselves that all the myriad factors that go into making oil or diamonds or state elites' insecurity or the culture of the United Nations are not gendered in any ways that "really matter." Yes, most oil workers, their corporate executives, and state allies are male. So what? Well, of course most of the people victimized by sexual assault in the militarized conflict are girls and women. Who would expect otherwise? Sure, most diamond miners and the traders who set their goods' international prices are male. That's not surprising. Yes, most national security officials and the aid agency directors with whom they are often at odds are male. Well, what's so interesting about that? The Big Picture thereby becomes—with each casual dismissal—a forest in which many of the trees and many of the relationships between those trees are made invisible. The resultant conventional Big Picture forest is a funny sort of forest.

It takes a feminist curiosity to make all of the trees visible, to accurately chart the full set of dynamics creating the relationships between the full set of trees, and so to present an alternative forest, an alternative Big Picture. To take seriously the testing of the possibility that in any given conflict the Big Picture is patriarchy, one must have access to scarce resources—time, money, staff, authority. Consequently, arguing for putting a feminist curiosity into practice takes institutional courage. It takes that capacity to break through the silence, to ask the surprising question when a sense of urgency pervades the room. Often, taking the lead in proposing that patriarchy might define the Big Picture—the basic causal dynamic—also means putting one's own status as a "serious professional" on the line.

That is a risk. It is not a risk that should be taken alone. What an edited volume such as this shows us all is how to create a supportive collaboration—between the editors and the contributors—that ensures that when any one of us does break the silence, when we do dare to suggest that gender, particularly in its sexist incarnation, is the Big Picture, we will not be alone. There will be others around the table who have gathered their own feminist-informed analyses and thus will be ready to chime in, "Maybe we should make the dismantling of violence-producing masculinities a principal goal of our policy here."

Appendix

(This list includes all international instruments and court cases referred to in the book manuscript)

International Instruments

"Agreement between the Government of the Commonwealth of Australia and the United States of America concerning the Status of United States Forces in Australia," May 9, 1963, *United Nations Treaty Series* 469: 56.

"Agreement under Article IV of the Mutual Defense Treaty between the United States and the Republic of Korea, regarding Facilities and Areas and the Status of United States Armed Forces in the Republic of Korea," July 9, 1969, *United Nations Treaty Series* 674: 164.

"Agreement under Article VI of the Treaty of Mutual Co-operation and Security between Japan and the United States, regarding Facilities and Areas and the Status of United States Armed Forces in Japan," January 19, 1960, *United Nations Treaty Series* 373: 248.

Beijing Declaration and Platform for Action, UN Doc. A/CONF.177/20 (September 15, 1995).

"Charter of the International Military Tribunal for the Far East," January 19, 1946, *Treaties and Other International Acts Series*, p. 1589, established by the Proclamation by the Supreme Commander for the Allied Powers, Tokyo (January 19, 1946), reprinted in *Crimes against Humanity under International Law* (Dordrecht: Martinus Nijhoff, 1992), 604.

"Charter of the International Military Tribunal, Annexed to the Agreement for the Prosecution and Punishment of Major War Criminals of the European Axis," August 8, 1945, *United Nations Treaty Series* 82: 279.

"Convention against Torture and Other Cruel, Inhuman or Degrading Treatment or Punishment," December 10, 1984, *United Nations Treaty Series* 1465: 85.

"Convention on the Prevention and Punishment of the Crime of Genocide," December 9, 1948, *United Nations Treaty Series* 78: 277.

"Convention on the Privileges and Immunities of the United Nations," February 13, 1946, *United Nations Treaty Series* 1: 16.

"Convention on the Rights of the Child," November 20, 1989, *United Nations Treaty Series* 1577: 3.

Declaration on the Protection of Women and Children in Emergency and Armed Conflict, General Assembly Resolution 3318 (XXIX) (December 14, 1974), *United Nations, Human Rights: A Compilation of International Instruments,* ST/HR/1/Rev.4 (1993).

"Draft Relationship Agreement between the Court and the United Nations," UN Doc. PCNICC/2001/1/Add.1 (January 8, 2002).

"Draft Statute of the Special Court for Sierra Leone," unpublished Security Council Draft (February 1, 2001).

"Finalized Draft Elements of Crimes," in *Report of the Preparatory Commission for an International Criminal Court,* UN Doc. PCNICC/2000/INF/3/Add.2 (July 6, 2000).

"Finalized Draft Rules of Procedure and Evidence," UN Doc. PCNICC/2000/1/Add.1 (November 2, 2000).

"Finalized Draft Text of the Elements of Crimes," UN Doc. PCNICC/2000/1/Add.2 (November 2, 2000).

"Finalized Draft Text of the Rules of Procedure and Evidence," UN Doc. PCNICC/INF/3/Add.1 (July 12, 2000).

Final Report of the Commission of Experts Established Pursuant to Security Council Resolution 780 (1992), UN Doc. S/1994/674 (May 27, 1994).

"Geneva Convention for the Amelioration of the Condition of the Wounded and Sick in Armed Forces in the Field," August 12, 1949, *United Nations Treaty Series* 75: 31.

"Geneva Convention for the Amelioration of the Condition of the Wounded, Sick and Shipwrecked Members of the Armed Forces at Sea," August 12, 1949, *United Nations Treaty Series* 75: 85.

"Geneva Convention Relative to the Protection of Civilian Persons in Time of War," August 12, 1949, *United Nations Treaty Series* 75: 287.

"Geneva Convention Relative to the Treatment of Prisoners of War," August 12, 1949, *United Nations Treaty Series* 75: 135.

"Hague Convention (IV) respecting the Laws and Customs of War on Land," October 18, 1907, *Bevans* 1: 631.

"Model Agreement between the United Nations and Member States Contributing Personnel and Equipment to United Nations Peace-Keeping Operations: Report of the Secretary-General," UN Doc. A/46/185 (May 23, 1991).

"Model Status-of-Forces Agreement for Peace-Keeping Operations: Report of the Secretary-General," UN Doc. A/45/594 (October 9, 1990).

"North Atlantic Treaty Status-of-Forces Agreement," June 19, 1951, *Canada Treaty Series* 13 (1953): 2.

President of the Security Council to the secretary-general, January 31, 2001, UN Doc. S/2001/95.

"Protocol Additional (I) to the Geneva Conventions of 12 August 1949, and Relating to the Protection of Victims of International Armed Conflicts," June 8 1977, *United Nations Treaty Series* 1125: 3.

"Protocol Additional (II) to the Geneva Conventions of 12 August 1949, and Relating to the Protection of Victims of Non-international Armed Conflicts," December 12, 1977, *United Nations Treaty Series* 1125: 609.

"Protocol between Australia, Canada, New Zealand, the United Kingdom of Great Britain and Northern Ireland, the United States and Japan on the Exercise of Criminal Jurisdiction over United Nations Forces in Japan," October 26, 1953, *United Nations Treaty Series* 2809: 260.

Report on the Situation of Human Rights in Kuwait under Iraqi Occupation [Kalin Report], prepared by Walter Kalin, special rapporteur of the Commission on Human Rights, in accordance with Commission Resolution 1991/67, UN Doc. E/CN.4/1992/26 (January 16, 1992), reprinted in Walter Kalin, *Human Rights in Times of Occupation: The Case of Kuwait* (London: Sweet & Maxwell, 1994).

Report on the Situation of Human Rights in Rwanda, submitted by Rene Degni-Segui, special rapporteur of the Commission of Human Rights, under paragraph 20 of Resolution S/-31 of May 25, 1994, UN Doc. E/CN.4/1996/68 (January 29, 1996).

Rome Statute of the International Criminal Court, UN Doc. A/CONF.183/9 (July 17, 1998), as corrected by the procès-verbaux of November 10, 1998, and July 12, 1999.

Rome Statute of the International Criminal Court, UN Doc. PCNICC/INF/3 (August 17, 1999).

Rules of Procedure and Evidence of the International Criminal Tribunal for the Former Yugoslavia, adopted February 11, 1994, as amended December 13, 2001.

Rules of Procedure and Evidence of the International Criminal Tribunal for Rwanda, adopted June 29, 1995, as amended May 31, 2001.

Secretary general to the president of the Security Council, January 12, 2001, UN Doc. S/2001/40.

United Nations Compensation Commission, *Recommendations Made by the Panel of Commissioners concerning Individual Claims for Serious Injury or Death (Category 'B' Claims)*, UN Doc. S/AC.26/1994/1 (May 26, 1994).

United Nations Security Council Resolution 1325, UN Doc. S/RES/1325 (October 31, 2001).

United Nations Security Council Resolution 868, UN Doc. S/RES/868 (September 29, 1993).

Vienna Declaration and Programme of Action, UN Doc. A/CONF.157/23 (July 12, 1993).

Cases

In the Matter of a Reference as to Whether Members of the Military or Naval Forces of the United States of America Are Exempt from Criminal Prosecutions in Canadian Criminal Courts [1943], S.C.R. 483.

International Military Tribunal for the Far East Judgment (November 1948), reprinted in Leon Friedman, ed., *The Law of War: A Documentary History*, vol. 2 (New York: Random House, 1972), 1029, 1038–39.

Prosecutor v. Akayesu, ICTR-96-4-I (Trial Chamber, September 2, 1998; Appeals Chamber, June 1, 2001).

Prosecutor v. Delalic et al., IT-96-21-T (Trial Chamber, November 16, 1998; Appeals Chamber, February 20, 2001).

Prosecutor v. Furundzija, IT-95-1-T (Trial Chamber, December 10, 1998; Appeals Chamber, July 21, 2000).

Prosecutor v. Kunarac, IT-96-23 and IT-96-23/1 (Trial Chamber, February 22, 2001).

Prosecutor v. Musema, ICTR-96-13 (Trial Chamber, January 27, 2000; Appeals Chamber, November 16, 2001).

Prosecutor v. Tadic, IT-94-1 (Trial Chamber, May 7, 1997; Appeals Chamber, February 27, 2001).

R. v. Brocklebank, 34 Dominion Law Review (4th) 377 (1996).

Index

About the Contributors

Erin K. Baines, Ph.D., has worked with the Women's Commission for Refugee Women and Children regarding women and armed conflict in Rwanda, as well as the Office of the Senior Coordinator for Refugee Children of the United Nations High Commissioner for Refugees in developing materials to assist children during and after armed conflict. She has published extensively on these topics, as well as on critiques of the role of international intervention, especially as it affects women and children. She is the recipient of numerous awards and fellowships to enable her research.

Barbara Bedont, J.D., is a lawyer from Canada who specializes in international humanitarian law and gender crimes. She has a master's degree in international relations from York University and a law degree from the University of Toronto. She practiced law in Toronto, Canada, for three years before entering into international human rights law. For the past three years, she has worked as an NGO representative on the development of an international criminal court. She was the legal text coordinator of the Women's Caucus for Gender Justice for the International Criminal Court. She was staff attorney and faculty at the International Women's Human Rights Law Clinic at City University of New York Law School. Bedont was recently a security fellow at the Canadian Department of Foreign Affairs and International Trade.

Cynthia Enloe, Ph.D., is widely considered to be among the leading international scholars on issues of militaries and militarism. Her books *Does Khaki Become You? The Militarization of Women's Lives, The Morning After: Sexual*

Politics at the End of the Cold War, and *Maneuvers: The International Politics of Militarizing Women's Lives* are foundational texts that expose the role of militarism in women's and men's lives and investigate gender during and after armed conflict. Dr. Enloe is a research professor of government and international relations at Clark University.

Tracy Fitzsimmons, Ph.D., is vice president for academic affairs and professor of political science at Shenandoah University, Winchester, Virginia. She holds a BA in politics from Princeton University, conducted graduate work in international relations at Universidad Catolica, Santiago, Chile, and holds an MA in Latin American studies and a Ph.D. in political science from Stanford University, California. Her book *Beyond the Barricades* examines the effect of democratization on women and civil society in Latin America. Her published articles and conferences papers address gendering new civilian police forces, women and security, and civil society. She has conducted field research throughout Latin America, as well as in Haiti, Croatia, and Bosnia.

Heidi Hudson, Ph.D., is an associate professor in the Department of Political Science, University of the Free State, South Africa. She teaches courses in the Governance and Political Transformation Programme of the department, including Global Governance, Contemporary Security and Strategy, International Political Risk Analysis, and Gender and the Politics of Security. Her current research interests are concentrated in the area of critical security studies with specific focus on critical perspectives regarding the impact of globalization and state-centric solutions to developing-world security problems. She has extensively published in the field of gender and security within the African context. Some of her most recent publications have explored the link between gender and peacekeeping in Africa.

Ruth Jacobson, Ph.D., is a research fellow at the Department of Peace Studies, University of Bradford. She has worked in the area of conflict and development since the early 1980s, when she spent three years with the Mozambican Ministry of Education and Culture. Since then, she has been a consultant for a number of governmental and nongovernmental aid agencies in Britain and Europe. Her most recent fieldwork and commissioned research in southern Africa has encompassed democratization, demobilization, and postconflict reconstruction in Angola. She was coeditor of *States of Conflict: Gender, Violence and Resistance* and has published review essays in the *International Feminist Journal of Politics* and *Signs*.

Sue Lautze is director of the Livelihoods Program at the Feinstein International Famine Center at Tufts University. Ms. Lautze has done extensive relief and development work in Africa and Asia, and has worked for various United Nations organizations and the USAID. Her current teaching responsibilities focus on the humanitarian, economic, political, and ethical aspects of external interventions in complex emergencies. Ms. Lautze's field research concerns strategic humanitarian responses in complex emergencies and the impact of violence on livelihoods systems, including patterns of trade across conflict zones. She is a researcher on a thermostable measles vaccine project at Tufts, and serves as a research scientist at the FXB Center for Health and Human Rights at the Harvard School of Public Health. Sue Lautze holds bachelor's degrees in agriculture and managerial economics from the University of California at Davis and a master's of public affairs from Princeton University's Woodrow Wilson School of Public and International Affairs. She is currently working toward her Ph.D. at Oxford University.

Ilja A. Luciak, Ph.D., J.D., is professor and chair in the Department of Political Science at Virginia Polytechnic Institute and State University. For the past twenty years he has conducted field research in Latin America, focusing on gender equality, reproductive rights, revolutionary movements, and democratization. He has published in North American, European, and Latin American journals and has been a guest professor/fellow at Cornell University, Stockholm University, Innsbruck University, and the Universidad Centroamericana in Managua, Nicaragua. His latest book, *After the Revolution: Gender and Democracy in El Salvador, Nicaragua, and Guatemala*, was published in 2001. He is currently concluding a multiyear study on gender equality and democratization in Central America and Cuba for the European Commission.

Angela Mackay graduated in English and history from the University of Wales and immediately began her career as a trainer of English to high school students in Botswana. She continued working in international development, primarily in Africa, working for NGOs, the British Council, and the government of Canada. In 1989, she joined CARE Canada as the training officer and later the media relations officer. This included a number of assignments in Somalia during the emergency in 1992; being the principal media anchor during the 1994 emergency in Rwanda; and a temporary secondment to the United Nations Development Program as an adviser in public relations to the Relief and Rehabilitation Commission of the government of Ethiopia. She was also the producer of a number of videos on the work of CARE in Peru and Bangladesh. In 1996, Mackay joined the Pearson Peacekeeping Centre in Canada as the director of programmes. In 1999, she went to Kosovo as the chief of training for the Organization for Security and Cooperation in Europe. Mackay has been working as a training adviser on the gender and peacekeeping project in the Training and Evaluation Service of the Department of Peacekeeping Operations since October 2000.

Dyan Mazurana, Ph.D., is a senior research fellow at the Feinstein International Famine Center, Tufts University. Dr. Mazurana is a primary author of *Women, Peace and Security: Study of the United Nations Secretary-General as Pursuant Security Council Resolution 1325*. She was a 2001–2002 peace and international security fellow, Kennedy School of Government, Harvard University, during which time she began the compilation of *Gender, Conflict, and Peacekeeping*. Her areas of specialty include women's human rights, war-affected children, armed conflict, postconflict, peace building, and peacekeeping. Dr. Mazurana has published more than thirty scholarly and policy books and essays on these subjects in languages that include Arabic, Albanian, Bosnian, Chinese, English, French, German, Russian, and Spanish. Her latest major works on these topics include essays in *Where Are the Girls? Girls within Fighting Forces in Northern Uganda, Sierra Leone, and Mozambique, Gender Mainstreaming in Peace Support Operations,* and *Women and Peacebuilding.* Her current fieldwork is in war-affected countries in sub-Saharan Africa and Afghanistan.

Cecilia Olmos was a high-ranking official in the United Nations Verification Mission in Guatemala who left the peace mission in December after several years of being in the front lines. She has extensive experience inside peacekeeping operations, in particular with regard to how those operations intersect with the interests of local women and in running disarmament, demobilization, and reintegration programs for former combatants.

Louise Olsson is a Ph.D. candidate and lecturer in the Department of Peace and Conflict Research at Uppsala University, Sweden. She was an associate of the United Nations project Mainstreaming a Gender Perspective in Multidimensional Peace Support Operations, 1999–2000. For the project, she wrote one report, published by the Department of Peace and Conflict Research, and two case studies, to be published by the Lessons Learned Unit of the Department of Peacekeeping Operations of the United Nations. Olsson has previously published on gender and peacekeeping in the *Journal of International Peacekeeping* (Autumn 2000; Summer 2001) and has coedited a special issue of the same journal, "Women and Peacekeeping," published in Summer 2001. Her ongoing thesis project analyzes the consequences of international peacekeeping for host societies' gender relations. She is also coediting a special issue on gender and security for *Security Dialogue.*

Valerie Oosterveld is a legal officer with the United Nations, Human Rights, and Economic Law Division of the Canadian Department of Foreign Affairs and International Trade. Her main areas of responsibility include the International Criminal Court, the International Criminal Tribunals for the Former Yugoslavia and Rwanda, the Special Court for Sierra Leone, and other international justice issues. She is a member of the Canadian delegation to the International Criminal Court's Assembly of States Parties and served on the Canadian delegation to the 1998 International Criminal Court Diplomatic Conference and the 1999–2002 Preparatory Commission. She has also served as adjunct faculty in the University of Toronto Faculty of Law (International Women's Human Rights Law with Professor Rebecca Cook) and the University of Ottawa Faculty of Law (Human Rights and International Protection). She has published numerous articles, chapters, and edited collections on international human rights and humanitarian law, including on gender issues in international law.

Jane Parpart, Ph.D., is professor of international development studies, history, and women's studies at Dalhousie University. She has had extensive experience with gender and development issues in Asia and Africa. Her primary interest has been the connection between development theorizing, gender issues, and development as practice. She is coeditor with Marianne Marchand of *Feminism/Postmodernism/Development* and with Kathy Staudt and Shirin Rai of *Rethinking Empowerment: Gender and Development in a Global/Local World*. She has a long-standing interest in urban problems in Africa, particularly the impact of gender and the role of the elite in urban life. She is currently carrying out a study on the emerging middle class in Bulawayo, Zimbabwe, with particular attention to constructions of modernity and progress and their impact on urban life.

Angela Raven-Roberts, Ph.D., is director of the Youth and Community Program at the Feinstein International Famine Center, Tufts University. Prior to her appointment at Tufts University, she served as a humanitarian officer for the United Nations Office for the Coordination of Humanitarian Affairs and as a senior project officer in the Policy Unit of the Office of Emergency Programs of the United Nations International Children's Fund, where she was responsible for policy development in Gender and Conflict Issues, Post-Conflict Recovery Program, and Internally Displaced Children. She has also served as project officer for the United Nations Development Program's Horn of Africa Emergency Refugee and Displaced Persons Unit. Prior to her work with the United Nations, Raven-Roberts was the program director for Save the Children and Oxfam America in Ethiopia. Raven-Roberts has worked extensively within the United Nations on issues surrounding gender, complex emergencies, and peacekeeping. Her most recent publication is "Participation, Citizenship and the Implications of Women's Activism in the Creation of a Culture of Peace," in *Women and a Culture of Peace*.

Martina Vandenberg, J.D., is currently an associate with the firm of Jenner and Block in Washington, DC. Prior to joining Jenner and Block, she was the Europe researcher for Human Rights Watch's Women's Rights Division. Before joining Human Rights Watch, Vandenberg worked as a researcher for the Israel Women's Network in Jerusalem, Israel, where she investigated the trafficking of women from the former Soviet Union to Israel for forced prostitution. From 1993 to 1996, Vandenberg lived in Russia, where she cofounded one of Russia's first rape crisis centers. She coordinated a small grants project and women's leadership training program in Russia and Ukraine as the NIS (Newly Independent States) coordinator of the NIS-US Women's Consortium, a coalition of regional women's organizations between 1994 and 1996. She also conducted conflict resolution seminars for women in Nazran, Ingushetia, during the war in Chechnya. Vandenberg has conducted research for Human Rights Watch in Bosnia and Herzegovina, the Russian Federation, Ukraine, Uzbekistan, and Kosovo. She is the primary author of the Human Rights Watch report *Kosovo: Rape as a Weapon of "Ethnic Cleansing."* Vandenberg, a Rhodes Scholar, has a bachelor's degree in international relations from Pomona College and a master of philosophy in Russian and East European studies from Oxford University. She graduated from Columbia Law School and has served as an adjunct faculty member at American University.

J. Zoë Wilson, Ph.D., completed her doctorate in political science at Dalhousie University. Wilson's chapter in this volume was born of fieldwork in Angola in 2001. Wilson is currently a postdoctoral fellow at the Centre for Civil Society at the University of KwaZulu Natal in Durban, South Africa, and a senior research fellow at the Institute for Research and Innovation in Sustainability (IRIS) at York University, Canada. Her current research projects seek to map the role of international actors and institutions in South Africa's municipal water delivery architecture. Recent and forthcoming publications include: "Paradoxes and Dilemmas of Institutional Change: Human Rights and Livelihoods in Remote Angola," *Journal of Peacebuilding and Development* 2, no.1 (December 2004); "Rights, Region and Identity: Exploring the Ambiguities of South Africa's Regional Human Rights Role," (with David Black) *Politikon* 31, no. 1 (May 2004); "Angola after Savimbi: Is There New Hope for the Region?" (with Arsene Mwaka) *New Regionalisms in Africa*, ed. Fred Soderbaum and Andrew Grant (2003).